22 - 5p

Understanding Supply Chains

Understanding Supply Chains

Concepts, Critiques, and Futures

Edited by
STEVE NEW and
ROY WESTBROOK

OXFORD
UNIVERSITY PRESS

OXFORD

UNIVERSITY PRESS

Great Clarendon Street, Oxford OX2 6DP

Oxford University Press is a department of the University of Oxford.
It furthers the University's objective of excellence in research, scholarship,
and education by publishing worldwide in

Oxford New York

Auckland Bangkok Buenos Aires Cape Town Chennai
Dar es Salaam Delhi Hong Kong Istanbul Karachi Kolkata
Kuala Lumpur Madrid Melbourne Mexico City Mumbai Nairobi
São Paulo Shanghai Taipei Tokyo Toronto

Oxford is a registered trade mark of Oxford University Press
in the UK and in certain other countries

Published in the United States
by Oxford University Press Inc., New York

British Library Cataloguing in Publication Data

Data available

Library of Congress Cataloging in Publication Data

Data available

ISBN 0-19-925932-1

ISBN 0-19-925933-x (pbk)

Typeset by Newgen Imaging Systems (P) Ltd., Chennai, India
Printed in Great Britain
on acid-free paper by

Biddles Ltd., King's Lynn, Norfolk

PREFACE

The future of supply chain management looks even more fantastic than the recent past (Quinn 2003: 5).

As we approach the 21st century, one thing becomes strikingly clear: Supply-chain management is not the wave of the future. It is a tsunami that will engulf everything in its path . . . (Institute of Management Accountants 1999: 48).

. . . Conventional ideas of 'supply chains' are a gross oversimplification that do more harm than good (Lamming 2001).

There is no doubt that the emergence of Supply Chain Management (SCM) has been a major development in management thinking and practice. It has become an established feature of management education, a professional field with its own magazines and journals, and is claimed by some to be 'a new way of thinking' (Quiett 2002; La Londe 2003). However, many writers observe that it is a field characterized by imprecise terminology, sloppily applied metaphors, and conflated or confused concepts. The slightest skim of the many of literatures that use the term reveals a wide range of interpretations: There are hundreds of different formulations, nuances, and taxonomies for the 'supply chain', and dozens of near-synonyms. In an earlier paper (New 1994), one of the editors of this volume mapped out different common usages of the term, including the flow of a product or commodity through a sequence of firms or locations, a web of commercial relationships (for a particular firm, or for a network of firms), a multi-echelon inventory/logistics system, a label for particular corporate management functions (e.g. warehousing, purchasing), an orientation towards cooperation and collective optimization between trading partners, a geographical or sectoral cluster of firms, or even as a synonym for 'chain store'. A single memorandum from the UK Department of Trade and Industry (DTI 2002) uses the phrase three ways—as a synonym for 'sector' (helping 'upskill [sic] the existing workforce while maintaining quality through-out the supply chain'), to describe firms working to improve their suppliers ('supply chain development'), and finally in a way which can only be read as empty jargon (helping the motor sports industry 'maintain its international expertise through capitalising on the supply chain linkages').

Nevertheless, it is clear that the supply chain remains a valid and important subject of academic attention. The purpose of the current volume is to help bring together insights from some of the leading researchers and thinkers on supply chain management to help move the field forward. While we do not claim that the contributions here definitely resolve the ambiguities and contradictions in the area, they do tackle aspects of the debate that are often neglected in articles in specialist journals.

The origins of this book lie in a seminar held in June 2001 at Hertford College, Oxford, at which most of the current contributors and a few others gathered to share their ideas about the key issues that would shape the development of supply chain research. The meeting encouraged us to think that a volume which collected together complementary, sometimes conflicting, but always well-researched views would prove a valuable resource for scholars and thinkers. We did not attempt to eliminate the differences of emphasis or impose a unified approach. What unites the contributions is a willingness to address the hard questions, and to take seriously the large body of relevant work that has been produced under other disciplinary headings.

We hope that three main audiences will find these contributions helpful. First, we think that researchers and teachers from several academic tribes—including operations management, marketing, strategy, industrial economics, and economic geography—will find the contributions illuminating and thought-provoking. Second, we particularly hope that the volume will become an important source for those studying supply chains as advanced students, or at the start of their research careers; and that they will find this book an important guide to the many relevant literatures, and a useful antidote to those textbooks in which the awkward questions are relegated to a footnote. Finally, we hope that the book finds interested readers among those practitioners and consultants for whom the prescriptive nostrums of the more popular literature seem rather strained.

Our thanks go principally, of course, to our contributors, but they are also due to the Saïd Business School, University of Oxford, for sponsoring our seminar, and to Mrs Farzana Sadat for secretarial support. We also add thanks to our colleagues Matthew Derbyshire and David Musson at Oxford University Press, who have understood our difficulties in implementing the concept of on-time delivery to our own supply chain.

SN and RW

References

Institute of Management Accountants (1999). *Statement on Management Accounting No. 411. Implementing Integrated Supply Chain Management for Competitive Advantage.* Montvale, NJ: IMA.

DTI (2002). Memorandum submitted by the Department of Trade and Industry to the Select Committee on Trade and Industry. COM 211. 14 June. London: The Stationery Office. Available at: http://www.parliament.the.stationery-office.co.uk/pa/cm20012/cmselect/omtridin/597/2031302.htm.

LA LONDE, B. (2003). 'Five Principles of Supply Chain Management'. *Supply Chain Management*, 7/3: 7–8.

QUIETT, W. F. (2002). 'Embracing Supply Chain Management'. *Supply Chain Management Review*, 6/5: 40–47.

QUINN, F. (2003). 'A Fantastic Future'. *Supply Chain Management Review*, 7/3: 5.

LAMMING, R. (2001). Quoted in 'Does Supply Chain Thinking Do More Harm Than Good?' 30th November 2001. www.manufacturingtalk.com/news.ssi/ssi107.html.

NEW, S. J. (1994). 'Supply Chains: Some Doubts'. *Proceedings of the Third International Conference of IPSERA*. 345–62.

CONTENTS

LIST OF FIGURES

LIST OF TABLES

LIST OF CONTRIBUTORS

John Bessant, Cranfield School of Management.

Nigel Caldwell, Centre for Research in Strategic Purchasing and Supply, School of Management, University of Bath.

Ani Calinescu, Oxford University Computing Laboratory.

Martin Christopher, Cranfield School of Management, Cranfield University.

Paul Cousins, Queen's School of Management and Economics, Queen's University, Belfast.

Simon Croom, Warwick Business School, University of Warwick.

Stephen Disney, Cardiff Business School, Cardiff University.

Janet Efstathiou, Department of Engineering Science, University of Oxford.

Mihalis Giannakis, Middlesex University Business School.

Christine Harland, Centre for Research in Strategic Purchasing and Supply, School of Management, University of Bath.

Luisa Huaccho Huatuco, Department of Engineering Science, University of Oxford.

P. Fraser Johnson, Richard Ivey School of Business, University of Western Ontario.

Robert D. Klassen, Richard Ivey School of Business, University of Western Ontario.

Louise Knight, Centre for Research in Strategic Purchasing and Supply, School of Management, University of Bath.

Richard Lamming, School of Management, University of Southampton.

Mohamed Naim, Cardiff Business School, Cardiff University.

Guido Nassimbeni, Dipartimento Di Ingegneria Elettrica Gestionale E Meccanica (DIEGM) via delle Scienze, University of Udine.

Steve New, Saïd Business School, University of Oxford.

Wendy Phillips, Centre for Research in Strategic Purchasing and Supply, School of Management, University of Bath.

Suja Sivadasan, RAND Europe.

Nigel Slack, Warwick Business School, University of Warwick.

Denis Towill, Cardiff Business School, Cardiff University.

Roy Westbrook, Saïd Business School, University of Oxford.

Supply Chain Paradigms

MIHALIS GIANNAKIS, SIMON CROOM, AND NIGEL SLACK

1. Introduction

... disciplines are distinguished by the general problem they address. (Tranfield and Starkey 1998)

Organizations do not exist in isolation. Any organization, whether a large corporation, public body, or small business aims to meet the needs of its various customers and stakeholders, will need resources in order to do this, and will acquire many of its materials, equipment, facilities, and supplies from other organizations. The performance of an organization is thus influenced to a greater or lesser degree by the actions of the organizations that make up the supply chain. The term supply chain management was first used in its popular sense by Oliver and Weber (1982) and then replicated by Houlihan in a series of articles (Houlihan 1984, 1985, 1988) to describe the management of materials flows across organizational borders. Since then several researchers have investigated the concept of supply chain management (Ellram 1991; Christopher 1992; Harland 1994; Lamming 1996; Handfield and Nichols 1999) establishing its theoretical and operational bases as we know them today. The influence of supply chain thought on organizational strategy has also been significant, reflecting, as Christopher (1992), Macbeth and Ferguson (1994), and others authors have succinctly claimed, '... that today ... competition takes place between Supply Chains rather than between individual companies'.

1.1. Challenges for a supply chain management discipline

In the literature a consensus on the meaning of supply chain management does not exist. A profusion of different terminologies can be found referring to: *supply network* (Nishiguchi 1994), *lean chain approach* (New and Ramsay 1995), *supplier integration* (Dyer, Cho, and Chu 1998), *buyer–supplier partnership* (Lamming 1993), *integrated purchasing strategy* (Burt 1984), *supply base management, strategic supplier alliances* (Lewis, Naim, and Towill 1997), *supply chain synchronization* (Tan, Kannan, and Handfield 1998), *network supply chain* (Nassimbeni 1998), *value-added chain* (Lee and Billington 1992), *supply pipeline management* (Farmer and van Amstel 1991), *value stream* (Jones 1994). In terms of the debate about the scope of supply chain management, Oliver and Webber (1982) considered it as *the planning and control of the total materials flow*; Ellram (1991) viewed it as *an alternative form to vertical integration*; and Christopher (1992) and Lee and Ng (1997) have defined it as *the management of a network of organizations or entities*.

These definitions do have different meanings or emphases, but they at least share one common theme—they all refer to phenomena relating to the management of operations across organizational boundaries. Furthermore, within this relatively diverse literature there is a common philosophy (or even ideology) that by understanding and managing the supply chain, organizations will gain commercial benefits (New 1996). The challenge, as New (1996) also notes, is that 'arguments about the precise metaphor are generally fruitless, as much writing in this area is based around a loose agreement on a general theme'.

In Table 1.1 we have highlighted a few definitions that have been used for the concept of supply chain management over the last 20 years in order to provide some indication of the changing emphasis and also the development of the literature in this important field. (For a more comprehensive review of supply chain definitions see, for example, Cooper, Lambert, and Pagh 1997.)

Such diversity is not an entirely negative factor. According to Anderson (1983) a subject's scientific status is enhanced if the knowledge base is widely dispersed, and there is a profusion of ideas and interpretations of its constitutional elements. Research relating to the management of supply chains is undoubtedly diverse and multidisciplinary and as we will show in this chapter, founded on a heritage of different antecedent bases. However, is it a cohesive and cogent body of thought that could be described as a supply chain management discipline? Is there a way in which such a discipline could be defined? How might such a discipline be delineated?

In this chapter we provide a review of the main theoretical antecedents that have informed the research behind the current body of supply chain management knowledge. We also discuss some of the key catalysts for the academic development of the subject, in particular the impact of a number of institutions in Europe and the United States and the contribution of two key research groups—the IMP and IMVP. We conclude this chapter by addressing the challenge for the development of supply chain management as an academic *discipline*, in which we outline the 3S Model as the framework for delineating and defining the general problem area for supply chain management. Using the well-known Benetton case study (Signorelli and Heskett 1984), we provide an illustration of the application of this framework.

Table 1.1. A sample of definitions of supply chain management

Authors	Definition
Oliver and Webber (1982)	Supply chain management covers the flow of goods from supplier through manufacturing and distribution chains to end-user
Jones and Riley (1987)	Supply chain management techniques deal with the planning and control of total materials flow from suppliers through end-users
Ellram (1991)	An integrative approach to dealing with the planning and control of the materials flow from suppliers to end-users
Christopher (1992)	Supply chain management is the management of a network of organizations that are involved, through upstream and downstream linkages, in the different processes and activities that produce value in the form of products and services in the hands of the ultimate consumer
International Center for Competitive Excellence (1994)	Supply chain management is the integration of business processes from end-user through original suppliers that provides products services and information that add value for customers
Harland (1994)	Supply chain management is defined as the management of the flow of goods and services to end customers to satisfy their requirements
Berry *et al.* (1994)	Supply chain management aims at building trust, exchanging information on market needs, developing new products, and reducing the supplier base to a particular original equipment manufacturer (OEM) so as to release management resources for developing meaningful, long-term relationships
Cooper *et al.* (1997)	An integrating philosophy to manage the total flow of a distribution channel from supplier to ultimate customer
Lee and Ng (1997)	(*The management of*) a network of entities that starts with the suppliers' supplier and end with the customers' customers for the production and delivery of goods and services
Handfield and Nichols (1999)	The supply chain encompasses all activities associated with the flow and transformation of goods from the raw materials stage (extraction), through to the end-user, as well as associated information flows. Material and information flow both up and down the supply chain. Supply chain management is the integration of these activities through improved supply chain relationships to achieve sustainable competitive advantage
Simchi-Levi *et al.* (2000)	Supply chain management is a set of approaches utilized to efficiently integrate suppliers, manufacturers, warehouses, and stores, so that merchandise is produced and distributed at the right quantities, to the right locations and at the right time, in order to minimize system-wide costs while satisfying service level requirements
Ayers (2001)	Supply chain management is the design, maintenance, and operation of supply chain processes for satisfaction of end-users

2. Theories that have influenced supply chain management thinking

In this section we examine the main antecedent theories that have informed the development of supply chain management thought.

2.1. Systems theory

Systems theory developed in physics and biology (von Bertalanffy 1950) but was very quickly adopted by management scholars to help explain the behaviour of processes, firms, and economies. The common usage of the term 'system' in organizational and management literature is perhaps a reflection of the pervasiveness of systems theory in modern management thought.

Systems theory views the world in terms of collections of resources and processes that exist to meet superordinate goals. (Systems are often described as *teleological*, which means they exist to serve an end goal or objective). A system may be constituted by material, people, information, and financial resources; configured into organizational or technical processes intended to deliver goods and services that enable the system to achieve some desired level of performance. The field of operations management (Slack, Chambers, and Johnston 2001) has been heavily influenced by systems theory, as has the field of organizational theory (see Trist and Bamforth 1951).

Utilizing the concepts of systems theory, the *Industrial Dynamics* approach developed by Forrester (1961) has been valuable for explaining the dynamic behaviour of industrial organizations and their supply systems. Based on the systems approach, Forrester claimed that industrial dynamics 'is the study of the information-feedback characteristics of industrial activity to show how organisational structure, amplification and time delays (in decisions and actions) interact to influence the success of the enterprise' (Wang and Seidmann 1995). The typical industrial dynamics model is a mathematical model for analysing stability and fluctuation in an industrial system—typically across the whole supply system.

Two particular aspects of systems theory are particularly pertinent for understanding the behaviour of supply chains:

Synergy: Synergy is the tendency to unify the power of two or more elements and the perception that 'the whole is greater than the sum of the parts that constitute it'. In other words, parts of a system (such as the firms constituting a supply chain) working together can achieve more than the sum of achievements that each one would achieve separately. Discussions of the 'beer game' and 'bullwhip effect' illustrate this characteristic ascribed to materials flow through the chain (Lee, Padmanabhan, and Whang 1997).

Entropy: Unless there is a continuous effort to feed back the system with the appropriate inputs a system has the tendency to debilitate. This gradual and continuous debilitation that leads the system to extinction is called entropy. Again, the phenomenon of the 'bullwhip effect' is a useful illustration of the debilitating effects of poor feedback across the chain.

2.2. Transaction cost economics

Transaction cost economics discusses the rationale behind the organization of production, specifically the determination of whether to produce or buy specific resources. In *Hierarchies and Markets*, Williamson (1975) presented an *institutional economics* perspective drawing on Coase's (1937) theorem of the firm in order to develop his theory for determining the most economical *governance structure* for a firm—that is, should the firm be vertically integrated (hierarchy) or should it use another firm (the market)? According to Williamson firms tend to choose vertical integration when the 'transaction costs' are high in order to control such costs through close supervision, but will resort to purchasing from the market when these costs are low. Williamson argued that there are three critical factors that determine the choice of governance structure: asset specificity, uncertainty, and frequency of transaction. Asset specificity refers to the degree of dedication of assets such as machines, facilities, and people to a single customer's requirement. Assets that are highly specific to only one use, he argued, would suggest a hierarchical governance structure. The second dimension of transaction costs is that of uncertainty, which refers to the limited competence, trustworthiness, and reliability of human agents. Williamson sees this as an important concern due to the existence of bounded rationality and opportunism. Employing Simon's (1960) view that individuals do not possess absolute rationality, but rather are perceived to have limited information processing capability ('bounded rationality'), Williamson assumes that individuals will act opportunistically, or will be 'self-interest seeking with guile'. Again, in this argument, a high degree of uncertainty suggests a hierarchical governance structure. Finally, frequency of transaction refers simply to the recurrence of transactions and Williamson's argument is fundamentally one of amortization of costs. The more frequent the transaction, the more viable is vertical integration.

2.3. Game theory

Game theory, originally developed by von Neumann and Morgenstern (1944), sets out to explore and explain the optimization of economic decisions involving more than one participant (e.g. a customer and supplier). Examples frequently cited in the literature include cooperative decisions such as pricing and investment decisions. They asserted that many economic decisions take the form of a strategic game involving the anticipation by one player of the other's actions. Game theory found fertile ground in the emergent field of operational research during the 1940s and 1950s and has utility for supply chain management in a wide range of decisions including inventory management, location decisions, pricing, and the development of strategic alliances (see Cox 1999*b*).

2.4. *Interorganizational relationships and industrial network theories*

Focusing on the nature of interaction between forms, Oliver (1990) developed a useful definition of an interorganizational relationship (IOR) as 'a relatively enduring transaction, flow and linkage that occurs among or between an organisation and one or more organisations in its environment'. Interorganizational research is predicated upon the perspective of interorganizational relationships as open systems (Kast and Rosenweig 1970; Morgan 1986), and that organizations are rational, taking conscious, intended decisions to enter into relationships (Simon 1960; Arrow 1974). Oliver's synthesis of the literature on IORs (1990) recognized that much of that literature was predicated on the view that IORs arise out of conscious, intentional decisions.

A major contribution to the development of this field was Van de Ven and Walker's (1984) research into interorganizational relationship development, which examined the dynamics of interaction in terms of building close relationships between parties. Their research emphasized the significance of the perceptions of parties to relationships. They concluded that the development of IORs over time was influenced by:

(1) perceptions of resource dependence in the short and long term;
(2) the contribution of communication to the formalization of the relationship over the medium term;
(3) the development of consensus among the parties in the medium to long term. Van de Ven and Walker's research draws attention to the perceptions of the parties to IORs, and the adaptations each may make to the other.

Following the increasing attention to interorganizational relationships brought about by new forms of organizations (alliances, joint ventures), the field of *Industrial Networks* developed out of Uppsala and Stockholm Universities. They conducted a series of comparative studies of buyer–supplier relationships within and across a number of European countries and examined the implications of these relationships in industrial markets. Their findings suggested that the nature of the relationships developed between the buyers and suppliers tended to have a very dynamic behaviour over time and concluded that industrial markets could be better understood if we consider and manage them. An industrial market thus could be seen as a network of relationships of actors that are interconnected through exchange relationships. Mari Sako's research (1992) further examined the way in which firms interact with each other, in particular, addressing the degree of trust between firms.

This research posited a continuum of relationship forms between the obligational contracting relation (OCR) characterized by high trust, cooperativeness, and long-term commitment, and arm's length contractual relation (ACR) where parties are principally independent and possibly adversarial.

The Interaction Model. The most important work in the industrial networks literature is the Interaction Model developed by the IMP group. The Interaction Model illustrated in Fig. 1.1 one is a dynamic model of buyer–supplier relationships in industrial markets in which the marketing and supply of industrial offerings is seen as an interaction between two parties (Ford 1990; IMP Group 1997).

This interaction is influenced by four groups of variables:

(1) variables describing the *parties* involved, as organizations, groups, and individuals;
(2) variables describing the *elements and process of interaction*;
(3) variables describing the *environment* within which the interaction takes place;
(4) variables describing the *atmosphere* affecting and affected by the interaction.

From the IOR and industrial network research, recognition that the complementary behaviour of firms across the supply chains is dependent on the way in which they relate and interact has made a significant contribution to the development of supply chain management.

2.5. The virtual organization—e-business and supply chains

More recently, advancements in IT, telecommunication, and specifically the use of Internet and web-based systems have impacted on the study and

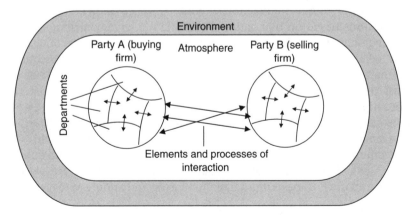

Fig. 1.1. The IMP model of interaction

development of the so-called '*virtual organisations*' (Evans and Wurster 1999), that is, an organization that has relatively few physical resources. Virtual organizations are technology driven and involve the development of a multitude of potential trading partners. With all its information technology it is the latest version of the new forms of strategic partnerships in a supply chain. It is believed that the virtual organization is the means of implementing the management of entire supply chains. Further research has emphasized the importance to e-business development of the management of supply chains through easier, quicker, and more comprehensive information and data flows across the supply chain (Malone and Yates 1989; Wise and Morrison 2000; Croom 2001).

3. Key events in the evolution of supply chain management thought

In this section we briefly review the main political, economic, and technological development that have served as an impetus for the development of supply chain managements thought, particularly in respect of empirical theory development. In Table 1.2 we have constructed a chronological assessment of the main conditions over the last 60 years that have triggered some of the major developments in the theoretical and empirical development of the field.

4. Institutions that contributed to the development of supply chain management

Without the financial and intellectual support of institutions and organizations that have specialized in promoting and conducting research in supply chain management and organizing conferences, some of the seminal research studies in supply chain management could not have been carried out. Organizations based on both sides of the Atlantic have contributed work in supply chain management from different perspectives. In this section we have identified eight such institutions that have played a major role in encouraging the generation and dissemination of knowledge in supply chain management issues: the IMP (Industrial Marketing and Purchasing) Group; the IMVP (International Motor Vehicle Programme) Programme; IPSERA (International Purchasing and Supply Education and Research Association); CAPS (the Center for Advanced Purchasing Studies) in Arizona; the department of Supply Chain Management at Arizona State University; the Department of Marketing and Supply Chain Management at Michigan State University; the Supply Chain Council; and the European Journal of Purchasing and Supply Management.

IMP Group. The work of the IMP Group began in the mid- to late 1970s and brought together researchers from Europe and the United States of America

Table 1.2. Chronological assessment of supply chain management developments

	Political	Economical	Technological	Key theoretical developments
1940s	The Second World War Split of Europe	Inflation pressures Marshall aid Resource scarcity	The transistor is invented in 1947 at Bell Laboratories	Total cost model Physical distribution and transportation Operational research logistics Game theory
1950s	Cold War and reconstruction of Eastern Europe First European attempt at unification	Economic growth Cost reduction Increasing wealth	1952—first digital computer for commercial applications is installed in GE Process innovations	Systems theory Contingency theory Industrial dynamics
1960s	Cold War Vietnam War	Economic growth Labour and consumer power	Computers are introduced for production control MRP systems Microchips are invented at Intel Laboratories	Contingency theory MRP
1970s	Emergence of European global influence Emergence of Japanese economy	Oil crisis Lean production Recession	CNC machine tools Digital computers are introduced MRP II	Transaction cost economics JIT, MRP II Best practices
1980s	End of Soviet Union Globalization	Deregulation of industries Increasing globalization Emphasis on quality	Intel launches the production of PCs (1981) Network development EDI Telecommunications advances	Supply chain management New organizational forms (Networks, alliances, mergers)
1990s	Gulf War EU integration	Oil crisis EU monetary union Technology-led innovation	IT advances Internet	Supply chain integration

who shared a common interest in business-to-business marketing, social networks, and, to a lesser extent, industrial purchasing. The Group remains today a loose collective rather than a formal organization, involving multiple collaborative projects and programmes and an annual conference. Undoubtedly on sheer volume of published output alone the IMP Group has had a major impact on our understanding of business markets. Furthermore, developing expertise in specific areas of their field (such as supply strategy and strategic account management), researchers have contributed to many aspects of supply chain management developments.

IMVP Programme. The International Motor Vehicle Programme, in contrast to the IMP Group, is a formal, funded global research group. Their first contribution was through the best-selling book *The Machine that Changed the World* (Womack, Jones, and Roos 1990) which introduced the lean operations concepts. Subsequently, various research units (notably Cardiff's Lean Enterprise Research Centre) and developments in supply chain thought (Lamming 1993; Womack and Jones 1996; Hines *et al.* 2000) have expounded on the lean concept. Undoubtedly the adoption of just in time or lean practices by many organizations has been remarkable and indicates the thirst for supply chain improvements that exists across global industries.

IPSERA. IPSERA was founded in 1990 by a group of academics financially supported by the Chartered Institute of Purchasing and Supply (CIPS) in the UK. It has over 200 members from fourteen different countries and is still growing rapidly. From its first conference in 1992 in Glasgow IPSERA has hosted an annual conference and provides regular workshops organized and hosted by local university centres/departments affiliated with IPSERA in most European countries. Other activities include a newsletter on a regular basis that keeps members informed of future events and provides feedback on events already run. It also provides a forum of exchange between members and presents relevant news items and information. Examination of the content and quality of conference proceedings since the first international conference provides a remarkable insight into the development of theoretical and empirical research in the field during the last decade.

CAPS. The Centre for Advanced Purchasing Studies (CAPS) is an independent, non-profit organization, affiliated with the US's National Association of Purchasing Management (NAPM) and the Arizona State University. It was founded in 1986 by NAPM and its mission is 'to help organisations achieve competitive advantage by providing them with leading-edge research and benchmarking information to support the evolution of strategic purchasing and supply management'. Over the past decade, the development of the CAPS has run parallel to a fundamental shift in the perceived role of the purchasing profession. CAPS (CAPS 1996) has provided these same professionals with the critical research data necessary to provide a solid basis for their recommendations.

As an independent research organization, CAPS provides companies and purchasing professionals with research and data from a perspective outside the normal business realm. This information is made available to companies as well as to their suppliers. By making this information available to all, CAPS believes that this research will benefit the widest audience over the long run. By distributing this information widely, CAPS enables organizations to avoid duplicating research activities across the profession.

ASU—Supply Chain Management. Arizona State University was one of the first universities to establish a substantial supply chain management department. Professor Joseph Carter, current director of the department, states that 'The name Supply Chain Management was selected in 1996 to reflect the development of graduate and undergraduate curricula with a clear inter-firm, integrated approach to managing the supply chain'. The department has over thirty academic members of faculty and provides a wide range of degree and executive programmes (including a B.Sc. programme) in Supply Chain Management. The Department is also affiliated with CAPS and CLM.

MSU Marketing and Supply Chain Management. The Department of Marketing and Supply Chain Management at Michigan State University was the result of the merger of the operations management and procurement faculty (formerly located in the Department of Management) with the faculty of the Department of Marketing and Logistics. Since 1980, these two faculties had cooperated in an inter-departmental programme, the Materials and Logistics Management Program, which integrated procurement, manufacturing, and logistics. Over the intervening years, this programme has achieved a dominant national reputation and strong demand for its products—knowledge, employees, and executive training.

Supply Chain Council (SCC). The Supply Chain Council is a professional organization formed in 1997 by a number of practitioners' initiative representing big multinational companies. It consists of many of the leading industrial companies, logistics, and distribution companies, and supply chain application software companies. It is in its mission statement that standard terminology, best practice models and benchmark metrics should be used for communicating supply chain management practices across companies in a model called the 'Supply Chain Operations Reference-model' (SCOR).

European Journal of Purchasing and Supply Management. The European Journal of Purchasing and Supply Management published its first issue in 1995. It is published quarterly by Elsevier/Butterworth-Heinemann. It is one of the few specialized journals on issues regarding supply chain management and has acheived great success within Europe. The journal covers every aspect of the purchasing of goods and services in all sectors.

5. The growth of supply chain management literature

Given the diversity of the field of supply chain management, attempting to quantify the size of the body of literature can be quite difficult. In order to simplify the process we concentrated on three main citation databases (Institute of Scientific Information, EBSCO, and ABI/Inform). In compiling our analysis we simply searched for the number of references including the term 'supply chain management' in the citation for each of the 11 years up to 2001. The results are represented below in Fig. 1.2.

The impact of seminal developments in management literature is not immediate—or at least not in terms of their citation in subsequent published works. Two factors influence this delay. First, the need by researchers to assimilate concepts, ideas, and theories into their research. Second, the lead time involved in writing and publication. Consequently a lag of 5–6 years between the emergence of seminal work and the adoption of its core precepts into other literature is typical. These data illustrate that supply chain management literature and research clearly emerged as a specific management topic in the mid-1990s. Reflecting, in large part, the gradual impact of the key antecedent theories and approaches developed during the late 1970s and 1980s that we have already discussed, we would also highlight the key role played in these developments by two bodies of research: the European IMP Group and the global IMVP. We would contend that the current developments in supply chain management continue to owe considerable debt to these two programmes. The IMP Group have contributed to much work on inter-firm relationships and the assimilation of ideas of network theory and transaction costs economics

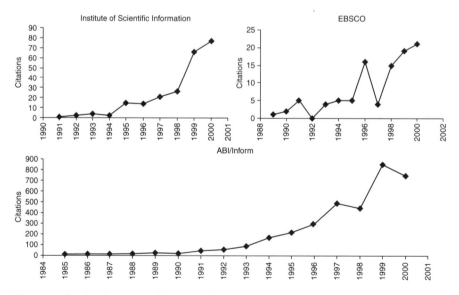

Fig. 1.2.   The development of a mass of literature—analysis of three citations databases

into the mainstream of supply chain literature. Their work is frequently cited in the literature and has stimulated the growth of multidisciplinary research, particularly among doctoral candidates across Europe. The IMVP programme has stimulated considerable developments in the logistics and application of industrial engineering to supply chains. Furthermore, the emergence of healthy debate around lean principles has helped to promote the development of alternative paradigms and research streams (see, for example, Cox 1999*a*; Hines *et al.* 2000).

6. Towards development of a cognate theoretical discipline

As we see, the importance of supply chain management to practitioners and researchers alike has grown considerably, particularly in the last decade of the twentieth century. However, one of the problems facing the academic development of a supply chain management discipline as argued by several researchers (see, for example, New 1994; Cox 1999*a*, *b*; Croom, Romano, and Giannakis 2000; Giannakis and Croom 2000) is the relative lack of theoretical work in the field, in stark contrast to a significant volume of empirical based research in the subject. Reflecting on our preceding discussion of the antecedent theories and evolution of the current body of supply chain thought, we conclude this chapter with an examination of the scope of a supply chain discipline through our proposed framework for describing the field which we call the '3S model'.

6.1. The 3S Model—synthesis, synergy, and synchronization

In supporting the case for recognition of supply chain management as a discipline in its own right we contend that it is necessary to be able to define, or map, the problem domain. First and vitally, it enables researchers to comprehend the relationship between streams of research and thus to be able to contribute to both theory building and theory testing. Second, through such classification it is possible to critically evaluate individual pieces of research and publications with existing knowledge. Third, it allows us to identify the development and progression of specific research trajectories. Fourth, it enables us to classify existing research and theory. At present there is a clear need for a framework that allows researchers and practitioners to locate and describe clearly the context and character of supply chain management problems. In this final section of the chapter we redress this gap in the theoretical development of a supply chain management discipline.

We have already seen that supply chain management is a concept that has been examined from different perspectives in a large number of different bodies of literature, disciplines, and research areas. We felt that although apparently disparate, it is possible to identify a few core dimensions to describe this body of work. In order to develop a framework for supply chain management we first conducted an extensive review of publications and then carried out a comprehensive survey of the views and opinions of supply chain and management academics. Our analysis then identified and delineated the supply chain management discipline according to three basic dimensions of supply chain decision-making which we contend relate to the *synthesis, synergy,* and *synchronization* of supply chains. Each of these three objective dimensions is described below.

6.2. *The synthesis of business and resource networks*

Synthesis is the term we use to describe strategic decisions related to the structure of supply chains primarily to reflect the importance of the characteristics relating to the construction of supply chains. Literature concerned with the issues of supply chain *synthesis* includes concern for:

1. The strategic governance of the firm in the supply chain (i.e. issues relating to vertical integration, such as what boundaries a firm should establish over its activities; make or buy decisions).
2. The physical and financial characteristics of resource structures (processes) within operations across the supply chain.
3. The physical and financial characteristics of logistics structures between and within organizations across the chain.
4. Decisions relating to the number, location, and size of suppliers to a firm for particular component or service.
5. The structural character of information networks in terms of their alignment and integration.

These 'anatomical' aspects of the supply chain build on the insights from a number of theoretical antecedents including transaction cost economics network theory, systems theory, and incorporate techniques and ideas from operational research and operations management.

6.3 *Determination of appropriate synergy between the actors in a supply chain*

Issues of *synergy* are concerned with the manner and form of interactions and relationships across supply chains. This has been a central area of development in the literature. We see acknowledgement of the importance of communication and joint decision-making for managing materials flows in order to address the Forrester or bullwhip effect (Lee, Padmanabhan, and Whang 1997). Also, the principles of lean supply relationships are predicated on the strategic advantages of integration between parties in the chain (Lamming 1993; Dyer 2000). In contrast, examination of the consequences and opportunities afforded through exploitation of the relative influence of different players in the chain also explores issues of supply chain synergy (Cox 1999a). These relational aspects of supply chain management are based on antecedent theories in the areas of interorganizational relationships, game theory, and strategic management. Such theories and research supports the examination and interpretation of issues relating to intra- and interorganizational relationships such as:

- the development and evolution of buyer–seller relationships
- the strategic returns from collaboration
- the economic value of market power
- identifying and responding to customer and supplier behaviour
- options in terms of managing major customers and suppliers.

6.4 Synchronization of the activities and operations across the supply chain

The dimension of *synchronization* is primarily concerned with the management and coordination of resource flows across supply chains. Such resource flows naturally concentrate on physical materials, but we would also see the flow of information and knowledge as key issues for the synchronization of supply chains. Examples of synchronization problems include:

- the scheduling of material flows across the supply chain
- the behaviour of logistics systems
- coordination of the operations processes of the involved actors
- creation and dissemination of knowledge among the supply chain members
- the contribution of interorganizational information systems to supply chain performance and behaviour.

Depending on the dimension, or combination of dimensions, being evaluated within any specific theoretical or empirical analyses, it is possible to clarify the characteristics and concerns of antecedent theory. For example, issues of synthesis are heavily influenced by transaction cost, social community, and governance theories; synergy issues (which are very much concerned with relational elements of organizational and supply chain behaviours) draw on game theory, behavioural theories, and elements of lean relationships; for example, issues relating to synchronization reflect the more operational and analytical concerns of operational research, systems behaviour, and IS integration.

The theoretical foundation of the 3S model is shown in Fig. 1.3 below, in which we map the development of key antecedent theories, concepts, and management phenomena since the 1940s to the three dimensions of synthesis, synergy, and synchronization. The objective with this map is to clarify the current and potential theoretical basis for research developments in supply chain management according to the problem domain of the research.

Thus, the 3S Model provides a simple, effective, and comprehensive framework for describing and deconstructing supply chain issues. To illustrate the application of this framework briefly we can employ it to analyse the Benetton

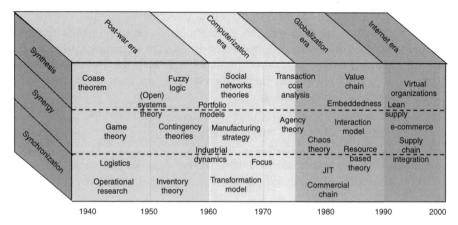

Fig. 1.3. Chronology of theoretical developments that influenced supply chain management

case study example (Harvard College 1984; Signorelli and Heskett 1984; Camuffo, Romano, and Vinelli 2001).

- *Synthesis* To support their core high volume, low variety production facilities, Benetton employ a core contractor network of approximately 220 employee-owned contractors, and a wider network of subcontractors, many of whom are 'casual' (i.e. paid on an ad hoc piece-rate basis). On the demand side, they employ a few regional agents who oversee a network of franchised, small retail outlets in primarily rented high throughput locations. Serving distribution Benetton operate large, automated warehouses utilizing advanced technology and standardized packaging.
- *Synergy* within the Benetton Network. On the supply side of the network Benetton's contractors have regular contact with the company, are an integral part of the work-in-process logistics system and have close family ties to employees. On the demand side, Benetton take a large responsibility for innovation in product design and analysis of retailing innovations. Their agents have a key responsibility for acting as intermediaries between manufacturing and the stores in their region, while retailers are franchised and closely connected (through information systems) to Benetton.
- *Synchronization* of the Benetton supply chain. Benetton operate a dual system of manufacturing and logistics, akin to Fisher's notions of functional and responsive supply chains (Fisher 1997): Signorelli and Heskett (1984) describe Benetton's two systems as 'speculation' and 'postponement'. Retailers have responsibility for ordering (from their agents) often as much as 8 months in advance of the season. Agents aggregate and often adjust these retail orders and order directly from Benetton manufacturing, allowing them to operate on a make-to-order master schedule. Contractors collect materials daily and to accommodate materials tracking, each consignment is clearly identified

according to retail order number. Completed work is returned to Benetton for quality checking and further operation. Integrating the whole materials flow across the supply chain is an advanced information system.

Benetton's success can be further understood through evaluation of the characteristics and interconnections between the synthesis, synergy, and synchronization of their supply chains. By concentrating on a few links between each stage of their supply chain (e.g. limited to around 220 local contractors on the supply side and regional agents on the demand side), lines of material and information flow are easier to facilitate and manage through the shorter lines of communications and logistics. Further, each stage in the chain is characterized by appropriate operations process choice—for example, while Benetton's own manufacturing is a high volume, low variety, high capital intensity process, contractors' operations are focused on a wider range, lower volumes, and lower capital intensity. Across the network this allows for 'flexible specialisation' (Piore and Sabel 1982) through optimization of process choice at each stage of the production supply chain. The close family ties between Benetton and their contractor network fosters obligational bonds encouraging greater adherence to schedules, clearer understanding of the characteristics of Benetton's systems, a dedication to product quality, and an appropriate priority response for urgent (postponement) orders (Sako 1992). The motivation for the franchised retail operation to bear significant forecasting risk in their commitment to ordering 8 months in advance of the season is enhanced by their opportunities to postpone colour choices until much later in the retail sales cycle and by the liberal financial regimes that Benetton provide for them.

Benetton's management of the total supply chain is distinctive in terms of their emphasis on the synthesis of the network—employing large-scale operations for centralized activities and small-scale operations to provide local focus yet at the same time provide flexibility at the level of the network. Their attention to the synergy between actors in the supply chain is reinforced by the use of employee family-owned contractors and franchised retailers. In both, a high degree of motivation and commitment to Benetton is fostered through appropriate financial as well as emotional reward. Their innovative use of a two-tier supply chain control methodology—the functional and responsive supply chains—offers clear advantages in coping with instability of demand.

Thus, the Benetton case offers a useful indication of the characteristics of each of the three dimensions of the 3S Model; it enable us to deconstruct the implications of their supply chain management practices and philosophies in order better to understand how it operates; and to analyse the contribution of each of the three dimensions singularly and in combination to Benetton's strategic success.

7. Conclusion

At the beginning of this chapter we cited Tranfield and Starkey's claim that disciplines are defined by their common problem domain. Supply chain management is naturally a diverse and multidimensional area of research. As we have tried to illustrate, the theoretical antecedents for much of current work in the field is founded in a number of existing theoretical antecedents—systems theory, transaction cost economics, and game theory in particular. It is apparent that research in supply chain management addresses a wide and diverse range of problems, involving very different theoretical approaches, and has developed a number of distinctive paths. In particular, the contribution of two major research programmes, the IMP Group and the IMVP programme, have been significant in terms of providing the foundation for the development of key streams of research concerned with network relationship analyses and lean operations, respectively.

However, the main challenge for support of a supply chain management *discipline* remains the issue of definition of the problem domain. In this respect we introduced the 3S Model, which we have found to have considerable utility as a device for defining the *ontology* of supply chain and consequently for establishing the confines and boundaries of supply chain management. While supply chain management has emerged and evolved as an area of important academic interest over the last fifteen or so years, it has done so in a relatively fragmented manner. This is potentially a good thing, for it at least ensures that a creative and innovative base of ideas has emerged through a diverse range of perspectives. We, like many readers presumably, hope for a robust and rigorous future for the development of a cognate discipline of supply chain management that continues to contribute to both intellectual debate and managerial practice.

References

ANDERSON, P. (1983). 'Marketing, Scientific Progress and Scientific Method'. *Journal of Marketing*, 47/4: 18–31.

ARROW, K. (1974). *The Limits of Organisation*. New York: Norton.

AYERS, J. (2001). *Handbook of Supply Chain Management*. Boca Raton, FL: St Lucie Press.

BERRY, D., TOWILL, D., and WADSLEY, N. (1994). 'Supply Chain Management in the Electronics Products Industry'. *International Journal of Physical Distribution and Logistics Management*, 24/10: 20–32.

BURT, D. (1984). *Proactive Procurement*. Englewood Cliffs: Prentice-Hall.

CAMUFFO, A., ROMANO, P., and VINELLI, A. (2001). 'Back to the Future: Benetton Transforms its Global Network'. *Sloan Management Review*, 43/1: 46–51.

CAPS (The Centre of Advanced Purchasing Studies) (1996). *The First 10 Years*. Tempe, Arizona: CAPS.

CHRISTOPHER, M. (1992). *Logistics and Supply Chain Management: Strategies for Reducing Costs and Improving Services*. London: Financial Times/Pitman.

COASE, R. H. (1937). 'The Nature of the Firm'. *Economica*, 4/16: 386–405.

COOPER, M. C., LAMBERT, D. M., and PAGH, J. D. (1997). 'Supply Chain Management: More than a New Name for Logistics'. *The International Journal of Logistics Management*, 8: 1–13.

COOPER, M. C., ELLRAM, L. M., GARDNER, J. T., and HANKS, A. M. (1997). 'Meshing Multiple Alliances'. *Journal of Business Logistics*, 18/1: 67–89.

COX, A. (1999a). 'A Research Agenda for Supply Chain and Business Management Thinking'. *Supply Chain Management*, 4/4: 209–11.

—— (1999b). 'Power, Value and Supply Chain Management'. *Supply Chain Management*, 4/4: 167–75.

CROOM, S. (2001). *Supply Chain Management in the E-Business Era*. Coventry: SC Associates.

—— ROMANO, P., and GIANNAKIS, M. (2000). 'Supply Chain Management: An Analytical Framework for Critical Literature Review'. *European Journal of Purchasing and Supply Management*, 6/1: 67–83.

DYER, J. H. (2000). *Collaborative Advantage. Winning Through Extended Enterprise Supplier Networks*. Oxford: Oxford University Press.

—— CHO, DONG SUNG, and CHU, WUJIN (1998). 'Strategic Supplier Segmentation: The Next "Best Practice" in Supply Chain Management'. *California Management Review*, 40/2: 57–77.

ELLRAM, L. M. (1991). 'Supply Chain Management: The Industrial Organisation Perspective'. *International Journal of Physical Distribution and Logistics Management*, 21: 13–22.

EVANS, P., and WURSTER, T. S. (1999). 'Getting Real About Virtual Commerce'. *Harvard Business Review*, 77/6: 85–94.

FARMER, D., and PLOOS VAN AMSTEL, R. (1991). *Effective Pipeline Management*. Aldershot: Gower.

FISHER, M. L. (1997). 'What is the Right Supply Chain for Your Product?' *Harvard Business Review*, 75/2: 105–16.

FORD, I. D. (1990). *Understanding Business Markets. Interaction, Relationships, Networks*. London: Academic Press.

FORRESTER, J. W. (1961). *Industrial Dynamics*. Cambridge, MA: MIT Press.

GEORGE, C. S. Jr. (1972). *The History of Management Thought*. New York: Prentice Hall.

GIANNAKIS, M., and CROOM, S. (2000). 'Towards the Development of a Supply Chain Management Paradigm: A Conceptual Framework'. *Proceedings of the IPSERA Conference, London Ontario*.

HANDFIELD, R. B., and NICHOLS, E. L. (1999). *Introduction to Supply Chain Management*. Upper Saddle River, NJ.: Prentice-Hall.

HARLAND, C. (1994). 'Perceptions of Requirements and Performance in European Automotive Aftermarket Supply Chains'. Ph.D. thesis, Warwick.

Harvard College (1984). *Benetton Factory Tour* Video 9-886-510.

HECKERT, J. B., and MINER, R. B. (1940). *Distribution Costs*. New York: The Ronald Press Company.

HELPER, S. (1991). 'How Much has Really Changed Between U.S. Automakers and Their Suppliers?' *Sloan Management Review*, 32/4: 15–28.

—— and SAKO, M. (1995). 'Supplier Relations in Japan and the United States: Are They Converging?' *Sloan Management Review*, 36/3: 77–85.

HILL, J. (1975). 'The Purchasing Revolution'. *Journal of Purchasing and Materials Management*, 11/2: 18–22.

HINES, P., LAMMING, R. C., JONES, D. T., COUSINS, P., and RICH, N. (2000). *Value Stream Management. Strategy and Excellence in the Supply Chain*. New York: Prentice Hall.

HOULIHAN, J. B. (1984). 'Supply Chain Management'. *Proceedings of the 19th Int. Tech. Conference BPICS*: 101–10.

—— (1985). 'International Supply Chain Management'. *International Journal of Physical Distribution and Materials Managemet*, 15: 22–39.

—— (1988). 'International Supply Chains: A New Approach'. *Management Decision*, 26: 13–19.

IMP Group (1997). 'An Interaction Approach, in International Marketing and Purchasing of Industrial Goods', in D. Ford (ed.), *Understanding Business Markets: Interactions, Relationships and Networks* (2nd edn). London: The Dryden Press, 3–22.

JONES, D. T. (1994). 'The Auto Industry in Transition: From Scale to Process'. *Journal of the Economics of Business*, 1/1: 139–50.

JONES, T. C., and RILEY, D. W. (1987). 'Using Inventory for Competitive Advantage through Supply Chain Management'. *International Journal of Physical Distribution and Materials Management*, 17: 94–104.

KAST, F. E., and ROSENWEIG, J. E. (1970). *Management and Organisation*. New York: McGraw-Hill.

LAMMING, R. C. (1993). *Beyond Partnership: Strategies for Innovation and Lean Supply*. Hemel Hempstead: Prentice-Hall.

—— (1996). 'Squaring Lean Supply with Supply Chain Management. (Lean Production and Work Organization)'. *International Journal of Operations and Production Management*, 16/2: 183–97.

LEE, H. L., and BILLINGTON, C. (1992). 'Managing Supply Chain Inventory: Pitfalls and Opportunities'. *Sloan Management Review*, 33/3: 65–78.

—— and NG, S. M. (1997). 'Introduction to the Special Issue on Global Supply Chain Management'. *Production and Operations Management*, 6: 191–2.

—— PADMANABHAN, V., and WHANG, S. (1997). 'The Bullwhip Effect in Supply Chains'. *Sloan Management Review*, 38/3: 93–102.

LEWIS, J. C., NAIM, M. M., and TOWILL, D. R. (1997). 'An Integrated Approach to Re-engineering Material and Logistics Control'. *International Journal of Physical Distribution and Logistics Management*, 27/3–4: 197–209.

MACBETH, D. K., and FERGUSON, N. (1994). *Partnership Sourcing. An Integrated Supply Chain Approach*. London: Pitman.

MALONE, T. W., and YATES, J. (1989). 'The Logic of Electronic Markets'. *Harvard Business Review*, 67/3: 166–75.

MORGAN, G. (1986). *Images of Organisation*. London: Sage Publications.

NASSIMBENI, G. (1998). 'Network Structures and Co-ordination Mechanisms: A Taxonomy'. *International Journal of Operations and Production Management*, 18/5–6: 538–54.

NEW, S. J. (1994). 'Supply Chains: Some Doubts'. *Proceedings of the Third Annual International Conference of IPSERA*, 345–62.

—— (1996). 'A Framework for Analysing Supply Chain Improvement'. *International Journal of Operations and Production Management*, 16/4: 19–34.

—— and RAMSAY, J. (1997). 'A Critical Appraisal of Aspects of the Lean Chain Approach'. *European Journal of Purchasing and Supply Management*, 3/2: 93–102.

NISHIGUCHI, T. (1994). *Strategic Industrial Sourcing: The Japanese Advantage*. Oxford: Oxford University Press.

OLIVER, C. (1990). 'Determinants of Interorganizational Relationships: Integration and Future Directions'. *Academy of Management Review*, 15/2: 241–65.

OLIVER, R. K., and WEBBER, M. D. (1982). 'Supply-Chain Management: Logistics Catches up with Strategy', in M. Christopher (ed.), *Logistics: The Strategic Issues*. London: Chapman and Hall, 63–75.

PIORE M. J., and SABEL, C. F. (1982). *The Second Industrial Divide: Possibilities for Prosperity*. New York: Basic Books.

SAKO, M. (1992). *Prices, Quality and Trust: Interfirm Relations in Britain and Japan*. Cambridge: Cambridge University Press.

SIGNORELLI, S., and HESKETT, J. L. (1984). *'Benetton' (A)*. Harvard Business School Case Study No. 9-685-014.

SIMCHI-LEVI, D., KAMINSKY, P., and SIMCHI-LEVI, E. (2000). *Designing and Managing the Supply Chain: Concepts, Strategies and Case Studies*. New York: Irwin McGraw-Hill.

SIMON, H. (1960). *The New Science of Management Decision*. New York: Harper Brothers.

SLACK, N., CHAMBERS, S., and JOHNSTON, R. (2001). *Operations Management* (3rd edn). London: FT Pitman.

TAN, K. C., KANNAN, V. R., and HANDFIELD, R. B. (1998). 'Supply Chain Management: Supplier Performance and Firm Performance'. *International Journal of Purchasing and Materials Management*, 34/3: 2–9.

TRANFIELD, D., and STARKEY, K. (1998). 'The Nature, Social Organization and Promotion of Management Research: Towards Policy'. *British Journal of Management*, 9/4: 341–53.

TRIST, E. L., and BAMFORTH, K. W. (1951). 'Some Social and Psychological Consequences of the Longwall Method of Coal-Getting'. *Human Relations*, 4: 3–38.

VAN DE VEN, A., and WALKER, G. (1984). 'The Dynamics of Interorganizational Coordination'. *Administrative Science Quarterly*, 29/4: 598–621.

VAN DEN BERG, J. P. (1999). 'A Literature Survey on Planning and Control of Warehousing Systems'. *IIE Transactions*, 37/8: 751–62.

VON BERTALANFFY, L. (1950). 'Theory of Open Systems in Physics and Biology'. *Science*, 111: 23–9.

VON NEUMANN, J., and MORGENSTERN, O. (1944). *Theory of Games and Economic Behavior*. New York: John Wiley and Sons Inc.

WANG, ERIC, and SEIDMANN, A. (1995). 'Electronic Data interchange: Competitive Externalities and Strategic Implementation Policies'. *Management Science*, 41/3: 401–17.

WILLIAMSON, O. (1975). *Markets and Hierarchies: Analysis and Antitrust Implications*. New York: The Free Press.

WISE, R., and MORRISON, D. (2000). 'Beyond the Exchange: The Future of B2B'. *Harvard Business Review*, 78/6: 86–96.

WOMACK, J., and JONES, D. T. (1996). *Lean Thinking: Banish Waste and Create Wealth in Your Corporation*. New York: Simon and Schuster.

—— —— and ROOS, D. (1990). *The Machine that Changed the World*. New York: Rawson Associates.

2

Supply Chains: A Marketing Perspective

1. Introduction

In this chapter we set out to explore the increasingly close connection between marketing strategy and supply chain design. Until recently, these two key business activities were conducted independently of each other and the idea of the supply chain as a source of potential competitive advantage was not well understood. Marketing strategies for many firms were based upon the conventional 'Four Ps' of product, promotion, price, and place. Indeed, for most companies there was little real consideration of the role of 'place' in the development of competitive strategies. There is now a changed perspective with the creation of customer and consumer value being seen as the key to success in the marketplace. At the same time the importance of relationship management is now more readily acknowledged as firms seek to utilize the strengths of other players in an extended value chain.

One of the most profound changes in the way that we think about competition has been the increasingly widely held view that it is the supply chain and not the individual organization that has become the source of competitive advantage (Christopher 1992; Webster 1992). For a century or more, the academic study of competition and markets has focused mainly around the firm (Marshall 1936; Stigler 1941). Equally, the prevailing tendency within businesses themselves was to perform as many of the value-creating activities as possible in-house. At its extreme this took the form of vertical integration, whereby the firm sought control through ownership of upstream suppliers and downstream distribution channels.

Today's thinking has tended to swing in the completely opposite direction. Now the emphasis is on organizations focusing on those core capabilities where they believe they have a differential advantage over competitors and to outsource all other activities which they perceive to be non-core.

Michael Porter (1980, 1985) has influenced much of our thinking about competitive advantage through his view that, essentially, differential advantage comes either through lower costs or greater customer value creation, that is, successful organizations perform activities 'cheaper' or 'better' than their competitors. Originally Porter's focus, and that of others, was on the individual firm's value chain. In other words, how could organizations become cost leaders or differentiated value providers? Now the focus has widened as the move to outsourcing non-core activities in the value chain accelerates. Thus, we are seeing, in effect, the supply chain become the value chain.

From this transformation comes the recognition that marketplace success is determined increasingly by the effectiveness of the supply chain and by the way in which the combined knowledge and capabilities of the individual entities in the chain can be leveraged. This view of the supply chain as the value chain is in stark contrast to the earlier concept of the firm seeking to establish control of its resources and its market through ownership. This was the concept of 'vertical' integration, best typified by Henry Ford I. Today's model is quite different. The focal firm still seeks integration of its extended value chain but that integration comes not through ownership, but by closer management of the interfaces of the supply chain through process alignment and shared information.

Achieving this alignment of processes and the wider transparency of information on demand and supply characteristics can only be achieved through a greater focus on relationship management upstream and downstream of the focal firm. Much attention has been paid in the academic literature over recent years to the ways in which relationships between organizations can be managed and leveraged for greater effect in the final marketplace. Pioneering work in this area emerged from the research output of the IMP Group. IMP (standing for Industrial Marketing and Purchasing) took as its stance the need to understand the context as well as the interaction between the participants in the buying/selling dyad (Ford 1990). Researchers in this area recognized that the 'atmosphere' within which the transaction takes place is a key to understanding how relationships are established.

Morgan and Hunt (1994) in researching the role of trust and commitment in relationship building within networks of organizations recognized the importance of resource sharing as the basis upon which enduring relationships are built. They concluded that in strong relationships there are neither 'buyers' or 'sellers', 'customers' nor 'key accounts', but only partners exchanging resources.

The linkage between the notion that marketing success is driven by strong *relationships* and the emerging idea of the supply chain as a *network* of closely connected organizations will be apparent. Effective supply chain management, it can be agreed, is one of the most powerful bases for the achievement of competitive advantage.

It will be apparent that supply chain management involves a significant change from the traditional arm's length, even adversarial, relationships that so often typified buyer/seller relationships in the past. The focus of supply chain management is on cooperation and trust and the recognition that properly managed 'the whole can be greater than the sum of its parts'.

Emerging from this idea is the author's definition of supply chain management: 'The management of upstream and downstream relationships with suppliers and customers to deliver superior customer value at less cost to the supply chain as a whole'. Thus, the focus of supply chain management is upon the management of relationships in order to achieve a more profitable outcome for all parties in the chain.

In parallel with the broadening of the definition of what constitutes the supply chain and the role of logistics within it has come recognition of the critical impact of logistics and supply chain management upon marketplace performance. This convergence of logistics and marketing has been termed, perhaps not surprisingly, *Marketing Logistics* (Christopher 1997).

The Marketing Logistics activity focuses upon the ways in which customer service can be leveraged to gain competitive advantage. It seeks to manage the interface between the marketing and logistics functions in order to align their respective strategies to enable market-driven logistics processes to be designed.

Marketing Logistics is thus primarily concerned with *availability* and *customer service*. It can be argued that markets are increasingly service sensitive customers and consumers have become more demanding of the service and support they receive from supplying organizations. Coincident with this pressure is the trend towards market 'maturity' that leads to a decline in brand loyalty and a tendency towards what might be described as 'commodity' markets.

The importance of availability as a key component of marketing success has been recognized by a few writers and researchers for many years. Bowersox (1961) argued that marketing and what was then termed 'physical distribution' should be merged conjointly. Stewart (1965) claimed that distribution service could generate additional sales through reduced out-of-stock situations and better customer relationships. Later writers such as Perreault and Russ (1976) put forward a procedure through which customers' distribution service preferences could be identified and 'packaged' as part of the service offer.

Today there is substantial evidence (see, for example, Sterling and Lambert 1987) that what we would now term logistics service can contribute significantly to competitive advantage. Unfortunately, this vital connection is not always fully recognized within organizations and so marketing and logistics are often quite separately managed.

2. The new rules of competition

Once, it seemed, all that was necessary for success in the marketplace was to ensure the delivery of 'the right product, at the right time, at the right price'. This simplistic view of the world was summarized as the 'Four Ps' of product, price, promotion, and place and has been the foundation for countless business education programmes and marketing textbooks. Now, this formula is increasingly becoming less effective as markets mature and customer and consumers become more knowledgeable and sophisticated.

In many cases we have seen the 'commoditization' of markets whereby customers and consumers see few real differences between competing products in terms of their characteristics and/or functionality. Brand loyalty has diminished and it seems that consumers now buy from a 'portfolio' of brands. While consumers may have a preference for a particular brand if it is not available they are quite willing to switch brands. Similarly in business-to-business marketing, competitive advantage is gained less through product quality and more and more through relationship quality (Christopher, Payne, and Ballantyne 1991). Customers in most industries today expect shorter order-to-delivery lead times and highly reliable just-in-time deliveries.

The evidence from many markets is that availability overcomes brand or supplier loyalty (Schary and Becker 1978). In consumer markets it can be argued that the battle now is not just for 'mind-space' but for 'shelf-space' (Corstjens and Corstjens 1995). Winning the shelf-space battle requires the supplier to focus on ways in which shelf-space profitability can be enhanced through more responsive service. The route to improved shelf-space profitability is through improved velocity which itself is driven by a more agile supply chain. The same can be said for business-to-business markets, where customers operating on a just-in-time basis need to know that they can rely upon their suppliers for rapid and reliable response. This is how companies compete today.

Clearly, none of the foregoing diminishes the continuing need for investment in innovative products and brand building. However, the point is that even the strongest, most innovative brand will suffer if it is not available at the time and place the customer or consumer requires it. This is the reality that

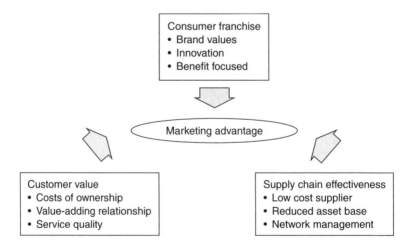

Fig. 2.1.   Marketing and logistics converge

underpins the idea of what some have termed 'time-based competition' (Stalk and Hout 1990).

The new model of competitive advantage that is emerging can be summarized as in Fig. 2.1 which emphasizes that relationships with customers are of equal importance as the relationships businesses have with consumers and that both of these need to be underpinned by superior supply chain management.

3. Competing through capabilities

As markets mature and customers and consumers become more knowledgeable and sophisticated, organizations are having to re-appraise their traditional definitions of strengths and weaknesses. The view now gathering ground is that the real opportunities for differential advantage come from capabilities or the things we excel at, our 'distinctive competencies'.

Thus in a market characterized by shortening life cycles, for example, the ability to get new products to market in ever-shorter time frames becomes a source of competitive advantage. Likewise, information systems that can capture demand as it happens and production systems that can respond rapidly are a major strength in a volatile market. Similar advantages accrue to organizations with order fulfilment and logistics systems that enable superior levels of customer service to be achieved.

The more that organizations come to recognize the importance of competing through capabilities, the more they will be forced to accept the need to switch the focus in business away from managing functions to managing the key activities or processes that create those capabilities. A major change that has taken place in the way in which we think about organizations has been the realization of the importance of processes. Processes are the ways in which firms create value for their customers, they are fundamental and, to a large extent, generic across business types. Processes are, in fact, capabilities.

In the fiercely competitive global telecommunications industry the success of Nokia underlines the importance of process excellence. In his annual letter to shareholders in 2000, the Chairman and CEO, Jorma Ollila, summarized it in this way:

Our experienced and unique way of operating is what we see as increasingly putting us ahead of the competition. As we move forward in this complex industry, *winning will be less about what we do and more about the way we do it* (emphasis added). This is what we firmly believe and this is also very much visible in our daily work.

Managing the flow of the 250 million components used daily in our mobile phone manufacturing means strict attention to logistics and scrutiny of every detail. In the networks business, it is our skill in timing parallel technology programmes, from the development phase right through to manufacturing and implementation, that allows us to provide customers with a competitive edge. (Nokia 2000)

Many companies have failed to recognize the need to invest in developing their logistics and supply chain capabilities. In some cases where there has been a focus on these critical issues it has tended to be driven by a need to reduce costs. While cost reduction will always be a goal in the typical business, an even greater priority should be the creation of enhanced *customer value*.

The customer value concept recognizes that marketplace success in the new competitive environment will require not only continued investment in the brand but also *investment in customers*. By 'customer' we mean the party or parties who actually buy the product as distinct from the consumer. The importance of this distinction is that much of marketing investment in the past has been aimed at consumers and not at the customer. Because of the shift in the balance of power in the distribution channels for most products it is important that we recognize that customers, not just consumers, have goals that they seek to achieve and that the role of the supplier is to help customers achieve those goals.

4. Defining customer value

What actually is customer value? Put very simply, customer value is created when the perceptions of benefits received from a transaction exceed the total costs of ownership. The same idea can be expressed as a ratio:

$$\text{Customer Value} = \frac{\text{Perceptions of Benefits}}{\text{Total Cost of Ownership}}$$

'Total cost of ownership' rather than 'price' is used here because in most transactions there will be costs other than price involved. For example, inventory carrying costs, maintenance costs, running costs, disposal costs, and so on. In business-to-business markets particularly, as buyers become increasingly sophisticated, the total cost of ownership can be a critical element in the purchase decision. 'Life-cycle costs', as they are referred to in the military and defence industries, have long been a critical issue in procurement decisions in those markets.

The marketing task is to find ways to enhance customer value by improving the perceived benefits and/or reducing the total costs of ownership. Thus, the goal of marketing and logistics strategy should be to seek to maximize this ratio relative to that of competitors. It could be argued that logistics is almost unique in its ability to impact upon both the numerator and the denominator of this ratio. In the case of business-to-business marketing, higher customer value can be delivered through superior logistics performance enabling our customers to service their customers better, but with less inventory and lower ordering costs, for example. The same rationale of enhanced customer value applies to selling to end-users where perhaps the benefits might come from, say, increased purchase convenience yet with lowered costs through improved payment terms.

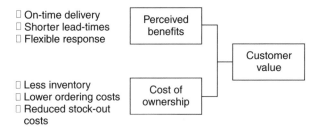

Fig. 2.2.   Logistics and customer value

The challenge within the supplying company is to identify unique ways to deliver this enhanced value that competitors will find difficult to imitate and thus providing a basis for sustainable competitive advantage. Figure 2.2 highlights some of the ways in which customer value can be enhanced by developing logistics processes that make it easier for the customer to service their customers while incurring less cost.

Often, it may be necessary to 'educate' the customer who often will not have fully understood the real costs of their existing systems and processes. For example, many organizations still do not recognize the true cost of carrying inventory. While they may place a nominal working capital charge upon departments in relation to the inventory they hold, that charge rarely reflects the actual costs. It has been estimated that it costs an organization at least 25 per cent p.a. of the book value of its inventory to carry it in stock (Lambert and Stock 1993). Inventory here includes raw materials, components, work-in-progress, finished product, as well as goods-in-transit. This figure of 25 per cent includes not only the cost of capital, but also the 'opportunity cost'. In other words, the cost of the forgone return that could be made by investing that capital elsewhere. In addition there are the costs of storage and handling, obsolescence, stock losses, insurance, and stock management.

Given that a medium to large organization will have inventory valued in £ millions the annual carrying cost at 25 per cent will be considerable. The benefit of any reduction in that inventory will be twofold: first, a once-off release of cash and then second, a continuing reduction in the annual cost of carrying that inventory which, other things being equal, should go direct to the bottom line.

5. Value in use

The whole issue of customer value is inevitably linked to price. Since price forms a part of the total cost of ownership it follows that there has to be a relationship between the price charged and the customer's perception of value. It also follows that the higher the perception of value the higher the price that can

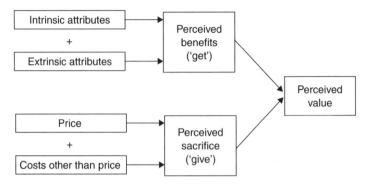

Fig. 2.3. The components of value

Source : Based on Naumann (1995).

be charged. Conversely, if price exceeds the perceived value sales will probably decline. It is important to have a clear understanding of the value that customers (and consumers) place on an organization's offer. This can be termed 'Value-in-Use' and it should be a priority for all marketing managers to better understand the key elements that comprise it. Figure 2.3 highlights the idea of value-in-use as a balance between perceived benefits (i.e. what the customer 'gets') and the perceived sacrifice (i.e. what the customer 'gives').

The perceived benefits derive from the hard, tangible elements of the offer—the intrinsic attributes—and the softer less tangible elements—the extrinsic attributes. The perceived sacrifice includes all those costs incurred by the customer, before, during, and after the sale. Again, not all of these costs may be 'hard', some may be 'soft' such as perceived risk or the costs associated with the time consumed in the purchase process, and so on.

6. Developing a market-driven logistics strategy

The connection between marketing and logistics is not always fully understood within the business. The purpose of the logistics process is to support the marketing strategy of the organization. Logistics impacts marketing effectiveness through the customer value that is created by superior service.

Typically, organizations have tended to manage those activities they see as 'demand creating' separately from those they consider to be concerned with 'demand satisfaction'. In other words, the classic approach to marketing has focused upon developing and managing the 'offer' and has sought to differentiate that offer through the manipulation of the marketing mix. On the other hand, the mechanisms by which demand is physically satisfied have tended to be seen as a separate responsibility within the business—often termed distribution management. More recently, however, companies have come to

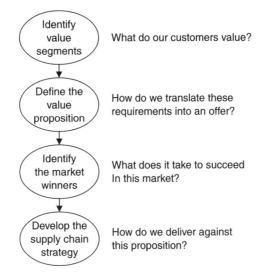

Fig. 2.4. Linking customer value to supply chain strategy

recognize that in today's markets the processes by which value is delivered to customers need to be managed alongside those by which it is created. Figure 2.4 suggests a four-stage process to creating a market-driven supply chain strategy. Let us examine each step in turn:

Identify value segments. It is important to recognize that in any given market there will probably be a number of customer segments that are quite different in their perceptions both of benefits and of sacrifice. In other words, the weights that individual customers or consumers place upon the attributes of the offer will differ as will their perceptions of actual performance.

By focusing on those things the customer attaches most value to, the supplying organization is more likely to win and retain business. To do this requires an in-depth knowledge of the customers' own value chain. Thus, for example, if the customer is another business organization how do they create value for *their* customers? What are their customers' costs and what are the opportunities for those costs to be reduced through our intervention? What are the characteristics of their business processes and what possibilities exist for a greater integration of those processes with our own?

The same philosophy holds for marketing to end-users. The supplying organization needs to understand the lifestyle of the consumer, the problems and pressures they face, the relative importance of time, the value they attach to convenience, ease of operation, and so on. In this way, a better targeting of customers can be achieved with value propositions that have specific relevance to the chosen segment. There may also be opportunities to emphasize total cost of ownership issues too: for example, a concentrated washing-up liquid that needs less liquid per wash, long-life light bulbs that need changing less often, paints that need no undercoats, and oils that run cooler so fewer engine oil changes are needed.

Defining the value proposition.   The value proposition is quite simply a statement of how, where, and when value is to be created for specific customers or market segments. The value proposition should form the guiding principles around which all the activities of the firm are based, from product development to order fulfilment. It should also be reflected in the marketing communications strategy as well as underpinning the internal values of the business.

For a value proposition to provide a strong foundation for competitive advantage it must be defined from the customer's viewpoint. In other words: what will our offer do for customers that they will recognize as relevant to their needs? It must also be set against the backdrop of the explicit or implicit value propositions of competing offers. Once the value proposition is agreed the challenge to logistics is to create and manage the processes that will deliver that value in a timely and consistent way. Linking logistics strategy and marketing strategy is, of course, the theme of this chapter, and yet only rarely do we see the two managed on an integrated, customer value focused basis.

Identify the market winners.   Hill (1993) has drawn our attention to the need to link manufacturing strategy to marketing strategy through the identification of what he terms 'order winning criteria'. Equally it is critical that the business needs to understand the links between perceived customer value and logistics strategy. It is important, therefore, to identify those key determinants driving the choice of supplier or product. These key drivers are what we might term the key success factors or 'market winners'. Sometimes it will be product performance or price that determines the decision. In other situations availability, responsiveness, and reliability may be the market winners. Understanding the nature of these key success factors is a vital pre-requisite for successful supply chain design.

The supply chain strategy adopted must be consistent with the achievement of those market winning goals. All too often, the supply chain design does not fit the market-winning strategy. It must also be recommended that organizations may address different markets or market segments with different market-winning criteria. In such situations 'one size will not fit all', and hence there will be a need for more than one supply chain. Many fast-moving consumer goods companies, for example, have differentiated their supply chains according to whether they are servicing 'every day low price' retailers or, alternatively, retail customers with frequent promotions demanding a more agile response.

Developing the supply chain strategy.   If the preceding three steps have been followed, the choice of supply chain strategy will usually be fairly apparent. However, there are a number of guidelines that can usefully be employed based upon the nature of the market. Markets can be characterized in a number of ways, but for the purposes of supply chain strategy determination, the issue of 'predictability' is important. If markets are predictable, then the main priority for supply chain design should be a focus on efficiency. In other words, demand can be forecast and the aim should be to construct a supply chain that can source, make, and deliver product to a requisite quality at lowest cost. This is the classic scenario for 'lean' thinking (Womack and Jones 1996) where the aim is to seek to reduce 'waste' to a minimum. This situation, where products are standard and where there is little volatility in demand, lends itself to such lean design strategies.

The contrasting market situation is where demand is volatile and where products are non-standard or where there are many variants. In situations such as this, it is harder to develop forecast-based supply chain strategies. Rather they must be demand-driven or customer-responsive. These are the type of circumstances where the concept of *agility* becomes applicable (Christopher 2000).

7. The agile supply chain

To be truly agile, a supply chain must possess a number of distinguishing characteristics as suggested in Fig. 2.5.

First, the agile supply chain is market sensitive. By this is meant that the supply chain is capable of reading and responding to real demand. Most organizations are forecast-driven rather than demand-driven. In other words, because they have little direct feed-forward from the marketplace by way of

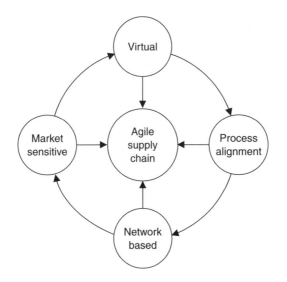

Fig. 2.5. The agile supply chain

data on actual customer requirements, they are forced to make forecasts based on past sales or shipments, and convert these forecasts into inventory. The breakthroughs of the last decade in the form of efficient consumer response (ECR), and the use of information technology to capture data on demand direct from the point-of-sale or point-of-use, are now transforming the organization's ability to hear the voice of the market and to respond directly to it.

Second, agile supply chains tend to be 'virtual'. That is, they are typified by information shared between upstream and downstream partners. Conventional logistic systems are based on a paradigm that seeks to identify the optimal amount of inventory and its spatial location. Complex formulae and algorithms exist to support this inventory-based business model. Paradoxically, we are now learning that once we have visibility of demand through shared information, the premise upon which these formulae are based no longer holds.

Shared information between supply chain partners can only be fully lever-aged through process alignment—the third characteristic of an agile supply chain. Process alignment means collaborative working between buyers and suppliers such as joint product development, vendor managed inventory, common systems, and synchronous operations. This form of cooperation in the supply chain is becoming ever more prevalent, as companies focus on manag-ing their core competencies and outsource all other activities.

The idea of a supply chain as a confederation of partners linked together as a network provides the fourth ingredient of agility. Whereas in the past, as we have noted, it was thought appropriate to seek to control all stages of the supply chain through ownership, now the pendulum has swung the other way. It has been suggested (Hedberg *et al.* 2000) that networks of smaller, specialist providers of resources, knowledge, and capabilities are inherently more agile than their vertically integrated predecessors. They are more easily reconfigured to meet the needs of a changing marketplace, for example. Equally, they are quicker on their feet because they are smaller and more likely to be market-oriented since their livelihood depends upon their customer responsiveness.

8. Managing relationships in the supply chain

It will be clear from our earlier definition that a key element of successful supply chain management is the way in which relationships between all the entities in the chain are managed. In the past it was more often the case that organizations were structured and managed on the basis of optimizing their own operations with little regard for the way in which they interfaced with sup-pliers or, indeed, customers. The business model was essentially 'transactional', meaning that products and services were bought and sold on an arm's length basis and that there was little enthusiasm for the concept of longer-term, mutually dependent relationships.

The emerging competitive paradigm is in stark contrast to the conventional model. It suggests that in today's challenging global markets, the route to sustainable advantage lies in managing the complex web of relationships that link highly focused providers of specific elements of the final offer in a cost-effective, value-creating network.

The key to success in this new competitive framework, it can be argued, is the way in which this network of alliances, suppliers, intermediaries—and sometimes competitors—are welded together in partnership to achieve mutually beneficial goals.

Previously, business organizations tended to perform most activities in-house. In the era of vertical integration, companies would seek to control through ownership of their entire value chain. Henry Ford I typified this concept. At one time Ford owned a power plant, a steel mill, a glass factory, and a rubber factory as well as mahogany forests. Today, our thinking has undergone a 180-degree change as corporations seek to focus on core competencies and outsource everything else. By definition, the more companies focus on those activities they believe they have a differential advantage in, the more they need to rely on others. As these external dependencies increase, it becomes vital that the nature of the relationship switches from arm's length, transactional mode to a collaborative, partnership mode.

The danger in outsourcing anything is the potential for loss of control. In fact, outsourced activities must be even more closely managed than if they were performed in-house. The maxim must be—outsource the *execution* of a process but never the *control* of that process. It could be argued that rather than talking about outsourcing we should use the term 'insourcing' instead.

'Outsourcing' implies we are putting something *outside* the business (as in subcontracting) whereas 'insourcing' suggests we are bringing a strength *into* the business—a strength we do not currently have.

It is this realization—that the organization no longer stands alone—that is prompting a new search for collaborative partnering. These partnerships may be with suppliers, distributors, retailers, specialist service providers, technology-sharing alliances, and increasingly, with competitors. Sometimes, the lines between suppliers, customers, and competitors become increasingly blurred.

For example, Dell and IBM compete in the PC market, but IBM is also a supplier to Dell (as well as providing components they also have a technology sharing agreement) and it has even been suggested that before long Dell might undertake certain assembly tasks for IBM!

This is a phenomenon which has been called by some 'co-opetition' (Nalebuff and Brandenburger 1996), that is collaborate to compete. The principle that underpins co-opetition is that it may well benefit organizations to collaborate in order to 'grow the pie', but to compete as to how to slice it. In many retail environments manufacturers of branded products compete with the retailers' own label products. Yet, the smart players in those markets have come to recognize the benefits of joint category planning in order to grow total demand within that category. Thus Coca Cola and Sainsburys compete for share of the cola market but work together to grow the total sales of carbonated soft drinks through joint category management.

In competing as a network it becomes apparent that the aim should be to maximize *collaborative advantage* rather than competitive advantage in its traditional, single-firm meaning. To release this collaborative advantage and to leverage the collective competitiveness and skills across the network means that knowledge must be shared and harnessed.

One of the most interesting developments in the practice of marketing has been the emergence of Customer Relationship Management (CRM) both as a philosophy and a set of tools. CRM can mean many things to many people, but the basic idea behind it is that the real focus of marketing should be upon the creation of enduring relationships with profitable customers. Successful CRM builds not only on the classic marketing principles of deep market understanding, but also on the recognition that building relationships with customers needs a different approach than that conventionally applied to building volume.

How can collaboration help in the creation of stronger customer relationships? Perhaps one of the best current examples comes from the packaged goods industry where manufacturers and retailers are combining to pool their knowledge of consumers and markets to create joint category plans. In many cases this activity has been widened to envelop the principles of collaborative planning, forecasting, and replenishment (CPFR).

CPFR programmes involve a high level of information sharing between partners in order to create forecasts that all parties agree to and then to manage supply and demand so that on-the-shelf availability improves. CPFR is an example of 'vertical' collaborative working leading to the delivery of greater customer and consumer value. 'Horizontal' collaborations between organizations marketing complementary products can also lead to stronger consumer appeal and greater value added. Coca Cola's long-standing global partnership with McDonalds is such an example.

Figure 2.6 suggests that the conventional idea of a predominantly vertical supply chain needs to embody a 'horizontal' dimension. Indeed, it can be argued that the supply chain has, in effect, become the value chain.

Perhaps one of the most powerful opportunities for creating competitive advantage through partnerships lies in innovation. For every organization the ability to enhance and accelerate innovation is critical to success in today's

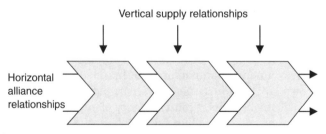

Fig. 2.6.   The supply chain becomes the value chain

markets. Already, it is evident that both product and process innovation is dependent, at least in part, on the contribution of partners. These partners will be both horizontal and vertical. The latter vertical partnerships are in the form of supplier involvement in the innovation process. For example, it is not uncommon today to see suppliers involved directly in the new market development process. The car industry provides a dramatic exemplar—ABS braking systems, improved engine management systems and advanced suspension systems owe as much to the suppliers as they do to the vehicle assemblers. Equally, improvements in supplier process technology enabling higher quality components or critical materials to be made available at lower cost on just-in-time time windows have added significantly to their customers' competitiveness.

At the same time, the greater willingness to embark upon horizontal relationships—often in the form of technology-sharing agreements with competitors—has made it possible for organizations to achieve levels of profitable innovation that previously would not have been thought possible. In telecommunications, for example, head-to-head competitors such as Nokia, Eriksson, and Motorola have combined to agree standards and to contribute to the development of the next generation of mobile communications equipment and products.

Time-to-market can be dramatically reduced by leveraging the capabilities of organizations who once operated as stand-alone entities, each duplicating each other's efforts at significant cost and with much longer development times.

Significant penalties are unnecessarily incurred if companies fail to exploit the potential for collaboration in the supply chain. In the first instance, organizations that do not connect with each other through shared information will inevitably carry additional inventory in the form of safety stock. Companies that do not communicate with each other are forced to buffer themselves against uncertainty through higher inventories. The cost of this lack of communication in turbulent markets is considerable. Second, and even more critical, this failure to connect means that there is little visibility from one end of the supply chain to the other, and hence agility is impaired. For example, if upstream suppliers cannot see what is happening at the downstream end of the pipeline they are forced to be forecast-driven rather than demand-driven. In today's turbulent markets, visibility of real demand is a vital component of competitive advantage. There are a growing number of examples of collaborative working in the supply chain—even among competitors. For example, for a number of years two direct competitors, Lever Fabergé and Colgate Palmolive have shared the same distribution centre in the United Kingdom and make combined deliveries to common customers. While clearly these two companies compete head-to-head in the marketplace, they would argue that they do not compete in the warehouse or on the truck—therefore, collaboration means that both benefit. Other emerging examples include competing airlines sharing inventories of high value spares, for example, aero engines. Often these types of collaboration are facilitated by third party logistics service providers who can provide a neutral platform.

Supply chain managers of the future will need to be much more aware of the competitive power of collaboration. The trends towards the virtual corporation are already evident and the implications are profound. Whereas in the past, when the firm competed as a stand-alone entity, it was sufficient for the business to have a corporate strategy, now—competing as a wider network—a collective strategy for value creation across connected organizations becomes a pre-requisite.

These strategies cannot be imposed, they must have buy-in from the participating players. New leadership skills are therefore demanded of those organizations that seek to endure and grow in this vastly changed competitive landscape.

9. The supply chain of the future

A number of powerful forces are changing the nature of supply chain management. There has been a fundamental shift from 'supplier push' to 'customer pull' as supply chains have been forced by competitive pressure to become more responsive to changing customer and consumer needs; whereas yesterday's market was typically a mass market best served by mass production, tomorrow's market is likely to be a 'one-to-one' marketplace with the emphasis on mass customization. Figure 2.7 summarizes this dramatic change in emphasis.

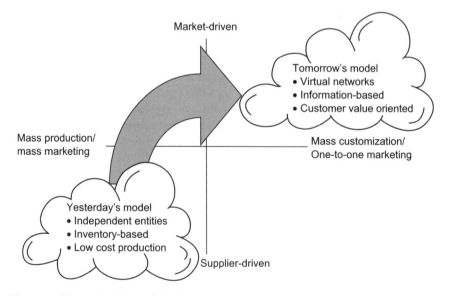

Fig. 2.7. The supply chain of the future

The suggestion is that previously the environment was characterized as supplier-driven based upon mass marketing and mass production philosophies. Independently suppliers, manufacturers, distributors, and other entities would seek to forecast demand from their immediate customers with no direct view of the final market. They would work on the basis of optimizing production, shipping and ordering quantities with the overriding goal of cost-minimization.

The new competitive framework that is emerging is quite different. Now the customer is firmly in the driving seat and customer responsiveness has become the order winner. At the same time markets have continued to fragment into niches and even 'segments of one', requiring suppliers to customize their offers to an even greater extent. Against such a backdrop, companies need to exhibit much higher levels of agility in order to compete. Hence, the growing likelihood that tomorrow's market leaders will most likely be virtual rather than vertical in their structures, be information-driven rather than inventory-based and will focus their supply chains around delivering superior customer value. The question remains: how will companies make this transition?

10. Making the transition

In many respects, supply chain management is change management. Guiding change of the sort we have described above requires particular influencing skills as well as a broad understanding of the multitude of issues that arise in managing the 'extended enterprise'.

Partly based upon a framework proposed by McKinsey (Ostroff and Smith 1992) a seven-step process is advocated to assist in the journey towards the creation of a market-driven supply chain.

Understand the value preferences of key market segments. Does the organization recognize the value preferences of key customers and segments and how they differ? Is this understanding widely diffused across the organization?

Realign the organization around the processes that deliver customer value. Most businesses still tend to be organized around functions rather than the processes that actually deliver value to customers. Examples of such processes are innovation, customer relationship management, and supplier development.

Engage customers and suppliers in end-to-end process management. Because supply chain excellence is highly dependent upon the collaboration of all players upstream and downstream of the focal firm, it is critical that they be involved in the planning and execution of supply-chain-wide processes.

Create cross-functional teams to manage those processes. In order to break through the functional silos that block the implementation of integrated supply chain management, cross-functional teams must be created to manage critical business processes.

Transform management's role from 'command and control' to 'process leadership'. Tomorrow's organizations will by definition be 'horizontal' and 'flat' as against 'vertical' and hierarchical'. A different type of management style is necessary to make these new structures effective.

Develop performance metrics to support cross-functional, customer-driven processes. One of the problems that halts organizational change of the type proposed here, is the fact that the main performance metrics utilized within the business are still functional in nature, for example, cost-per-unit rather than cost-to-serve or capacity utilization rather than throughput times.

Promote multiple competencies in individuals. It will be apparent that to be a successful member or leader of a market-facing cross-functional process team, managers will require new skills. They will need to have a wider understanding of supply chain processes and move beyond their original functional focus. There are significant implications for management training and development.

The achievement of change of this magnitude may seem to be a daunting task. However, there will be little choice for those organizations that seek to thrive in the increasingly turbulent and unpredictable markets that are fast becoming the norm. The creation of market-facing and customer-responsive supply chains must become the goal as the rules of competition change dramatically and we enter the era of supply chain competition.

11. An agenda for research

While the idea of creating market-driven supply chain strategies is undoubtedly appealing, there still remain a number of crucial areas where further research is needed to help move forward its real world implementation. The following issues might repay more detailed study:

How closely are marketing and supply chain management integrated at the strategic level in organizations? Initial observation suggests that rarely are supply chain strategies developed specifically to support marketing strategies. Understanding the barriers to a closer linkage would help in identifying the way forward towards the creation of market-driven supply chains.

How do companies identify and respond to customer value preferences in their supply chains? Well-established tools exist in market and consumer research for the evaluation of customer value preferences but the evidence is that these tools are rarely used in the development of supply chain strategies. However, even if customer value preferences are clearly understood how well are these converted into differentiated supply solutions?

Since supply chain agility is key to success in today's more volatile market place, what are the inhibitors and enablers of agility? In some cases, there could well be organizational challenges to be met, for example, the predominance of functional silos. In other cases lack of collaborative working upstream and downstream of the focal firm may be the stumbling block.

In fast-moving consumer goods markets what is the impact of lack of availability (e.g. stock-outs on the shelf or long waiting times for delivery) on consumer behaviour? There is growing evidence that consumers are less brand loyal, and hence might readily switch brands if their preferred brand is not available. Is their response consistent across product categories or are there some areas where product availability is more crucial than others?

Finally, and closely connected to the previous point, in business-to-business markets what is the impact of logistics service on the choice of preferred supplier? This is an important question in a growing number of industries as companies seek to reduce their supplier base. What are the 'market winners' that enable businesses to become and remain preferred suppliers?

There are, undoubtedly, many other issues that could be nominated for further research but the five we have listed seem to lie at the heart of the search for competitive advantage through the design and management of world-class supply chains.

References

BOWERSOX, D. J. (1961). 'The Role of the Marketing Executive in Physical Distribution in Effective Marketing Co-ordination' G. L. Baker (ed.), Chicago: American Marketing Association.

CHRISTOPHER, M. (1992). *Logistics and Supply Chain Management* (1st edn). London: Pitman Publishing.

—— (1997). *Marketing Logistics*. London: Butterworth Heinemann.

—— (2000). 'The Agile Supply Chain: Competing in Volatile Markets'. *Industrial Marketing Management*, 29/1: 37–44.

—— PAYNE, A., and BALLANTYNE, D. (1991). *Relationship Marketing* (1st edn). London: Butterworth Heinemann.

CORSTJENS, J., and CORSTJENS, M. (1995). *Store Wars*. Chichester: John Wiley.

FORD, I. D. (ed.) (1990). *Understanding Business Markets: Interaction, Relationships, Networks*. London: Academic Press.

HEDBERG, B., DAHLGREN, G., HANSSON, J., and OLVE, N. (2000). *Virtual Organizations and Beyond*. Chichester: John Wiley.

HILL, T. (1993). *Manufacturing Strategy: Text and Cases* (2nd edn). London: Macmillan Press.

LAMBERT, D., and STOCK, J. (1993). *Strategic Logistics Management* (3rd edn). Homewood, IL. Richard Irwin.

MARSHALL, A. (1936). *Principles of Economics* (8th edn). London: Macmillan Press.

MORGAN, R. M., and HUNT S. D. (1994). 'The Commitment–Trust Theory of Relationship Marketing'. *Journal of Marketing*, 58/3: 20–38.

NALEBUFF, B., and BRANDENBURGER, A. M. (1996). *Co-opetition*. New York: Doubleday.

NAUMANN, E. (1995). *Creating Customer Value*. London: International Thomson Publishing.

NOKIA, *Insight/Business Review 2000*.

OSTROFF, F., and SMITH, D. (1992). 'The Horizontal Organization'. *McKinsey Quarterly*, 1: 148–68.

PERREAULT, W. D., and RUSS, F. A. (1976). 'Quantifying Marketing Trade-offs in Physical Distribution policy Decisions'. *Decision Sciences*, 7/2: 186–201.

PORTER, M. E. (1980). *Competitive Strategy*. New York: The Free Press.

—— (1985). *Competitive Advantage*. New York: The Free Press.

SCHARY, P. B., and BECKER, B. W. (1978). 'The Impact of Stock-Out on Market Share: Temporal Effects'. *Journal of Business Logistics*, 1/1: 31–45.

STALK, G., and HOUT, T. (1990). *Competing Against Time*. New York: The Free Press.

STERLING, J. U., and LAMBERT, D. M. (1987). 'Establishing Customer Service Strategies with the Marketing Mix'. *Journal of Business Logistics*, 8/1: 1–30.

STEWART, W. M. (1965). 'Physical Distribution: Key to Improved Volume and Profits'. *Journal of Marketing*, 29/1: 65–70.

STIGLER, GEORGE. J. (1941). *Production and Distribution Theories*. London: Macmillan.

WEBSTER, F. E. (1992). 'The Changing Role of Marketing in the Corporation'. *Journal of Marketing*, 56/4: 1–17.

WOMACK, J., and JONES, D. (1996). *Lean Thinking*. New York: Simon and Schuster.

3

Supply Chains: A Network Perspective

GUIDO NASSIMBENI

1. Introduction

For some years the idea has been emerging that the locus of value creation is the chain, the network, and not the firm. The belief is that competition occurs between systems of enterprises, rather than single firms, as in modern economies it is unlikely that a single company could, on its own, develop all the resources needed. It can, indeed it *must*, develop some resources and competencies, some areas of excellence. However, such areas of excellence must then join with other areas of excellence so that the enterprise can face the competitive challenge. Thus, they must build a network, according to the principle of complementariness between inner and external abilities. In other words 'no business is an island' (Håkansson and Snehota 1989).

This progressive awareness of the importance of relationships is particularly visible in the field considered in this book: supply chain management (SCM). We are witnessing an interesting evolution of perspectives passing from attention being mostly focused on the inner flows to attention extended to the total logistic network, that is, to the entire system composed of producers, suppliers, and customers. SCM is, in fact, a natural development of the studies on *logistics management*. The term *chain* has immediately taken root in management literature; however, it has been criticized because it gives the impression of a linear, unidirectional flow, a sort of pipeline. In reality it is generally different. Supply systems are characterized by bi-directional flows, lateral ties, and paths that are often segmented and articulated (Lamming *et al.* 2000). Companies are crossed by a variety of simultaneous flows, being nodes of branched supply networks.

In spite of the importance of the topic and the abundance of literature, our knowledge of networks, their shapes, and the principles that regulate their processes is limited. The topic is so wide that even a summary cannot be presented in the narrow space of a chapter. My intention here is simply to outline the constituent elements of a network and underline some of the more important issues. I have tried to clarify a concept that is not novel but still needs—at least in part—a theory, that of supply networks. The literature, in fact, focuses on some forms of networking, in particular alliances and joint ventures. In addition, it tends to develop along its own specialized lines as the organization scholars focus on organizational aspects of networks, economists probe economic variables and efficiency assessments of the various forms, operations management experts highlight the problematic of integration and management of the operations at the network level. In this chapter I have tried to knit together contributions of various matrices, such as economic, organizational, and operative, with the ambitious objective of jointly declining these different views of analyses. However, more space has been intentionally given to the non-OM literature, since these chain or network operational aspects are widely covered in other parts of this book.

The chapter is organized as follows. The initial step in the work was to identify a sufficiently general definition of the network concept (Section 2). Then the specificity of supply (production) networks and the characteristics that render them different from other network typologies are identified (Section 3). The reasons for the current increasing needs for networking in supply environment are pointed out (Section 4). Finally, some important directions of research are presented (Section 5).

2. Network: some concepts

The term system or network of companies generally refers to a vast range of interorganizational relations. What are, and what characterizes these forms? Notwithstanding the extensive body of papers, no definition able to capture the multiplicity of situations and inter-firm architecture that fall under the term 'network' is provided. Nohria (1992), reiterating an observation made by others, stated 10 years ago that network literature is a 'terminological jungle in which any newcomer can plant a tree'. This affirmation can probably be repeated today, if it is true, as Oliver and Ebers (1998) observe, that 'the increase in the number of studies has contributed to a rather messy situation marked by a cacophony of heterogeneous concepts, theories, and research results'.

The definition of a network itself is a debated question. If there are no doubts that networks are constituted by two or more agents, the form and modalities of this relationship governance are, instead, an open question. Which modalities of interaction characterize networks? According to most authors, interorganizational network relationships are characterized by continuity, informality, and social embeddedness. For example, Sydow and Windeler (1998) define 'inter-firm networks' as a 'complex arrangement of reciprocal, co-operative rather than competitive relationships'. Jones, Hesterly, and Borgatti (1997) maintain that networks refer to 'interfirm co-ordination that is characterised by organic and informal social systems, in contrast to bureaucratic structures within firms and formal contractual relationships between them'.

This type of agreement is also called 'relational contracting' (MacNeil 1985). However other authors think that it is only the presence of an interaction between organizations—and not also the governance form—which characterizes networks. In other words, the sole existence of an exchange gives origin to a network, independently of the type of contractual agreement between the parties. Social network analysis, for example, considers the network to be a sort of 'mother' of all organizational forms, since it is a system of nodes and ties that can assume various configurations.

Another issue concerns the elements that distinguish networks from other organizational forms, in particular hierarchy and market. As is well known, according to the Transaction Cost Theory (Williamson 1975, 1985), networks of companies represent an intermediary solution between the integrated manufacturer and the 'market', that is, the complex of independent manufacturers with whom exclusively short term ('spot') transactions are established. When compared with hierarchical relations, networks are more loosely coupled, rely to a greater extent on self-organizing processes and competitive pressures (Ring and Van de Ven 1994). When compared to the market, they provide denser information channels, demand more loyalty and trust, show a higher degree of social embeddedness, and are more stable (MacMillan and Farmer 1979).

The use of the Williamsonian categories and the definition of networks by differences from extreme ones (market and hierarchy) have been criticized for various reasons. First, because these forms are in reality excessively stylized. For example, the market is described as a set of coordination mechanisms based on price and on unilateral and optimizing decisions (Machlup 1978). Grandori (1999) observes that if the market is the ideal mechanism depicted by economists, and if the hierarchy is defined as the ideal type of Weberian bureaucracy, then nearly all the governance forms constitute a network. Second, because this approach compartmentalizes the variety of forms into a few structural alternatives, when, instead, the real world shows a multiplicity of shading situations. Finally, because the diversity of the various forms (network, hierarchy, and market) are emphasized, while in reality they exhibit also some common elements. For example, firms can use pricing and other 'market-based' mechanisms even within their boundaries, while networks may use hierarchical and formalized (procedures, programmes) coordination devices. Even if criticized several times over, the Williamsonian categories continue to recur in the literature. Evidently they maintain their own explanatory valence and distinct identities. The elements that make up this identity are summarized in the following section.

Those reported above are just a few of the questions. This debate is fed by the indeterminatess of the network concept. At this point, however, it is opportune to assume a definition of network to which reference can be made in the continuation of the chapter.

2.1. Definition

For the purpose of this chapter, an inter-firm network can be loosely defined as 'two (dyad) or more agents, at least in part autonomous, which give rise to an exchange relationship, according to certain modalities and forms' (Table 3.1).

The definition reported in Table 3.1 points out the following constituent dimensions:

The agents (two or more) involved, which are legally independent but economically interdependent. They can be individuals, groups of individuals, or organizations, though in general (and also in the following) the latter (organizations) are considered. Each of these nodes is related to other nodes (agents) and the whole set of nodes and ties composes the overall structure (*architecture*) of these systemic relationships. Thus, the first dimension refers to the parties (*Who*) that are engaged in the relationship and the ways in which the parties are linked;

The presence of an exchange relationship. Various proposals can be found in the literature concerning the contents of a relationship. At first glance we can distinguish between transactions of products or services, social or affective exchanges, and resource association or sharing. This distinction brings to mind that proposed by Tichy, Tushman, and Fombrun (1979) between: (*a*) the exchange of goods (work flow networks); (*b*) the exchange of information and ideas (communication networks); (*c*) affect or linking (friendship networks). It recalls also the distinction proposed by Grandori (1995) between 'transactional' and 'associative' interdependencies. The first refer to the transfer of goods or services across a technologically separable interface (Williamson 1985).

Table 3.1. Definitions of networks

Definition	Network basic dimensions	
Inter-organizational networks are composed of		
Two (dyad) or more agents, at least in part autonomous	The *structure* (architecture)	*Who* is engaged in the relationship (individuals, groups, and organizations) and the overall architecture of these systemic relationships
which give rise to an exchange relationship	The *content* (task) of the relationships	*What* is exchanged (Soda, 1996): —products or services (transactions) —social or affective exchange —resource association or sharing
according to certain modalities and forms	The *governance*	*How* to adapt, coordinate, and safeguard exchanges

Instead, associative interdependencies imply joint efforts, aligned behaviour, and common actions. In these networks a sale–purchase contract does not occur; however, a type of exchange does take place: the benefits connected with network membership require a corresponding compensation, in terms of behaviour and action, by the members. Thus, this second dimension refers to the presence and the content (*What*) of the exchange;

The modalities of exchange governance. The use of interfirm relationships implies that some activities and tasks are divided among the parties. Each partner assumes certain obligations, gives up some rights and gains others through explicit and implicit, formal and informal agreements (Sobrero and Shrader 1998). Thus, the governance form specifies *how* activities and tasks are divided up among the parties, how to organize, structure, and guide the parties' behaviour. In other words, it specifies how to *govern* (adapt, coordinate, and safeguard) the exchange.

2.2. Network basic dimensions

The proposed definition emphasizes the main dimensions of a network, which often recur in the literature. The *Who*, the *What*, and the *How* can be declined in various ways, giving rise to different reticular forms, that are more or less connected, more or less extended, and more or less stable. It is, therefore, opportune to explode each of these dimensions, in order to understand which properties and characteristics they assume. The Table 3.2 shows an obviously not exhaustive summary of these properties and characteristics.

The *content* (*What*) of the exchange regards primarily materials, services, information, and resources, but also knowledge or expertise or even agreements on actions and results to be achieved. Various theories have identified and extended the properties of the content. The transaction cost theory (Williamson 1975, 1985) is probably the most frequently applied. It assumes, as is well known, that the specificity (idiosyncrasy) of the content is one of the determinants of the contract agreement. Other important, correlated but independent properties, include the innovation and the complexity of the object exchanged.

Governance (*How*)—as shown in Table 3.2—distinguishes between two main categories, inter-firm relationships and inter-firm operations governance. The former contains two categories of governance mechanisms: formal (contractual and bureaucratic) and informal (social) mechanisms. Governance here is intended in the broad sense, while the theoretical definitions and empirical operationalizations primarily refer to the contractual dimension (see Jones *et al.* (1996) for a review on this topic). Contractual coordination mechanisms are used to define the legal boundaries of the relationships. They involve the choice of the legal form governing the agreement, its length, the extent to which parties are bound (e.g. exclusivity clauses, penalties, etc.) (Sobrero and Schrader 1998).

Table 3.2. Network dimensions and elements

Network basic dimensions

Content (*What*)		Governance (*How*)		Structure (*Who*)	
Object	Properties	Inter-firm relationships	Inter-firm operations	Boundaries	Properties
Materials	Object	Institutional	Technological	Make or buy	Centrality,
Services	specificity	mechanisms:	and managerial	decisions	spatial
Information	(customization)	*Formal*	infrastructure:	Level of	distance,
Resources	Object	*mechanisms*	Kind and level	chain cover	position
Knowledge,	innovation	Contractual	of technological	Relevant	Density,
expertise	Object	(legal)	and managerial	relational	number of ties
(Joint)	complexity	agreements	resources	environment	Redundancy
actions		(rights	through which		(structural holes)
Purposes		distribution)	logistics,		Stability/
		Bureaucratic	production,		dynamicity
		control	and design		Directions
		(programmes and	connections are		(horizontal/vertical/
		procedural rules)	achieved		lateral) of ties
		Informal (social)			Versus of ties
		mechanism			(kind of
		Culture and			interdependence)
		macro-culture			Exclusivity
		(shared values			(openness of
		and goals,			strategic blocks)
		unwritten norms)			
		Trust			
		Collective			
		sanction			
		Reputation			
		Industry customs			

This coordination mechanism is therefore formalized in a written agreement between the parties, as are any programmes and procedural rules (bureaucratic control) that can be defined in order to coordinate activities. Beside these formal mechanisms other informal ones act, especially in the presence of relational ties: trust, reputation, shared values, goals, and customs that make up the culture and macrocultures where relationships develop. Also these unwritten and usually tacit aspects govern the behaviour of the parties. A rich literature on economic sociology explains how economic actions may be influenced by the social (cognitive, institutional, and cultural) patterns of ties within which they are embedded (e.g. Granovetter 1985).

The distinction between formal and informal coordination mechanism is quite frequent in the literature, that is, in Smith, Carrol, and Ashford (1995) and in Bates, Nassimbeni, and Hollingworth (2001). It must be noted that social (informal) and formal governance devices should be considered complementary and mutually reinforcing rather than alternative.

The *network structure* (*Who*) is a dimension that has been studied in depth by a specific line of studies: Network Analysis (cf. Aldrich and Whetten 1981;

Burt 1982; Wellmann and Berkowitz 1988). It assumes a structurationist perspective, focusing on the architectural characteristics of networks and the corresponding measures. For example, the measure of the centrality refers to the number of relations that directly or indirectly connect an enterprise to the other network members. It describes the extension of the basin of critical resources from which a firm can draw, thus denoting its degree of attractiveness. This structurationist perspective has been cross-bred in recent times with the Network Strategic Approach, giving particularly interesting results. For a review on the studies that analyse the relationship between structural characteristics (network density, structural holes, structural equivalence, firm location) and profitability of industries and firms see Gulati (1998) and Gulati, Nohria, and Zaheer (2000).

After this brief characterization of the three constituent dimensions of a network and their elements, it is opportune to return to the proposed definition (Table 3.1): This definition needs some comments and specifications.

First, a network originates when *at least two parties* interact. It should be noted that cooperation dynamics were initially considered with respect to dyadic (bilateral) relations and subsequently extended to the collective actions of a plurality of subjects. The reconsideration of the organizational problem from the dyadic to the network level is based on the awareness that the relations between two subjects are conditioned by the relations they have with third parties (Håkansson and Snehota 1989).

Second, the *agents* who interact must be—at least in part—*autonomous* (legally independent). It is precisely this separation of the property rights, Grandori (1999) observes, that distinguishes networks from hierarchies, where parties interact within a sole ownership structure. In other words, there is only one *Who* within hierarchies, since parts are not independent. What instead distinguishes networks—at least networks constituted by relational ties—from markets is the *How*, that is, the transactions governance. Networks are similar to markets with respect to the ownership structure (separated in both cases), but differ in terms of governance making a greater use of informal (social) coordination mechanisms. In fact, the relationship continuity that characterizes 'relational ties' provides incentives to collaborate even in the presence of possible contractual incompleteness, that is, in front of needs (contingencies) not formalized (forecasted) *ex ante*. Moreover, relationship stability gives social mechanisms space and time to develop. Vice versa incentives for collaboration are weaker in markets so here the need exists to formalize the agreement as much as possible. This does not mean that informal mechanisms are totally absent. The neoclassical idea of a market exchange as an a priori discrete event, entirely regulated by contractual clauses and price mechanisms is rather unlikely. Apart from the formal duration of the contract, the expectation of continuity usually accompanies any supply relation whatever, and price does not exhaust all the informative requirements of the parts.

These considerations anticipate a third comment on the proposed definition. Generically, it concerns some modalities and forms to regulate the exchange between the parties, without reducing the field to cooperative modalities, that is, to previously introduce 'relational contracts'. This does not mean that the role of relational valences is denied here. It simply means admitting that in the strategic plan of an enterprise that resorts amply to external transactional environments even more unstable and formal relations can find a precise, 'designed' positioning. This is true especially now in the digital era. With modern information and communication technologies nowadays it is possible for a firm to connect up with a number of external interlocutors and, with relative facility, activate or interrupt a wide range of relations. These technologies do not permit social exchange, which is possible only when there are direct interactions, mutual acquaintance, and a history of past relations. However, they can render the geometry that characterizes the network structure even more variable than it was in the past.

2.3. The two theoretical poles

Impressive research work has been carried out on the network dimensions and their constituent elements. For reviews on the main theoretical lines regarding interorganizational relations and networks see Oliver and Ebers (1998), Grandori and Soda (1995), Schrader and Sobrero (1998), to mention just a few. I only want to point out here that the three constituent dimensions—the *Who*, the *What*, and the *How*—provide the readers with a rough map so they can find their way through this huge body of theories.

As Oliver and Ebers (1998) observe in their interesting meta-analytic paper on interorganizational research, studies 'seem to stretch out between two focal points: a social network perspective at one pole, and a governance perspective at the other'. Researches applying the social network perspective employ the formal apparatus of social network analysis in order to examine how *structural properties* (actor positioning, connectivity, interactions, structural equivalence, etc.) influence organizations and their members. At the opposite pole we find the *governance perspective*, broadly defined as 'all theoretical approaches that study the institutional mechanisms by which inter-organisational relationships are initiated, negotiated, designed, co-ordinated, monitored, adapted and terminated'. According to Oliver and Ebers, this governance perspective comes in two variants. The first shows how the institutional environment (political, legal, cultural, and industry conditions) impacts the likelihood of interorganizational network formation and their forms. The second variant focuses on how to forge networking relations so that actors gain access and make best use of external resources.

3. Supply networks

What are and what distinguishes supply networks from other typologies? While still referring to the network definition given above, the distinctive elements of supply networks are as follows.

They are made up of 'transactional' rather than 'associative' ties. By definition they regard supply relations, that is, exchanges of goods or services. 'A transaction occurs when a good or service is transferred across a technologically separable interface. One stage of processing or assembly activity terminates, and another begins' (Williamson 1985). It follows that the parties are essentially enterprises (economic agents), the motivations of the exchange are primarily related to economic convenience (at least in the long run), their interaction is normally accompanied by a formal agreement (even if not necessarily exhaustive) and regulated by commercial law.

The object of exchange concerns goods and services used for industrial purposes. Supply networks are sometimes called 'production' networks since the input coming from the net units enters into an industrial transforming process. Notwithstanding the fact that service supply networks deserve as much attention as those that move materials, the literature mainly concentrates on the latter. The reason is clear, these papers originated from SCM studies, which are primarily addressed to the management of the physical flow. The fact that the exchanged object constitutes an industrial input determines an important consequence: it is a *hard, visible exchange* (Harland and Knight 2001), if for no other reason than defining the exchange in a contractual sitting. In other kinds of networks, that is, professional communities or trade associations, vice versa, the exchange concerns more intangible elements. The industrial purpose of the exchange determines another decisive characteristic. Resuming Håkansson's (1990) classification regarding the forms of dependence among network members (technical, knowledge, social, and logistic), it is obvious that technical and logistic dependencies characterize supply network. It follows that the importance of *technological and managerial infrastructure* is significantly higher here.

They usually have a hierarchical character and structure. In most of these networks it is possible to individuate an actor that decides how to divide the work (at least in correspondence of the main production stages), selects the external interlocutors, etc. This actor is often defined as the 'focal firm' and its role is highlighted by various definitions. For example, Zheng *et al.* (1999) write 'The boundary of a supply network [. . .] can be drawn from the perspective of a focal firm to include all upstream and downstream organisations from the original source of raw materials or services to the ultimate end customers'. Thus, the focal firm in some way defines the watershed between the sourcing flows of the networks, governing their convergence and coherence. Usually—but not necessarily—the focal firm is the buying company that is placed at the end of the production spinneret. The crucial role of the focal firm is particularly evident in engineering-to-order environments, especially of large projects. The main contractor is the barycentre of the system, it contracts external units to produce parts of the product and manages the outward flow. The hierarchical character of supply networks does not imply that coordination between the units is achieved only through *hierarchical* mechanisms. On the contrary, it is likely that the number and variety of coordination instruments required go hand in hand with the informative and operational complexity of the project. When the object exchanged is complex, the need for mutual adaptations, constant interactivity, jointly reached choices, and shared objectives increases (Håkansson and Snehota 1995). Anyway, even in this case the role of the members is unlikely to be equal: the decision and control rights—even if results of a negotiation process—are not equally distributed.

They are constituted by vertical relationships. With respect to the focal firm, the units of a supply network are engaged in production activities at neighbouring stages of the value chain. They give rise to relations that are different from horizontals ones (parties engaged in similar activities, that is, located at the same stage of the value chain) and diagonals (enterprises that work on technologically distinct but potentially synergistic chains). The distinction between vertical, horizontal, and diagonal linkages is explained by Noteboom (1999), among others. Therefore, a vast casuistry of alliances and joint ventures is excluded, where the joining elements between the network members are the 'functional' synergies (exchange of expertise and skills) rather than the material flows. For example, we exclude commercial agreements between enterprises regarding the sharing of commercial resources or R and D agreements when the parties intend to share research and development efforts obtaining size advantages, sharing the risks and lowering the costs. The fact that vertical relationships are a distinctive feature of supply networks does not mean that relations have only one direction. Horizontal (i.e. two suppliers cooperate to fulfil logistical requirements), lateral (a supplier supplies a customer and at the same time a customer's supplier), and circular relationships are likely to arise (De Toni and Nassimbeni 1995; Pfohl and Buse 2000). Lamming *et al.* (2000) observe: 'The supply network describes lateral links, reverse loops, two-way exchanges and so on, encompassing the upstream and downstream activity, with the focal firm as the point of reference'.

They usually cut across industry boundaries. Particularly in the last five years an intense process of industry cross-fertilization has taken place: materials that originate within an industry find an outlet in several others. Let us think about electronic or oil-compounded materials. Probably there are no sectors that do not utilize some electronic or plastic materials. Consequently, focal firms must relate with suppliers belonging to dissimilar part categories and with clients operating in very distant sectors. These various supply chains intersect in the purchasing department of the focal firm so their competitive priorities, logistic requirements, information exchange, etc. may significantly vary from supplier to supplier and customer to customer, determining a wide and complex *relationship portfolio*.

4. Networking needs in current supply environments

The networking needs, and more specifically the need for stable and cooperative relations (relational contracting) with the units at the upper and lower end of the value chain, have grown remarkably in recent years. Before explaining the reasons, it is opportune to summarize the 'traditional' supply management approach and its disadvantages.

'Traditional' supply management is characterized by four elements (Jackson 1985). First, the buyer interacts with many suppliers (order fragmented into several sources), so as to maintain multiple market alternatives and promote bidding competition among them. Second, the supply relationship is short term, since the buyer wants to retain the possibility of switching the actual supply relationships quickly and opening new ones depending on favourable market opportunities. Third, price is the main vendor selection criterion, determined by competitive pressure in the supply market. Fourth, the customized effort of sources is kept low, since the buyer wants to have source replacement possibilities ready. This approach has obvious advantages but also some strict limitations (Table 3.1).

In the past these limitations were widely tolerated, or in any case they were not so strong as to convince 'traditional' buyers to resort to pure market logic in the relationships with the suppliers, logic so deeply rooted in their culture and managerial praxis. On the other hand, this logic is justified when the exchanged object is not specific and suppliers are replaceable without difficulties. However, modern production and flow management systems have rendered these two conditions less and less probable. Management systems such as Just in Time (JIT) and Concurrent Engineering require the adoption of quality control procedures that are homogenous and coherent along all the process steps, the implementation of integrated coordination practices along the entire flow of materials, and collaboration between all actors (inner and external) involved in the development of a new product and its constituent components. Returning to Table 3.2, we can assert that the supply *content* has changed, becoming more customized, needing better quality and service. At the same time the *governance* has changed too. Supply policies based on multiple sources, on short-term relations, on price as the basic vendor selection criterion appear impracticable in the presence of strong operational buyer–suppliers interdependencies. The latter require adequate incentives for collaboration, in particular greater exclusivity and a longer time horizon of the relationship (De Toni and Nassimbeni 1999, 2000). However, even the 'co-operative' approach has several disadvantages (Table 3.3).

The challenge faced by the focal firm is to maintain efficiency within a supply system characterized by bilateral specific investments, and more exclusive, long-termed relationships. In other words, this is a *challenge of governance* that consists in a sophisticated equilibrium of cooperation and competition between the units of the net.

If we analyse the Japanese automotive supply system, a paradigmatic example of advanced buyer–supplier relationships, we realize that its stability and efficiency depend to a large extent on the *governance capability* of the focal firm, that is on the actions this firm has developed in order to control possible

Table 3.3. 'Spot market' and 'relational contracting': stylized elements and disadvantages

Spot markets	Relational contracting
Stylized elements	
Supplier selection based on price	Supplier selection based on multiple
Multiple sourcing	criteria
Spot transactions (short-term relationships)	Single sourcing or reduced supply base
	Long-term relationships
Disadvantages	
Difficulty of boosting the supplier to the acquisition and development of relational-specific assets	Greater risks of unilateral reinforcement (empowerment) of the partner which can stimulate opportunistic behaviour
Difficulty of generating joint product or process innovation	
Difficulty in supplying of components tailored for the buying firm's production process	Higher switching costs and greater source replacement problems—higher dependency from the sources
Difficulty of improving the productive and logistic chain (by means of adoption of compatible and interacting production planning system, of proper packaging procedures, of compatible identification (bar-coding) systems, . . .)	Higher buyer's operational vulnerability
	Higher insensitivity towards the evolutionary trends in the supply markets
Higher variability of purchased materials	
Incompatibility with the 'continuous improvement' and TQM perspectives	More complex and expensive supplier selection
Exposure to operational inefficiencies (=necessity of buffer inventories to face supplier's unreliability, need of receiving inspection on entry flows, greater planning time horizons, . . .)	
Superior supplier's rigidity to customer's requirements (concerning quality, volumes, deliveries, . . .)	
Greater risk of contentions on quality, quantity and time requirements and greater risk of price renegotiations	

Source: De Toni and Nassimbeni (1999).

opportunistic behaviour and maintain cooperative attitudes within the pool of suppliers (Richardson 1993; Mariotti 1996). In other words, the invisible hand of the market is substituted by the visible and informed hand of the buyer which imposes a competitive discipline on the suppliers, restoring margins of contestability to a 'market' however limited to a narrow and selected group of sources.

This discipline uses several formal mechanisms, for example, (*a*) sophisticated and transparent vendor assessment and monitoring systems, whose purpose is to maintain an adequate competitive pressure within the pool of suppliers and to hand out rewards (attribution of increased supply quotas or of the most remunerative orders) or punishments, (*b*) use of dual or parallel sourcing (even the Japanese buyer tries to avoid dependency on a single supplier), and (*c*) contractual norms of profit and risk sharing.

This discipline is also obtained using some social mechanisms deliberately developed by the buyer through meetings, newsletters, and other means of public comparison. On these occasions a supplier's reputation is at stake in front of the community and tacit collective norms form and consolidate. The clan culture—an element to some extent typical of Japan—offers a particularly favourable environment to cooperation, both inside and between organizations.

Moreover, the Japanese supply system cannot be fully understood without considering its *structure* too. It is shaped like a pyramid where every tie has a specific profile and role; in addition, this supply system is part of a larger network (keiretsu) where important complementariness of business exists. Nowadays, the Japanese supply model is facing a situation of economic crisis that is bringing some of its elements under discussion (Lamming 2000). However, it is obvious that this model, so often hastily explained in terms of simple cooperative harmony is, in reality, the result of a sophisticated, effective governance system and of an original structural configuration.

Following Japanese competitors' performances, western producers—not only in the automotive sector—have tried to reproduce their supply practices and polices, but not always with success. The difficulty in reproducing the Japanese model is substantially imputable to (*a*) the actual difficulty in developing, and above all governing, a supply system with longevity and exclusive features; (*b*) the difficulty in replicating some specific conditions (keiretsu, clan cultures); (*c*) a deeply rooted business culture that ascribes the risk of inefficiencies to supply relation stability and evaluates purchasers mainly in terms of cost reduction. Therefore, the Japanese model does not offer indications that can be rigidly generalized.

5. Research directions

Why did networks emerge? There have been a number of theories, that is, transaction cost theory (cf. Williamson 1975, 1985), resource-based (cf. Barney 1991; Hamel 1991) and resource-dependence (cf. Pfeffer and Salancik 1978) theories, the institutional theory (cf. DiMaggio and Powell 1983), location and regional development theories, social networks theory, agency theory, property rights theory, game theory, contingency theories, population ecology theory, etc. and there is no doubt that the motivations of networking have been abundantly developed in the literature. However, the theoretical and empirical efforts have not explored forms and outcome of networking to the same extent. Oliver and Ebers (1998) observe that 'Research has centred on the driving forces behind inter-organisational networking, rather than on the possible consequences'. Similar conclusions can be found, for instance, in Sobrero and Schrader (1998) and Sydow and Windeler (1998). Moreover, even less research exists that has passed the phase of network description and analysis and reached the phase of network design, offering indications, to some extent normative, for their construction. Lorenzoni and Lipparini (1999) note that past work has tended to consider networks as a given context, rather than a structure that can be deliberately designed. After all, resuming the three network constituent dimensions previously introduced, we can say that the central question 'Which network (content, governance, and structure) for which outcomes under which circumstances?' has received only partial answers up to now.

In this section the areas where research on interorganizational networks, in particular supply networks, needs to be most thorough are pointed out. Before this, however, two preliminary questions and warnings, related to the central problem reported above, need to be underlined.

Can networks be 'disassembled' into basic dimensions and components? Table 3.2 takes this disassembly for granted. But is it really the case? This question is turning up in all the literature on networks. Put in a simple way, we can identify two currents of thought. On one hand there is the 'reductionist' view. According to this networks, even if representing complex systems where technical and social aspects intersect, exhibit some constitutive recurrent elements with their own valence, which is, at least in part, independent from the system they belong to. On the other hand we find what we can call the 'holistic' vision. It asserts that it is impossible to (rigorously) circumscribe each network dimension and sub-dimension, splitting network structure, governance modalities, interaction practices, and individuals that accomplish these practices. Social structures, simultaneously constituted by actors and their practices, exist and manifest themselves at the moment in which they act.

Even accepting the existence of basic network 'components', is it possible to conceptualize the relationships between them? In this case also, we can try to identify two extreme theoretical positions. On one hand there is the 'deterministic' vision that asserts that some regularities in the network phenomena exist. These regularities identify distinct network configurations, or at least distinct patterns of behaviour. Evidently, there is in this view the underlying idea that a deductive–nomothetic search for regularities inside network phenomena can be applied. On the other, we find the 'relativist' vision. According to this, social structures cannot be described in terms of causes and effects, like an operating mechanism of actions and reactions, a stable

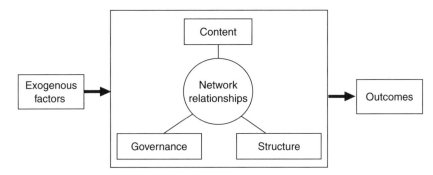

Fig. 3.1.   The reference model

macro-phenomenon which can, to some extent, be predicted. In addition, network processes have cumulative effects and depend also on past history. 'The links, ties and bonds which are developed in one relationship [. . .] are the source as well as the effects of change' (Håkansson and Snehota 1995). Finally, the private, invisible nature of ties renders the network inimitable, and thus the information they provide too (Gulati, Nohria, and Zaheer 2000).

This stylized contraposition between various currents of thought confirms once again the width and complexity of the theme and points out the need for researchers to avoid oversimplified deterministic models. At the same time it highlights the need for comprehensible and normative suggestions for organizational design, though without forgetting the appeal of the holistic and relativist visions. Figure 3.1 graphically translates the central question reviewed above.

The list of the research directions which are summarized in the following sections is by no means comprehensive but simply reflects some broadly defined areas where I see the greatest potential for research.

5.1. The basic network dimensions

The first research direction refer to each of the three network dimensions, examined individually.

The content. As far as the content is concerned, in my opinion it does not seem to be adequately profound, above all, in non-OM literature. The property most frequently considered is *idiosyncrasy*, that is its specificity with respect to partner requirements. As already pointed out, this specificity is a basic construct in the transaction cost theoretical framework. However, in most of the studies this specificity remains a generic, abstract feature, without a clear comprehensive explanation of the real (site, physical, or human) determinants. More generally there is the need, particularly under a supply network perspective, to better understand the nature and form of buyer–supplier operational interdependencies.

The governance. Governance is probably the most critical network dimension since a system with distributed abilities and competencies can work effectively only where governance mechanisms are adequately configured. Uzzi (1996) observes that 'although network governance is widely acknowledged and is seen as producing important economic benefits, the mechanisms that produce these benefits are vaguely specified and empirically still incipient'. Much remains to be understood of the procedures and mechanisms that produce network disciplines, the incentives that can enforce liability and induce cooperative, proactive behaviour. In particular social mechanisms, as their intrinsic nature is more difficult to capture, need further research (see Jones, Hesterly, and Borgatti 1997 and Gulati 1998 on this topic). How can a common culture (values, norms, and beliefs shared across firms) be developed and which (collective) sanctions and rewards should be used?

More in general, which relational capabilities are required to network members, in particular to the focal firm? The development of a network demands additional organizational capabilities, various called 'integrating' or 'systemic' capabilities (Pfohl and Buse 2000) or a firm's 'alliances capability' (Kale, Singh, and Permutter 2000). An important topic of research concerns the processes (learning, knowledge transfer, personnel exchange, etc.) able to build or reinforce social mechanisms. Once these points have been cleared, however, another question emerges: what is the relationship between various governance mechanisms and the adaptive fit of the network? It is reasonable to think of an inverted U-shape. In fact, on one hand, these mechanisms should not be so rigid as to tightly bind the nodes. Otherwise, one of the winning features of networks would collapse, that is, the flexibility of the nodes due to the involvement of integrated and independent units. On the other hand, these mechanisms should be able to render the activities and behaviour of each coherent with the strategic project of the system (Nassimbeni 1998). Thus, which is the optimal level of structural embeddedness, where parties are neither too tightly connected to fragment relational integration (think, for instance, about the weakening of competitive dynamics, the 'not-invented here' syndrome, the 'closed system' mentality), nor so loosely connected as to be to unaware of the requirements of other parties? Cohesion exhibits not only advantages (capillary dissemination of information, involvement, social control, confidence), but also disadvantages (cost, informative redundancy, strategic myopia, risk of knowledge expropriation). For example, Dyer and Nobeoka's (2000) analysis of Toyota's supplier network demonstrates that ties that are too close cause performance deterioration. Similar conclusions can be found in studies on German (Grabher 1993) and Italian (Nassimbeni, 2003) industrial districts.

These questions bring one back to the basic problem of network governance, that is the correct and difficult *balance between* specialization and integration, dependence and independence, fragmentation and cohesiveness, homogenization and diversity, market and hierarchy.

Governance seems to be particularly complex within supply networks. As already pointed out, firms are usually integrated in various chains with different characteristics in terms of supply object specificity, structure of the supply market, and need for interactions. How can one harmonize the various supply chain designs and dynamics? This problem is particularly relevant for the focal firm, which must develop and govern simultaneous relations that have different characteristics. The implications of the simultaneous and possibly conflicting influence of multiple supply channels (and the correspondent multiple economic and social networks) have yet to be systematically examined. Moreover, there are problems of coordination and control of the operations of supply networks that do not occur in other network typologies. The role of information systems (for information exchange and the development of a common language), planning and control systems (for strategic objectives sharing), and human resource management systems (in order to orient the actions and behaviour best suited for network maintenance) is critical here.

The structure. Reconstructing the ramifications of a network can be an arduous task, particularly in presence of inter-sector ties. However, this is an obligatory passage if one truly wishes to understand the competitive forces and dynamics that forge network processes and behaviour. Since external relationships provide access to key resources, the structure of relationship networks describes the asymmetric access that rivals have to raw materials, information, technology, and markets (Madhavan, Koka, and Prescott 1998). One of the more promising lines of research regards the strategic blocks, that is the analysis of the structure of cooperative relations inside and between industries. It first emerged in the works of Harrigan (1985), and is based on the observation that in several sectors cooperative constellations develop that exhibit structural similarities. We have already mentioned the automotive industry (Nohria and Garcia-Pont 1991), but also in many other sectors (banks, insurance, etc.) it is possible to recognize this phenomenon.

As far as supply networks are specifically concerned, a critical question refers to the structure, not of the external relationships, but of the internal organization. How is the matching between internal and external networks achieved? The literature tends to focus on the external transactional environment, while obviously the internal organization (especially that of the focal firm) should be modified in order to support the relational requirements of the network form. How do the boundary-spanning units change, that is, those units that constitute the bridge between the inside and the outside?

Specifically, how does the purchasing function change, now that it must play a proactive role in the identification of procurement needs, the development of partners, and in the crucial collection of information?

5.2. The connection between the basic network dimensions

To specify the connection between network content, governance, and structure is equivalent to specifying the configuration of the network. Several network classifications of such configurations (typologies) have been proposed, and some of them are mentioned in Table 3.4. Evidently, the underlying assumption of these classifications is that it is possible to recognize some 'regularities' (some recurrent patterns) within the variegated universe of network forms. The configurational approach, that is, the identification of ideal types or empirical archetypes that show a recurrent and coherent combination of organizational elements, has been criticized (cf. Grandori 1999). Fundamentally the criticism is 'relativist' in nature and concerns the positivist idea that some generative mechanisms exist in the network phenomena that produce the same effects under the same conditions. In my opinion the risk of fixed or pre-emptory generalizations actually exists, however research in this ambit cannot avoid the identification (with all precautions) of the connections between the basic network dimensions and their possible regularities, on an empirical base.

If we analyse the different classifications proposed in the literature, we can see that usually the various network classifications focus on specific content, governance, or structural issues. However, a valid classification should point out the connection between these dimensions. A good organizational network design should match structural (centrality, density, number, and direction, location of ties, etc.), governance (coordination mechanisms, communication processes, etc.), and content issues. The literature lacks a truly comprehensive classification framework, particularly where supply networks are concerned.

In this ambit we can still find an important direction that needs in-depth study, that is, network configuration in the current e-business environment. Virtual markets, with their unprecedented reach, connectivity, and low-cost information processing power, open entirely new possibilities for value creation through the structuring of transaction in novel ways (Amit and Zott 2001). Value creation opportunities in virtual markets may result from new combinations of information, physical products or services, innovative configurations of transactions, and the reconfiguration and integration of resources, capabilities, roles and relationships among suppliers, partners, and customers. In other words, the virtual environment impacts on content, governance, and structure of networks, which becomes wider and more transient. However, according to Amitt and Zott (2001), we still do not have adequate conceptual instruments for understanding and modelling these transformations.

Table 3.4. Network classifications

Authors	Network basic dimensions				
	Content		Governance		Structure
	Object	Properties	Inter-firm relationships	Inter-firm operations	Boundaries Properties
Achrol and Kotler (1999)	Internal, vertical, intermarket, opportunity networks				—
Nassimbeni (1998)	Supply networks, agreements and joint ventures, regional industrial systems		—		—
Belussi and Arcangeli (1998)		—		—	Steady, retractile, evolutionary
Rowley (1997)		—		—	Compromiser, subordinate, commander, solitarian
Rosenfeld (1996)	Hard, soft	—	—		—
Grandori and Soda (1995)	—		Social, bureaucratic, proprietary		—
Hinterhuber and Levin (1994)		—		—	Internal, vertical, horizontal, diagonal
Miles and Snow (1992)		—		—	Internal, stable, dynamic
Supply (production) network typologies:				—	—
Patterson *et al.* (1999)		—	Transcendental, transitional, transactional		—
Pfhol and Buse (2000)					Strategic, virtual, regional, operative
Lamming *et al.* (2000)	Supply networks of: (*a*) innovative and unique products; (*b*) functional products				

5.3. *Network dimensions, external contingencies, and outcomes*

The analysis of the relationships between exogenous forces (input factors), network designs (content, governance, and structure), and performances (output) needs further research. There is an enormous amount of research on the motivation for alliance formation, the factors which influence the firm's proclivity to enter alliances, and the choice of the partner (see Gulati 1998 for a review). However, many economic, political, and cultural exogenous forces need to be further investigated (Ebers and Jarillo 1998). In addition, most of these studies refer to horizontal alliances, while vertical alliances have received, with few exceptions, less attention (Martin, Mitchell, and Swaminath 1995).

On the output side, the main studies on inter-firm relationship performance have been to establish the link between some types of relational behaviour and aspects (in particular long-term versus spot transactions) and performance (O'Toole and Donaldson 2000). However, research should better identify the possible consequences not only of dyadic buyer–supplier relationship forms, but of networking, and especially which form of networking (Provan and Milward 1995). Recently, a number of researchers have examined different aspects of a firm's network—such as strength of ties, geographical extension, centrality (Zaheer and Zaheer 1997), and redundancy (McEvily and Zaheer 1999)—and certain network performance outcomes. In addition, some outcome categories are better considered than others. In economic studies, cost efficiency and innovation prevail, while in sociological studies power is the most frequently considered variable (Oliver and Ebers 1998).

The advantages of networking are quite clear: networks potentially provide a firm with access to information, resources, markets, and technologies, with benefits from learning, scale, and scope economies, and allow firms to achieve strategic objectives, such as risk sharing and outsourcing value-chain stages and organizational functions (see, for example, Gulati, Nohria, and Zaheer 2000). The disadvantages of networking (increased dependency, strategic rigidities, cost of coordination, new skills required, loss of critical knowledge, etc.) are discussed in many papers too, though more emphasis is placed on positive rather than on negative outcomes (Ebers and Grandori 1997; for the costs of networking see Smith 1999; and Madhok and Tallman 1998).

It should be noted that the research directions reported above—related to network dimensions, their reciprocal connection and the influence on environmental factors—need to be examined *in dynamic terms*. Networks are changing organisms, with inherent dynamics features, characterized by a continuous organizing process (Håkansson and Snehota 1995). Despite the number of contributions appearing in recent times, important questions still remain concerning the evolutionary process of interfirm tie formation and how networks evolve and change over time (Madhavan, Koka, and Prescott 1998; Grandori and Soda 1995). Also for these studies, it can be useful for separating the literature into two branches (Benson-Rea and Wilson 2000), that is, the *evolutionary* and the *revolutionary* perspectives. The former assumes that incremental adaptations move networks—which have an equilibrium-seeking nature—towards a steady state. The latter maintains that in the current turbulent environment organizational needs become more complex, and different types of networks will be required so that initial configurations can be rapidly and drastically modified. These two perspectives are based on a different hypothesis regarding the speed of the external changes and the organizational inertia of networks. Apart from this hypothesis, important fields of research concern: (*a*) origin, nature, speed, sequence, and diffusion (domino effects) of changes; (*b*) patterns of transformation; (*c*) actions and reactions; (*d*) path dependency of changes. How networks develop over time, particularly in situations of crisis (as in Japan) is an argument of extreme importance and has not been adequately explored.

5.4. Some 'dominant' perspectives

In this section certain perspectives of analysis that in some ways dominate current research and limit its development are pointed out. These are:

The focal-firm dominated perspective. That related to the focal firm is certainty a privileged visual angle, however it is not exhaustive. The points of views of the supplier and the suppliers' supplier are often neglected. Let us consider, for example, JIT practices along the supply chain. The literature frequently emphasizes the performance improvement for focal firms, while in many cases—as empirically documented (Sako, Lamming, and Helper 1995)— suppliers complain about the fact that 'JIT only transfers inventory responsibility from customers to suppliers'. Besides, in some industries, particularly in some e-businesses, the architecture for the product, service, and information flows, as well as the set of business actors, are continuously changing. So it is difficult to identify a barycentre for the network, a focal firm. The central element is not the company that purchases materials and delivers the finished product to consumers, but the business model that combines various products and services in continuously changing ways.

The buyer–supplier dyad dominated perspective. This point is linked to the previous one, with the difference that in this case the unit of analysis is represented not only by the focal firm, but also by its direct suppliers or customers. Vice versa, it is important to consider the overall structure of the network, rather than the exchange dyads. This limitation is often connected to the methodological difficulty of individuating all relevant relationships and developing and combining measures related to different nodes of the same unit of analysis (the network).

The automotive-industry dominated perspective. The automotive sector historically represents the reference point for the development and validation of advanced managerial models. However, this industry evidently presents some specificities, linked to the product, manufacturing process, and market environment. Therefore, the indications it provides cannot be rigidly generalized, but much of current research on this topic refers to this industry (Zheng *et al.* 1999).

The 'co-operative harmony' dominated perspective. One of the criticisms of the literature on enterprise cooperation regards the excessive emphasis on elements such as mutual involvement, reciprocity, and confidence, while neglecting a series of tensions and friction that unavoidably accompany cooperative processes (Padula 2000). These tensions have also a competitive valence. As pointed out, effective network management demands a sophisticated balance between cooperation and competition (New and Ramsay 1997). For this reason, the concepts of 'co-opetition' (Nalebuff and Brandenburger 1997), 'learning racing' (Hamel 1991), and 'multifaceted relationships' (Dowling *et al.* 1996) merit more profound investigation.

The network members' 'homogenization' perspective. Often the literature evidences the need for network members to be *homogeneous*, that is, exhibiting the same behaviour and culture (values, beliefs, and experiences). The nodes of the network—by definition at least in part independent and therefore having their own competitive individuality—must, in fact, integrate within a common strategic project that demands a certain degree of values, language, and culture sharing. However, the overemphasis on the behaviour and culture alignment of network members tends to cloak the positive effects of variety and diversity. After all, the attractiveness of a network resides precisely in its diversity.

The lean-practices dominated perspective. As noted in Section 3, modern production and flow management systems, in particular JIT, Concurrent Engineering, and Total Quality Management practices, have determined the increase in the networking needs of firms. However, in current competitive environments, Lamming *et al.* (2000) observe, the requirements for agility may call for extra resources to be made available, above what might be termed 'lean'. For this reason a growing number of networks imply a firm furnished with redundant resources (Belussi and Arcangeli 1998). More generally, it is not just a problem of practices, whether lean or not. This term is the proper one to describe the *operations* between network members, that is the production–logistic interdependencies and coordination modalities. However, the governance of interorganization relationships is equally important (Table 3.2): it is constituted in a large part by informal mechanisms such as culture, trust, and reputation. In this ambit it is not so much a matter of procedures and practices, rather of relational sensibility, behaviour, and social capital.

6. Conclusions

In this chapter, the first step was to develop a sufficiently general definition of network to which reference could be made. The proposed definition individuates the three fundamental dimensions of a network, which then have been divided into their constituent elements and properties. Evidently even this is a simplifying and 'reductionist' passage, thus one can fully appreciate the multidimensionality that characterizes networks in general, and supply networks in particular. Here, in fact, technical, economic, and organizational variables interlace and merge. A large part of the research on supply networks has, up to now, focused on one or a few categories of elements. Vice versa, analysing the supply chain according to a network perspective means that this complexity, this multidimensionality must be faced. The analysis has to be extended beyond the horizon of *operations* invading economics, sociology, and organization, that is the disciplines that, up to now, have claimed leadership in the topic here analysed. Here, therefore, an attempt was made to analyse supply networks according to a multidisciplinary approach. The remaining chapters of this book offer useful insights into many of the aspects that have been simply introduced here.

References

ACHROL, R. S., and KOTLER, P. (1999). 'Marketing in the Network Economy'. *Journal of Marketing*, 63/4: 146–63.

ALDRICH, H., and WHETTEN, D. A. (1981). 'Organization-sets, Action-sets, and Networks: Making the Most of Semplicity', in P. C. Nystrom and W. H. Starbuck (eds.), *Handbook of Organizational Design*. Oxford: Oxford University Press, 385–408.

AMIT, R., and ZOTT, C. (2001). 'Value Creation in E-business'. *Strategic Management Journal*, 22/6–7: 493–520.

BARNEY, J. B. (1991). 'Firm Resources and Sustained Competitive Advantage'. *Journal of Management*, 17/1: 99–120.

BATES, K. A., NASSIMBENI, G., and HOLLINGWORTH, D. G. (2001). 'A Longitudinal Study of the Institutionalization of Japanese-oriented Supplier Management Outside Japan'. *2001 Rotman Working Papers Series*, University of Toronto.

BELUSSI, F., and ARCANGELI, F. (1998). 'A Typology of Networks: Flexible and Evolutionary Firms'. *Research Policy*, 27/4: 415–28.

BENSON-REA, M., and WILSON, H. I. (2000). 'Performance and the Lifecycle of the Firm and Its Network'. 16th IMP Conference on Interactions and Relationhips. University of Bath.

BURT, R. S. (1982). *Toward a Structural Theory of Actions*. New York: Academic Press.

DE TONI, A., and NASSIMBENI, G. (1995). 'Supply Networks: Genesis, Stability and Logistics Implications'. *OMEGA—International Journal of Management Science*, 23/4: 403–18.

—— —— (1999). 'Buyer–supplier Operational Practices, Sourcing Policies and Plant Performances: Results of an Empirical Research'. *International Journal of Production Research*, 37/9: 597–619.

—— —— (2000). 'Just-In-Time Purchasing: An Empirical Study of Operational Practices, Supplier Development and Performance'. *OMEGA—International Journal of Management Science*, 28/6: 631–51.

DIMAGGIO, P., and POWELL, W. (1983). 'The Iron Cage Revisited: Institutional Isomorphism and Collective Rationality in Organizational Fields'. *American Sociological Review*, 48: 147–60.

DOWLING, M. J., ROERING, W. D., CARLIN, B. A., and WISNIESKI, J. (1996). 'Multifaceted Relationships Under Co-opetition. Description and Theory'. *Journal of Management Inquiry*, 5: 155–67.

Dyer, J. F., and Nobeoka, K. (2000). 'Creating and Managing a High Performance Knowledge-sharing Network: The Toyota Case'. *Strategic Management Journal*, 21/3: 345–67.

Ebers, M., and Grandori, A. (1997). 'The Forms, Costs, and Development Dynamics of Inter-organizational Networking'. in M. Ebers (eds.), *The Formation of Inter-organizational Networks*. Oxford: Oxford University Press, 265–86.

—— and Jarillo, J. C. (1998). 'The Construction, Form and Consequences of Industry Networks'. *International Studies of Management and Organization*, 27/4: 3–21.

Grabher, G. (1993). 'The Weakness of Strong Ties', in G. Grabher (ed.), *The Socially Embedded Firm*. London: Routledge, 255–77.

Grandori, A. (1995). *L'organizzazione Delle Attività Economiche*. Bologna: Il Mulino.

—— (1999). 'Interfirm Networks: Organizational Mechanisms and Economic Outcomes', in A. Grandori (ed.), *Interfirm Networks*. London: Routledge, 1–14.

—— and Soda, G. (1995). 'Inter-firm Networks: Antecedents, Mechanisms and Forms'. *Organization Studies*, 16/2: 183–214.

Granovetter, M. (1985). 'Economic Action and Social Structure: The Problem of Embeddedness'. *American Journal of Sociology*, 91/3: 481–510.

Gulati, R. (1998). 'Alliances and Networks'. *Strategic Management Journal*, 19/4: 293–317.

—— Nohria, N., and Zaheer, A. (2000). 'Strategic Networks'. *Strategic Management Journal*, 21/3: 203–15.

Håkansson, H. (1990). 'Product Development in Networks', in D. Ford (ed.), *Understanding Business Markets: Interactions, Relationships and Networks*. London: Academic Press. 487: 507.

—— and Snehota, I. (1989). 'No Business is an Island: The Network Concept of Business Strategy'. *Scandinavian Journal of Management*, 5/3: 187–200.

—— —— (1995). *Developing Relationships in Business Networks*. London: Routledge.

Hamel, G. (1991). 'Competition for Competence and Inter-partner Learning Within International Strategic Alliances'. *Strategic Management Journal*, 12/4: 83–103.

Harland, C. M., and Knight, L. A. (2001). 'Supply Network Strategies. Role and Competence Requirements'. *International Journal of Operations and Production Management*, 21/4: 476–89.

Harrigan, K. R. (1985). *Strategies for Joint Ventures*. Lexington, MA: Lexington Books.

Hinterhuber, H. H., and Levin, B. M. (1994). 'Strategic Networks: The Organisation of the Future'. *Long Range Planning*, 27/3: 43–53.

Jackson, B. (1985). *Winning and Keeping Industrial Customer*. Lexington, MA: Lexingon Books.

Jones, C., Hesterly, W. S., and Borgatti, S. P. (1997). 'A General Theory of Network Governance: Exchange Conditions and Social Mechanisms'. *Academy of Management Review*, 22/4: 911–45.

Kale, P., Singh, H., and Permutter, H. (2000). 'Learning and Protection of Proprietary Assets in Strategic Alliances: Building Relational Capital'. *Strategic Management Journal*, 21/3: 217–37.

Lamming, R. (2000). 'Japanese Supply Chain Relationships in Recession'. *Long Range Planning*, 33/6: 757–78.

—— Johnsen, T., Zheng, J., and Harland, C. (2000). 'An Initial Classification of Supply Networks'. *International Journal of Operations and Production Management*, 20/6: 675–91.

LORENZONI, G., and LIPPARINI, A. (1999). 'The Leveraging of Interfirm Relationships as a Distinctive Organizational Capability: A Longitudinal Study'. *Strategic Management Journal*, 20/4: 317–38.

MACHLUP, F. (1978). 'Ideal Types, Reality and Construction', in F. Machlup (ed.), *Methodology of Economics and Other Social Sciences*. New York: Academic Press, 345–67.

MACMILLAN, K., and FARMER, D. (1979). 'Redefining the Boundaries of the Firm'. *Journal of Industrial Economics*, 27/3: 277–85.

MACNEIL, I. R. (1985). 'Relational Contract: What We Do and Do Not Know'. *Wisconsin Law Review*, 3: 483–525.

MADHAVAN, R., KOKA, B. R., and PRESCOTT, J. E. (1998). 'Networks in Transition: How Industry Events (Re)Shape Interfirm Relationships'. *Strategic Management Journal*, 19/5: 439–59.

MADHOK, A., and TALLMAN, S. B. (1998). 'Resources, Transactions and Rents: Managing Value Through Interfirm Collaborative Relationships'. *Organization Science*, 9/3: 326–39.

MARIOTTI, S. (1996). *Mercati Verticali Organizzati e tecnologie dell'informazione— L'evoluzione dei rapporti di fornitura*, Roma: Quaderni della Fondazione Adriano Olivetti.

MARTIN, X., MITCHELL, W., and SWAMINATH, A. (1995). 'Recreating and Extending Japanese Automobile Buyer Supplier Links in North America'. *Strategic Management Journal*, 16/8: 589–619.

MCEVILY, B., and ZAHEER, A. (1999). 'Bridging Ties: A Source of Firm Heterogeneity in Competitive Capabilities'. *Strategic Management Journal*, 20/12: 1133–58.

MILES, R. E., and SNOW, C. C. (1992). 'Causes of Failure in Network Organizations'. *California Management Review*, 34/4: 53–72.

NALEBUFT, B. J., and BRANDENBURGER, A. (1997). *Co-opetition*. London: Prolific Books.

NASSIMBENI, G. (1998). 'Network Structures and Co-ordination Mechanisms: A Taxonomy'. *International Journal of Operations and Production Management*, 18/6: 538–54.

—— (2003). 'Local Manufacturing Systems and Global Economy: Are They Compatible? The Case of the Italian Eyewear District'. *Journal of Operations Management*, 21/2: 151–72.

NEW, S., and RAMSAY, J. (1997). 'A Critical Appraisal of Aspects of the Lean Chain Approach'. *European Journal of Purchasing and Supply Management*, 3/2: 93–102.

NOHRIA, N. (1992). 'Introduction: Is a Network Perspective a Useful Way of Studying Organizations?', in N. Nohria and R. G. Eccles (eds.), *Networks and Organizations*. Boston, MA: Harvard Business School Press, 1–22.

—— and GARCIA-PONT, C. (1991). 'Global Strategic Linkages and Industry Structure'. *Strategic Management Journal*, 14/3: 179–91.

NOTEBOOM, B. (1999). 'The Dynamic Efficiency of Networks', in A. Grandori (eds.), *Interfirm Networks. Organization and Industrial Competitiveness*. London: Routledge, 91–118.

OLIVER, A. L., and EBERS, M. (1998). 'Networking Network Studies: An Analysis of Conceptual Configurations in the Study of Inter-organisational Relationships'. *Organisation Studies*, 19/4: 549–83.

O'TOOLE, T., and DONALDSON, B. (2000). 'Relationship Governance Structure and Performance'. *Journal of Marketing Management*, 16/4: 327–41.

PADULA, G. (2000). 'Reti di Imprese e Processi Competitivi', *Finanza Marketing e Produzione*, 20/3: 39–88.

PATTERSON, J. L., FORKER, L. B., and HANNA, J. B. (1999). 'Supply Chain Consortia: The Rise of Transcendental Buyer–supplier Relationships'. *European Journal of Purchasing and Supply Management*, 5/2: 85–93.

PFEFFER, J., and SALANCICK, G. R. (1978). *The External Control of Organizations*. New York: Harper and Row.

PFOHL, H. C., and BUSE, H. P. (2000). 'Inter-organizational Logistics Systems in Flexible Production Networks'. *International Journal of Physical Distribution and Logistics Management*, 30/5: 388–408.

PROVAN, K. G., and MILWARD, H. B. (1995). 'A Preliminary Theory of Interorganizational Network Effectiveness'. *Administrative Science Quarterly*, 40/1: 1–33.

RICHARDSON, J. (1993). 'Parallel Sourcing and Supplier Performance in the Japanese Automobile Industry'. *Strategic Management Journal*, 14/5: 339–50.

RING, P. S., and VAN DE VEN, A. (1994). 'Development Process of Co-operative Interorganizational Relationships'. *Academy of Management Review*, 19/1: 90–118.

ROSENFELD, S. A. (1996). 'Does Co-operation Enhance Competitiveness? Assessing the Impacts of Inter-firm Collaboration'. *Research Policy*, 25/2: 247–63.

ROWLEY, T. J. (1997). 'Moving Beyond Dyadic Ties: A Network Theory of Stakeholder Influences'. *Academy of Management Review*, 22/4: 887–910.

SAKO, M., LAMMING, R. C., and HELPER, S. M. (1995). 'Supplier Relationship in the UK Car Industry: Good News–Bad News'. *European Journal of Purchasing and Supply Management*, 2/1: 35–48.

SMITH, K. G., CARROL, S. J., and ASHFORD, S. J. (1995). 'Intra- and Interorganizational Co-operation: Toward a Research Agenda'. *Academy of Management Journal*, 38/1: 7–23.

SMITH, P. S. (1999). 'The Cost of the Networked Organization', in A. Grandori (eds.), *Interfirm Networks. Organization and Industrial Competitiveness*. London: Routledge.

SOBRERO, M., and SCHRADER, S. (1998). 'Structuring Inter-firm Relationships: A Meta-analytic Approach'. *Organization Studies*, 19/4: 585–615.

SYDOW, J., and WINDELER, A. (1998). 'Organizing and Evaluating Interfirm Networks: A Structurationist Perspective on Network Processes and Effectiveness'. *Organization Science*, 9/3: 265–84.

TICHY, N. M., TUSHMAN, M. L., and FOMBRUN, C. (1979). 'Social Network Analysis for Organizations'. *Academy of Management Review*, 4/4: 507–19.

UZZI, B. (1996). 'The Sources and Consequences of Embeddedness for the Economic Performance of Organizations: The Network Effect'. *American Sociological Review*, 61/4: 674–98.

WELLMANN, B., and BERKOWITZ, S. D. (eds.) (1988). *Social Structures: A Network Approach*, Cambridge, England: Cambridge University Press.

WILLIAMSON, O. E. (1975). *Market and Hierarchies: Analysis and Antitrust Implications*. New York: The Free Press.

—— (1985). *The Economic Institutions of Capitalism*. New York: The Free Press.

ZAHEER, A., and ZAHEER, S. (1997). 'Catching the Wave: Alertness, Responsiveness, and Market Influence in Global Electronic Networks'. *Management Science*, 43/11: 1493–509.

ZHENG, J., HARLAND, C., JOHNSEN, T., and LAMMING, R. (1999). 'Methodological Issues in Inter-Organisational Supply Network Research', in E. Bartezzaghi, R. Filippini, G. Spina, and A. Vinelli (eds.), *Managing Operations Network*. Proceedings of the 6th EurOMA Conference, SGE Padova, 1999: 111–19.

4

Supply Chains: Construction and Legitimation

STEVE NEW

1. Introduction

What is going on when we talk of 'supply chains'? Rather than merely enumerating the many potential definitions, or even proposing new ones, this chapter analyses the foundations that underpin the supply chain concept. It examines the senses in which supply chains can be said to exist in the first place (the 'ontology' of the chain) and shows how the idea serves particular interests.

In contemporary philosophy, ontology ('the science of being') is associated with the study of formal logic and the use of rather technical language: how can we decide what exists, or not? In computer science, ontology means models of entities and their relations that define specific domains of knowledge (and in some quarters, 'supply chain ontology' has a precise technical meaning concerning the design of interorganizational information systems: see Haugen and McCarthy 2000; Smith 2000). Here, however, ontology refers to the way in which an abstract concept is imputed with meaning, and used to imply the real existence of something. Other parallel terms might include 'reification' and 'social construction'.

Merely to observe that supply chains are socially constructed is not much of a contribution; the label can be applied in many different ways, and there are considerable definitional problems in determining whether we mean, for example, the flow of goods relating to a particular product, or the network of commercial relationships connected to a particular firm (New 1994). Any attempt to talk about, for example, 'Hewlett-Packard's supply chain' or the 'steel supply chain' involves some kind of projection of a boundary; as this is not 'given' in any objective sense, then clearly we are talking about something that people *choose* to define in particular ways. So to point out that supply chains are some kind of social construction in this sense is neither controversial, nor particularly interesting.

However, what becomes more intriguing is *why* people make the definitional choices they do: what interests are being served? What function does the concept fulfil? Why take what could be treated as a series of independent commercial relationships, and construe it as a 'supply chain' entity? This line of thinking means that, rather than agonizing over which of the many definitions of the supply chain is the 'right' one, it becomes interesting to ask why the supply chain idea has taken such purchase in the minds of managers and academics. Beneath the surface discussion of cooperation, integration, and optimization, are there other agendas at work?

The argument below will proceed as follows. Section 2 expands on the idea of social construction, exploring the idea from the perspective of practice and theory. Section 3 considers attempts to conceive of the supply chain as some kind of structure, while Section 4 reviews approaches based on the idea of the integration of process. Section 5 moves on to review how the supply chain idea serves to legitimate certain kinds of power relationship, and considers, in turn, the use of language, the concept of legitimation, and the nature of supply chain power. Section 6 concludes the chapter with a discussion of the implications of this analysis.

2. Social construction in practice and theory

The notion of 'deconstruction' is well established within management studies and social sciences more generally. The origins of the approach are complex, and its evolution has involved varying amounts of overlap with interpretivist and anti-managerialist agendas, and has developed in loose coordination with an interest in the nature of 'discourse' in other fields (notably social psychology, literary theory, and political science; see Mills 1997). Lynch (2001) claims that the idea of social construction has become stretched across so many disciplines that it may be too diffuse for coherent discussion. However, here the idea will be summarized in two ways: on the one hand, in regard to the reality experienced by practitioners and actors; on the other, as the reality as imagined by research.

In the first case, it is non-controversial to observe that how ordinary people conduct themselves depends on their perceptions of reality—and it is this that is socially constituted as part of some collectively negotiated order, and exists in a reflexive relationship to language. There are many origins of this insight, including Wittgenstein's analysis of the fundamentally *constructive* role of language (Wittgenstein 1953), and Austin's (1962) description of the *performative* role of language. In linguistics and literary criticism, writers such as Saussure (1974) and Bakhtin (1986) problematized the nature of communication, emphasizing the constructive role of the listener/reader. These ideas have fed into a stream of cultural/philosophical studies including the contributions of Foucault (1972), Lincoln (1989), and many others, which themselves find influence in the anthropologies of Evans-Pritchard (1940), Malinowski (1954), Lévi-Strauss (1964), and Maus (1967).

For sociology, a key inspiration was that provided by Mead's (1934) introduction of 'symbolic interactionism' in which the very notion of the 'self' is constructed in social interaction. March and Simon (1958) argued that managers focus on simplified models of the environment, and that their choices regarding what was in or out of the models were significant. The seminal work of Berger and Luckmann (1966) drew together many of these emerging strands, influencing a generation of organizational theorists. Weick (1969, 1985) outlined how decision-makers 'enact' the environment and engage in 'sensemaking', a concept that has become a cornerstone of research in organizational behaviour (see Tushman and Scanlan 1981; Starbuck 1982). Thompson (1980) explored the organization's role in reality construction (see also Hines 1988). The social construction of market relationships was highlighted by Granovetter (1973, 1985—see also Olkkonen, Tikkanen, and Alajoutsijärvi 2000), and this has been a significant element of francophone economic sociology (see especially the work of Callon 1998). One related development, Actor–Network theory, has proven to be especially applicable in studies relating to innovation and technology (e.g. Harrison and Laberge 2002). Other significant contributions include Garfinkel (1967); Douglas (1986); Geertz (1973, 1975); Gergen (1985, 1994, 1999); Harré (1979); and Campbell (2000).

These various strands of analysis vary in many important ways, but converge on the key insight that the 'reality' experienced by economic and managerial actors cannot be read at face value (Harré 1979; Lakoff and Johnson 1980; Draper 1988; Kendall and Kendall 1993). The 'common-sense' interpretations of managers—and the prognostications of consultants and journalists—arise from a complex interplay of social processes and sectional interests (Harré and Secord 1972; Buckley and Chapman 1997).

This point leads to the consideration of the second mode of social construction as applied to management: the reification of theoretical entities by researchers and thinkers—abstract artefacts that become the building blocks of academic inquiry. In Economics, much of the debate at the margins of the discipline focuses on the value of the use of key concepts (e.g. economic growth, natural rates of unemployment) whose meaning, empirical clarity, and ideological content are open to debate. Keita (1992), for example, pillories the scientific aspirations of conventional economics for its lack of 'empirically identifiable content'—see also Gibson-Graham (1996); Lawson (1997). In management studies, the work of Burrell and Morgan (1979) fed into a thriving field of critical engagement with management theory, crystallizing in a 'movement' of Critical Management Studies, in which a major element has been the understanding of the way in which individuals interact with prevailing narratives of management and control (Alvesson and Willmott 1992*a*, *b*). An important aspect of this evolving and tangled stream of work was to highlight the importance of language and metaphor (e.g. Morgan 1986; see also Tsoukas 1991; Rigney 2001).

The construction of the world as perceived by research has become a fertile area of investigation in its own right. Abrahamson (1991) considers the role of fads in management practice and research in terms of the diffusion of innovations. Barley and Kunda (1992) sketch patterns of managerial discourse and link them with broadly alternating ideologies of control (see also Gill and Whittle 1992; Grint 1994, 1997; Mizurchi and Fein 1999; Griseri 2002). However, although these debates tend to rumble on at the edges of academic discourse, it is fair to say that—in the spirit of Kuhnian 'normal science'—such debates are often marginalized by the mainstream of research practice. For example, mainstream microeconomics can proceed happily according to its own mode of discourse, effectively oblivious to the various debates about the social construction of 'markets' (Lawson 1997; Mäki 2000).

Social construction, then, can be seen to be going on at the level of practice and theory. However, as Whitley (1984a, b) points out, the nature of management studies' peculiar relation to practice means that two domains have an interactive and reflexive existence; and this presents a serious challenge to any attempt at detailed deconstruction. This point is made by Shenhav (1995) in his analysis of the rise of the systematization movement of the late nineteenth and early twentieth centuries: '. . . Academic and non-academic texts should not be read as external to the practice of organizations but, rather, as discursive practices that are intertwined with organizational practices' (p. 582). For example, the use of language by managers and consultants cannot be ignored, even if it is incoherent or at odds with the formal definitions used by academics. Researchers in management do not have the luxury of dismissing the conceptualizations offered in, for example, the trade press or in consultants' PowerPoint™ slides as being simply 'wrong', as these constructions are to some extent formative of managerial reality, and are important in guiding and justifying practice in both direct and complex ways. Clark and Salaman (1999) provide a helpful review of this point (see also Kallinkos 1996; Heracleous and Hendry 2000; Clark and Fincham 2002). There is growing interest, however, in the mechanisms of this interplay, and, in particular, in the consequences of casual reification. Carrier and Miller (1998) outline the nature of what they term 'virtualism'—the ascription of existence to abstract concepts creating 'a kind of virtual reality': 'when people take this . . . not just to be a parsimonious description of what is really happening, but prescriptive of what the world ought to be' (Carrier 1998: 2). In various ways, the contributors to Carrier and Miller's book highlight the problem that what might begin as a tentative and simplified abstraction for the conceptual convenience of academics can rapidly translate into a normative trope; mediated by the way 'knowledge' is represented in academic papers, textbooks (and maybe policy papers and newspaper editorials), a speculative model can rapidly make the transition between 'might be' to 'ought'. This chapter argues that this is what has happened with supply chains.

3. The supply chain as 'structure': three theoretical perspectives

The supply chain is more than a metaphor. A supply chain is, in fact, a series of links between suppliers and their customers until a product or service reaches its ultimate end-user. (Infoteria Corporation 2001).

When supply chains are seen in terms of structure, the implied ontology is one of some system of links and nodes—for example, Lee and Billington (1992) define the supply chain as a network of 'sites'. For some authors these are literal geographic sites, and for others these may be commercial entities or even departments or business units. Julka, Srinvasan, and Karimi (2002, emphasis added) claim that 'More enterprises now consider the *entire supply chain structure* while taking business decisions'. Many textbooks and introductory articles begin with a simple diagram of box representing a firm, linking to one or more boxes in either direction representing customers and suppliers. This holds out two enticing possibilities: that 'real' chains might be formally mapped and plotted out, and that such a plotting will enable the understanding of 'the system'. Lillenfeld (1988) argues that all 'systems thinking' is built on the idea of diagrams purporting to show the relationship between entities (see also Peery 1972; Berlinksi 1976; Bloomfield and Best 1992; Kendall and Kendall 1993).

Disappointingly, however, it is an important observation that diagrams of all but the most simple 'actual' supply chains (in this sense) are *almost entirely absent* from the literature. Generally, exceptions are either simplified or figurative rather than specific, or—where detail is provided—illustrate distribution and manufacturing within a unitary organization. There are two straightforward reasons for this: the complexity of many real systems (in terms of the numbers of products and components, suppliers, locations, and so on), and commercial confidentiality. Information about who supplies whom is generally sensitive, and not generally accessible for research destined for the public domain. Chapman (1973), for example, illustrates that mapping the flow of materials through the petrochemical industries—a sector often portrayed by textbooks as consisting of flows of relative simplicity—is very difficult. He comments: '. . . the different approaches to corporate growth . . . have superimposed a behavioural variable on their technical structure' (p. 33). Cisic, Kesic, and Jakomin (2000) present some theoretical tools for assessing the 'structure' of supply chains—but provide no real applications. More importantly, even large organizations with well-developed 'supply chain management' may not have good information as to the structure of their own chains: Choi and Hong's pioneering (2002) study of Honda, Acura, and DaimlerChrysler is fascinating not least for the effort required to produce even simple diagrams of the chain, but also for the observation that the information about the structure of the second tier of the chain held by the assembler was surprisingly inaccurate. Fawcett and Magnan (2002) comment on the relative difficulty of finding firms whose supply chain activities go beyond their immediate trading partners.

Nevertheless, three interconnected streams of academic investigation have risen to the challenge of tackling this kind of conception of the 'structural' supply chain: within mainstream economics, what might be called the '*Vertical Economy*' school has considered questions of vertical integration and its alternatives; the '*Marketing Channel*' school has focused on the mechanisms of corporate interaction between trading partners and the choices firms make (in particular regarding the structure of 'downstream' distribution); and, finally, the '*Commodity Chain*' approach has tended to address broader questions of political economy. These distinct academic approaches have arisen in a curious fashion; while there is a degree of cross-citation, and frequent (and often imprecise) swapping of terminology, there has been surprisingly little genuine cross-fertilization of ideas between these important movements. In all three cases, there can be seen as a broad ambition of tackling the 'structural' supply chain, and the rather embarrassed—but understandable—retreat to a more modest agenda. In each case, the causes of this trajectory are similar: the empirical complexity, and the fundamentally 'constructed' nature of the putative object of study.

The study of vertical integration—broadly defined—is a central theme of contemporary economics, and its various debates are the best theorized and documented of any of the academic approaches to the idea of an objective supply chain (e.g. Williamson 1971, 1979; Klein, Crawford, and Alchian 1978; Casson 1984; Hennert 1988; Vickers and Waterson 1991; Holmstron and Roberts 1998). Spulber (1996) adds that microeconomic theory has failed to fully grapple with the role of the industrial intermediary (in contrast to the extensive literature on financial intermediaries).

Perhaps more important, however, is that economics' key conceptual apparatus for thinking about the structure of the chain—Principal–Agent theory and Transaction Cost Economics—both ultimately rely on intangible and contestable concepts such as 'perceived risk' and 'trust'. As such, attempts to provide a modelling-driven, predictive economic science constantly butt up against the unavoidably 'constructed' nature of human interpretation. The consequence is that, while there are many studies which declare themselves interested in explaining industrial 'structure', work in this paradigm tends to collapse to either purely theoretical models, or extremely limited (normally dyadic or small network) studies.

In the same way, the vast 'marketing channel' literature, while frequently drawing on some of the underlying ideas of economic ideas (e.g. transaction costs), has also struggled to come to terms with early ambitions. In his extensive review of the development of the marketing channel concept, Wilkinson (2001) locates the conceptual origins in the work of mainstream economists such as, *inter alia*, Marshall (1889, 1919), Coase (1937), and Schumpeter (1947). The channels literature takes on its own identity, however, when it begins to develop these ideas around the strategic questions facing managers in regard to how they get their products to market (e.g. Artle and Berglund 1959). Thus, whereas the mainstream economics agenda has been largely driven to explain the 'supply chain' in order to provide insight into regulatory questions (e.g. retail price maintenance), the marketing channel literature has been more oriented towards the concerns of participants in the chain. Indeed, the term 'distribution channel' is used as a frequent synonym for 'marketing channel', particularly in cases where a manufacturer downstream is concerned with the progress of goods 'downstream' towards the final consumer (McVey 1960; Lewis 1968; Main 1976).

The extensive work on marketing channels has ranged over a wide range of subsidiary areas—indeed, the perspective coincides with early definitions of the field of marketing itself: '. . . marketing is the performance of business activities directed toward, and incident to, the flow of goods and services from producer to consumer or user' (American Marketing Association 1948: 202). Wilkinson points to the underlying epistemological problems in the ontology of marketing channels (Reve and Stern 1979; Stern and Reve 1980). Attempts to move beyond a single company raises the question of *perspective*; a buyer and supplier may simply not see a relationship in the same way, and indeed may have entirely divergent views on both the existence and character of the channel. This issue has immense importance for any presumed ontology of the chains, channels, or networks—and brings the question of 'social construction' immediately to the fore (New and Mitropoulos 1995; Lindgreen 2001; Blois 2003; Lemke, Goffin, and Szwejczewski 2003). Holmlund and Strandvik (1999) identify in literature thirty studies, both conceptual and empirical, on participants' perception of buyer–seller relationships.

The third approach which starts from construing the supply chain as some kind of objective entity is Commodity Chain analysis—an approach that has developed almost entirely outside the orbit of management studies and mainstream economics, and instead has arisen in the fields of development economics, social and economic geography, political economy, and cultural studies. Hopkins and Wallerstein (1986) define commodity chains as the 'network of labour and production processes whose end result is a finished commodity'— a definition in essence identical to definitions of the supply chain and the marketing channel in other contexts.

The field is quite diffuse (there is no journal with 'Commodity Chain' in the title, nor many books) and its origins are difficult to trace. However, an important source has been the francophone 'Filière' tradition (Raikes, Jensen, and Ponte 2000; occasionally 'vivrières', Doel 1999). This originated in attempts to develop statistical analyses of economic activity based on input/output tables (Montfort and Dutailly 1983), but has evolved to incorporate both an attempt to understand the actions and strategies of the actors in the system, and also with the use of French convention and regulation theory to understand different patterns of economic coordination for a product or group of products (De Bandt 1985; Lenz 1997; Wilkinson 1997). Although the commodity chain approach has been applied to a wide variety of empirical settings, the highest concentration of commodity chain analysis is found in studies related to food (e.g. Barrett *et al.* 1999; Jarosz 2000; Murdoch, Marsden, and Banks 2000).

Two observations can be made about the approach. First, many elements of the commodity chain literature follow much of the thematic agenda of the supply chain and marketing channel literatures. Second, however, the distinctive flavour of this work has often been an interest in placing an understanding of the operation of the chain in a broader political, geographic, and sociological agenda, especially in regard to developing countries. For example, Kaplinsky (2000) uses value chain analysis in regard to explaining global economic inequality. The approach also tends to take seriously work in fields such as the sociology of consumption, and the associated concerns of class and gender (McKendrick, Brewer, and Plumb 1982; Fullerton 1988; Fine and Leopold 1993; Crang and Malbon 1996; McRobbie 1997; Leslie and Reimer 1999). This has been both the key advantage and crucial weakness of the approach; in seeking both broad applicability and theoretical richness, the various commodity chain studies have found it difficult to build a cumulative body of research, or to produce systematic comparisons between different 'chains'.

The commodity chain perspective, like those of the vertical economy and 'marketing channel' schools, presents something of a paradox. On the one hand, in all three of these approaches, there is a serious interest in what seems to be an appealing and intuitive model of analysing the flow of goods through the economy. It is, in some senses, obvious that these 'flows' or structures or channels or chains exist, and it is clear that it would be something like intellectual cowardice for social scientists not to want to engage with them. On the other hand, once one begins to investigate these assumed artefacts of the commercial world, problems of ontology and epistemology surface and make progress very difficult. The narrowly microeconomic approach finds the complexity of the real world too demanding for its elegant theory; the inclusive and holistic commodity chain approach finds the vast range of potential narratives it can invoke an obstacle to methodical progress; the marketing channel literature faces the fundamental epistemic and ontological problem of making sense of the socially constructed channel.

These three perspectives are important intellectual foundations for the supply chain idea, even if the supply chain motif is not used directly. But what of the operations-management-oriented literature which explicitly identifies itself as to do with 'supply chains' and 'supply chain management'? Here, a paradox arises; although the idea of the *structural* supply chain is repeatedly invoked in this literature, with frequent mention of the 'the whole supply chain' and even 'supply chain structure', there is almost nothing of substance said about what these structures look like, or any empirical attempt to define them. Rennie (2001) comments: 'The phrase "a company's supply-chain" doesn't even make sense according to these omnipotent perspectives that define the term.' In the words of supply chain 'guru' Jim Tompkins, 'Supply chain management is not really about the supply chain—it is about being linkable' (Davies 2002).

Instead, the supply chain motif is applied to a separate concept—not a network of nodes and links per se, but the *integration of processes* among some adjacent stages.

4. The supply chain as 'process': three types of integration

The distinction between the 'objective entities' and 'process' views of the supply chain has been highlighted by a number of writers, including Harland (1996) and Croom, Romano, and Giannakis (2000). The 'process view' will be taken here to refer to the way in which stages in the industrial process are 'integrated' or mutually coordinated, and this may or may not be across organizational boundaries (Stevens 1989; Searcy 2002). Bowman (1997) reports a definition of supply chains developed by PRTM for the US Supply Chain Council: '... from your customer's customer to your supplier's supplier. Beyond that ... the supply chain consists of four core processes: plan, make, source and deliver.' The UK Institute of Logistics and Transport (www.iolt.org.uk) use: 'The total sequence of business processes, within a single or multiple enterprise environment, that enable customer demand for a product or service to be satisfied'.

This integration can be understood in three main senses: first, there is the *operational integration* which coordinates separate business units. This usually concerns inventory management, scheduling, transport, marketing, new product development, and so on. Second, there is the notion of *functional integration*, in which the activities of different managerial functions (e.g. purchasing and inventory management, or quality and shipping) are managed such that departmental or professional boundaries do not introduce dysfunctional effects (in other words, avoiding the so-called 'silo mentality'). Finally, there is the *relational integration* of seeking to increase the effectiveness of inter-unit interaction by improving relations at the boundary—by avoiding unnecessary conflict and waste, removing adversarial activity, and reifying a notion of shared interest and mutual responsibility.

4.1. Operational integration

The idea of stages in the chain integrating the 'machinery' of their operations for overall advantage is a core concern for much of what is written and practised under the supply chain motif. Under this heading, two broad streams of thought and activity can be identified, although there is significant interplay between them: one emphasizes the need for modelling, and can be characterized as an 'operations research' (OR)-driven agenda; the other emphasizes simplicity and interdependence, and might be labelled as the Total Quality Management (TQM)/'lean' approach, and draws its insights from the Toyota Production System and in part from the quality 'gurus' such as Deming and Juran. The fundamental premise of both is very simple. Complex operations systems are highly vulnerable to local sub-optimization—and holistic approaches often yield considerable advantages. This can apply to a wide range of issues, including logistics, inventory management, scheduling, product design and research and development, and quality systems. The unifying idea of operational integration is that the systems need to be optimized and managed as a whole.

The heritage of both these streams again predates supply chain terminology. The OR perspective is illustrated by Madigan (1937) in regard to the need for complex coordination within a multi-echelon enterprise. Other important contributions arose from work in transport economics, especially in regard to the need for holistic approaches to the exploitation of air freight (see Heckert and Miner 1940; Lewis 1956; Farris 1997). The mathematical approaches applied to this task have varied, but the two dominant strands have been simulation and optimization. Simulations (often drawing on the work of Jay Forrester 1961, and the emergence of the so-called 'industrial dynamics') have provided considerable insight into the advantages of coordinating planning and distributive processes, such as the well-known 'Beer Game' illustrating the 'Bullwhip' effect (Lee, Padmanabhan, and Whang 1997*a*, *b*; Metters 1997). However, it is probably fair to observe that the problems are more diagnosed than solved (Buffa and Dyer 1977). By far the most common use of these tools has been modelling idealized or imaginary systems, raising some difficult issues about the validation and verification of the conclusions drawn.

Mathematically oriented investigations of supply chain optimization have produced a vast body of research, and for many sets of researchers this constitutes what supply chain management *is*. The key paper in this field is the seminal work of Clark and Scarf (1960); Scarf (2002) credits Clark (1958) with the coining of the term 'multi-echelon'. Burns and Sivazlian (1978) are early users of the supply chain label, using it to refer to a variant of the multi-echelon inventory system.

However, the problems of multi-echelon inventory modelling are extraordinarily complex (Meyer and Groover 1972; Muckstadt 1973; Silver 1981), and it is only in the last few years—with the improvement of firms' IT capabilities and the development of the so-called Advanced Planning and Scheduling (APS) tools, and the widespread use of interorganizational electronic linkages such as electronic data interchange (EDI; see Williams 1994; Hill and Scudder 2002)—that the deployment of sophisticated optimization has significantly impinged on practice. Important contributors to this stream of work include Joseph Cavinato (1991, 1992), Hau Lee (Lee and Billington 1992; Lee, Padmanabhan, and Whang 1997*a*, *b*; Lee and Whang 1999, 2000) and Dennis Towill (Towill 1991; Towill, Naim, and Wikner 1992; Towill 1997*a*, *b*, 2000).

The TQM/'Lean' perspective on operational integration has relied less on mathematical modelling, and pointed to empirical evidence of integration of firms eliminating waste in chains, particularly in regard to quality, logistics, and new product development (Lascelles and Dale 1989; Ansari and Modarress 1990;

Womack, Roos, and Jones 1990; Scott and Westbrook 1991; Lamming 1993). Childerhouse and Towill (2003) present case studies which illustrate simplification in material flow, and this can be contrasted with an emphasis on sophisticated computation. Much of this research is descriptive, and some adopts an explicitly prescriptive tone (e.g. Taylor 1999). One key question for this paradigm is the extent to which the practices it celebrates are dependent on particular cultural and economic contexts, and the extent to which they depend on high degrees of commercial interdependency (Helper 1991; Shiomi 1995).

Two comments need to be made about these interpretations of the supply chain concept. First, the overall idea is compelling and appears to be demonstrated by the experiences of many organizations (see, for example, Fernie 1995; Jones and Riley 1987). That collaboration between organizations or organizational units can sometimes generate *mutual* advantage is supported by a great deal of empirical and theoretical work. The second point, however, is that the broadly technicist and polemical literature has often ignored the questions of (*a*) what happens when the distribution of 'pain' and 'gain' in these activities is unequally divided, and (*b*) what degree of coordinating intelligence is required to permit operational integration. For some of the OR-oriented literature, this problem is assumed away by the assumption that a 'side payment' can be made to make the division of spoils 'fair', or that optimality is ensured by the presence of central coordination. Corbett (2001: p. 487) writes: 'Traditionally, the multi-echelon inventory control literature has assumed the existence of a central planner for the entire supply chain, with perfect information about cost structure and demand patterns and with the power to impose a globally optimal inventory policy on the echelons'. Alternatively, some researchers have focused on the need for 'the rules of the game' or other mechanisms to encourage jointly optimal behaviour (examples include Lee and Whang 1999, 2000; and Porteus 2000). Corbett's own work is an example of recent attempts to apply a more sophisticated, game-theoretic, approach to the issue, observing that 'equilibrium' falls short of the 'optimality' trumpeted by the more simplistic literature. The TQM/Lean approach also struggles with the same issue of the division of spoils, and in general places great reliance on the need for relational integration (discussed below) as a necessary means for operational integration. These issues of control and fairness will turn out to be central to the discussion that follows.

4.2. Functional integration

The idea of functional integration relates to how management functions within an organization work together to further the organization's mission. For supply chain management, an early manifestation of this can be seen in the term 'materials management', which emerged early in the late 1960s to mean the formal integration of purchasing and inventory management within manufacturing firms, and popularized most notably by Zenz (1969) and Ammer (1968), although the term was in common use much earlier (e.g. Lewis and Livesey 1944). The argument has constantly been remade in different forms, and the principles can be seen in Business Process Reengineering (Hammer and Champy 1993), and is a regular feature of the organization of procurement within organizations (Farmer 1975; Pooler and Pooler 1981; Davenport and Short 1990; Trent and Monczka 1994).

Although functional integration proves to be a major element of how many firms operationalize the idea of the supply chain, it will not play a major part in the current discussion; in this sense, it is the mere relabelling of an approach which is well established. For many authors, the issues of operational and functional integration are closely intertwined: only by effective functional integration can operational integration be accomplished (Thomas and Griffin 1996; Singhal and Singhal 2002). It is worth noting that consultants and software vendors occasionally talk in the language of the inter-company 'structural' supply chain, when in fact they mean the integration of internal processes: when Songini (2003) reports 'end-to-end supply chain' software, it refers to functional integration of process rather than anything to do with integrating a multi-company chain.

4.3. Relational integration

Since the 1970s, a major theme of the supply chain management literature has been collaborative (as opposed to adversarial) relationships between trading partners. Although it was observed by several writers that certain firms worked in relatively stable interdependence on each other (Houssiaux 1957; Blois 1972), it was probably Farmer (1976; although foreshadowed by Wind 1970), who, using Williamson's language of opportunism and transaction costs, first clearly elaborated the argument that supply chain collaboration could be pursued as a managerial policy. This idea did not emerge in a vacuum, however, and in other contexts important work such as MacNeil's (1980) 'relational contract' influenced many writers. By the mid-1980s the idea was well established, not least because of the growing interest in Japanese subcontracting systems. An enormous literature has developed under various labels: much (often highly prescriptive) work emerging from the operations and purchasing communities has used labels such as 'partnership sourcing' and 'vendor partnering' (Leenders and Blenkhorn 1988; Carlisle and Parker 1989; Moody 1993; Stuart 1993; Macbeth 2002). Within marketing, a vast body of descriptive research has intertwined with the marketing channels literature on the nature of buyer–supplier relationships (Hånkansson 1982; Dwyer, Schurr, and Oh 1987; Blois 1997, 1999). These have tended to draw heavily (but often loosely) on the language and conceptual apparatus not only of microeconomics (especially transaction costs and game theory), but also of the sociology of trust (see, for example, Walker and Poppo 1991; Sako 1992; Lane and Bachman 1996; Nooteboom 1999).

Three types of critique of this perspective can be identified. For Ramsay (1990, 1996*b*) and Sheridan (1992), the idea of partnership is fundamentally flawed as it denies an essential tension arising from the distinct commercial interests of buyers and sellers. For both of these writers, 'partnerships' are a potentially dangerous excuse for purchasers to be lazy, or sloppy, or both.

A second body of criticism has arisen which has pointed to the divergence between the rhetoric of non-adversarial relationships and empirical data: firms may indeed claim to co-operate, and indeed may do so up to a point, but warm words may conceal a highly brutal, stressful, and in some cases inequitable arrangement. Barringer (1997) points out that relational exchange may have many negative consequences for small businesses. Examples of discussion of this point include: Lamming (1993); Szymankiewicz (1994); Koufteros and Kunnathur (1996); Parker and Hartley (1997); New (1998); Cox, Sanderson, and Watson (2000); Emiliani (2003).

A final criticism arises from an expanding and technically impressive body of work on the nature of contracts. There remains some discomfort with the vagueness of the 'relational' contract; possibly because it threatens some cherished notions of the (even bounded) rationality of economic behaviour. This points to analytical approaches based on the formal language and formulae of contractual modelling. Examples include Corbett and Tang (1999); Tsay, Nahmias, and Agrawal (1999); Ha (2001); Baiman and Rajan (2002); Wang (2002). This literature tends to draw on the more abstract theory of contracts (and especially incomplete contracts); see Hart (1988) and Tirole (1999).

5. The supply chain as legitimation device

5.1. *Decoding supply chain language*

The chapter has so far concentrated on the range of alternative constructions and emphases for the supply chain concept. In the worlds of both practice and research, these ideas are jumbled together. But so what? Does it matter? If it were the case that coming together of this diversity of ideas under a common label was nothing more than the rather sloppy use of metaphors, then there would not be very much to say. However, two points need to be made which present a case for exploring what might lie beneath these ideas.

The first of these is that a great deal of that which is written about supply chains *makes no sense*. This is not to write off all the valuable and important insights that have arisen in the field, and nor is it a pious and sweeping condemnation of the people who spend their lives working, writing, and consulting under the supply chain rubric. It merely recognizes that the idea of reifying the multi-company 'supply chain' as either a generic, abstract ideal, or as an objectively existing, empirical entity, is fraught with logical difficulties and crippling ambiguities. Patterns of buying and selling are highly diffuse, and the structure of these chains almost impossible to plot. If buyers share common suppliers, and if knowledge about the structure beyond the first tier of relationships is rather fragmentary, the value of the chain as an abstraction becomes suspect. The supply chain as 'a structure' is in most cases impossible to delineate without narrowing the discussion to a very precise locus, within which the 'supply chain' label, let alone the most common adjectives (total, end-to-end, integrated), adds no value over other more modest labels (a physical distribution system, a buyer–seller relationship). Furthermore, there is no general empirical support for the frequently asserted claim of a general shift from standard competition to 'competition is at the level of the chain'—as there are almost no empirically reported 'chains'. Many of the writers who demur from the supply chain label (and subsequently substitute 'nets' or 'webs', or 'streams' as their metaphor of choice) have then continued to valorize the idea of the 'chain', producing analyses that differ only in vocabulary. The distinction made in the preceding section regarding operational, functional, and relational integration is useful inasmuch as it helps clarify the great extent to which these concepts are almost deliberately obfuscated; arguments about the importance of relational integration are bolstered by claims about operational integration and vice versa.

The second point is the importance of supply chain language. Much political discourse operates at the level of high rhetoric; concepts are rarely communicated with cold precision, but instead presented in emotive terms that engage the subjectivity and identity of the listener. Economic discourse is no different, and there is a growing academic interest in the growth of lay understanding of economic ideas. One major issue in this debate is that economic language is unavoidably wrapped up in tacit notions of morality and justice: notions of 'good' and 'bad' play a key role in how economic ideas are formulated and transmitted. Once expressed in this way, it can become difficult to separate the core idea from its moral framing.

In much talk about the supply chain, 'integration' is implicitly something that is intrinsically and obviously good—something like harmony, unity, or peace. In contrast, boundaries, barriers, and separation are bad. Gourdin (2001: 214) comments:

The premise espoused throughout this text is that integrated supply chain management will result in logistical system performance in the channel of distribution (or supply) superior to that of channels not employing such integrating approaches

The words are seductive: it seems obvious that an integrated system must be more efficient than a fragmented one. Who can be against 'integration', or for disintegration or boundaries? The language of the supply chain is appealing both for what it promises and what it seems to be against. In a volume entitled *Leading Beyond the Walls*, Hesselbein (1999: 6) writes:

The security of the old walls and the relevance of the gated enterprise are slowly diminishing. There is a new energy as leaders of the future embrace the vast opportunities for

leadership in this wider world of building community where the old barriers and boundaries, both psychological and physical are fading . . . Partnerships are defining a new
order that is marked by open lines of communication among organizations working to
build a healthy, vibrant society.

In the same volume, Collins (1999: 27) writes: 'The most progressive corporations have jettisoned the idea that they can exist in a walled-off cocoon of private activity'. This realization has almost Gnostic value: according to Ulrich
(1999: 103) 'Leaders who blur the inside with the outside understand why things
happen'; Helgesen (1999: 49) writes 'Only those who understand the phenomenon of dissolving boundaries and its implication for the future will be able to
shape events as they unfold; only those comfortable in the zone beyond the
walls will be able to assume leadership in the years ahead'.

Similar observations about the loaded nature of language have been made in
regard to other areas of management studies, notably Information Technology
(IT). Hirschheim and Newman (1991) are among many in a stream of research
which has emphasized the importance of the symbolic in understanding of IT
within organizations; the totemic potency of computing as a representation of our
modernity is such that the narratives which surround IT are at least as significant
as the technology itself. Waring and Wainwright (2000) provide an insightful discussion of the role of 'integration' as an enveloping narrative for IT implementation, and highlight that the word can be applied to both integrating components
of IT and also with integrating the functions of IT with organizational goals.

5.2. What is legitimation?

The first proposition to be considered here is that supply chain ideas and language can serve a purpose of legitimation. The idea that reification of concepts
and deployment of language can be used to permit, justify or provide a mandate
for certain types of action is well established in the social sciences and cultural
theory; Richardson and Dowling (1986: 91) describe the 'processes by which
power relations are mystified through the manipulation of symbols'. Lincoln
(1989: 5) writes that discourse is '. . . strategically employed to mystify the
inevitable inequities of any social order and to win the consent of those over
whom power is exercised, thereby obviating the need for the direct coercive use
of force and transforming simple power into "legitimate authority" '. For example, politicians and chief executives routinely attempt to reify particular types of
crises to provide the grounds for particular policies: threats from competitors or
regulators may provide a narrative which makes mass redundancies possible;
dangers from international terrorism may be used by governments to make permissible restrictions on personal freedom (Suchman 1995; Granlund 2002).
Whether such threats are 'real' in some fundamental sense is not necessarily
the salient issue: what is clear is that social actors are active in generating reality, and that this process does not occur in some politically neutral vacuum.

Brown (1978) gives a good summary of this idea:

Formal organizations are essentially processes of organizing enacted by persons. Given this view, the factors by which the organization is analysed, such as power, authority, or technology, can be translated into actions that people engage in or order to generate and maintain various features of the situation . . . The study of reality creation is the study of power, in that definitions of reality, normalcy, rationality, and so on serve as paradigms that in some sense govern the conduct permissible within them. . . . Instrumental reason displaces attention from the appropriateness of pre-given ends and the class interests that they serve (Brown 1978: 371).

This notion is a central element in what Bradshaw-Camball and Murray (1991) describe as the interpretive perspective on politics, and may also be seen as a major strand of the Critical Theory of the Frankfurt School. In particular, the reification of social constructs in ways which come to govern human behaviour is a core idea within the Habermasian concept of 'technocratic consciousness': it 'conceals behind a façade of objective necessity the interests of classes and groups that actually determine the function, direction and pace of technological and social developments' (Held 1980: 265). Other studies which have dealt with this approach have tended to focus on the justification or rationalization of organizational change, and the operation of particular mechanisms within organizations (especially management accounting). These include those by Dent (1991); Macintosh and Scapens (1991); Preston, Cooper, and Coombs (1992); Brunsson (1993); Marsden (1993); Fligstein (1998); and Granlund, Lukka, and Moutitsen (1998).

The application of this notion to the domain of the supply chain requires an explicit recognition of the human character of interorganizational behaviour: rather than leaving the granularity of the description of phenomena at the level of the organization, it is necessary to acknowledge that real people conduct the business of organizations, and, furthermore, real people operating at levels at which nuance, rhetoric, context, and meaning are significant. In other words, the notion of 'exchange' between organizations is as amenable to analyses of social signification and symbolism as the exchanges between the remote tribes in anthropological studies (see, for example: Davis 1992; Polodny 1994; Kranton 1996; Burnes and New 1997; Price 1997). There is a distinction, however, between an observation that the symbolism of interorganizational discourse is merely 'rich' and 'interesting', and one that draws a connection with issues of power and the pursuit of particular interests. As Lincoln (1989: 3) writes, 'No consideration of discourse is complete that does not also take account of force'. A vital concept, then, is the idea of 'power' in the chain.

5.3. Supply chain power: who does the 'M' in SCM?

One of the most significant points of ambiguity in regard to the various visions of the extended supply chain is the question of who in the chain is supposed to be doing the managing. Who has the power, and who reaps the benefits? For the current argument, two key points need to be made about the nature of supply chain power: it is important, and it is not well understood.

First, supply chain power—whatever it is—is clearly massively important for the ordinary conduct of business. It is an obvious and frequently made point that not all firms have the same degree of leverage over their trading partners, and discussion of 'buying power' is a common element of business analysis from Porter's famous five forces (1980) to newspaper articles about mergers between firms. Businesses' strategies are heavily influenced by their perceptions of commercial risk and dependency, and firms make large efforts to manage such risks, both in supplier and customer relations. This may involve the formation of cartels and trade associations for sellers, and the use of single or consolidated sourcing, and 'user' groups (Miles 1991) for buying. The idea of the exercise and impact of this power, and the relational turbulence as firms jockey for advantage, is a central theme of the marketing channel literature (Robbins, Speh, and Mayer 1982). The issue has been the focus of considerable attention from legislators (as in the US Robinson–Patman Act of 1936: see Vaile *et al.* 1939; Gatty 1981; Posner 1986; Bean 1996), and activists concerned at the perceived growth of power of major companies (e.g. Wal-Mart—see Quinn 2000). Supply chain power of some kind is a pre-requisite for the notion of interfering in the internal operations of a trading partner, for example, in supplier development (Leenders 1966; Bache *et al.* 1987; Burt 1989; MacDuffie and Helper 1997; Krause *et al.* 1998).

Second, despite being the subject of a considerable literature, there are no easy metrics or even entirely robust conceptual frameworks for understanding the relative power of trading partners, nor for considering the way in which supply chains might be 'owned by', attributed to, or managed by a particular participant organization. To examine the paucity of theory in this area, it is useful to consider the analyses of supply chain power that emerge first from economics and then from the marketing channel, 'supply chain' and 'network' literatures.

While there is vast and sophisticated economics-based literature on monopoly practices—and an established legal framework in which powerful sellers must operate—there is relatively little literature in regard to the powerful buyer (Clarke *et al.* 2002 give a useful and concise summary of the extant theory). This disparity is illustrated by the massive imbalance in the weight of theory between monopoly and monopsony effects, despite the repeated observation of the necessary conceptual symmetry between the two (e.g. Stigler 1966: 205–8). Since the introduction of the term 'monopsony' by Robinson in 1933, the trajectory of research in the this area has been largely dominated by analyses of labour markets (where large employers are monopsonist buyers of labour—see Rothschild 1943; Litwinski 2001; Manning 2003). Theorists since Adelman (1949) have pointed out that, unlike with consumer-facing markets, price data in industrial markets can be difficult to obtain, and there are complex dynamics (e.g. in regard to technology development) that stretch the ability of standard economic modelling. Other relevant research on this issue includes: Perry (1978) who examines the cases in which it is sensible for a monopsonist to vertically integrate; Gabel (1983), who examines the effect of buyer power on supplier cartels; Cowley (1985), who considers the balance of buyer and supplier power in the plastics industry, and its effects on profitability; Raper and Love (2000), who attempt to apply econometric modelling to unpicking the relative balance of buyer and supplier power in the US tobacco market; and, Gilligan (1986), who reviews the issues related to retail price maintenance. Galbraith (1952) posited that large and powerful buyers emerged as an expression of 'countervailing power' to large sellers, although this proved to be a complex notion in terms of welfare arguments (see Whitney 1953; Stigler 1954; Bork 1978; Sherman 1989), empirical support (Lustgarten 1975; LaFrance 1979; OECD 1981; McAfee 2001), and also cut across some of the underlying ideological positions of neoclassical economics (see Galbraith 1981: 281–5). Perhaps the best example of the failure of standard economic analysis of supply chain power is the difficulty of applying economic analysis to the regulation of powerful retailers: this has been a complex issue in the United States and elsewhere, in regard to, among other issues, questions of slotting fees (Borghesani, de la Cruz, and Berry 1997; FTC 2001; FMI 2002; Renhoff 2002) and retail price maintenance (see the 'A&P Case'—Dirlam and Kahn 1952; Adelman 1953; Everton 1986; Kahn 1988). A major study of the UK supermarket sector, reputedly costing £20 million, was widely held to be inconclusive in its analysis of the question of vertical power (see Competition Commission 2000; Clarke *et al.* 2002). While the curve drawing of standard economic theory produces models that are coherent in their own terms, there are some fundamental reasons why orthodox economics fails to deliver an *applicable* critique. Before exploring these, it is sensible to examine alternative approaches to examining supply chain power.

For the marketing and supply chain literatures, the idea of understanding organizational relationships from the perspective of a 'focal firm' can be traced at least as far as Evan (1966). Farmer (1978) invokes the idea of firms proactively managing their 'supply chain', although previously he had referred to the same idea as 'supply base' (1975). But what sort of power a firm could exercise on such a chain or base remains difficult to describe, despite a large body of research seeking to identify or measure relative supply chain power (e.g. Hunt and Nevin 1974; McMillan 1990; Cho and Chu 1994; Ramsay 1996a). Although a broad progression towards increasing realism and sophistication can be seen in these analyses, it remains difficult to generate an applicable formula that combines the plausible input variables (such as measures of financial dependency, or estimates of switching costs) into some predictive measure of supply chain power. The difficulties are threefold: a lack of theoretical frameworks; a huge number of factors to be considered; and, the fundamental importance of the perceptions of the actors. This last problem is key: how 'powerful' a firm is in relation to its trading partners seems to depend on difficult-to-quantify issues such as faith and trust, levels of optimism, perceived scope for innovation, and so on. As Provan and Gassenheimer (1994) point out, buyer–supplier power is more than just dependency—norms of cooperation and long-term commitment must be taken into account. Even Porter's (1980) perspective is one in which intrinsic bargaining power combines with managers' propensity to use it, and this is clearly something to do with perceptions, values, and beliefs.

It is worth observing that much of the literature on interorganizational relationships and organizational networks (Alter and Hage 1993; Ring and Van de Ven 1994; Grandori and Soda 1995) transpires to be of limited applicability to supply chain relationships because it ignores or minimizes the existence and consequences of supply chain power. For example, Snow and Miles (1992) deal with the governance of networks by invoking the depoliticized roles of broker, caretaker, lead-operator, and manager–architects:

With regard to the grid of potential network firms, the caretaker may engage in nurturing and disciplinary behavior. For example, a caretaker may notice that a particular firm appears to be falling behind technologically, or in some other way devaluing its usefulness to the grid. Appropriate actions could be taken to rectify the situation. An even more troublesome case occurs when a firm exploits its position in the grid—for example, by obtaining some short-run gain at the expense of its actual or potential partners. Here the caretaker's challenge is to point out the dysfunctional effects of such behaviour on the overall system and teach the offending firm how to behave more appropriately for the common good (p. 17).

Similarly, Chisholm (1996: 216) writes:

Network organizations are controlled by members, not by a centralized source of power. Members are responsible for developing a purpose, mission, and goals, and for initiating and managing projects and work activities. The organization is self-regulating (members direct and control activities) and rests on a shared understanding of issues.

Santoro (1999) echoes this by describing an initiative to construct virtual enterprise structures with no regard for the political dimension, casting the role of coordination (and presumably discipline) of the network to a vaguely described 'Business Integrator'. Lowrie (1997) attempts to sketch out a model (Self Imposed Network Discipline) to account for the exercise of power in networks—but, like other efforts, ultimately relies on the notion of some form of enlightened self-interest. As Provan (1983) pointed out, when many writers deploy the 'chain' or the 'network', they are perhaps really talking about a 'federation' (see also Whicker and Walton 1996). This de-politicization of the interaction between organizations can be seen as representing an heroic attempt to generalize from non-commercial settings to an abstract general case (a large chunk of the inter-organizational literature arises from analyses of voluntary and public sector bodies), or, in other cases, a bald prescriptive injunction ('firms ought to collaborate to mutual advantage'). Jarillo (1988) designates 'strategic networks' as collections of firms which reap individual advantage by working in concert with each other.

The difficulties of construing useful and applicable frameworks for evaluating supply chain power arise in part from the complexity of the world, and in part from some of the underlying assumptions that underpin economic and management thinking. On the first point, a major issue for the economic analysis of supply chain power is the focus on a single (and simplistic) variable—price (see Becker 1997). For understandable reasons, when economists consider the trading relationship, the prime question tends to be whether the price mechanism of market exchange is working 'properly'. This is useful for modelling, but hopeless for capturing the complexity of business-to-business relationships. On the other hand, those approaching the relationship from other perspectives (such as operations or marketing) are likely to have a more textured view in which the 'fairness' of the relationship, reflecting the more complex interactions at the commercial interface, such as the innovations in product development and logistics systems associated with operational and relational integration described above. Thus, the distribution of 'pain and gain' involved in such initiatives as Vendor Managed Inventory (e.g. see Kaipia, Holmström, and Tanskanen 2002), in Efficient Consumer Response (Kurnia and Johnston 2001), in the preparations for the 'millennium bug' (Dewhurst, Spring, and Arkle 2000), or in the adoption of long-term 'partnerships' in general (Kalwani and Narayandas 1995), becomes a better indicator of the exercise of supply chain power. In these cases, buyers and suppliers stand to invest and benefit from the initiatives differentially, and the balance of that difference is a reflection—at least in part—of supply chain power. A more fundamental issue, however, is that the idea of supply chain power unfairly exercised by a powerful buyer over its suppliers is a fundamentally awkward proposition for traditional economic thinking: supply chain power is difficult to model and even to engage with, because traditional economic thinking finds it difficult to posit a supply relationship in which there is duress upon the supplier. To understand this, it is useful to return to the concepts of monopoly and monopsony. It is clear that a monopolist seller can exploit his position, if the product or service is a genuine need; the buyers have nowhere else to go. In the case of a monopsony, however, if sellers do not like the terms of a trade, they can simply choose not to engage with the exchange or to sell something else. In other words, in a free economy, sellers cannot be forced to sell something; as independent economic agents, they are not bound to the monopsonist in the same way that a powerless and needy buyer is to the monopolist. To illustrate, a consumer might complain that they are obliged to buy from a powerful retailer who dominates the market; a supplier, on the other hand, could always shut up shop and go and do something else. In practice, however, this freedom to 'walk away' may not exist (see Fried 2003). This point is also suggested by Dawson and Shaw (1989) and Howe (1998), and is an observation that goes back at least to MacGregor (1906) and the Webbs' (1902) *Industrial Democracy*.

This point has profound implications for understanding the nature of supply chain power. One of the few writers to acknowledge and explore this point is Zeitz, in a largely ignored paper from 1980. Zeitz comments that the (then) prevailing positivist approach to interorganizational research had led to it failing to develop satisfactory theory, and this was because it failed to address its own fundamental assumptions. He points out that exchange theory often presumes that exchange is intrinsically efficient and consistent with distributive justice, and this hampers the development of a more realistic and dialectical understanding of interorganizational exchange. He cites the foundations of standard exchange theory as:

(1) exchanging parties have equality of status (either legal or equality of opportunity);
(2) exchange brings about mutual benefit;
(3) exchange decisions are made voluntarily;
(4) parties have adequate knowledge of costs and benefits.

Zeitz (1980) criticizes Blau's (1964) seminal work on exchange, which although acknowledging the existence of power and authority has systems of power emerging from and potentially replacing exchange rather than leading to systems of leading to increasingly unequal exchange. While Blau allows for dominance in an exchange relationship, the dominant partners get that way by simply contributing more resources, and taking a 'fair' amount of utility. Zeitz comments, 'There is thus no consideration of the possibility that dominant partners may use their position to alter the exchange ratio in their favor' (p. 81). This line of argument is also partially reflected in Heath's (1976) analysis of exchange theories. Prasch (1995) reinforces this view in his discussion of the foundations of the notion of 'exchange' in conventional economics; he argues that the whole structure of economics is premised on a notion of essentially homogeneous actors—he cites Menger's (1871) example of two farmers happily exchanging surplus goods: 'No sense of urgency is expressed in this vision of the exchange relation. This autonomy is not merely a simplifying assumption . . . it is integral to the neoclassical theory of the market' (p. 811). Grant (2002) echoes this: 'A trade involves voluntary action by all parties concerned to bring about a result that is beneficial to all parties concerned. If these conditions were not met, the trade would simply not occur' (p. 111). In other words, if one makes the right assumptions, one can always arrive at a position where there can be no way in which sellers to a powerful buyer are exploited. This is the fundamental reason why attempts to tackle supply chain power from the position of orthodox economics tend to run out of intellectual steam; to address this problem, and to acknowledge that there is indeed scope for exploitation of a supplier, one needs to relax the core assumptions that make the traditional approach tractable.

However, if exploitative commercial relations are acknowledged as really existing, then this means it is necessary to consider the nature of the 'unfreedom' which might apply to an exploited supplier. If the supplier has made significant customer-specific investments, or cannot choose alternative suppliers

or enter new markets in time, then there is a real sense in which choice and freedom are limited. A bullying dominant customer may make demands, and genuinely exploit its position. As interorganizational relationships are often
multi-threaded (e.g. with multiple products and services being bought and sold,
or with different organizational subunits interacting with one another), there
may be simultaneous incidences of this genuine conflict with real cooperation
and mutual advantage. Where does this analysis lead? To summarize this part of
the argument: supply chain power is a vital business issue, but is poorly understood because of both its complexity and also the way it sits uneasily with standard economic thinking, premised on particular, abstract and idealized notions
of the freedom of economic agents. If, however, one concedes that such free-
doms might not always apply, and that supply relationships *can* occur in an
environment of exploitation and coercion, then one might look for ways in
which such coercion might be dressed up or rationalized. It is at this point that
we return to the notion of the supply chain, and the way in which the concept
may be deployed to legitimize certain types of commercial relationship.

5.4. *Legitimizing power with the 'Supply Chain'*

The language of the supply chain permits a narrative construction in which the
goals and aspirations of the component firms are in some sense subsumed
within the larger entity. The logic goes that this is driven by mutual benefit; just
as in any other 'imagined community', the benefits of membership are held to
outweigh the costs. In this way, the language of the chain deflects questions of
power, control, exploitation, and interests. For example, Govil and Proth (2002)
declare: 'In a supply chain, partners should be allowed to freely make their own
decisions, assuming that these decisions meet the internal policy accepted by
all the partners' (p. 8). They go on to say:

A perfect supply chain calls for a fair collaboration between all the participants, from suppliers to customers. This requires a clear definition of the collaboration rules between the
partners, especially if they are competitors. Such a set of rules is called a sharing process
and it enables participants to share risks and benefits. Such a sharing process has to be
defined during the design of the supply chain, long before conflicts occur among partners. It can be expressed in terms of contracts between all the partners, the goal of such
contracts being to guarantee the best work practices among partners while allowing for
healthy competition. (p. 15).

There are three main ways in which this 'subliminal message' is encoded in
supply chain language. First, it is assumed that the role of an individual company is to support the success of the chain. The best example of this is the
notion that competition occurs in the economy at the level of the chain rather
the firm (Schill and McArthur 1992; Cox 1997). As discussed above, whether this
makes sense depends a great deal on the nature of the industry, and structural

features of the supply chain (i.e. how neatly do the chains line up; do they over-lap), but such messy questions are occluded by the neatness of the metaphor.

Second, there is the idea that the chain itself has an 'objective' (typically the satisfying of an 'ultimate consumer' whose demands become ever more urgent, and who confers a rationale for existence and action for the constituent mem-bers) and which, in turn, constitutes an iron imperative (see, for example, Pearce 1996; Harreld and Jones 2001). One might make a connection here with the reification of the consumer (in Du Gay and Salaman's 1992 phrase) as the 'cult(ure) of the customer', which played a central role in various interpreta-tions of 'choice and freedom' in the economic rhetoric of the 'new right'.

The supply chain concept, then, reflects a well-established logic—almost a technological determinism—that the firms in the chain are subject to forces which they *must* obey: Whewell (1997) presents an analysis of the supply chain couched in terms of laws of nature (making parallels with the laws of thermo-dynamics) in which 'suppliers *must* give their customers increased choice, flex-ibility and value from the service they provide if they wish to win increased market share from competitors' (p. 24, emphasis added). Vonchek (1995, empha-sis added) comments: 'To remain competitive in the face of global competition and mounting cost pressures, firms *must* view the supply chain as an integrated enterprise of closely-linked locations, with the flow of products along the supply chain drive by demand'. The rhetoric spans the divide between practitioners and academia: an advertisement for a software company declares that the satis-fying the ultimate customer depends on 'every link in the chain performing effec-tively' (Amethyst Group 2001); Vis and Roodbergen (2002) write: 'Supply chains have to be improved continuously to remain competitive and to be able to fulfil the wishes of customers'. A consultant from software company JD Edwards writes: 'Companies must move from operating as islands of automation and embrace the concept of information sharing with partners, suppliers and cus-tomers across the entire supply chain using secure and integrated technologies' (Stubbs 2002). Blackwell (1997) raises the customer-oriented imperative to almost religious pitch: 'Rather than building and operating their supply chains from manufacturer to market, the best firms in the next century will form their supply chains from the mind (of the customer) to market, creating chains based on consumers' needs, wants, problems, and lifestyles' (p. xviii). Firms need to embrace the change to demand-driven chains: 'In that embrace lies their salva-tion and their route to success' (p. 239). The same message—in slightly more measured tones—finds it way into a US National Research Council study on the effect of supply chain integration on small and medium-sized enterprises: 'SMEs *cannot* ignore the supply chain revolution and remain competitive' (NRC 2000, emphasis added). Govil and Proth (2002: 56) declare: 'As empha-sized throughout this book, the ultimate goal of the supply chain is customer satisfaction'.

Third, there is the notion that, for some, a privileged place in the supply chain confers status and the right to take the lead; for others, their 'natural' role is one of subservience, and their expectations of reward should be lower. This idea predates the specific language of the chain: Markin (1971) talked of an eco-logical analogy with the survival of retailers being 'often a function of their understanding of their role and contribution in the distribution chain'. This concept is frequently regurgitated in the trade press and in the accounts of practitioners: one magazine article comments: 'Admitting where you are in the chain, both with regard to customers and suppliers, can be a humbling experi-ence. You may well wield significant leverage with suppliers, but with cus-tomers you may not be such a big cog' (Flott 2001: 47–8). Peake (2003) writes that mid-sized companies ' . . . are not the masters of their own destinies. They play the role of cog in the within value chains defined by the channel masters'. Clapperton (2002, emphasis added) describes the problem: 'Those *smaller people*—the component manufacturers, the servicing companies—are norm-ally part of a chain of supply, rather than at the top; as such, they don't get to dictate the shape of the chain. Instead they just get told, "You're doing it like this" so that's how they do it.' Practical examples of this include the way in which larger buying firms might exert pressure on suppliers, for example, to adopt particular practices or technologies. Examples of this include the role played by large organizations in imposing technologies. In regard to EDI, Kavanagh (1993) quotes a manager of Tesco, a major UK retailer: 'We see EDI as a cornerstone in the effective management of our supply chain and those of our suppliers . . . our insistence might sometime come across as bullying'. Similar comments are currently commonplace in regard to the introduction of Radio Frequency Identification (RFID: Thomas 2003). Knight (1993) describes suppliers' discontent at having to provide detailed information regarding environmental credentials (see also New 1999).

This notion of subservience and obedience extends to common assump-tions about profitability:

Even through the heyday of the late '90s, when automakers such as Ford Motor Co. and General Motors Corp. were posting record profits, the suppliers had to settle for table scraps. There was no gravy train for them. There were several reasons for this disparity: Many suppliers, at the behest of their automaker customers, had taken on too much debt to acquire other parts makers in an attempt at consolidation. Suppliers would have to invest in new plants in developing markets and begin shouldering more expenses for tooling and product engineering. And even though automakers were raking in money on high-profit SUVs, they couldn't stomach such profitability for their suppliers, so they demanded aggressive price cuts from them as a condition of getting future business. (Murphy 2001: 44)

The rhetoric of the chain legitimates certain types of business practices: powerful buyers can make demands of suppliers about technology invest-ments, the expansion of service provision, or engagement in interorganiza-tional development projects (such as supplier development, or information sharing, or changes to prices and pricing arrangements). Managers in a buying firm can rationalize and defend policies which otherwise might seem brutal, interfering, or even unethical by appealing to a narrative about the existence of the 'chain'. That which might be questionable becomes more acceptable if dressed in appealing language; that which might be inexplicable becomes comprehensible if located in a convincing narrative.

6. Conclusions

This chapter has examined the way in which the supply chain idea may be interpreted—at least in part—as vehicle for a diffuse set of interests. Beneath the technocratic narrative of the integrated chain, there lurk complex stories about the exercise of power, and the nature of the organization of economic activity. Having examined the foundations of the supply chain idea—as a structure, as integrated process—it is possible to see how it legitimates the exercise of certain kinds of interorganizational power, and has the effect of partially smothering the potential for debate and resistance. The word 'partially' here is important, as it would be naive to assume that practitioners universally accept the supply chain language or rhetoric at face value—there is considerable cynicism, and even those who adopt the language may do so with a degree of irony, scepticism, and even sarcasm. Much practitioner discussion of 'partnerships' makes extensive use of the quotation marks; much of the breathless paeans to the chain acknowledge that the concept of the integrated 'chain' remains a 'dream' (e.g. Zuckerman 2002). Thomson (1995) points out that supply chain integration requires some kind of 'equality'—but points out with rather charming understatement this is 'something which has hitherto proved difficult'.

It is important not to mistake this critique as a rejection of the supply chain concept; it remains a valuable contribution to management and economic thought. The argument does not say that supply chains do not exist, merely that the supply chain does not exist in the simplistic way in which much of the literature conceives it. The argument does not imply that supply chain managers are wasting their time, nor that software sold under the supply chain label is wrong-headed; it does say that the way we explain managers' behaviour, or conceptualize the problems faced by manufacturers, retailers, and distributors, can be framed in different ways. It does not imply that the painstaking modelling of idealized supply systems is pointless; it does imply that we ought to be wary about ignoring the implicit assumptions that can be unwittingly smuggled into our elegant simulations. Perhaps the key point is that the analysis does not imply that people have been unwittingly duped by some shadowy conspiracy; the supply chain idea may be convenient for the powerful, but this does not mean it is their deliberate concoction. Just as TQM may end up serving a subtle ideological purpose in the workplace, supply chain management may serve to provide a convenient cloak for powerful companies. But it is simplistic and naïve to cast either as being principally a tool of oppression.

It is also important, however, not to forget that the world in which academics and theorists operate is not automatically harmonious and rational;

real people and real organizations have real and divergent interests. It is also worth pointing out that there are several parties for whom the language of the supply chain is convenient as a legitimizing device, beyond the managers of powerful buying organizations. The supply chain idea also provides supplying firms and their managers with a narrative framework in which actions and policies may be justified. The other 'beneficiaries' may have less subtle interests: management consultants and software providers have both reaped considerably from the 'imperative' of supply chain integration. Academics have built careers in a subject area in which the harsh corners of commerce are blunted by the soft padding of words like 'cooperation', 'community', and 'relationship'. It is only by holding up our theorizing to uncomfortable analysis, and by recognizing the way in which interests can skew our vision, that genuine progress is possible.

References

ABRAHAMSON, E. (1991). 'Managerial Fads and Fashions: The Diffusion and Rejection of Innovations'. *Academy of Management Review*, 16/3: 586–612.

ADELMAN, M. A. (1949). 'The Large Firm and its Suppliers'. *The Review of Economics and Statistics*, 31/2: 113–18.

—— (1953). 'Dirlam and Kahn on the A&P Case'. *Journal of Political Economy*, 61/5: 436–41.

ALTER, C., and HAGE, J. (1993). *Organisations Working Together*. Newbury Park, CA: Sage.

ALVESSON, M., and WILLMOTT, H. (1992a). 'On the Idea of Emancipation in Management and Organisation Studies'. *Academy of Management Review*, 17/3: 432–64.

—— —— (eds.) (1992b). *Critical Management Studies*. London: Sage.

American Marketing Association (1948). 'Report of the Definitions Committee'. *Journal of Marketing*, 13/2: 202–17.

Amethyst Group (2001). Advertisement in *Distribution Business*, September 2001, 23.

AMMER, D. A. (1968). *Materials Management*. Homewood, IL: Irwin.

ANSARI, A., and MODARRESS, B. (1990). *Just-In-Time Purchasing*. New York: Free Press.

ARTLE, R., and BERGLUND, S. (1959). 'A Note on Manufacturers' Choice of Distribution Channels'. *Management Science*, 5/4: 460–71.

AUSTIN, J. L. (1962). *How to Do Things with Words*. Oxford: Oxford University Press.

BACHE, J., CARR, R., PARNABY, J., and TOBIAS, A. M. (1987). 'Supplier Development Systems'. *International Journal of Technology Management*, 2/2: 219–28.

BAIMAN, S., and RAJAN, M. V. (2002). 'Incentive Issues in Inter-Firm Relationships'. *Accounting, Organizations and Society*, 27/3: 213–38.

BAKHTIN, M. M. (1986). *Speech Genres and Other Late Essays* (trans. V. W. McGee). Austin, TX: University of Texas Press.

BARLEY, S. R., and KUNDA, G. (1992). 'Design and Devotion: Surges of Rational and Normative Ideologies of Control in Managerial Discourse'. *Administrative Science Quarterly*, 37: 363–99.

BARRETT, H. R., ILBERY, B. W., BROWNE, A. W., and BINNS, T. (1999). 'Globalization and the Changing Networks of Food Supply: The Importation of Fresh Horticultural Produce from Kenya into the UK'. *Transactions of the Institute of British Geographers*, 24/2: 159–74.

BARRINGER, B. R. (1997). 'The Effects of Relational Channel Exchange on the Small Firm: A Conceptual Framework'. *Journal of Small Business Management*, 35/2: 65–79.

BEAN, J. J. (1996). *Beyond the Broker State: Federal Policies Toward Small Business, 1936–1961*. Chapel Hill: University of North Carolina Press.

BECKER, G. (1997). 'Market power', in R. McAuliffe (ed.), *The Blackwell Encyclopaedic Dictionary of Managerial Economics*. Oxford: Blackwell, 121–3.

BERGER, P., and LUCKMAN, T. (1966). *The Social Construction of Knowledge*. Garden City, NY: Doubleday.

BERLINSKI, D. (1976). *On Systems Analysis: An Essay Concerning the Limitations of Some Mathematical Methods in the Social, Political, and Biological Sciences*. Cambridge, MA: MIT Press.

BLACKWELL, R. D. (1997). *From Mind to Market: Reinventing the Retail Supply Chain*. New York: Harper Business.

BLAU, P. (1964). *Exchange and Power in Social Life*. New York: Wiley.

BLOIS, K. (1997). 'Are Business-to-Business Relationships Inherently Unstable?' *Journal of Marketing Management*, 13: 367–82.

—— (1999). 'Trust in Business to Business Relationships: An Evaluation of its Status'. *Journal of Management Studies*, 36/2: 197–216.

—— (2003). 'B2B "relationships"—a Social Construction of Reality? A Study of Marks & Spencer and One of its Major Suppliers'. *Journal of Marketing Theory*, 3/1: 79–95.

—— (1972). 'Vertical Quasi-Integration'. *Journal of Industrial Economics*, 20: 253–71.

BLOOMFIELD, B., and BEST, A. (1992). 'Management Consultants, Systems Development, Power, and the Translation of Problems'. *Sociological Review*, 40/3: 533–60.

BORGHESANI, W. H., DE LA CRUZ, P. L., and BERRY, D. B. (1997). 'Controlling the Chain: Buyer Power, Distributive Control and New Dynamics in Retailing'. *Business Horizons*, 40/4: 17–24.

BORK, R. (1978). *The Antitrust Paradox: A Policy at War with Itself*. New York: Basic Books.

BOWMAN, R. J. (1997). 'The State of the Supply Chain'. *Distribution*, 96/2: 28–36.

BRADSHAW-CAMBALL, P., and MURRAY, V. V. (1991). 'Illusions and Other Games: A Trifocal View of Organizational Politics'. *Organization Science*, 2/4: 379–98.

BROWN, R. H. (1978). 'Bureaucracy as Praxis: Toward a Political Phenomenology of Formal Organizations'. *Administrative Science Quarterly*, 23/3: 365–82.

BRUNSSON, N. (1993). 'Ideas and Actions: Justification and Hypocrisy as Alternatives to Control'. *Accounting, Organizations and Society*, 18: 489–506.

BUCKLEY, P. J., and CHAPMAN, M. (1997). 'The Use of Native Categories in Management Research'. *British Journal of Management*, 8: 283–99.

BUFFA, E. S., and DYER, J. S. (1977). 'Managerial Use of Dynamic Structural Models'. *Decision Sciences*, 8/1: 73–81.

BURNES, B., and NEW, S. J. (1997). Collaboration in Customer–Supplier Relationships: Strategy, Operations and the Function of Rhetoric'. *International Journal of Purchasing and Materials Management*, 33/4: 10–17.

BURNS, J. S., and SIVAZLIAN, B. D. (1978). 'Dynamic Analysis of Multi-Echelon Supply Design'. *Computers and Industrial Engineering*, 2/4: 181–93.

BURRELL, G., and MORGAN, G. (1979). *Sociological Paradigms and Organisational Analysis*. London: Heinemann.

Burt, D. N. (1989). 'Managing Suppliers up to Speed'. *Harvard Business Review*, 67/4: 127–35.

Callon, M. (ed.) (1998). *The Law of the Markets*. Oxford: Blackwell.

Campbell, D. (2000). *The Socially Constructed Organization*. London: Karnac Books.

Carlisle, J., and Parker, R. C. (1989). *Beyond Negotiation: Redeeming Customer–Supplier Relations*. Chichester: John Wiley.

Carrier, J. G. (1998). 'Introduction', in J. G. Carrier and D. Miller (eds.), *Virtualism: A New Political Economy*. Oxford: Berg, 1–24.

—— and Miller, D. (eds.) (1998). *Virtualism: A New Political Economy*. Oxford: Berg.

Casson, M. (1984). 'The Theory of Vertical Integration: a Survey and Synthesis'. *Journal of Economic Studies*, 11/2: 3–43.

Cavinato, J. L. (1991). 'Identifying Interfirm Total Cost Advantages for Supply Chain Competitiveness'. *International Journal of Purchasing & Materials Management*, 27/4: 10–15.

—— (1992). 'A Total Cost/Value Model for Supply Chain Competitiveness'. *Journal of Business Logistics*, 13/2: 285–301.

Chapman, K. (1973). 'Agglomeration and Linkage in the United Kingdom Petro-Chemical Industry'. *Transactions of the Institute of British Geographers*, 0:60 (November) 33–68.

Childerhouse, P., and Towill, D. (1993). 'Simplified Material Flow Holds the Key to Supply Chain Integration'. *OMEGA*, 31/1: 17–27.

Chisholm, R. F. (1996). 'On the Meaning of Networks'. *Group & Organization Management*, 21/2: 216–35.

Cho, D.-S., and Chu, W. (1994). 'Determinants of Bargaining Power in OEM Negotiations'. *Industrial Marketing Management*, 23: 343–55.

Choi, T. Y., and Hong, Y. (2002). 'Unveiling the Structure of Supply Networks: Case Studies in Honda, Acura and DaimlerChrysler'. *Journal of Operations Management*, 20: 469–93.

Cisic, D., Kesic, B., and Jakomin, L. (2000). *Research of The Power in the Supply Chain*. Working Paper. http://econwpa.wustl.edu/eps/it/papers/0004/0004002.pdf.

Clapperton, G. (2002). 'Chain of Command'. *The Guardian*, 31 October. Special Supplement on Business Solutions, 7.

Clark, A. J. (1958). *A Dynamic, Single-Item, Multi-Echelon Inventory Model*. Santa Monica: Rand Corporation.

—— and Scarf, H. (1960). 'Optimal Policies for a Multi-Echelon Inventory Problem'. *Management Science*, 6: 475–90.

Clark, T., and Fincham, R. (eds.) (2002). *Critical Consulting: New Perspectives on the Management Advice Industry*. Oxford: Blackwell.

—— and Salaman, G. (1998). 'Telling Tales: Management Gurus' Narratives and the Construction of Managerial Identity'. *Journal of Management Studies*, 35/2: 137–61.

Clarke, R., Davies, S., Dobson, P., and Waterson, M. (2002). *Buyer Power and Competition in European Food Retailing*. Cheltenham: Edward Elgar.

Coase, R. H. (1937). 'The Nature of the Firm'. *Economica*, 4: 365–405.

Collins, J. (1999). 'And the Walls Came Tumbling Down', in F. Hesselbein, M. Goldsmith, and I. Somerville (eds.), *Leading Beyond the Walls*. San Francisco: Jossey Bass, 19–36.

Competition Commission (2000). *Supermarkets: A Report on the Supply of Groceries from Multiple Stores in the United Kingdom*. London: The Stationary Office.

Corbett, C. J. (2001). 'Stochastic Inventory Systems in a Supply Chain with Asymmetric Information: Cycle Stocks, Safety Stocks and Consignment Stocks'. *Operations Research*, 49/4: 487–500.

—— and TANG, C. S. (1999). 'Designing Supply Contracts: Contract Type and Information Asymmetry', in S. Tayur, R. Ganeshan, and M. Majayine (eds.), *Quantitative Models for Supply Chain Management Research*. Boston: Kluwer, 267–97.

COWLEY, P. R. (1985). 'Modelling the Effects of Buyer and Seller Power on the Margins of Commodity Plastics'. *Strategic Management Journal*, 6/3: 213–22.

COX, A. (1997). *Business Success*. Midsomer Norton, Bath: Earlsgate Press.

—— SANDERSON, J., and WATSON, G. (2000). 'Wielding Influence'. *Supply Management*, 5/7: 30–3.

CRANG, P., and MALBON, B. (1996). 'Consuming Geographies: A Review Essay'. *Transactions of the Institute of British Geographers*, 21: 704–11.

CROOM, S., ROMANO, P., and GIANNAKIS, M. (2000). 'Supply Chain Management: An Analytic Framework'. *European Journal of Purchasing and Supply Management*, 6: 67–83.

DAVENPORT, T. H., and SHORT, J. E. (1990). 'The New Industrial Engineering: Information Technology and Business Process Redesign'. *Sloan Management Review*, 31/4: 11–27.

DAVIES, M. (2002). 'Six Steps to Heaven'. *Distribution Business*, 15/4: 12–14.

DAVIS, J. (1992). *Exchange*. Milton Keynes: Open University Press.

DAWSON, J. A., and SHAW, S. A. (1989). 'Horizontal Competition in Retailing and the Structure of Manufacturer–Retailer Relationships', in L. Pellegrini and S. K. Reddy (eds.), *Retail and Marketing Channels*. London: Routledge, 22–35.

DE BANDT, J. (1985). 'La Filière de Production Comme Catégorie de la Méso-Dynamique Industrielle'. *Cahiers du CERNEA*, 16: 12–23.

DENT, J. (1991). 'Accounting and Organisational Cultures: A Field Study of the Emergence of a New Organisational Reality'. *Accounting, Organisations and Society*, 16: 693–703.

DEWHURST, F., SPRING, M., and ARKLE, N. (2000). 'Environmental Change and Supply Chain Management: A Multi-Case Study Exploration of the Impact of Y2000'. *Supply Chain Management: An International Journal*, 5/5: 245–61.

DIRLAM, J. B., and KAHN, A. E. (1952). 'Antitrust Law and the Big Buyer: Another Look at the A&P Case'. *Journal of Political Economy*, 60/2: 118–32.

DOEL, C. (1999). 'Towards a Supply-Chain Community? Insights from Governance Processes in the Food Industry'. *Environment and Planning A*, 31/1: 69–85.

DOUGLAS, M. (1986). *How Institutions Think*. Syracuse: Syracuse University Press.

DRAPER, S. W. (1988). 'What's Going On in Everyday Explanation?', in C. Antaki (ed.), *Analysing Everyday Explanation*. Beverly Hills: Sage, 15–42.

DU GAY, P., and SALAMAN, G. (1992). 'The Cult(ure) of the Customer'. *Journal of Management Studies*, 29/5: 615–633.

DWYER, F. R., SCHURR, P. H., and OH, S. (1987). 'Developing Buyer–Supplier Relationships'. *Journal of Marketing*, 51: 11–27.

EMILIANI, M. L. (2003). 'The Inevitability of Conflict Between Buyers and Sellers'. *Supply Chain Management*, 8/2: 107–15.

EVAN, W. M. (1966). 'The Organisation-Set: Towards a Theory of Interorganisational Relations', in J. D. Thompson (ed.), *Approaches to Organization Design*. Pittsburgh: University of Pittsburgh Press, 173–91.

EVANS-PRITCHARD, E. E. (1940). *The Nuer*. Oxford: Oxford University Press.

EVERTON, A. R. (1986). *The Legal Control of Buyer Power*. London: National Federation of Newsagents.

FARMER, D. (1975). 'Drawing Lessons from History'. *Purchasing*, October, 16–18.

—— (1976). 'Voluntary Collaboration vs "Disloyalty" to Suppliers'. *Journal of Purchasing and Materials Management*, 12/4: 3–9.

FARMER, D. (1978). 'Developing Purchasing Strategies'. *Journal of Purchasing and Materials Management*, 14/3: 6.

FARRIS, M. T. (1997). 'Evolution of Academic Concerns with Transportation and Logistics'. *Transportation Journal*, 37/1: 42–50.

FAWCETT, S. E., and MAGNAN, G. M. (2002). 'The Rhetovic and Reality of Supply Chain Integration'. *International Journal of Physical Distribution and Logistics Management*, 32/5: 339–61.

FERNIE, J. (1995). 'International Comparisons of Supply Chain Management in Grocery Retailing'. *Service Industries Journal*, 15/4: 134–7.

FINE, B., and LEOPOLD, E. (1993). *The World of Consumption*. London: Routledge.

FLIGSTEIN, N. (1998). 'The Politics of Quantification'. *Accounting, Organisation and Society*, 13: 325–31.

FLOTT, L. W. (2001). 'Understanding Supply Chains'. *Metal Finishing*, August, 47–50.

FMI (2002). *FMI Backgrounder: Slotting Allowances in the Supermarket Industry*. FMI. Washington, DC: Food Marketing Institute.

FORRESTER, J. (1961). *Industrial Dynamics*. New York: Wiley.

FOUCAULT, M. (1972). *The Archaeology of Knowledge*. New York: Pantheon.

FRIED, B. H. (2003). ' "If You Don't Like It, Leave It": The Problem of Exit in Social Contractarian Arguments'. *Philosophy and Public Affairs*, 31/1: 40–70.

FTC (2001). *Report on the Federal Trade Commission Workshop in Slotting Allowances and Other Marketing Practices in the Grocery Industry*. Washington, DC: Federal Trade Commission.

FULLERTON, R. (1988). 'How Modern is Modern Marketing?' *Journal of Marketing*, 52/1: 108–25.

GABEL, H. L. (1983). 'The Role of Buyer Power in Oligopoly Models: An Empirical Study'. *Journal of Economics and Business*, 35/1: 95–108.

GALBRAITH, J. K. (1952). *American Capitalism: The Concept of Countervailing Power*. Boston: Houghton Mifflin Company.

—— (1981). *A Life in Our Times*. Boston: Houghton Mifflin Company.

GARFINKEL, H. (1967). *Studies in Ethnomethodology*. Englewood Cliffs: Prentice Hall.

GATTY, B. (1981). 'Antitrust Goal: "Economic Rationality" '. *Nation's Business*, 69/10: 59–62.

GEERTZ, C. (1973). *The Interpretation of Cultures*. New York: Basic Books.

—— (1975). 'On the Nature of Anthropological Understanding'. *American Scientist*, 63: 47–53.

GERGEN, K. (1985). 'The Social Constructionist Movement in Modern Psychology'. *American Psychologist*, 40: 266–75.

—— (1994). *Realities and Relationships: Soundings in Social Construction*. Cambridge, MA: Harvard University Press.

—— (1999). *An Invitation to Social Construction*. London: Sage.

GIBSON-GRAHAM, J. K. (1996). *The End of Capitalism (as We Knew It)*. Oxford: Blackwell.

GILL, J., and WHITTLE, S. (1992). 'Management by Panacea: Accounting for Transience'. *Journal of Management Studies*, 30/2: 281–95.

GILLIGAN, T. W. (1986). 'The Competitive Effects of Retail Price Maintenance'. *The RAND Journal of Economics*, 17/4: 544–56.

GOURDIN, K. N. (2001). *Global Logistics Management*. Oxford: Blackwell.

GOVIL, M., and PROTH, J.-M. (2002). *Supply Chain Design and Management: Strategic and Technical Perspectives*. San Diego: Academic Press.

GRANDORI, A., and SODA, G. (1995). 'Inter-Firm Networks: Antecedents, Mechanisms and Forms'. *Organization Studies*, 16/2: 182–214.

GRANLUND, M. (2002). 'Changing Legitimate Discourse: A Case Study'. *Scandinavian Journal of Management*, 18: 365–91.

—— LUKKA, K., and MOUTITSEN, J. (1998). 'Institutional Justifications of Corporate Action: Internationalisation and EU in Corporate Reports'. *Scandinavian Journal of Management*, 14: 433–58.

GRANOVETTER, M. (1973). 'The Strength of Weak Ties'. *American Journal of Sociology*, 78/6: 1360–80.

—— (1985). 'Economic Action and Social Structure: The Problem of Embeddedness'. *American Journal of Sociology*, 91/3: 481–510.

GRANT, R. (2002). 'The Ethics of Incentives: Historical Origins and Contemporary Understandings'. *Economics and Philosophy*, 18: 111–39.

GRINT, K. (1994). 'Reengineering History: Social Resonances and Business Process Reengineering'. *Organization*, 1/1: 179–201.

—— (1997). 'TQM, BPR, JIT, BSCs and TLAs: Managerial Waves or Drownings'. *Management Decision*, 35/10: 731–8.

GRISERI, P. (2002). *Management Knowledge: A Critical View*. Basingstoke: Palgrave.

HA, A. Y. (2001). 'Supplier–Buyer Contracting: Asymmetric Cost Information and Cutoff Level Policy for Buyer Participation'. *Naval Research Logistics*, 48/1: 41–64.

HAMMER, M., and CHAMPY, J. (1993). *Re-engineering the Corporation: A Manifesto for Business Revolution*. New York: Harper Business.

HARLAND, C. M. (1996). 'Supply Chain Management: Relationships, Chains and Networks'. *British Journal of Management*, 7/1(Special issue): S63–S80.

HARRÉ, R. (1979). *Social Being*. Oxford: Blackwell.

—— and SECORD, P. F. (1972). *The Explanation of Social Behaviour*. Oxford: Basil Blackwell.

HARRELD, H., and JONES, J. (2001). 'Supply-Chain Collaboration'. *InfoWorld*, 19th December. Available at http://archive.infoworld.com/articles/fe/xml/01/12/24/011224fesccollab.xml.

HARRISON, D., and LABERGE, M. (2002). 'Innovation, Identities and Resistance: The Social Construction of an Innovation Network'. *Journal of Management Studies*. 39/4: 497–522.

HART, O. (1988). 'Incomplete Contracts and the Theory of the Firm'. *Journal of Law, Economics and Organisation*, 4: 119–39.

HAUGEN, R., and McCARTHY, R. (2000). 'REA, a Semantic Model for Internet Supply Chain Collaboration'. Paper presented to the *Business Object Component Workshop VI: Enterprise Application Integration*. Available at www.jeffsutherland.org/oopsla2000/mccarthy/mcarthy.htm.

HEATH, A. (1976). *Rational Choice and Social Exchange*. Cambridge: Cambridge University Press.

HECKERT, J. B., and MINER, R. B. (1940). *Distribution Costs*. New York: The Ronald Press Company.

HEIDE, J., and MINER, A. S. (1992). 'The Shadow of the Future: Effects of Anticipated Interaction and Frequency of Contact on Buyer–Seller Cooperation'. *Academy of Management Journal*, 35/2: 265–91.

HELD, D. (1980). *Introduction to Critical Theory: Horkheimer to Habermas*. London: Hutchinson.

HELGESEN, S. (1999). 'Dissolving Boundaries in the Era of Knowledge and Custom Work', in F. Hesselbein, M. Goldsmith, and I. Somerville (eds.), *Leading Beyond the Walls*. San Francisco: Jossey Bass, 49–55.

HELPER, S. (1991). 'How Much Has Really Changed Between US Automakers and their Suppliers?'. *Sloan Management Review*, Summer, 15–28.

HENNERT, J. F. (1988). 'Upstream Vertical Integration in the Aluminium and Tin Industries: a Comparative Study of the Choice between Market and Intrafirm Coordination'. *Journal of Economic Behaviour and Organisation*, 9/3: 281–99.

HERACLEOUS, L., and HENDRY, J. (2000). 'Discourse and the Study of Organization: Towards a Structurational Perspective'. *Human Relations*, 53/10: 1251–86.

HESSELBEIN, F. (1999). 'Introduction: The Community Beyond the Walls', in F. Hesselbein, M. Goldsmith, and I. Somerville (eds.), *Leading Beyond the Walls*. San Francisco: Jossey Bass, 1–6.

—— GOLDSMITH, M., and SOMERVILLE, I. (eds.) (1999). *Leading Beyond the Walls*. San Francisco: Jossey Bass.

HILL, C. A., and SCUDDER, G. D. (2002). 'The Use of Electronic Data Interchange for Supply Chain Coordination in the Food Industry'. *Journal of Operations Management*, 20: 375–87.

HINES, R. D. (1988). 'Financial Accounting: In Communicating Reality, We Construct Reality'. *Accounting, Organizations and Society*, 13/3: 251–61.

HIRSCHHEIM, R., and NEWMAN, M. (1991). 'Symbolism and Information Systems Development: Myth, Metaphor and Magic'. *Information Systems Research*, 2/1: 29–62.

HOLMLUND, M., and STRANDVIK, T. (1999). 'Perception configurations in business relationships'. *Management Decision*, 37/9: 686–96.

HOLMSTROM, B., and ROBERTS, J. (1998). 'The Boundaries of the Firm Revisited'. *Journal of Economic Perspectives*. 12/4: 73–94.

HOPKINS, T., and WALLERSTEIN, I. (1986). 'Commodity Chains in the World Economy Prior to 1800'. *Review*, 10: 157–70.

HOUSSIAUX, J. (1957). 'Le Concept de Quasi Integration et le Role des Sous-Traitants dans l'Industrie'. *Revue Economique*, March, 94–113.

HOWE, W. S. (1998). 'Vertical Market Systems in the UK Grocery Trade: Analysis and Government Policy'. *International Journal of Physical Distribution and Logistics Management*, 26/6–7: 212–25.

HUNT, S., and NEVIN, J. R. (1974). 'Power in a Channel of Distribution: Sources and Consequences'. *Journal of Marketing Research*, 11: 186–93.

Infoteria Corporation (2001). *The Complexity of Information Flows in Global Supply Chains*. Beverley, MA: Infoteria. www.infoteria.com/pdf/WP_BizViz_v3.pdf.

JARILLO, J. C. (1988). 'On Strategic Networks'. *Strategic Management Journal*, 9/1: 31–41.

JAROSZ, L. (2000). 'Understanding Agri-Food Networks as Social Relations'. *Agriculture and Human Values*, 17/3: 279–83.

JONES, T. C., and RILEY, D. W. (1987). 'Using Inventory for Competitive Advantage through Supply Chain Management'. *International Journal of Physical Distribution and Materials Management*, 17: 94–104.

JULKA, N., SRINVASAN, R., and KARIMI, I. (2002). 'Agent-based Supply Chain Management—1: Framework'. *Computers and Chemical Engineering*, 26/12: 1755–69.

KAHN, A. E. (1988). *The Economics of Regulation: Principles and Institutions*. Cambridge, MA: MIT Press.

KAIPIA, R., HOLMSTRÖM, J., and TANSKANEN, K. (2002). 'VMI: What Are You Losing If You Let Your Customer Place Orders?' *Production Planning and Control*, 13/1: 17–25.

KALLINKOS, J. (1996). 'Mapping the Intellectual Terrain of Management Education', in C. Grey and R. French (eds.), *Rethinking Management Education*. London: Sage, 36–53.

KALWANI, M. U., and NARAYANDAS, N. (1995). 'Long-Term Manufacturer–Supplier Relationships: Do They Pay Off For Supplier Firms?' *Journal of Marketing*, 59: 1–16.

KAPLINSKY, R. (2000). 'Globalisation and Unequalisation: What Can be Learned from Value Chain Analysis?' *Journal of Development Studies*, 37/2: 117–46.

KAVANAGH, J. (1993). 'Supermarket Pioneer'. *Financial Times*, 11 March, Supplement: Software at Work, 15.

KEITA, L. D. (1992). *Science, Rationality and Neoclassical Economics*. London: Associated University Press.

KENDALL, J. E., and KENDALL, K. E. (1993). 'Metaphors and Methodologies: Living Beyond the Systems Machine'. *MIS Quarterly*, 17/2: 149–71.

KLEIN, B., CRAWFORD, R. G., and ALCHIAN, A. A. (1978). 'Vertical Integration, Appropriable Rents and the Competitive Contracting Process'. *Journal of Law and Economics*, 21/2: 297–326.

KLOSE, A., SPERANZA, M. G., and WASSENHOVE, L. N. V. (eds.) (2002). *Quantitative Approaches to Distribution Logistics and Supply Chain Management*. Berlin: Springer.

KNIGHT, P. (1993). 'Business and the Environment: Demands from the Suppliers'. *Financial Times*, 10 March, 18.

KOUFTEROS, X. A., and KUNNATHUR, A. (1996). 'A Study of Cooperative and Coercive JIT Relationships Between Small Suppliers and Big Buyers'. *International Journal of Vehicle Design*, 17/3: 221–39.

KRANTON, R. E. (1996). 'Reciprocal Exchange: A Self-Sustaining System'. *American Economic Review*, 86/4: 830–51.

KRAUSE, D. R., HANDFIELD, R., and SCANNELL, T. V. (1998). 'An Empirical Investigation of Supplier Development: Reactive and Strategic Processes'. *Journal of Operations Management*, 17: 39–58.

KURNIA, S., and JOHNSTON, R. B. (2001). 'Adoption of Efficient Consumer Response: The Issue of Mutuality'. *Supply Chain Management: An International Journal*, 6/5: 230–41.

LAFRANCE, V. A. (1979). 'The Impact of Buyer Concentration—An Extension'. *Review of Economics and Statistics*, 61/3: 475–6.

LAKOFF, G., and JOHNSON, M. (1980). *Metaphors We Live By*. Chicago: The University of Chicago Press.

LAMMING, R. (1993). *Beyond Partnership*. London: Prentice Hall International.

LANE, C., and BACHMANN, R. (1996). 'The Social Constitution of Trust: Supplier Relations in Britain and Germany'. *Organisation Studies*, 17: 365–95.

LASCELLES, D. M., and DALE, B. G. (1989). 'The Buyer–Supplier Relationship in Total Quality Management'. *Journal of Purchasing and Materials Management*, Summer: 10–19.

LAWSON, T. (1997). *Economics and Reality*. London: Routledge.

LEE, H. L., and BILLINGTON, C. (1992). 'Managing Supply Chain Inventory: Pitfalls and Opportunities'. *Sloan Management Review*, 33/3: 65–73.

—— and WHANG, S. (1999). 'Decentralized Multi-Echelon Supply Chains: Incentives and Information'. *Management Science*, 45/5: 633–40.

—— —— (2000). 'Information Sharing in a Supply Chain'. *International Journal of Technology Management*, 20/3–4: 373–87.

—— PADMANABHAN, V., and WHANG, S. (1997a). 'Information Distortion in a Supply Chain: The Bullwhip Effect'. *Management Science*, 43/4: 546–58.

—— —— —— (1997b). 'The Bullwhip Effect in Supply Chains'. *Sloan Management Review*, 38/3: 93–102.

LEENDERS, M. R. (1966). 'Supplier Development'. *Journal of Purchasing*, 2/4: 47–62.

—— and BLENKHORN, D. L. (1988). *Reverse Marketing: the New Buyer–Seller Relationship*. New York: The Free Press.

LEMKE, F., GOFFIN, K., and SZWEJCZEWSKI, M. (2003). 'Investigating the Meaning of Supplier–Manufacturer Partnerships: An Exploratory Study'. *International Journal of Physical Distribution and Logistics Management*, 33/1: 12–35.

LENZ, B. (1997). 'The Filiere Concept as an Heuristic Instrument for Analysing the Organizational and Spatial Patterns of Production and its Distibution'. *Geographische Zeitschrift*, 85/1: 20–33.

LESLIE, D., and REIMER, S. (1999). 'Spatializing Commodity Chains'. *Progress in Human Geography*, 23/3: 401–20.

LÉVI-STRAUSS, C. (1964). *Totemism*. London: Merlin Press.

LEWIS, E. H. (1968). *Marketing Channels: Structure and Strategy*. New York: McGraw-Hill.

LEWIS, H. T. (1956). *The Role of Air Freight in Physical Distribution*. Boston: Graduate School of Business Administration, Division of Research, Harvard University.

—— and LIVESEY, C. A. (1944). 'Materials Management in the Airframe Industry'. *Harvard Business Review*, 22/4: 477–94.

LILLENFIELD, R. (1988). *The Rise of Systems Theory: An Ideological Analysis*. Malabar, FL: Robert E. Kreiger Publishing Company.

LINCOLN, B. (1989). *Discourse and the Construction of Society*. Oxford: Oxford University Press.

LINDGREEN, A. (2001). 'A Framework for Studying Relationship Marketing Dyads'. *Qualitative Market Research: An International Journal*, 4/2: 75–88.

LITWINSKI, J. A. (2001). 'Regulation of Labor Market Monopsony'. *Berkeley. Journal of Employment and Labor Law*, 22/1: 49–98.

LOWRIE, A. (1997). 'The SIND Concept of Power: A Model for Managing Non-Owned Networks'. IPSERA Conference, University of Naples, Po5.1–Po5.12.

LUSTGARTEN, S. H. (1975). 'The Impact of Buyer Concentration in Manufacturing Industries'. *Review of Economics and Statistics*, 57/2: 125–32.

LYNCH, M. (2001). 'The Contingencies of Social Construction'. *Economy and Society*, 30/2: 240–54.

MACBETH, D. K. (2002). 'Emergent Strategy in Managing Cooperative Supply Chain Change'. *International Journal of Operations and Production Management*, 22/7: 728–40.

MACDUFFIE, J. P., and HELPER, S. (1997). 'Creating Lean Suppliers: Diffusing Lean Production through the Supply Chain'. *California Management Review*, 39/4: 118–51.

MACGREGOR, D. H. (1906). *Industrial Combination*. London. Reprinted 2001 Kitchener, Ontario: Batoche Books.

MACINTOSH, N. B., and SCAPENS, R. (1991). 'Management Accounting and Control Systems: A Structuration Theory Analysis'. *Journal of Management Accounting Research*, 3: 131–58.

MACNEIL, I. R. (1980). *The New Social Contract: An Inquiry into Modern Contractual Relations*. New Haven, CT: Yale University Press.

MADIGAN, J. J. (1937). 'Securing Lowest Total Freight Costs in the Movement of Packing House Products'. *Harvard Business Review*, 15/3: 352–60.

MAIN, J. (1976). 'The Chain Reaction that's Rocking Industrial Distribution'. *Sales and Marketing Management*, 116/3: 41.

MÄKI, U. (2000). 'Reclaiming Relevant Realism'. *Journal of Economic Methodology*, 7/1: 109–25.

MALINOWSKI, B. (1954). *Magic, Science and Religion and Other Essays*. New York: Doubleday.

MANNING, A. (2003). *Monopsony in Motion*. Princeton: Princeton University Press.

MARCH, J. G., and SIMON, H. (1958). *Organizations*. New York: Wiley.

MARKIN, R. J. (1971). 'The Retailer in the Vertical Marketing Network—an Ecological Analogy'. *Business Review*, 31/1: 39.

MARSDEN, R. (1993). 'The Politics of Organisational Analysis'. *Organization Studies*, 14/1: 93–112.

MARSHALL, A. (1898). *Principles of Economics*. New York: Macmillan.

—— (1919). *Industry and Trade*. New York: Macmillan.

MAUS, M. (1967). *The Gift*. New York: Norton.

McAFEE, R. P. (2001).'Measuring Anticompetitive Effects of Mergers when Buyer Power is Concentrated.' *Texas Law Review*, 79/6: 1621–39.

McKENDRICK, N., BREWER, J., and PLUMB, J. H. (1982). *The Birth of a Consumer Society*. Bloomington: Indiana University Press.

McMILLAN, J. (1990). 'Managing Suppliers: Incentive Systems in Japanese and US Industry'. *California Management Review*, Summer: 38–55.

McROBBIE, A. (1997). 'Bridging the Gap: Feminism, Fashion and Consumption'. *Feminist Review*, 55: 73–89.

McVEY, P. (1960). 'Are Channels of Distribution what the Textbooks Say?' *Journal of Marketing*, 25: 61–5.

MEAD, G. H. (1934). *Mind, Self and Society*. Chicago: University of Chicago Press.

MENGER, C. (1981[1871]). *Principles of Economics* (trans. James Dingwall and Bert Hoselitz). New York: New York University Press.

METTERS, R. (1997). 'Quantifying the Bullwhip Effect in Supply Chains'. *Journal of Operations Management*, 15: 89–100.

MEYER, U., and GROOVER, M. P. (1972). 'Multiechelon Inventory Systems Using Continuous Systems Analysis and Simulation'. *AIIE Transactions*, 4/4: 318–27.

MILES, R. (1991). 'Collective Voices Suppliers Cannot Afford to Ignore'. *Computing*, 20 June, 20.

MILLS, S. (1997). *Discourse*. London: Routledge.

MIZURCHI, M. S., and FEIN, L. (1999). 'The Social Construction of Organizational Knowledge: A Study of the Uses of Coercive, Mimetic, and Normative Isomorphism'. *Administrative Science Quarterly*, 44: 653–83.

MONTFORT, M. J., and DUTAILLY, J. C. (1983). *Les Filieres de Production*. Archives et Documents no. 67. Paris: INSEE.

MOODY, P. E. (1993). *Breakthrough Partnering*. Essex Junction, VT: Oliver Wight Publications.

MORGAN, G. (1986). *Images of Organization*. London: Sage.

MUCKSTADT, J. A. (1973). 'A Model for a Multi-Item, Multi-Echelon, Multi-Indenture Inventory System'. *Management Science*, 20/4 (part 1): 472–88.

MURDOCH, J., MARSDEN, T., and BANKS, J. (2000). 'Quality, Nature and Embeddedness: Some Theoretical Considerations in the Context of the Food Sector'. *Economic Geography*, 76/2: 107–25.

MURPHY, T. (2001). 'The Pain Spreads Wide'. *Ward's Auto World*, 37/12: 44–5.

NEW, S. J. (1994). 'Supply chains: some doubts', in *Proceedings of the Third Annual Conference of IPSERA*, Cardiff, April, 345–62.

—— (1998). 'The Implications and Reality of Partnership' in: B. Burnes and B. Dale (eds.), *Working in Partnership: Best Practice in Customer–Supplier Relationships*. Aldershot: Gower, 9–20.

—— (1999). 'Understanding Supplier Resistance: Overcoming Obstacles to Supply Innovation' in: S. Ho (ed.), *TQM and Innovation: Proceedings of the Fourth International Conference on ISO9000 and TQM*. Hong Kong: Hong Kong Baptist University, 419–24.

—— and MITROPOULOS, I. (1995). 'Strategic Networks: Morphology, Epistemology and Praxis'. *International Journal of Operations and Production Management*, 15/11: 53–61.

NOOTEBOOM, B. (1999). *Inter-firm Alliances: Analysis and Design*. London: Routledge.

NRC (2000). *Surviving Supply Chain Integration: Strategies for Supply Chain Integration*. Washington, DC: National Academy Press.

OECD (1981). *Buying Power: The Exercise of Market Power by Dominant Buyers: Report of the Committee (178P)*. Paris: OECD.

OLKKONEN, R., TIKKANEN, H., and ALAJOUTSIJÄRVI, K. (2000). 'The Role of Communication in Business Relationships and Networks'. *Management Decision*, 38/6: 403–9.

PARKER, D., and HARTLEY, K. (1997). 'The Economics of Partnership Sourcing Versus Adversarial Competition: A Critique'. *European Journal of Purchasing and Supply Management*, 3/2: 115–25.

PEAKE, A. (2003). 'Mid-Market: Redefining Value Chain Roles'. *Manufacturing and Logistics IT*, May, 14–18.

PEARCE, A. M. (1996). 'Efficient Consumer Response: Managing the Supply Chain for "Ultimate" consumer satisfaction'. *Supply Chain Management*, 1/2: 11–17.

PEERY, N. S. Jr. (1972). 'General Systems Theory: An Inquiry into its Social Philosophy'. *Academy of Management Journal*, 15/4: 495–510.

PERRY, M. K. (1978). 'Vertical Integration: The Monopsonist Case'. *American Economic Review*, 68: 562–70.

POLODNY, J. M. (1994). 'Market Uncertainty and the Social Character of Economic Exchange'. *Administrative Science Quarterly*, 39: 458–83.

POOLER, V. H., and POOLER, D. J. (1981). 'Purchasing's Elusive Conceptual Home'. *Journal of Purchasing and Materials Management*, 17/2: 13–18.

PORTER, M. (1980). *Competitive Strategy*. New York: The Free Press.

PORTEUS, E. L. (2000). 'Responsibility Tokens in Supply Chain Management'. *Manufacturing and Service Operations Management*, 2/2: 203–19.

POSNER, R. A. (1986). *The Robinson-Patman Act: Federal Regulation of Price Differences*. Washington, DC: American Enterprise Institute for Public Policy Research.

PRASCH, R. E. (1995). 'Toward a "General Theory" of Market Exchange'. *Journal of Economic Issues*, 29/3: 807–28.

PRESTON, A. M., COOPER, D., and COOMBS, R. W. (1992). 'Fabricating Budgets: A Study of the Production of Management Budgeting in the National Health Service'. *Accounting, Organisations and Society*, 17: 561–93.

PRICE, H. (1996). 'The Anthropology of the Supply Chain'. *European Journal of Purchasing and Supply Management*, 2/2–3: 87–105.

PROVAN, K. (1983). 'The Federation as an Interorganizational Linkage Network'. *Academy of Management Review*, 8/1: 79–89.

—— and GASSENHEIMER, J. (1994). 'Supplier Commitment in Relational Contract Exchanges with Buyers: A Study of Interorganizational Dependence and Exercised Power.' *Journal of Management Studies*, 31/1: 55–68.

QUINN, B. (2000). *How Wal-Mart is Destroying America and The World and What You Can Do About It*. Berkeley, CA: Ten Speed Press.

RAIKES, P., JENSEN, M. F., and PONTE, S. (2000). 'Global Commodity Chains and the French Filiere Approach: Comparison and Critique'. *Economy and Society*, 29/3: 390–417.

RAMSAY, J. (1990). 'The Myth of the Cooperative Single Source'. *Journal of Purchasing and Materials Management*, Winter, 2–5.

—— (1996*a*). 'Power measurement'. *European Journal of Purchasing & Supply Management*, 2/2–3: 129–43.

—— (1996*b*). 'The Case Against Purchasing Partnerships'. *International Journal of Purchasing and Materials Management*, 32/4: 13–19.

RAPER, K. C., and LOVE, A. H. (2000). 'Determining Market Power Exertion Between Buyers and Sellers'. *Journal of Applied Econometrics*, 15/3: 225–52.

RENHOFF, A. (2002). *A Theoretical and Empirical Investigation of Slotting Allowances in the Grocery Industry*. Working Paper. www.people.virginia.edu/~adr2n.

RENNIE, R. (2001). 'The Supply-Chain Defined'. *SC News*, August, www.thesupplychain.com/eng/news/scnews/2001_08.as.

REVE, T., and STERN, L. W. (1979). 'Interorganisational Relations in Marketing Channels'. *Academy of Management Review*, 4/3: 405–16.

RICHARDSON, A. J., and DOWLING, J. B. (1986). 'An Integrative Theory of Organizational Legitimation'. *Scandinavian Journal of Management Studies*, 3/2: 91–109.

RIGNEY, D. (2001). *The Metaphorical Society: An Invitation to Social Theory*. Oxford: Rowman and Littlefield.

RING, P. S., and VAN DE VEN, A. H. (1994). 'Developmental Processes of Cooperative Interorganisational Relationships'. *Academy of Management Review*, 19/1: 90–118.

ROBBINS, J. E., SPEH, T. W., and MAYER, M. L. (1982). 'Retailers' Perceptions of Channel Conflict Issues'. *Journal of Retailing*, 58/4: 46–67.

ROBINSON, J. (1933). *The Economics of Imperfect Competition*. London: Macmillan.

ROTHSCHILD, K. W. (1943). 'Monopsony, Buying Costs and Welfare Expenditure'. *The Review of Economic Studies*, 10/1: 62–7.

SAKO, M. (1992). *Prices, Quality and Trust*. Cambridge: Cambridge University Press.

SANTORO, R. (1999). 'The Procurement Process in the Virtual Vertical Enterprise Scenario: The Point of View of Large Enterprises'. *Human Systems Management*, 18/3–4: 187–91.

SAUSSURE, F. (1974 [1916]). *Course in General Linguistics* (trans. W. Baskin). London: Fontana/Collins.

SCARF, H. (2002). 'Inventory Theory'. *Operations Research*, 50/1: 186–91.

SCHILL, R. L., and McARTHUR, D. N. (1992). 'Redefining the Strategic Competitive Unit: Towards a New Global Marketing Paradigm,' *International Marketing Review*, 9/3: 5–24.

SCHUMPETER, J. (1947). *Capitalism, Socialism and Democracy*. New York: Harper.

SCOTT, C., and WESTBROOK, R. (1991). 'New Strategic Tools for Supply Chain Management'. *International Journal of Physical Distribution and Logistics Management*, 21/1: 23–33.

SEARCY, D. L. (2002). *Facilitators and Impediments in Moving Firms Toward Supply Chain Management: A Qualitative Field Study*. Ph.D. dissertation. The University of Tennessee, Knoxville.

SHENHAV, Y. (1995). 'From Chaos to Systems: the Engineering Foundations of Organisation Theory, 1879–1932'. *Administrative Science Quarterly*, 40: 557–85.

SHERIDAN, D. (1991). *Negotiating Commercial Contracts*. London: McGraw-Hill.

SHERMAN, R. (1989). *The Regulation of Monopoly*. Cambridge: Cambridge University Press.

SHIOMI, H. (1995). 'The Formation of Assembler Networks in the Automobile Industry: the Case of Toyota Motor Company. 1955–1980', in H. Shiomi and K. Wada (eds.), *Fordism Transformed*. Oxford: Oxford University Press, 28–48.

SILVER, E. A. (1981). 'Operations Research in Inventory Management: A Review and Critique'. *Operations Research*, 29/4: 628–45.

SINGHAL, J., and SINGHAL, K. (2002). 'Supply Chains and Compatibility Among Components in Product Design'. *Journal of Operations Management*, 20: 289–302.

SMITH, H. (2000). 'The Role of Ontological Engineering in B2B Net Markets'. Available at www.ontology.org/main/papers/csc-ont-eng.html.

SNOW, C. C., and MILES, R. E. (1992). 'Managing 21st Century Network Organizations'. *Organizational Dynamics*, 20/3: 5–20.

SONGINI, M. L. (2003). 'SAS Pushes End-to-End Supply Chain Analytics Suite'. *Computerworld*, 11 February, www.computerworld.com/softwaretopics/erp/story/0,10801,78458,00.html.

SPULBER, D. F. (1996). 'Market Microstructure and Intermediation'. *Journal of Economic Perspectives*, 10/3: 135–52.

STARBUCK, W. (1982). 'Congealing Oil: Inventing Ideologies to Justify acting Ideologies Out'. *Journal of Management Studies*, 19/1: 3–27.

STERN, L. W., and REVE, T. (1980). 'Distribution Channels as Political Economies: A Framework for Comparative Analysis'. *Journal of Marketing*, 44: 52–64.

STEVENS, G. C. (1989). 'Integrating the Supply Chain'. *International Journal of Physical Distribution and Materials Management*, 19/8: 3–8.

STIGLER, G. J. (1954). 'The Economist Plays with Blocks'. *American Economic Review: Paper and Proceedings*, 44: 7–14.

—— (1966). *The Theory of Price*. New York: Macmillan.

STUART, F. I. (1993). 'Supplier Partnerships: Influencing Factors and Strategic Benefits'. *International Journal of Purchasing and Materials Management*, 29/4: 22–8.

STUBBS, E. (2002). 'Achieving Collaborative Supply Chains'. *Logistics Manager*, 9/10: 26–7.

SUCHMAN, M. C. (1995). 'Managing Legitimacy: Strategic and Institutional Approaches'. *Academy of Management Review*, 20: 571–610.

SZYMANKIEWICZ, J. (1994). 'Supply-Chain Partnerships—Who Wins?' *Logistics Focus*, 2/10: 8–11.

TAYLOR, D. (1999). 'Parallel Incremental Transformation Strategy: An Approach to the Development of Lean Supply Chains'. *International Journal of Logistics: Research and Applications*, 2/3: 305–24.

TAYUR, S., GANESHAN, R., and MAGAZINE, M. (eds.) (1999). *Quantitative Models for Supply Chain Management Research*. Boston: Kluwer.

THOMAS, D. (2003). 'Wal-Mart's RFID Plan Too Aggressive for Suppliers'. *Computer Weekly*, 1 July, 10.

THOMAS, D. J., and GRIFFIN, P. M. (1996). 'Coordinated Supply Chain Management'. *European Journal of Operational Research*, 94/1: 1–15.

THOMPSON, K. (1980). 'Organizations as Constructors of Social Reality', in G. Salaman and K. Thompson (eds.), *Control and Ideology in Organizations*. Cambridge, MA: MIT Press, 216–36.

THOMSON, I. (1995). 'Future Supply Chain Strategy'. *Logistics Manager*, 2/2: 12–16.

TIROLE, J. (1999). 'Incomplete Contracts: Where Do We Stand?' *Econometrica*, 67: 741–81.

TOWILL, D. R. (1991). 'Supply Chain Dynamics'. *International Journal of Computer Integrated Manufacturing*, 4/4: 197–208.

—— (1997a). 'FORRIDGE: Principles of Good Practice in Materials Flow'. *International Journal of Production Control*, 8/7: 622–32.

—— (1997b). 'The Seamless Supply Chain: The Predator's Strategic Advantage'. *International Journal of Technology Management*, 13/1: 37–56.

—— (2000). 'A Route Map for Substantially Improving Supply Chain Dynamics'. *International Journal of Manufacturing Technology and Management*, 1/1: 94–112.

—— NAIM, M., and WIKNER, J. (1992). 'Industrial Dynamics Simulation Models in the Design of Supply Chains'. *International Journal of Physical Distribution and Logistics Management*, 22/5: 3–13.

TRENT, R. J., and MONCZKA, R. M. (1994). 'Effective Cross-Functional Sourcing Teams: Critical Success Factors'. *International Journal of Purchasing and Materials Management*, 30/1: 2–11.

TSAY, A. A., NAHMIAS, S., and AGRAWAL, A. (1999). 'Modeling Supply Chain Contracts: A Review', in S. Tayur, R. Ganeshan, and M. Magazine (eds.), *Quantitative Models for Supply Chain Management Research*. Boston: Kluwer, 299–336.

TSOUKAS, H. (1991). 'The Missing Link: A Transformational View of Metaphors in Organizational Science'. *Academy of Management Review*, 16/3: 566–85.

TUSHMAN, M. L., and SCANLAN, T. J. (1981). 'Boundary Spanning Individuals: Their Role in Information Transfer and their Antecedents'. *Academy of Management Journal*, 28/2: 289–305.

ULRICH, D. (1999). 'Maximising Creative Collaboration', in F. Hesselbein, M. Goldsmith, and I. Someville (eds.), *Leading Beyond the Walls*. San Francisco: Jossey Bass, 91–103.

VAILE, R. S., COVER, J. H., GRETHER, E. T., and BOWEN, E. R. (1939). 'Changing Distribution Channels'. *The American Economic Review*, 29/1: 104–8.

VICKERS, J., and WATERSON, M. (1991). 'Vertical Relationships: An Introduction'. *Journal of Industrial Economics*, 39/5: 445–50.

VIS, I. F. A., and ROODBERGEN, K. J. (2002). 'Examining Supply Chains from Practice', in A. Klose, M. G. Speranza, and L. N. V. Wassenhove (eds.), *Quantitative Approaches to Distribution Logistics and Supply Chain Management*. Berlin: Springar, 3–18.

VONCHEK, A. (1995). 'The Components of Supply Chain Management'. *Logistics Focus*, 3/3: 12.

WALKER, G., and POPPO, L. (1991). 'Profit Centers, Single-Source Suppliers and Transaction Costs'. *Administrative Science Quarterly*, 36: 66–87.

WANG, C. X. (2002). 'A General Framework of Supply Chain Contract Models'. *Supply Chain Management: An International Journal*, 7/5: 302–10.

WARING, T., and WAINWRIGHT, D. (2000). 'Interpreting Integration with respect to Information Systems in Organizations—Image, Theory and Reality'. *Journal of Information Technology*, 15: 131–48.

WEBB, S., and WEBB, B. (1902). *Industrial Democracy*. Longmans: London.

WEICK, K. E. (1969). *The Social Psychology of Organizing*. Reading, MA: Addison-Wesley.

—— (1985). *Sensemaking in Organizations*. London: Sage.

WHEWELL, R. (1997). 'Turning up the Heat under the Supply Chain'. *Logistics Focus*, 5/4: 18–24.

WHICKER, L., and WALTON, J. (1996). 'Logistics and the Virtual Enterprise'. *Logistics Focus*, 4/8: 7–10.

WHITLEY, R. (1984*a*). 'The Fragmented State of Management Studies: Reasons and Consequences'. *Journal of Management Studies*, 21/3: 331–48.

—— (1984*b*). 'The Scientific Status of Management Research as a Practically-Oriented Social Science'. *Journal of Management Studies*, 21/4: 371–89.

WHITNEY, S. N. (1953). 'Errors in the Concept of Countervailing Power'. *The Journal of Business of the University of Chicago*, 26/4: 238–53.

WILKINSON, I. (2001). 'A History of Network and Channels Thinking in Marketing in the Twentieth Century'. *Australian Journal of Marketing*, 9/2: 23–53.

WILKINSON, J. (1997). 'A New Paradigm for Economic Analysis?' *Economy and Society*, 26/3: 305–39.

WILLIAMS, G. (1994). 'A Shopper's Tale: Supply Chain Integration'. *Manufacturing Engineer*, 73/5: 222–5.

WILLIAMSON, O. (1971). 'The Vertical Integration of Production: Market Failure Considerations'. *American Economic Review*, 6: 112–23.

—— (1979). 'Transaction Cost Economics: The Governance of Contractual Relations'. *Journal of Law and Economics*, 22: 233–62.

WIND, Y. (1970). 'Industrial Source Loyalty'. *Journal of Marketing Research*, 8: 433–36.

WITTGENSTEIN, L. (1953). *Philosophical Investigations*. Oxford: Blackwell.

WOMACK. J., ROOS, D., and JONES, D. (1990). *The Machine That Changed the World*. New York: Rawson Associates.

ZEITZ, G. (1980). 'Interorganizational Dialectics'. *Administrative Science Quarterly*, 25: 72–88.

ZENZ, G. J. (1969). 'The Personnel Equation in Materials Management'. *Personnel Journal*, 48/9: 683–90.

ZUCKERMAN, A. (2002). 'From the Supply Chain to a Supply Network'. *World Trade*. 1 October. Available at www.worldtrademag.com/wt/cda/articleinformation/features/bnp_features_item/0,3483,85707,00.html.

5

Supply Chain Dynamics

MOHAMED NAIM, STEPHEN DISNEY, AND DENIS TOWILL

1. Introduction

There is currently a considerable preoccupation with the impact of electronic innovations in various environments including business, commerce, and manufacturing. In particular, the Internet and related information and communication technologies (ICT) have recently enabled the cost-effective dissemination of information between disparate parties in the supply chain. New supply chain strategies, such as Vendor Managed Inventory (VMI), Collaborative Planning Forecasting and Replenishment (CPFR), or Efficient Consumer Response (ECR), have begun to exploit these new communication channels (Disney 2001), principally at the retail end of the supply chain. The impact of the ICT enabled supply chain on manufacturers and materials/component suppliers is, however, less well understood and exploited.

Advances in ICT enable a radical rethink in how products and services are marketed (Peppers and Rogers 1998). The shift, already seen in embryonic form by companies such as Dell Computers and Domino Pizza, is from traditional mass marketing strategies towards customer-driven marketing. The former is based on identifying a set of 'average' customer wants (Christopher and Towill 2000) and 'pushing' the product and services to as many people as possible who may have those wants. The latter requires an enterprise (possibly as a single entity but almost certainly a virtual one or as part of a supply chain) to establish a '1–2–1' interactive relationship with each of its customers. While the enterprise treats all its customers equally it must also prioritize its resources and efforts to its most valued customers based on each customer's lifetime value to the enterprise. With most enterprises ultimately fulfilling the needs of thousands or millions of end customers, there is a need to develop efficient but flexible methods of customer interaction and product or service delivery. This is in line with contemporary thinking in Operations Management (Hill 2000).

While ICT in the form of eBusiness is advocated as an enabler to the '1–2–1' enterprise (Peppers and Rogers 1998), by allowing marketplace information to be shared by all businesses in the supply chain, there is little analytical or quantifiable evidence that it will actually improve overall performance of the enterprise in delivering customer wants. Most of the research to date has been via empirical research studies (Holmström 1997). It is usually proposed that passing marketplace information on to all businesses in the supply chain via ICT will improve performance. In fact, recent research (e.g. Hong-Minh, Disney, and Naim 2000) has shown, via a supply chain management game, that simply passing information on to businesses can have a detrimental effect. This is due to the fact that, in addition to information transparency, there is a need to coordinate the separate logistics planning and control systems. Our conclusion is that such notions as VMI, ECR, and CPFR are bandied about with little understanding and assessment of their capabilities.

2. The problem

The origins of the systems approach to generic problem solving may be traced back to the work of von Bertalanffy (in Kramer and de Smit 1977) who proposed the General Systems Theory (GST) in 1932. GST suggests that 'the whole is greater than the sum of its individual parts' and that suboptimal solutions do not yield true total optima—this is often referred to as 'gestalten'. The dangers of suboptimization is highlighted by what is known as Braess' Paradox (Shapiro 2001).

If a part of a management system is re-engineered, then the odds are:

25% that the system performance is improved

50% that the system performance will not change significantly

25% that the system performance will actually get worse

GST has generic applicability and one of its aims is to develop a unified approach that transcends disciplinary boundaries. One of the unifying principles of GST is that any system is in dynamic interaction with its environment. For systems to be efficacious and effective they must be 'open' and aim to reach an equilibrium with their environment. This interactivity, resulting in feedback flows between system and environment and the delays that are inherent in any system results in dynamic behaviour.

Much of the pioneering work into aspects of supply chain dynamics was undertaken by Forrester in the late 1950s (Forrester 1958), using a simple but representative simulation model of a production distribution supply chain. Originally developed as a detailed case study incorporating the DYNAMO simulation language, Forrester's work has been widely quoted, and misquoted in business and academic literature. Based on a series of simulation experiments, Forrester revealed a number of important behavioural features of the supply chain model that were concluded as having relevance to real-world supply chains:

a. Demand in the marketplace becomes a delayed and distorted order pattern moving upstream through a supply chain.

 a.1. At any one point in time, processes in various companies in the chain may be moving in different directions to each other and to the market.

 a.2. Supply chain designs tend to 'amplify' marketplace variations. The magnitude of the variations in orders placed on the factory is greater than the variations in marketplace demand.

 a.3. Supply chain designs can introduce 'periodicity', or rogue seasonality which can be misinterpreted as a consequence of seasonal variations in the marketplace, rather than a property of the supply chain design.

b. Attempts to reduce poor supply chain dynamic behaviour can exacerbate the problem. Counter-intuitive behaviour often occurs because the causes of the behaviour are obscured from the decision-makers in the chain. Consequently learning opportunities are restricted.

Point 'a' above has been historically termed 'The Law of Industrial Dynamics' (Burbidge 1984) but the same phenomenon has more recently been described as 'bullwhip' (Lee *et al.* 1997*a*, *b*). Bullwhip is an important measure as it is symptomatic of a poorly performing supply chain (Jones and Simons 2000). Bullwhip is a surrogate measure of production adaptation costs (Stalk and Hout 1990) and implies the inclusion of 'just-in-case' stock holding to buffer against uncertainties. Evidence, in many forms, suggests that the 'bullwhip' effect and Forrester's empirical conclusions are highly applicable to the vast majority of supply chains. Typical are the results observed in a global mechanical precision products supply chain (McCullen and Towill 2001). The ability to recognize the 'bullwhip' effect, its impact on business and supply chain performance and ways to eliminate or cope with it have been a key issue in a number of current management paradigms including

- Time compression (Stalk and Hout 1990)
- Lean Thinking (Womack and Jones 1996)
- Mass customization (Pine 1993)
- Supply chain management (Houlihan 1987)
- Agile production (Kidd 1994).

An example of the 'bullwhip' effect in just one echelon of a real-world automotive supply chain is given in Fig. 5.1. This shows customer demand coming into a business and the resulting supplier orders. The ratio in variance between the supplier order and customer demand is 2:1! Point 'b' above forms a critical research agenda for this chapter as we determine whether the application of ICT in the supply chain may lead to counterintuitive behaviour, hence what are our research priorities and to what extent innovative research platforms have to be developed.

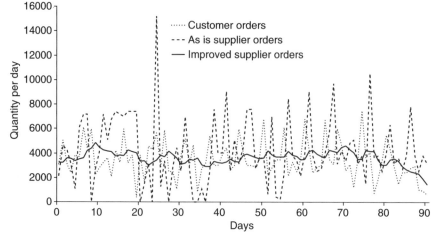

Fig. 5.1. Sample bullwhip curve

3. What we know: current state of knowledge

There is a 40+ year history embedded in the theories of systems thinking and cybernetics. Research on improving the dynamic behaviour of individual manufacturing businesses and supply chains is well known. Most recent research may be categorized under the following headings.

Management games: Such as the Beer Game that was originally developed at MIT at the end of the 1950s (Sterman 1989) are useful tools to illustrate the benefits of different supply chain strategies. Games are limited in the sense that generally nothing can be rigorously proved from the game in itself. But they do provide a valuable source of experiential evidence and are a good learning device. Other authors have since extended or computerized the Beer Game including van Ackere, Larsen, and Morecroft (1993), Kaminsky, and Simchi-Levi *et al.* (2000), Lambrecht and Dejonckheere (1999*a*, *b*).

Empirical studies: A number of authors have investigated the impact of ICT on the supply chain including Holmström (1998), Fransoo and Wouters (2000), Kaipia, Holmström, and Tanskanen (2000). However, this type of contribution looks at quantifying the improvement performance of a known strategy after its implementation; that is, there is no predictive element and the focus of the research is to identify best practices. Unfortunately, it is not always possible to compare ICT implementation strategies directly due to the varying nature of the environments in which they have been implemented.

Statistical analysis: This type of contribution typically provides statistical insights about the impact of demand properties such as standard deviation and auto-correlation, and supply chain properties such as lead times and information paths, on inventory costs and the bullwhip effect, or demand amplification.

Statistical methods are often used to quantify performance of real situations. These methods, however, fail to show how to reduce or eliminate the detrimental dynamic effects, such as 'bullwhip', and insights into the causes and effects of system structure on performance are rarely obtained in depth from the technique. Recent significant contributions of this type include Lee, So, and Tang (2000), Chen *et al.* (2000), and Chen, Ryan, and Simchi-Levi (2000).

Simulation and system dynamics: This was advocated by Forrester (1961) as a method of investigating the dynamic effects in large non-linear systems as a means of avoiding resorting to complicated mathematical control theory based models (Edghill and Towill 1989). Simulation approaches alone suffer from being cumbersome, time-consuming, and only provide limited insight (Popplewell and Bonney 1987), but they do have the advantage of being able to model non-linearities while avoiding complicated mathematics. Previous work using simulation is very prolific and includes (but is by no means limited to) Forrester (1961), and Coyle (1982), who studied traditional supply chain structures, Cachon and Fisher (1997), and Waller, Johnson, and Davis (1999) who studied VMI.

Continuous control theory techniques: For production and inventory control, this was first recognized by the Nobel Prize for Economics Winner in 1978 (for his work on organizational dynamics), Herbert Simon. Simon (1952) described how to use linear deterministic control theory for production and inventory control. This was transformed into 'good practice' format by Towill (1982). Axsäter (1985) presents a useful review paper of early work, summarizing the advantages and limitations of the field. He concludes that control theory 'illustrates extremely well dynamical effects and feedback', but cannot incorporate sequencing and lot-sizing issues. Grubbström (1996) and other colleagues at Linköping Institute of Technology have been applying the Laplace transform and economic techniques such as Net Present Value to MRP systems. Continuous control theory suffers from the fact that some scheduling and ordering scenarios are inherently discrete and the continuous representation of discrete time delays is mathematically complicated.

Discrete control theory: This is a very powerful way of investigating sampled data systems (i.e. a scheduling and ordering systems and computer system which are inherently discrete). Vassian (1955), inspired by Simon's work in the continuous domain, studied a production-scheduling algorithm using discrete control theory. DeWinter (1966), in possibly one of only two contributions that consider novel supply chain structures, looks at a form of centralized inventory control used in naval supply chains. Deziel and Eilon (1967) describe a significant application. Burns and Sivazlian (1978) consider a four level traditional supply chain using z-transforms. Bonney and Popplewell (1988) have investigated MRP systems. Dejonckheere *et al.* (2003) have been using z-transforms and Fourier transforms to investigate the bullwhip performance of common forecasting mechanisms within common control structures. Disney (2001) has been using discrete control theory to investigate VMI supply chains. The disadvantages of discrete control theory is that the mathematics often involves lengthy and tedious algebraic manipulation.

Classical OR/management science: At about the same time as the seminal work of Simon (1952) and Vassian (1955) this separate but parallel strand of research established a dynamic programming approach to the inventory control problem. Arrow (2002) gives a recap of the genesis of the search for the 'optimal inventory policy'. While not actually investigating structural dynamics, this approach aims to establish optimal policies for inventory control. Inherent in this approach is the assumption that there are an infinite number of possible policies and it tries to identify the best one for a given set of assumptions. For example, the assumptions may be concerned with the cost structure, demand pattern, lead times, and planning horizons. An objective function has to be defined and it is usually based on inventory holding and shortage costs. Key works in the field include Karlin (1960), Scarf (1960), Veinott (1965), and Johnson and Thompson (1975). Such an approach rarely considers the generation of order upstream from the point of inventory control, and therefore may be regarded as a suboptimal approach. Towill *et al.* (2003) have undertaken a detailed comparison of the control theory and OR approach to Decision Support System (DSS) design for managing supply chain dynamics.

The hybrid approach: Naim and Towill (1994) brought together the separate elements above into a contingency-based methodology. Control theory models coupled with simulation (such as Disney, Naim, and Towill 1997) and statistical methods (Griffiths, Hafeez, and Naim 1993) have enabled a systematic approach (such as Evans, Naim, and Towill 1998) to understanding the linear, time invariant, and the non-linear, time varying dynamic behaviour of production and inventory control systems (Cheema 1994). Solutions have been similarly proposed to improved customer service levels and increased stock turns through action-based research (Lewis 1997). The analytical studies have also been related to empirical survey findings. Berry, Evans, and Naim (1998) applied this approach to model the delivery performance of a health care vendor with an active catalogue of 6000 products covering 'A', 'B', and 'C' classified items.

There is little explicit analytical evidence of the impact of ICT on supply chain dynamics. In fact, counterintuitive behaviour has resulted from our playing of the Beer Game. For example, transparency of marketplace demand transmitted along the supply chain can easily have an overall detrimental effect if no holistic strategy is in place (Hong-Minh, Disney, and Naim 2000). It would clearly be impossible to examine all the above approaches in this chapter. What we will do is to develop some of the concepts regarding supply chain dynamics based on key published material that help to define a framework for future research.

4. Supply chains and complexity

In the 1960s Mark Gardner and Ross Ashby in research undertaken in what is now Cardiff University were concerned with the general behaviour of large dynamical systems (Gardner and Ashby 1970). 'Large' was arbitrarily defined

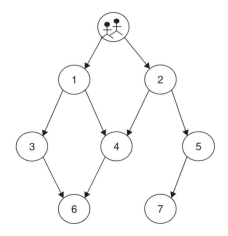

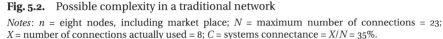

Fig. 5.2. Possible complexity in a traditional network

Notes: n = eight nodes, including market place; N = maximum number of connections = 23; X = number of connections actually used = 8; C = systems connectance = X/N = 35%.

with examples given as airport traffic congestion due to 10^2 aeroplanes, group activities involving 10^4 people and the human brain with 10^6 neurones. Via simulation Gardner and Ashby made a significant contribution to our understanding of the behaviour of complex systems. This resulted from the careful design and subsequent analysis of a set of experiments based on the number of variables in a system and the way in which these variables interact.

Figure 5.2 shows a possible configuration for a traditional supply network where communication proceeds in just one path from the marketplace upstream to the suppliers. Each numbered node represents both an operation in the network plus the end consumers, here seen as an aggregate marketplace node. Gardner and Ashby undertook a number of experiments in which the number of nodes and the number of connections actually used were varied. The latter, representing information flows in the supply network, were selected at random both in number and sign. By repeating the experiments many times the probability of stable operation of the network was established. This showed the existence of 'switching lines' between stable and chaotic behaviour and contains a stark message for anyone concerned with the design and operation of supply chains.

Figure 5.3 shows a summary of the simulation results as depicted by Towill (1997). The axes of the graph are the probability of stable behaviour of the system and the 'system connectance', which is the percentage of the system nodes randomly connected to each other. Two important phenomena are manifestly evident:

1. As the number of nodes increases the probability of a stable operation decreases dramatically.

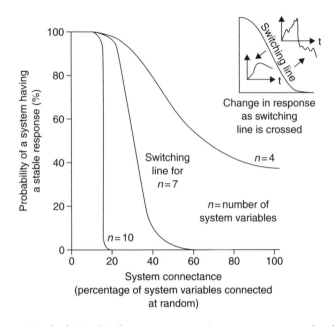

Fig. 5.3. Empirical relationship between system size, connectance, and stability

Source: From Towill (1997), based on the simulation results of Gardner and Ashby (1970).

2. As the system connectance increases the network swiftly crosses the switching line and enters the unstable operations region.

The implications for supply chain networks and any supporting strategy of passing on information, say via EPOS, are obvious. Figure 5.4 shows the same supply network of Fig. 5.1 but with EPOS data now transferred from the first echelon (say, equivalent to the retailers in the grocery sector) through to the third echelon (say, the raw food suppliers delivering goods to the food processors). Thus, the number of connections increases to ten and the system connectance thereby increases to 43 per cent making the probability of stable response much lower. Hence, it is clear that the supply network must be properly designed and not allowed to grow in an 'ad hoc' manner. *Otherwise, using the wrong information at the wrong node in the wrong way may suddenly cause the network to become unstable and chaos to reign throughout the system.*

These results concur with the seminal work of Shannon, Oliver, and Pierce (1948) that Kramer and de Smit (1977) have embedded in other research in the field of chaos and information availability. It is important to realize that data transfer on its own is not information. Kramer and de Smit (1977) have noted that data may be transferred between a sender and a receiver, but it only contains information if and when it removes uncertainty in some way. Thus, in a supply system scenario, additional data is insufficient unless the receiver knows what to do with it. It also does not help that a lack of coordination between the

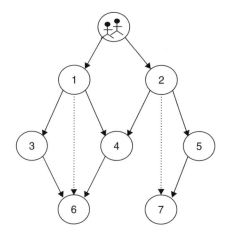

Fig. 5.4.   Possible increased complexity in an ICT enabled network

Notes: e-enabled supply chain: n = eight nodes, including market place; N = maximum number of connections = 23; X = number of connections actually used = 10; C = systems connectance = X/N = 43%.

nodes in the system means that the receiver is still unaware of the consequences of their own actions. The same argument also applies to the likely actions taken by the other nodes, taken to hopefully improve their situation.

5. Supply chains and human behaviour

The MIT 'Beer Game' (Senge 1990) represents a four-echelon supply chain including a retailer, a wholesaler, a distributor, and a factory. A flow of information (orders) goes from the retailer to the factory and a flow of product returns. The game involves different delays: 2 weeks delay for the order to reach the next echelon and 2 weeks transport delay from the inventory of an echelon to the next as shown in Fig. 5.5. Usually the players (representing one echelon) cannot speak to each other. A customer demand is inputted at the retailer level and after having satisfied the order, the retailer must decide the quantity needed to be ordered from the wholesaler. Each echelon has to pass an order to its supplier in order to fulfil the order of its immediate customer.

The aim of the game is to minimize cumulative costs over the length of the game due to excess inventory and stock outs. To set up a performance metric it is commonly assumed that for each unit inventory costs are £0.50 and stock outs costs are £1. It is considered that even if the supplier cannot satisfy the demand during one or several weeks, the products ordered are still required by the customer, thus, a backlog is created. The inventory cost is an important measure as it ultimately determines the extent to which we satisfy the customer as well as determining the risk of stock obsolescence. The severity of backlog cost is justified because, no

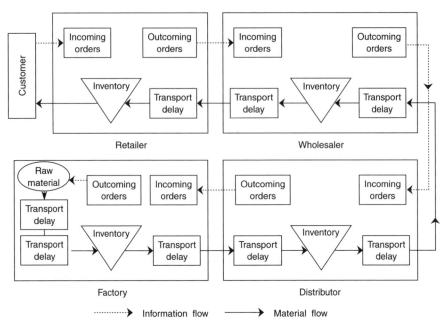

Fig. 5.5. Schematic of the Beer Game

matter how well we control the degree of volatility in the supply chain, if we do not satisfy the end consumer then we will eventually go out of business.

The goal of the game is to demonstrate to the players the existence of the bull-whip phenomenon and that it is not induced by external disturbances but is due to the lead times in the supply chain coupled with the players' feedback-based decision-making. While traditionally the 'Beer Game' is utilized as a mechanism for allowing participants to experience the demand amplification phenomenon for themselves it may also be used to test different supply chain re-engineering scenarios (Mason-Jones 1998). For the specific purposes of this chapter we have taken the results from Hong-Minh *et al.* (2000) and Disney *et al.* (2002*a*) to high-light the implications of ICT strategies.

Disney *et al.* (2002*a*) analysed the impact of four ICT enabled scenarios by investigating the bullwhip effect using two different delivery management approaches and comparing them to a traditional supply chain. The first approach is based on an analysis of the results of the management flight simu-lator, the Beer Game. The second approach is based on a quantitative *z*-transform analysis using the tools highlighted by Disney and Towill (2002*b*).

The five supply chain strategies considered are:

traditional—in which there are four 'serially linked' echelons in the supply chain. Each echelon only receives information on local stock levels and sales.

Each echelon then places an order onto its supplier based on local stock, sales, and previous 'orders placed but not yet received'.

e-shopping—the scenario where the manufacturer receives orders directly from the end consumers (possibly via the Internet like Dell) and ships the product directly to them after the production and distribution lead time. Thus, this simple supply chain strategy has exactly the same fundamental structure as a single echelon traditional supply chain.

echelon reduction—where an echelon in the supply chain had been removed. This is representative of, say, the Amazon.com supply chain, where the retailer echelon is bypassed. This is a supply chain that has used ICT to eliminate an echelon in the supply chain. Wikner, Towill, and Naim (1991) have identified echelon removal as an effective mechanism for improving supply chain dynamics.

Vendor Managed Inventory (VMI)—that is simulated by developing a protocol positioned between two businesses in the supply chain that gives the necessary inventory and sales information, authority, and responsibility to the supplier in order to manage the customer's inventory.

Electronic Point of Sales (EPOS)—where information from the marketplace is transmitted to all enterprises in the supply chain. This is equivalent to the situation in many grocery supply chains, where the EPOS data is available electronically via the Internet, either directly from the retailer or via a third party, which can be used by supply chain members to generate their own forecasts. Specifically, in this strategy, the end consumer sales may be used by each echelon for their own planning purposes, but each echelon still has to deliver (if possible) what was ordered by their immediate customer. A full-scale investigation of this strategy has been conducted using z-transforms by Dejonckheere *et al.* (2001*b*) inspired by the simulation approach of Mason-Jones (1998).

6. Analysis of before game results

The five supply chain scenarios researched are summarized in Fig. 5.6. Hong-Minh, Disney, and Naim (2000) analysed the results from four different teams playing different supply chain management strategies, one of which was the EPOS scenario previously described. Even though the research literature implies great benefits for information sharing (Mason-Jones and Towill 1997), surprisingly the EPOS strategy yielded the worst result. While the EPOS strategy limited the degree of bullwhip in the supply chain this was at the expense of long periods of backlogs (negative net stock). It was concluded that, although market information was shared with all echelons in the supply chain without any delays, each player of the supply chain had their own insular ordering rule. That is, there was no collaboration between the different players.

To test the hypothesis that although sharing market information is potentially a good thing it will only yield benefits as part of an agreed overall supply

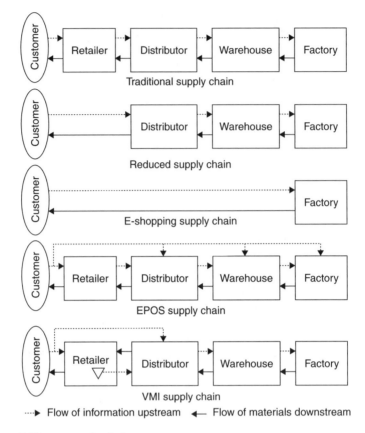

Fig. 5.6. Different supply chain structures
Source: Disney *et al.* (2002).

chain decision-making strategy (Mason-Jones 1998), the EPOS strategy was rerun by Disney, Naim, and Potter (2002*a*) but with the added characteristic that all players were involved in collaborative planning, forecasting, and replenishment; in other words, CPFR.

While different measures of performance were collected from the game they have been summarized according to Equation 1 (Chen *et al.* 2000):

$$\text{Bullwhip}^i = \frac{\sigma^2_{\text{ORATE}^i}/\mu_{\text{ORATE}^i}}{\sigma^2_{\text{CONS}}/\mu_{\text{CONS}}} = \frac{\sigma^2_{\text{ORATE}^i}}{\sigma^2_{\text{CONS}}} \tag{1}$$

which gives the bullwhip measure, the coefficient of variation, at echelon *i*, where σ^2 is the variance and μ is the mean of the end consumer sales (CONS) or the order rate (ORATE) at echelon *i*.

Table 5.1. Sample Beer Game results

Supply chain	Inventory cost ranking	Bullwhip			
		Retailer	Distributor	Warehouse	Factory
e-shopping	First	—	—	—	1.50
Reduced	Second	1.00		0.99	0.93
EPOS–CPFR	Third	1.92	1.37	0.99	0.49
VMI	Fourth		3.42	4.68	4.44
EPOS–no CPFR	Not applicable	1.85	0.83	0.55	0.69

Source: Disney *et al.* (2002), rankings based on cumulative inventory costs over length of a game.

Summary results from the game are shown in Table 5.1. The inventory costs are shown as a relative ranking achieved and normalized so as to be independent of the number of actual echelons in a particular supply chain strategy. We are, therefore, penalizing those supply chains with fewer echelons. Also, two EPOS results are shown. The first is that played in the research described in this paper and has been defined as EPOS–CPFR. The second (named EPOS–no CPFR) is based on the results recorded by Hong-Minh, Disney, and Naim (2000).

EPOS–CPFR again does well at minimizing, and in fact is reducing, bullwhip in the supply chain. But, as with EPOS–no CPFR, a price is paid in inventory costs, which is primarily attributable to the supply chain having long periods of stock out. Despite the normalization of the inventory costs it is evident that a strategy that eliminates an echelon, or a number of echelons, still outperforms alternatives. As has been previously reported (see, for example, Wikner, Towill, and Naim 1991) eliminating an echelon removes both a decision point and reduces total lead times in one fell swoop. Clearly this double benefit has been achieved.

Even more surprising than the EPOS–CPFR result is that the VMI scenario had both the worst inventory holding costs and the worst bullwhip. It was evident in the game de-briefing that, despite the provision of well-documented protocols, the players had problems in implementing the concept. It is also evident that even in a CPFR scenario if too much focus is given to a single measure (in these scenarios, bullwhip) then this can be to the detriment of other performance indices such as stock holding and product availability.

Disney, Naim, and Potter (2002*a*) took two different approaches to understand the impact of ICT on supply chain dynamics. The *z*-transform analysis indicates that there is an expectation that the innovative use of ICT will outperform alternative strategies. But the Beer Game results have indicated that ICT adds a degree of complexity to human decision-making that is difficult to cope with even if well-defined protocols are provided. There is simply too much information and too many calculations for the human scheduler to manage.

The Beer Game also indicates that poor management of the ICT protocols leads to increased inventory costs. We conclude that although the Beer Game is a simulated and simplified environment, much like the real world people have to make decisions the consequences of which are not immediately known. As Sterman (1989) has indicated, people are not good at making decisions in such an environment. In using the passing-on-order algorithm as a benchmark, Sterman (1989) demonstrated that the majority of human decision-makers in his large sample performed much worse than this target in terms of stock fluctuations along the chain.

But the good news is that he also established via the same criterion, that a few human decision-makers performed much better than this standard. So the search is always for this top performance to be modelled and automated by a DSS. This is particularly important when the business is dealing with many thousands of stock keeping units all of which need to be kept under control. In such a situation the DSS need to operate automatically for the mast majority of items. While ICT offers the opportunity for greater supply chain transparency it also creates an even more complex environment so that when people do have to intervene, the decision-making is even more difficult.

7. What we do not know: gaps in our understanding and priorities for research

We still do not understand the dynamic implications of ordering structures and rules afforded by different ICT current and future scenarios. Historically, a number of authors have developed dynamic model representations of innovative system structures and have described their behaviour. Although a number of these models were physically infeasible or too costly to implement at the time, with current ICT innovations there is a need to revisit them.

An example of a hierarchy within a known system structure for a decision rule within a single business unit of analysis (managing many process streams) is given in Fig. 5.7 (Evans, Naim, and Towill 1998). Figure 5.7 shows the progressive development of the system structure. Each additional information source added in the system structure, while having the potential for improved dynamic behaviour, increases complexity. Therefore, the benefits of increased information flow must outweigh the potential for the system to go unstable either if it is not

- designed properly
- robust to parameter drift.

A comprehensive hierarchical suite of system structures needs to be derived and tested that determine the ordering and inventory policy requirements for various units of analysis with due consideration of varying market and operational environments. This coincides with Hill's (2000) order-winner and

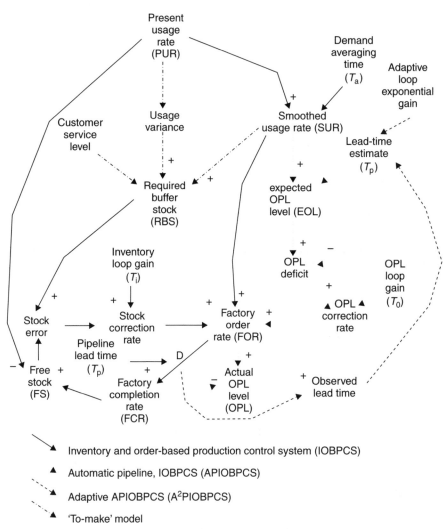

Fig. 5.7. Hierarchy within an adaptive ordering and inventory control model

Source: Evans *et al.* (1998).

order-qualifier criteria and the trade-off considerations required in process choice. The latter has recently been consolidated within a supply chain context and related to the lean and agile characteristics (Naylor, Naim, and Berry 1999).

Different units of analysis need to be considered. At the lowest level we may analyse individual activities that constitute a work process which in themselves aggregate to a business process (Watson 1994). Further aggregation yields an

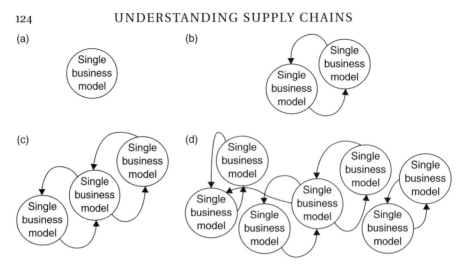

Fig. 5.8. Supply system units of analysis (a) Single Unit, (b) dyadic structure, (c) supply chain structure, and (d) network structure

Source: Based on Harland (1996).

entire business unit, dyadic relationship, supply chain and ultimately a whole supply network as indicated in Fig. 5.8 (based on Harland 1996).

8. Future key developments

This chapter highlights the need for systematic approaches to the introduction of ICT in the supply chain. An important phase in many change programmes is the need to simplify existing complex operations. As a Director of Reckitt and Colman stated (Parmenter 1989), 'Good managers can manage complexity but better managers simplify'.

The simplicity paradigm is a powerful model but only within an overall systematic regime. Failure to understand what needs to be simplified, can again be detrimental to effective operations (de Bono 1998).

We propose the approach recently highlighted by Thomke (2001) in the area of product design innovation but to be applied here in the area for supply system design innovation. The ability to develop synthetic environments via behavioural, analytical, and simulation tools allows 'crashes' to be performed early on in the innovation process prior to their piloting or implementation in the 'real-world'. An innovation process should develop synthetic environments to allow experimentation with different supply system architectures to aid in detecting counterintuitive behaviour (Sterman 1989; Thomke 2001) and spurring even greater innovation. Thomke (in line with the system dynamics movement, for example, Wolstenholme 1990) also highlights the impact of synthetic environments in developing the spirit of enquiry in multidisciplinary teams.

Appropriate, sustainable, and adaptable innovation processes will thus be developed incorporating strategic design tools. It may be feasible to develop the models outside of the innovation process and implement them within the planning and operation order fulfilment process. Thus, 'real-time' models, interfacing with the latest ICT developments that capture information of the different supply system states, such as production rates, inventory levels, and work-in-progress levels, will ensure the efficient, efficacious, and effective flow of materials throughout the supply chain. Novel and innovative system structures and evaluation tools need to be developed that consider the dichotomy of increased information flows versus increased complexity in the supply system. These will challenge or validate the suppositions of complexity theory and ascertain the role of control theory in deriving 'optimal' solutions.

By 'optimal' we mean systems that meet a number of criteria including satisfying customer value requirements (summarized as cost, lead time, service, and quality), making the best use of operational capabilities (such as capacity limitations and human resource capabilities) and ensuring robustness to exogenous and endogenous perturbations.

Through the development of archetypes a 'system of systems' will be developed. Each level of aggregation will have defined dynamic behaviour characteristics related to organizational behaviour models, ICT frameworks, management principles, and various financial forms. A case based scheme that manages to incorporate the intricacies of the archetypes needs to be developed. Artificial intelligence tools, with the associated theoretical infrastructure, such decision theories, probability theory, and set theory, will have to be developed to manage the possible complexity of the archetype knowledge base.

The substantive theory underpinning this chapter, and indeed the whole book, is GST. This may be summarized as 'Gestalt'—the whole is greater than the sum of the individual parts. GST should pervade all branches of science and all human endeavours. It should encompass not only our working environment but also all our social relationships. Within the specific area of supply chain dynamics modelling and simulation there are specific technical core competencies that either have to be embedded within an organization or 'bought in' through appropriate routes. This means the development of system engineers with the ability to relate GST, analytical studies, and practical operations.

9. The scope model as a research platform

A robust research framework, based on an holistic approach, is required to support the above future research needs. The unit of analysis previously described is just one dimension of the scope of the research platform we propose. Supply chain dynamics research is, in reality, a three-dimensional

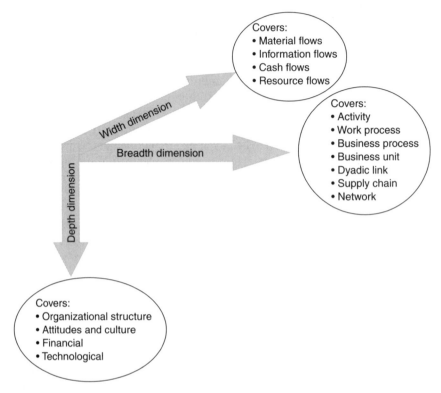

Fig. 5.9. The Scope Model as a platform for supply system dynamics research
Source: Based on Evans *et al.* (1999).

problem. Figure 5.9 shows the *Scope Model* developed for this purpose (Evans, Mason-Jones, and Towill 1999) that describes

breadth—the primary axis that determines the unit of analysis as already discussed;
width—that determines the flows to be considered in any given unit of analysis;
depth—the change management factors that enable the implementation of innovative solutions.

The depth dimension highlights the need for multidisciplinary teams in undertaking the research.

This Scope Model emphasizes that tackling individual elements in a supply chain will have limited benefit to the chain as a whole (Hall, Rosenthal, and Wade 1993). Instead, a holistic approach is required which integrates along each dimension, and yet simultaneously welds the activities across dimensions. The Scope Model makes it transparent, for example, that material flows cannot be managed in isolation of each other. But neither can they be managed just within discrete functional silos if the total chain is to benefit. And all this is pointless without the right supporting organizational, financial, technological, and cultural infrastructure.

Computer packages, coupled with increased computing power are now available that are specifically designed to study the dynamic performance of supply chains. This allows a step change in sophistication that can be incorporated into a control systems analysis. This has come at a time when computers have also enabled sophisticated control systems to be developed (such as VMI), as ICT allows efficient gathering and distributing of large amounts of information.

Such research will, for the first time, quantify the benefits of ICT technologies, such as e-business, on product delivery from raw materials to the end customer. It will take 'hard' analytical studies and relate them to the current and future scenarios envisaged for ICT enabled customer-driven enterprises. A research process will have to be defined that incorporates fundamental concepts and theories, action research and development, implementation change programmes, and monitoring studies.

10. Consequences and conclusions

This chapter has indicated the extent of our current knowledge base in the field of supply chain dynamics. There is an abundant and rich history to the modelling and synthesis of supply control systems going back at least 50 years. Mathematical and simulation techniques originally developed for the design and control of hardware systems have found applications in production, inventory and ordering systems.

It is our view that the 'social capital' associated with our field of endeavour is almost lost to us as the technical knowledge base of the United Kingdom, and in fact much of the Western world, has differentiated between 'engineering' and 'management'. A number of organizations do have the competencies to undertake the analytical studies required and implement them in their operations. Unfortunately, such organizations are few and far between. As Sir Karl Popper said, 'It is often better to be vaguely right than precisely wrong'. In focusing on computers for data processing we may be in danger of overlooking those principles of system design which guarantee stable and successful operation. In other words we see the detail at the expense of the architecture.

The problem of system complexity is very real and as we have shown has the potential to increase with the addition of ICT enabled data flows. Solutions have to be developed that not only strive to cope with complexity but also must endeavour to simplify where possible. Horizontal research studies will not shed any light on such matters due to averaging effects (Fisher 1997). Vertical and longitudinal action research is required to address the operational realities of organizations (Coughlan and Coghlan 2002). Emerging paradigms will be tested using a procedure already evaluated on the Time Compression Principle (Towill 1999).

The research will require a breadth of disciplines and approaches involving both observation and problem solving. The research will bring together

- Business and management studies
- Systems and process thinking
- Engineering and technology.

That is, there is a need for Business Systems Engineering of ICT enabled supply systems.

References

ARROW, K. J. (2002). 'The Genesis of Optimal Inventory Policy'. *Operations Research*, 50/1: 1–2.

AXSÄTER, S. (1985). 'Control Theory Concepts in Production and Inventory Control'. *International Journal of Systems Science*, 16/2: 161–69.

BERRY, D., EVANS, G. E., and NAIM, M. M. (1998). 'Pipeline Information Survey: A UK Perspective'. *Omega*, 26/1: 115–131.

BONNEY, M. C., and POPPLEWELL, K. (1988). 'Design of Production Control Systems: Choice of Systems Structure and Systems Implementation Sequence'. *Engineering Costs and Production Economics*, 15: 169–73.

BURBIDGE, J. (1984). 'Automated Production Control With a Simulation Capability'. Copenhagen: Proc. IPSP Conf. WG 5–7.

BURNS, J. F., and SIVAZLIAN, B. D. (1978). 'Dynamic Analysis of Multi-echelon Supply Systems'. *Computer and Industrial Engineering*, 2/4: 181–93.

CACHON, G., and FISHER, M. (1997). 'Campbell Soup's Continuous Replenishment Program: Evaluation and Enhanced Inventory Decision Rules'. *Production and Operations Management*, 6/3: 266–76.

CHEEMA, P. (1994). 'Dynamic Analysis of an Inventory and Production Control System with an Adaptive Lead-time Estimator'. Ph.D. Dissertation, Cardiff University.

CHEN, F., DREZNER, Z., RYAN, J. K., and SIMCHI-LEVI, D. (2000). 'Quantifying the Bullwhip Effect in a Simple Supply Chain: The Impact of Forecasting, Lead-times and Information'. *Management Science*, 46/3: 436–43.

—— RYAN, J. K., and SIMCHI-LEVI, D. (2000). 'The Impact of Exponential Smoothing Forecasts on the Bullwhip Effect'. *Naval Research Logistics*, 47/4: 269–86.

CHRISTOPHER, M., and TOWILL, D. R. (2000). 'Supply Chain Migration From Lean and Functional to Agile and Customised'. *International Journal of Supply Chain Management*, 5/4: 206–13.

COUGHLAN, P., and COGHLAN, D. (2002). 'Action Research for Operations Management'. *International Journal of Operations and Production Management*, 22/2: 220–40.

COYLE, R. G. (1982). 'Assessing the Controllability of a Production and Raw Materials System'. *IEEE Transactions on Systems, Man and Cybernetics*, SMC-12/6: 867–76.

DE BONO, E. D. (1998). *Simplicity*. London: Viking, Penguin Books.

DEJONCKHEERE, J., DISNEY, S. M., LAMBRECHT. M. R., and TOWILL, D. R. (2003). 'Measuring the Bullwhip Effect: A Control Theoretic Approach and Avoiding. *European Journal of Operations Research*, 147/3: 567–90.

—— —— —— —— (2004). 'The Impact of Information Enrichment on the Bullwhip Effect in Supply Chains: A Control Engineering Perspective'. *European Journal of Operations Research*, 153/3: 727–50.

DeWinter, R. E. (1966). 'Inventory Applications of Servo-mechanism Models', M.Sc. Thesis, United States Naval Postgraduate School.

Deziel, D. P., and Eilon, S. (1967). 'A Linear Production-inventory Control Rule'. *The Production Engineer*, 43: 93–104.

Disney, S. M. (2001). 'The Production and Inventory Control Problem in Vendor Managed Inventory Supply Chains', Ph.D. Thesis, Cardiff University, UK: Cardiff Business School.

—— —— and Potter, A. (2002a). 'Assessing the Impact of E-business on Supply Chain Dynamics'. Proceedings of the Twelfth International Working Conference on Production Economics, Igls, Austria.

—— and Towill, D. R. (2002b). 'A Discrete Linear Control Theory Model to Determine the Dynamic Stability of Vendor Managed Inventory Supply Chains'. *International Journal of Production Research*, 40/1: 179–204.

—— Naim, M. M., and Towill, D. R. (1997). 'Dynamic Simulation Modelling for Lean Logistics'. *International Journal of Physical Distribution and Logistics Management*, 27/3: 174–96.

Edghill, J. S., and Towill, D. R. (1989a). 'The Use of Systems Dynamics in Manufacturing Systems'. *Trans Inst MC*, 11/4: 208–16.

Evans, G. N., Naim, M. M., and Towill, D. R. (1998). 'Application of a Simulation Methodology to the Redesign of a Logistical Control System'. *International Journal of Production Economics*, 56–7: 157–68.

—— Mason-Jones, R., and Towill, D. R. (1999). 'The Scope Paradigm of Business Process Re-engineering'. *Business Process Management Journal*, 5/2: 121–35.

Fisher, M. (1997). 'What is the Right Supply Chain for Your Product?' *Harvard Business Review*, 75/2: 105–16.

Forrester, J. (1958). 'Industrial Dynamics: A Major Breakthrough for Decision Makers'. *Harvard Business Review*, 36/4: 37–66.

—— (1961). *Industrial Dynamics*. Cambridge, MA: MIT Press.

Fransoo, J. C., and Wouters, M. J. F. (2000). 'Measuring the Bullwhip Effect in the Supply Chain'. *Supply Chain Management: An International Journal*, 5/2: 78–89.

Gardner, M., and Ashby, W. R. (1970). 'Connectance of Large Dynamic (Cybernetic) Systems: Critical Values for Stability'. *Nature*, 228/12: 784.

Griffiths, M., Hafeez, K., and Naim, M. M. (1993). *Use of Statistical Techniques in the Dynamic Modelling of an Industrial Supply Chain*. UMIST, Manchester UK: 30th MATADOR Conference, 413–22.

Grubbström, R. W. (1996). 'Stochastic Properties of a Production-Inventory Process with Planned Production Using Transform Methodology'. *International Journal of Production Economics*, 45/1–3: 407–19.

Hall, G., Rosenthal, J., and Wade, J. (1993). 'How to Make Re-Engineering Really Happen'. *Harvard Business Review*, 71/6: 119–31.

Harland, C. M. (1996). 'Supply Chain Management: Relationships, Chains and Networks'. *British Journal of Management*, 7 (Special Issue): S63–S80.

Hill, T. (2000). *Operations Management: Strategic Context and Managerial Analysis*. Basingstoke: MacMillan Business.

HOLMSTRÖM, J. (1997). 'Product Range Management: A Case Study of Supply Chain Operations in the European Grocery Industry'. *Supply Chain Management*, 2/3: 107–15.

—— (1998). 'Business Process Innovation in the Supply Chain: A Case Study of Implementing Vendor Managed Inventory'. *European Journal of Purchasing and Supply Management*, 4/2–3: 127–31.

HONG-MINH, S. M., DISNEY, S. M., and NAIM, M. M. (2000). 'The Dynamics of Emergency Transhipment Supply Chains'. *International Journal of Physical Distribution and Logistics Management*, 30/9: 788–815.

HOULIHAN, J. B. (1987). 'International Supply Chain Management'. *International Journal of Physical Distribution and Materials Management*, 17/2: 51–66.

JOHNSON, G., and THOMPSON, H. (1975). 'Optimality of Myopic Inventory Policies for Certain Dependent Demand Processes'. *Management Science*, 21/11: 1303–7.

JONES, D. T., and SIMONS, D. (2000). 'Future Directions for the Supply Side of ECR', in D. Corsten and D. T. Jones (eds.), *ECR the Third Millennium—Academic Perspectives on the Future of Consumer Goods Industry*, 34–40.

KAIPIA, R., HOLMSTRÖM, J., and TANSKANEN, K. (2000). 'VMI: What Are You Losing if You Let Your Customer Place Orders'. Working Paper, Dept of Industrial Management. Finland: Helsinki University of Technology.

KARLIN, S. (1960). 'One Stage Inventory Models With Uncertainty', in K. Arrow, S. Karlin, and P. Suppes (eds.), *Mathematical Methods in the Social Sciences*. Stanford, CA: Stanford University Press.

KIDD, P. (1977). *Agile Manufacturing: Forging New Frontiers*. Great Britain: Addison-Wesley.

KRAMER, N. J. T. A., and DE SMIT, J. (1977). *Systems Thinking*. Leiden: Martinus Nijhoff Social Sciences Division.

LAMBRECHT, M. R., and DEJONCKHEERE, J. (1999a). *A Bullwhip Effect Explorer, Research Report 9910*, Katholieke Universiteit, Leuven, Belgium: Department of Applied Economics.

—— —— (1999b). 'Extending the Beer Game to Include Real-Life Supply Chain Characteristics'. *Proceedings of EUROMA International Conference On Managing Operations Networks*: 237–43.

LEE, H. L., PADMANABHAN, P., and WHANG, S. (1997a). 'Information Distortion in a Supply Chain: the Bullwhip Effect'. *Management Science*, 43/4: 546–58.

—— —— —— (1997b). 'The Bullwhip Effect in Supply Chains'. *Sloan Management Review*, 38/3: 93–102.

—— So, K. C., and TANG, C. S. (2000). 'The Value of Information Sharing in a Two-Level Supply Chain'. *Management Science*, 46/5: 626–43.

LEWIS, J. C. (1997). 'An Integrated Approach to Re-Engineering Material Flow Within a Seamless Supply Chain: The Evolutionary Development of a Human-resource Centred Approach to Managing Material Flows Across the Customer–Supplier Interface', Ph.D. Thesis, Cardiff University.

MASON-JONES, R. (1998). 'The Holistic Strategy of Market Information Enrichment Through the Supply Chain', Ph.D. Thesis, Cardiff University.

—— and TOWILL, D. R. (1997). 'Information Enrichment: Designing the Supply Chain for Competitive Advantage'. *International Journal of Supply Chain Management*, 2/4: 137–48.

McCULLEN, P., and TOWILL, D. R. (2001). 'Achieving Lean Supply Through Agile Manufacturing'. *International Journal of Manufacturing Technology and Management*, 12/7: 524–33.

NAIM, M. M., and TOWILL, D. R. (1994). 'Establishing a Framework for Effective Materials Logistics Management'. *International Journal of Logistics Management*, 5/1: 81–8.

NAYLOR, J. B., NAIM, M. M., and BERRY, D. (1999). 'Leagility: Integrating the Lean and Agile Manufacturing Paradigms in the Total Supply Chain'. *International Journal of Production Economics*, 62/1–2: 107–18.

PARMENTER, O. (1989). *Restructuring and Manufacturing Strategy*. Manufacturing Strategy and Success Conference, London: The Strategic Planning Society.

PEPPERS, D., and ROGERS, M. (1998). *Enterprise 1–2–1: Tools for Building Unbreakable Customer Relationships in the Interactive Age*. London: Piatkus.

PINE, B. J. (1993). *Mass Customisation*. Cambridge, MA: Harvard Business School Press.

POPPLEWELL, K., and BONNEY, M. C. (1987). 'The Application of Discrete Linear Control Theory to the Analysis of Multi-product, Multi-level Production Control Systems'. *International Journal of Production Research*, 25/1: 45–56.

SCARF, H. (1960). 'The Optimality of (s,S) Policies in the Dynamic Inventory Problem', in K. Arrow, S. Karlin, and P. Suppes (eds.), *Mathematical Methods in the Social Sciences*. Stanford, CA: Stanford University Press.

SENGE, P. M. (1990). *The Fifth Discipline*. London: Century Business Books.

SHANNON, C. E., OLIVER, B. M., and PIERCE, J. R. (1948). 'The Philosophy of Pulse Code Modulation'. *Proceedings of the IRE*, 36/11: 1324–31.

SHAPIRO, S. M. (2001). *24/7 Innovation—A Blue Print for Surviving and Thriving in an Age of Change*. New York: McGraw-Hill.

SIMCHI-LEVI, D., KAMINSKY, P., and SIMCHI-LEVI, E. (2000). Designing and Managing the Supply Chain. Boston: Irwin McGraw-Hill.

SIMON, H. A. (1952). 'On the Application of Servomechanism Theory to the Study of Production Control'. *Econometrica*, 20/1: 247–68.

STALK, G., and HOUT, T. M. (1990). *Competing Against Time: How Time-based Competition is Reshaping Global Markets*. New York: The Free Press.

STERMAN, J. (1989). 'Modelling Managerial Behaviour: Misperceptions of Feedback in a Dynamic Decision Making Experiment'. *Management Science*, 35/3: 321–39.

THOMKE, S. (2001). 'Enlightened Experimentation: the New Imperative for Innovation'. *Harvard Business Review*, 79/2: 67–76.

TOWILL, D. R. (1982). 'Dynamic Analysis of an Inventory and Order Based Production Control System'. *International Journal of Production Research*, 20/6: 369–83.

—— (1997). 'FORRIDGE—Principles of Good Practice in Material Flow'. *International Journal of Production Planning and Control*, 8/7: 622–32.

—— (1999). 'Management Theory—is it of Any Practical Use?' *IEE Management Journal*, 9/3: 111–21.

—— LAMBRECHT, M. R., DISNEY, S. M., and DEJONCKEERE, J. (2003). 'Explicit Filters and Supply Chain Design'. *Journal of Purchasing and Supply Management*, 9/2: 73–81.

VAN ACKERE, A., LARSEN, E. R., and MORECROFT, J. D. W. (1993). 'Systems Thinking and Business Process Redesign: An Application to the Beer Game'. *European Management Journal*, 11/4: 412–23.

VASSIAN, H. J. (1955). 'Application of Discrete Variable Servo Theory to Inventory Control'. *Journal of the Operations Research Society of America*, 3/3: 272–82.

VEINOTT, A. F. Jr. (1965). 'Optimal Policy for a Multi-product, Dynamic, Non-stationary Inventory Problem'. *Management Science*, 12/3: 206–22.

WATSON, G. H. (1994). *Business Systems Engineering: Managing Breakthrough Changes for Productivity and Profit*. New York: John Wiley and Sons Inc.

WALLER, M., JOHNSON, M. E., and DAVIS, T. (1999). 'Vendor Managed Inventory in the Retail Supply Chain'. *Journal of Business Logistics*, 20/1: 183–203.

WIKNER, J., TOWILL, D. R., and NAIM, M. M. (1991). 'Smoothing Supply Chain Dynamics'. *International Journal of Production Economics*, 22/3: 231–48.

WOLSTENHOLME, E. (1990). *System Enquiry: A System Dynamics Approach*. Chichester: JohnWiley.

WOMACK, J. P., and JONES, D. T. (1996). *Lean Thinking*. New York: Simon and Schuster.

6

Supply Chain Complexity

SUJA SIVADASAN, JANET EFSTATHIOU, ANI CALINESCU, AND
LUISA HUACCHO HUATUCO

1. Introduction

The concept of the supply chain as an entity that enables companies and commercial organizations to carry out business functions has become well established. The enablers and inhibitors of those business functions may also be identified within the social and economic relationships that exist between the many participants in the network of suppliers and customers that fulfil the goal of delivering goods to the ultimate consumer.

Modern views of supply chain management emphasize the need for close integration between suppliers and customers, moving away from the adversarial relationships of the past. Adversarial relationships were seen as causing, among other things

(1) poor quality goods;
(2) delays in movement of goods and information along the supply chain;
(3) lack of commitment and therefore investment by suppliers;
(4) lack of incentive to innovate and improve processes and products;
(5) poor understanding of customers' and suppliers' constraints.

The movement away from adversarial relationships towards closer integration and partnerships helped to alleviate many of these problems, but as companies sought to integrate their manufacturing, scheduling, and communications, the old problems were replaced with new problems. Many of the new problems were worse for being unanticipated and of an altogether different nature from those seen in the past.

A project was undertaken as a collaboration between the Universities of Oxford and Cambridge to see if it would be possible to measure some of the features of organizations that would contribute to the integration difficulties of willing supply chain partners. The project was undertaken by members of the Engineering Departments of both universities, rather than academics from Business Schools or other Social Science departments. As a result, the project emphasized rigorous mathematical modelling of the process of communicating along the supply chain with the development and application of an objective process of carrying out the measurement process. The goal was to develop a methodology that could

(1) be applied rigorously and formally by any organization;
(2) identify the causes of problems in the flow of information and/or material along the supply chain;
(3) enable organizations to understand aspects of their own behaviour and those of their partners that caused difficulties in achieving smooth integration;
(4) support organizations to remove these problems and assess the likely improvements that would follow as a result.

The model that was developed as a result of this project is based on the application of entropy and information theory to the modelling of the supply chain. Information theory is used to quantify the expected amount of information that would be needed to describe deviations in production and delivery of products along the supply chain. When deviations occur or are anticipated, organizations need to take action to protect onward deliveries to their customers. In essence, these actions are different versions of strategies to cope with the extra entropy that is caused as a result of the deviations from plan.

This chapter will present in some detail our model and findings from a project to help understand transactions along the supply chain. Principally, we present an information theoretic method for integrating the measurement of information and material flows. Section 2 presents background material and the role of complexity in supply chains. Section 3 introduces information theory and develops the formal mathematical background to descriptions and analysis of complexity. Section 4 develops the model, showing how complexity is transferred along the supply chain. Of particular relevance are the ways in which complexity can be imported and exported to organizations, and the implications for organizations that are participating in a supply network. Policies that organizations may adopt for protecting themselves from the undesirable aspects of complexity are discussed in the concluding paragraphs of Section 4.4. Section 5 introduces briefly a methodology for measuring complexity in a supply chain and presents some generic findings from a case study recently completed. The chapter ends with a summary and conclusion.

2. Background

2.1. Models of supply chains

The simplest possible model of a supply chain is of a linear structure of suppliers and customers, with one supplier to each customer and one customer for each

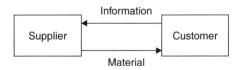

Fig. 6.1. The simplest possible model of a supply chain

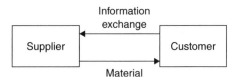

Fig. 6.2. Several stages of information exchange occur at the interface before the material transfer stage

supplier. Information flows from the customer to the supplier and goods flow from the supplier to the customer (see Fig. 6.1). However, reality is more complex than that. The structure of the supply chain is more like a network, with many suppliers to each customer and many customers for each supplier, and the pattern of communication between supplier and customer consists of more than one-way opposed flows of information and material.

In a commodity-based supply chain, it may happen that the products are freely available, and the customer places a request to the market for a quantity of standard products, which are delivered to the agreed quantity and at the agreed time, price, and location. However, for more specialized products, negotiation may take place prior to the agreement of the order, with requirements being communicated by the customer, followed by quotes from the supplier. At some point a contract is specified and agreed.

However, the transmission of information does not end there, with further two-way communication between customer and supplier still possible after placement of the contract. The supplier may communicate to the customer with progress reports on the agreed schedule of delivery, providing warning of any foreseen delays or difficulties with meeting agreed quantities or times of delivery. The customer may also initiate requests to the customer for changes to the agreed quantity or time, or even with requests for a different product altogether. The supplier will then respond to these change requests from the customer, establishing another round of negotiation and communication. The contact between customer and supplier, prior to delivery of goods, may be summarized as in Fig. 6.2. Between agreement of contract and delivery of goods, the communication may be summarized as transmission of schedules from the supplier to the customer and change requests or responses to schedule changes passing from the customer to the supplier.

But the story does not end with the delivery of the goods. The goods might not be what the customer was expecting, because they are the wrong product, or have been delivered in the wrong quantity in the wrong place at the wrong time. The customer might not agree to pay the price originally understood by the supplier, so the final stage of the contract (the exchange of money) may also require further communication. Money may have to be sent back from supplier to customer as a result of penalty clauses being invoked or the customer returning faulty or unwanted goods.

To summarize, the communication of information, material, and finance is much more complex than that suggested by the usual simple model of opposed flows of information and goods. The issue of interest in this chapter is how to identify and measure the impact of these complex flows and their value to the participating organizations.

2.2. The transmission of complexity

Our model of the flow of information and material along the supply chain focuses on the deviations between what was planned or expected to happen, and what actually happened. These deviations may be identified by examining the records kept or documents generated, by the participating organizations, often in the form of schedules or updating reports.

This approach recognizes the fact that when one organization introduces a change to a planned state of affairs, the organizations with which it does business, be they customer or supplier, will also have to bear the consequences of this change. These changes may have severe effects on organizations, since they do not have the resources to cope with the changes that are being imposed upon them. We have long been aware of the Beer Game (Sterman 1992) and the effects it demonstrates. A small change in the orders requested by the consumer at the end of the supply chain induces huge swings in the orders placed at the factory located at the other end of the chain.

The kinds of effects that are caused by changes in the schedules or orders can be far-reaching and expensive. Changes to orders may have to be made to other suppliers upstream, and other supply chain partners may have their deliveries affected in an effort to accommodate the requested changes. Internally, the organization may have to adjust its schedules, moving other customers' orders later or changing the lot sizes, routings, specifications, etc. Other effects will be discussed in more detail in Section 3.1.

However, an organization can choose not to transmit or absorb complexity. By refusing to accept change requests, it can reduce the amount of complexity it accepts, although it may still be prone to complexity transmission from its suppliers, who may be unable to deliver as scheduled. This may not be a widely accepted situation, since an organization would need to be capable of performing predictably and consistently to a very high level before its trading partners would be willing to accept a very rigid 'no changes' policy. Typically, organizations have a *quid pro quo* working arrangement, where minor problems or deviations from schedule by either side are overlooked.

2.3. *Supply chain complexity*

Complexity can be associated with systems that are difficult to understand, describe, predict, or control. We will define complexity in a precise formal sense in Section 3, but this section will consider the contributing aspects of complexity within an organization. In general, the complexity of a supply chain can be described in terms of several interconnected aspects of the supply chain system, including

(1) number of elements or subsystems;
(2) degree of order within the structure of elements or subsystems;
(3) degree of interaction or connectivity between the elements, subsystems and the environment;
(4) level of variety, in terms of the different types of elements, subsystems, and interactions; and
(5) degree of predictability and uncertainty within the system.

For the purposes of analysis, two classes of complexity can be defined: structural and operational. The structural complexity is defined by Frizelle and Woodcock (1995) as that associated with the static variety characteristics of a system and by Deshmukh (Deshmukh, Talavage, and Barash 1998) as that linked to the static design dimensions of the system. Operational complexity can be defined as the uncertainty associated with the dynamic system (Frizelle and Woodcock 1995; Frizelle 1998; Sivadasan *et al.* 1999*a*). A measure of operational complexity should accordingly capture behavioural uncertainty of the system with respect to a specified level of control.

In a dynamic environment such as the supply chain, even basic supplier–customer systems with structurally simple information and material flow formations have a tendency to exhibit operational complexity. The operational complexity of supplier–customer systems is associated with the uncertainty of information and material flows within and across organizations (Sivadasan *et al.* 1999*b*, 2002*a*). Operational complexity can be observed within organizations on a daily basis in the form of *ad hoc* orders, unreliable deliveries, changes to what has been ordered, alterations to specifications, and other unpredicted variations in information and material flows across supplier–customer interfaces (Sivadasan *et al.* 1999*a*, 2000).

Supply chains are inherently complex from both structural and operational perspectives. Supply chains display the characteristics of complex systems in that a large number of firms operate simultaneously with many supply partners, interacting through a variety of information and material flows in an uncertain way. These characteristics of supply chains also govern the complex nature of individual supplier–customer systems.

The complexity of a supply chain can be examined further by considering

(1) the complexity of the internal organization;
(2) the complexity at the supplier–customer interface; and
(3) the complexity associated with the dynamic environment.

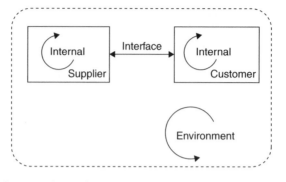

Fig. 6.3. Complexity analysis of supplier–customer systems

Please see Fig. 6.3. We shall discuss these three aspects of supply chain complexity below.

Complexity of the internal organization. The internal complexity of manufacturing organizations can be considered in terms of the individual complexities of product characteristics, of operational processes, and of organizational structures.

The internal complexity of a manufacturing system is closely tied to the characteristics of the products that it manufactures, both in terms of the variety of product categories and the intrinsically complex nature of the products. Organizations including Procter and Gamble and Unilever have focused on reducing product variety through product range rationalization and pack standardization. For managing intrinsic product complexity, the factors to be considered include:

(1) hierarchy of the product structure, which is influenced by the number, variety, and level of product subsystems, as defined in the Bill of Materials (BOM);

(2) degree of technological novelty, which captures the extent of incomplete information;

(3) grade of functionality, which includes the number, nature, and degree of user variety and specificity;

(4) level of interconnectivity, which includes the relationships across subsystems in terms of components and across disciplines;

(5) project constraints, which include constraints on lead times and resources.

In practice, organizations deal with a mix of these product characteristics, across a variety of products, which change over time.

Complex products embody more information than simple products and so require closer monitoring and greater control. Organizations on the one hand may reduce product complexity with regards to variety, design, manufacture, and management, but on the other hand are constrained to manage the product complexity required by the customer, to meet the requirements of flexibility.

The nature of internal operational processes can precondition an organization to certain types of complex behaviour. The type of manufacturing layout primarily determines the level of process complexity. Complex processes are ones that require a larger volume of information monitoring. Some examples that illustrate this are considered next.

1. *Flexible Manufacturing Systems* (*FMS*) consist of a group of machines under computer control with the automatic movement of products between machines. The operational features of FMS (including varying lot sizes, machine rates, routes, and independence between machines) make them inherently complex, requiring large volumes of information to be monitored.
2. *Job Shops* consist of machines grouped together by type, and are often used for products with a mix of process sequences, servicing products in small batches. Job shops tend to be difficult to manage, with progress 'chasers' often needed to monitor the system. This behaviour is a consequence of the high complexity associated with this kind of arrangement.
3. *Cell-based layouts* having machines grouped according to product family are less complex than Job Shops.
4. *Just In Time* (*JIT*) flowlines are structurally simple systems and often operationally reliable (with uniform machine rates, well-defined linkage between machines, and balanced lot sizes).

Two other internal process characteristics that influence the complexity of the system are

(1) degree of control and flexibility in the scheduling processes, which determines the responsiveness of the system to disturbances;
(2) level of organizational and management structure of the organization, which influences the complexity associated with both administrative and decision processes.

As with product complexity, organizations on the one hand may reduce process complexity by altering the manufacturing layout and control structure, but on the other hand are limited to manage the process complexity which is often required to meet the flexibility requirements of the product or customer.

The internal complexity of manufacturing systems can also be influenced by organizational characteristics such as strategic objectives, human interactions, and structural design.

The strategic objectives that underpin an organization often define the level and nature of complexity that the organization will experience. For example, the level and nature of the complexity that result within an organization whose strategic objective is to minimize cost will be different to an organization whose strategic objective is to meet customer responsiveness requirements and expectations.

Concerning the human aspect of organizational complexity, even the most predictable system will be prone to complexity where it interfaces with people. This is particularly the case within manufacturing organizations where the control and management of complexity ultimately rests with human decision-makers.

To consider the influence of an organization's departmental and personnel structure on its complexity, a comparison between a hierarchical organization and a project-based organization can be made. In the hierarchical design, there is a well-defined hierarchy of control, with continuous reporting to management. By contrast, within the project-based organizational structure there is one project team for each task, where any employee can work on a number of projects and teams at any one time. The primary difference in terms of complexity between the hierarchical and project-based structural designs is with regards to the level of interaction and the extent of information exchange.

The management of internal complexity from an organizational perspective can be difficult due to the embedded nature of organizational structure. However, organizations as a whole do evolve and transform over time, directed or otherwise, in response to internal or external stimuli.

Complexity across the supplier–customer interface. Complexity across the supplier–customer interface can be considered in terms of the nature of the supplier–customer relationship, material flow, and information flow.

Supplier–customer interfaces are built on relationships between separable organizational entities, whether at the level of the top-level management board, department, project, or on an individual basis. These relationships can be characterized by a set of behavioural traits that include trust, power, and cultural alignment.

Organizations unite to share information and technology for mutual benefit, as trust across the supplier–customer interface increases. This can lead to lower levels of uncertainty and can reduce the amount of complexity resulting from misunderstandings and other wasteful activities. This would suggest that operational complexity could be reduced through effectively enhanced supplier–customer partnerships.

Acknowledging power relationships is important in understanding the complexity across supplier–customer interfaces because organizations will operate in a given manner according to the relative power regimes within which they operate. Powerful organizations may be in a position to extract unfair advantage from weaker members of the chain by exporting complexity onto partners as an easy means of coping with uncertainty. This means that the less powerful players within the chain are often forced to absorb any transmitted complexity.

Cultural misalignments are not restricted to cross-border trading interfaces, where complexity can arise due to language, national customs, legislation, and working practices. In fact, all organizations come with their own corporate culture and business image, which like the personalities of people may not always match perfectly, even if they are located in the same national or geographical area.

At the interface, the more tangible element of complexity exists in the form of uncertainty associated with the quantity and timing of product deliveries. Unreliability of supply can have an immediate and direct impact on customer performance. Material flow between organizations can be considered in terms of the complexity associated with the product category, the type of material flow interface and the inventory holding policies at the interface.

In general, a manufactured product may fall into the categories of supplier standard, black box parts and detailed control parts. These product categories can have different levels of information exchange and complexity associated with them at the supplier–customer interface. Another product categorization is where products can be grouped by their functional or innovative nature, where functional products may be regarded as being operationally less complex than innovative products. Fisher (1997) proposes that the best match is where functional products operate within efficient supply interfaces and innovative products operate within responsive supply chains. Puttick (1994) identifies four industrial segments by mapping low and high product complexity onto low and high environmental uncertainty as given in Fig. 6.4. It may be regarded that high complexity products operating in high uncertainty environments, such as capital goods, will be operationally more complex than low complexity products operating in low uncertainty environments, such as commodities.

The nature of the material flow, and the complexity relating to it, depends on the type of supplier–customer interface that exists, which include single sourcing, preferred supplier agreements, tiered supplier interfaces, outsourcing subassemblies, and contracting out services. These sourcing policies work to reduce the overall complexity of the system either through simplification, as in the first three cases, or by paying a premium to some external party for managing the unwanted uncertainty, as in the last two cases. The choice of interface type for any particular organization will depend on the relative levels of risk and reward.

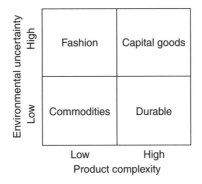

Fig. 6.4. Puttick's (1994) classification of product complexity by environmental uncertainty

Different types of inventory systems have different implications for the complexity of the material flow at the supplier–customer interface. Inventory holdings often exist as an insurance against the uncertainty that propagates through the supply chain. In essence, the unpredictability of stock buffers between organizations can contribute to an increase in operational complexity. This unpredictability will vary across industries and along the different tiers of the supply chain.

Information can be regarded as the controlling signal within supplier–customer systems (Mason-Jones and Towill 1998, 1999). Operational complexity associated with information flows can be related to the quality of information flows that exist, as well as the means of managing information flows.

The transfer quality of information between firms within a supply chain remains a key determinant of supply chain complexity. Poor quality information transfer between organizations can amplify and become more uncertain as information undergoes transformations, delays, and losses as it travels through the chain (Forrester 1961). Poor quality of the definitions of products, orders, payments, and general logistics can result in amplifying levels of uncertainty and unreliability within the supply chain.

Information Technology has the potential to facilitate tighter inter-firm links through information sharing, increased speed and reduced delays in information processing. IT systems have been sold as a means of coping with the variations caused by customers, suppliers, and the manufacturing system's own variability. Nearly all organizations use IT systems to some extent for managing their data and information flows, but there are marked differences in the performance related to these IT systems. The information-related complexity of an organization can increase where organizations fall into the trap of becoming a slave to technology.

Dynamics of the market. The dynamics of the market are important in determining the level of operational complexity that supplier–customer systems must manage. The operational complexity experienced often depends on the market environment in which the product is traded. This means that standard products can also be operationally complex as a result of unpredictable market conditions. Different types of market will have different levels of inherent complexity, with regard to how predictable the market conditions are. The dynamics of the environment in which supplier–customer systems operate can be considered in terms of their location within the supply chain, and the amplification and uncertainty demand functions that characterize the system.

The location of the organization within the supply chain (whether it is located towards the final customer or towards the raw material end) is governed by the different interactions that exist at various tiers within the chain. This means that the nature of the complexity experienced by supplier–customer systems will vary along the supply chain. As the positioning of supplier–customer systems moves away from the consumer end of the network, there is greater potential for amplification (Forrester 1961) and greater dissatisfaction (Harland 1996), and second, the greater the number of tiers, the greater the amplification will be towards the raw material supplier end. Adding more stages to a system increases the complexity because each additional tier within the supply chain acts as a further obstacle to flow (Frizelle 1998).

One of the biggest sources of unpredictability within the supply chain is due to demand amplifications. This amplification of demand as it passes between organizations in the supply chain is often described as the Forrester effect (Forrester 1961) or the Bullwhip effect (Lee, Padmanabhan, and Whang 1997). Due to the complex linkages that exist across the supply chain, it is difficult for any individual organization to control the uncertainty of demand. By passively or actively participating in working away from the schedule, organizations are in fact contributing to the transmission of uncertainty across the supplier–customer interface. This can often result in highly variable inventory holdings, fluctuating capacity utilization, and long 'safety' lead times throughout the supply chain.

The evidence suggests that supply chains are complex. The complex characteristics of supply chains impact all suppliers and customers that exist within the chain, having implications across all interfaces.

3. Information theory

Information theory provides a means of quantifying complexity. The complexity of a system increases with increasing levels of disorder and uncertainty. Therefore, a higher complexity system requires a larger amount of information to describe its state (Efstathiou *et al.* 1999; Calinescu *et al.* 2000; Sivadasan *et al.* 2002c). From an information-theoretic perspective, entropy is defined as the amount of information required to describe the state of the system (Shannon 1948; Shannon and Weaver 1949). Hence, an increase in the complexity of a system, through increased disorder and uncertainty, will increase its entropy, which can be measured as an increase in the expected amount of information required to describe the state of the system.

Shannon (Shannon 1948; Shannon and Weaver 1949) introduced the concept of measuring the quantity of information, by means of entropy, in his work on a mathematical theory of information or general theory of communication. The basic form for defining the entropy H of a system S is given by Equation 1. According to information theory, the entropy is defined as the expected amount of information necessary to describe the state of a system, comprising alternative countable states or events i ($i = 1, \ldots, n$), with an associated probability p_i that state i occurs, where $p_i \geq 0$, $\sum_{i=1}^{n} p_i = 1$ and $\log_2(0) = 0$. The uncertainty of the system is captured through the probability distributions (p_i) across the states.

$$H(S) = -\sum_{i=1}^{n} p_i \log_2 p_i \qquad (1)$$

From information theory, a common interpretation of Equation 1 is as a measure of 'uncertainty', 'choice', or 'surprise'. Four aspects of this measure are listed next.

1. $H(S)$ attains its maximum value $(\log_2 n)$, in the case of an equiprobable system, where all p_i are equal $(p_i = 1/n)$. As all outcomes are equally likely, this is the case where each observation is equally unpredictable. For a given number of possible events, n, this is the most uncertain situation, where the entropy increases as the number of possible events, n, increases.

2. $H(S)$ is zero in the case of absolute certainty, where one of the states $(i = 1, \ldots, n)$ gives $p_i = 1$. In terms of information theory, observations of a 'certain' system provide the least information. With only one possible outcome of absolute certainty, observations of the system do not add any information.

3. As an additive measure, the entropy associated with a number of independent flows is the sum of the entropy associated with each independent flow.

4. The logarithm is to the base 2, yielding bits as the unit of measure, where one bit is the amount of information required to distinguish between two equiprobable events.

Information-theoretic measures are flexible and adaptable, as demonstrated through their application within fields other than Manufacturing, including Medicine, Biology, Decision Risk Theory, and Sociology. Within the Manufacturing Systems research area, information theory has been widely developed to measure product variety, estimate the risk of managing projects, measure manufacturing flexibility, measure software complexity, and quantify decision-making complexity. Information theory provides a basis to measure the operational complexity of supplier–customer links within the supply chain.

3.1. Application of information theory to measure supply chain complexity

The operational complexity across the supplier–customer system can be defined as the amount of information required to describe the state of the system, given the level of control and the detail of monitoring, in terms of the quantity or time variations across expected and actual material flows and information flows.

This section will describe the application of this technique to the study of a customer–supplier relationship. Many of the details of the application are specific to this case study, but the technique may be generalized. For the supplier–customer system investigated, a simplification of the relationship is illustrated in Fig. 6.5. The variables that were considered in measuring the operational complexity are listed next.

1. *The Flow Variations monitored.* The proposed Flow Variations that were monitored at the interface are (Order − Forecast) and (Actual Delivery − Order), and the internal Flow Variations are (Actual Production − Scheduled Production). For each Flow Variation, time variations and

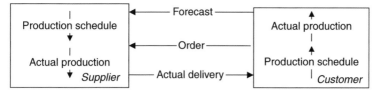

Fig. 6.5. Material and information flows in a supplier–customer system

quantity variations can be measured. For other supply chains, different flows may be identified, and alternative names may be used for the same flows.

2. The products across which the variations are monitored. Products can be monitored and classified by the product family group to which they belong or by some other common factor such as common processes.

3. Where variations are recorded, the state of the variation must be defined with respect to control decisions, by considering the severity of the variation as defined by the Controller. This is a process by which the measured variations are categorized into groups according to the control action required. It is not a weighting process. For example, the Controller of the Flow Variation (Order − Forecast) is responsible for managing that Flow Variation and so defines which category of severity any variation would fall within. The controller defines the boundaries for one in-control state variation and five out-of-control states according to the degree of control required.

4. Once the measured Flow Variations are categorized by the type of control action required, the reason for the variation must also be noted. The reasons for variations may be due to external factors such as Customers or Suppliers, or internal factors such as Machine Breakdown.

5. The frequency at which the Flow Variation is monitored is also recorded for comparability across flows that are monitored at different frequencies. Where one Order and one Forecast document is sent once a week, the Controller responsible for (Order − Forecast) monitors this Flow Variation once per week. Similarly, where there are fifty deliveries per week against one Order document, the Controller responsible for (Actual Delivery − Order) monitors this Flow Variation fifty times per week.

Based on this model, an information-theoretic measure of supplier–customer operational complexity is derived from Equation 1 (Sivadasan 2001; Sivadasan *et al.* 2002). The proposed equation for measuring the operational complexity across supplier–customer systems, $H_0(SC)$, is given in Equation 2.

$$H_0(SC) = -\sum_{i-1}^{F} c_i \sum_{j-1}^{U} (1 - P_{ij}) \sum_{k=1}^{R} \sum_{l=1}^{NS} p_{ijkl} \log_2 p_{ijkl}, \qquad (2)$$

where

F: Number of Flow Variations, in both material and information,

c_i: The frequency at which the Flow Variation i is monitored by the Controller over the same period of time (with reference to point iv above),

U: Number of products monitored,

R: Number of reasons investigated,

P_{ij}: Probability of product j across Flow Variation i being in the in-control (scheduled) state,

NS: Number of out-of-control (non-scheduled) states across flow i for product j and reason k,

p_{ijkl}: Probability of product j across flow i being in an out-of-control (non-scheduled) state l due to reason k.

The form of Equation 2 is such that monitoring an additional element across any of the variables i, j, or k of a system (such that, for example, F, U, or R increase by 1) will increase the complexity value of that system. This is based on the assumption that the relative probability distributions across the original out-of-control states remain unchanged. There are cases where this assumption of unchanged probability distributions does not hold. In such cases the operational complexity of the supplier–customer system does not necessarily increase with the number of elements considered within the variables monitored, but instead it depends on the nature of the monitored variations and defined states.

Regardless of the number of Flow Variations considered, the operational complexity of a system will increase with the frequency at which any Flow Variation is monitored. This is indicated in Equation 2 by the c_i term. Organizations can control the amount of operational complexity that they manage by defining the monitoring frequency of Flow Variation. Internal to the production system the monitoring frequency is often determined by the detail of the schedule.

The ways in which operational complexity can be managed depend on the source of the complexity itself. The constituent components of complexity by source can be calculated by considering the reasons for variations. In Equation 2, this can be calculated for each reason k. Internal to the production system, this can be used to identify the relative information demands placed on the system due to self-generated complexity and due to the amount of complexity absorbed within the system from external sources. At the supplier–customer interface, the reason-based analysis can be used to identify the extent to which organizations import and export complexity.

Another factor that has a direct impact on the complexity of the supplier–customer system is the in-control probability P_{ij} of the system, where given a set out-of-control probability distribution, the operational complexity decreases with increasing values of P_{ij}. Organizations can work to control the amount of operational complexity that they manage either by defining and operating within wider in-control state boundaries which will increase the value of P_{ij}, or given a narrow in-control boundary, work to ensure that the variations fall within this state. In the first instance, the policies of managing the operational complexity rest with accepting and accommodating a larger in-control variation state. In the second instance, the complexity management policies would focus on tighter control and greater predictability of the out-of-control variations that occur. Policies available to organizations for managing operational complexity are detailed in Section 4.4.

On the basis that supplier–customer systems are controlled by people, the operational complexity of the system is measured with respect to the amount of information required to describe the state of the system within the boundaries defined by the Controller. This is considered in Equation 2 through the state definitions into which the observed variations are categorized. These states are defined according to the severity and manageability of the variations. The complexity can be assessed with respect to the Controller responsible for managing that Flow Variation. This analysis allows organizations to assess the information demands placed on any Controller against the information resources available to them.

The adaptability and comparability of Equation 2 is made possible by the information-theoretic form of the measure. The measure is adaptable in terms of the level and scope of analysis that it provides. It is comparable due to the units of measure being in bits per unit time or bits per observation. The quantification provided by the application of this measure allows the principal supplier–customer issues to be identified, quantified, and prioritized.

Information theory goes beyond counting complexity elements by measuring the essence of complexity: the information content. Overall, information-theoretic measures are appropriate to investigate supply chain complexity because they can capture the colloquial characteristics of the complexity of the system in one measure, which can be used to compare different aspects of systems.

4. Transfer of complexity

In this section, we shall consider some of the mechanisms by which complexity occurs within an organization and is transmitted to its trading partners within the supply network.

Complexity internal to the organization manifests itself as the uncertainty between scheduled and actual production. The internal operational complexity of the production system can be measured as the amount of information required to describe the state of the variations across the scheduled and actual production. Internal operational complexity must be considered in terms of both external variations that are absorbed and internal variations that are generated within the system. External variations imported from customers and suppliers depend on the level of responsiveness required by customers and that available from suppliers. Internal variations can be generated in production or within the scheduling function.

Complexity within the production system can be due to processes and products. Some processes are intrinsically more unpredictable than others due to unreliability, unplanned rework loops or other factors. The operational complexity by process, or by similar work-centre, can be evaluated using an information-theoretic measure. Equation 2 gives $H_0(SC)$ across Flow Variation (Actual Production − Scheduled Production) by each process. Similarly, some products are operationally more complex than others due to structural details, interaction with processes or susceptibility to external factors. The complexity by product across the supply interface can also be evaluated with Equation 2 by measuring and comparing $H_0(SC)$ across the Flow Variation (Actual Production − Scheduled Production) for each product. This allows organizations to rank operational complexity variables such as products or processes by their complexity characteristics.

The role of the scheduling function in dealing with complexity within an organization will be discussed in Section 4.1, the dynamics of importing and exporting complexity are discussed in Section 4.2 and the implications for managing complexity will be discussed in Section 4.3. Then Section 4.4 will consider the methods and policies available to organizations for coping with or managing complexity.

4.1. Role of the scheduling function

The scheduling function is limited in the amount of information it can manage, by the quality of the information with which it makes decisions and by the constraints within which it must operate. The measured complexity associated with the internal production process is dependent on several factors including the detail, horizon and frequency of scheduling.

The greater the desired level of production control, the greater the prescribed detail (information content) of the schedule. The detail of schedules can be illustrated by considering two schedules, both of which cover a 5-day period and specify that a total of 1,000 units of Product A and 2,000 units of B be produced by the end of the 5 days. In the case of a low detail schedule this is the only information that it contains, whereas a high detail schedule specifies how may units of each product need to be produced each day. In the former case the production facility need only be monitored against the schedule once over this period, at the end of the fifth day. In the latter case the production facility would need to be monitored against the schedule every day over the 5 days. This is considered in Equation 2 through c_i, which in the former case is 1 and in the latter case is 5. This is because, with all other things remaining the same, the likelihood of deviating from the schedule increases with increasing scheduling detail. This is similar to stating that the more detailed the schedule,

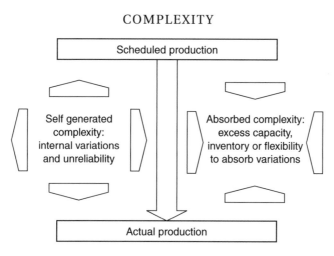

Fig. 6.6. Internal transfer of operational complexity framework

the more often it needs to be monitored and hence the more operational complexity the system is likely to experience.

For many organizations, the flexibility of the scheduling task determines how effectively the imported complexity is absorbed and self-generated complexity is managed within the system. This flexibility rests with the characteristics of the production system being scheduled and on the decision-making capacity of the scheduler. There are real costs associated with this task, such as the costs associated with information management, monitoring, and negotiating.

From these discussions, two classes of operational complexity transfer are identified within the internal system: generating operational complexity and absorbing operational complexity. A framework that illustrates how organizations absorb and generate complexity is shown in Fig. 6.6. Organizations can generate internal operational complexity through unreliable processes or procedures and absorb uncertainty through internal flexibility, high inventories, or excess capacity.

Qualitatively identifying and quantitatively analysing the internal complexity of the system within this framework provides organizations with a valuable tool for assessing their internal predictability and internal susceptibility to external variations.

4.2. Dynamics of importing and exporting complexity

In general, with reference to Fig. 6.7, the sources of complexity at the interface can be attributed to

(1) immediate supplier or customer (1,2);
(2) parallel suppliers or customers of the same tier (3,4); and

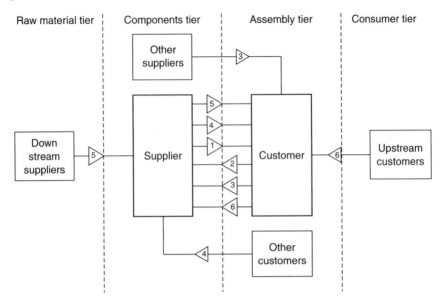

Fig. 6.7. Sources of operational complexity at the supplier–customer interface

(3) other upstream or downstream suppliers or customers, where variations
are transmitted through the immediate or parallel categories of suppliers and customers (5,6).

The relative contributions of each of these sources of operational complexity
at the supplier–customer interface can be calculated by analysing $H_o(SC)$
as given in Equation 2, with respect to each of the R reasons for the measured
variations. This identifies organizations that export complexity and the nature
of the complexity exported. Complexity exported by any source, such as customers, is associated with the amount of information required to describe the
state of quantity and time variations across the interface due to that reason.

A striking distinction between complexity exported by customers and that
exported by suppliers is that complexity exported by customers is often
expected and tolerated by the suppliers, whereas complexity exported by suppliers is often penalized by the customers. This attitude surfaces from two
aspects: first, the notion that the 'customer is always right', and second, the
misconception that variations in information flows, due to their intangible
nature, are less detrimental to the effective operation of the interface than variations in material flows. These two factors often act to institutionalize complexity exported by customers while that exported by suppliers continues to be
unacceptable.

Complexity exported by customers generally consists of variations in information flows alone, whereas complexity exported by suppliers consists of variations
in information and material flows. A framework by which the transmission of

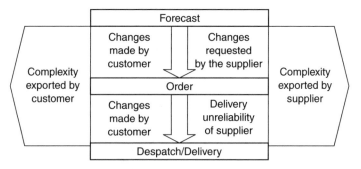

Fig. 6.8. External transfer of operational complexity framework

complexity between organizations can be analysed is summarized in Fig. 6.8, from which it may be broadly generalized that

(1) customers largely export complexity to suppliers through unpredictability between Forecast and Order; and
(2) suppliers largely export complexity to customers through unpredictability between Order and Dispatch.

The first case represents information-to-information discrepancy and the second case represents information-to-material discrepancy.

Within the supply chain there is often an imbalance between partners in importing and exporting complexity. For example, a net importer may receive unpredictable variations between Forecasts and Orders from customers but still manage to provide predictable delivery to its customers, thereby transmitting lower levels of complexity than those received. A net exporter would amplify the complexity through unpredictable material and information transfers. These concepts are quantifiable using information-theoretic measures.

In a supplier–customer relationship where both organizations have a tendency to export complexity, the interface will be highly unpredictable. This presents a situation where there is a potential mismatch between the supplier and the customer. In this case, high supply side complexity exported by the supplier can feed on high demand complexity imported from the customer and conversely, high demand side complexity exported by the customer can feed on high supply complexity imported from the supplier and so, the cycle of complexity exchange would continue within the supplier–customer partnership. Based on this supplier–customer interaction, a supplier–customer mismatch matrix is illustrated in Fig. 6.9.

At the supplier–customer interface, the situation where both the customer and the supplier have a tendency to export complexity exposes a mismatch in the relationship, as given by the top-right quadrant of Fig. 6.9. In such a case, the information monitoring demands at the interface would be high. Partnerships with low information monitoring demands at the interface would

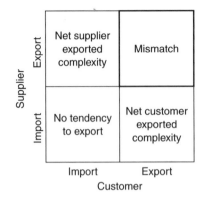

Fig. 6.9. Supplier–customer mismatch matrix based on tendency to export and import complexity

fall into the bottom-left quadrant where neither of the two parties have a tendency to export complexity. However, the majority of supplier–customer relationships exist under some form of export–import imbalance, as given by the top-left and bottom-right quadrants of Fig. 6.9. The export–import imbalance is often a reflection of the supplier–customer power imbalance, as discussed by Cox (Macbeth and Ferguson 1994; Cox 1999, 2001; Evans 2001).

The mismatch matrix and conceptual framework provide the foundation for understanding the dynamics of operational complexity. The ability to quantify these complexity transfer models by measuring the operational complexity at the supplier–customer interface provides organizations with a measure that prioritizes by source of complexity and highlights complexity issues at the interface. The conceptual models, supported by actual measured values, provide a means by which the supplier–customer system can work towards agreements on the amounts of complexity exported and imported for a mutual supply chain advantage.

4.3. Implications for managing complexity

Categorizing organizations according to their internal and interface characteristics of operational complexity provides some insights into how they might operate within supplier–customer systems. Organizations that act as complexity sources and those that act as complexity sinks can be identified by their internal and interface operational complexity characteristics as identified on the matrix given in Fig. 6.10. Complexity sinks are net importers of complexity at the interface and net absorbers of complexity internally. Complexity sources are net internal generators of complexity as well as net exporters of complexity at the interface.

The complexity of supplier–customer systems has implications for management practice and, conversely, management practice has implications for the

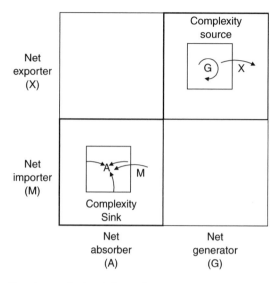

Fig. 6.10. Operational complexity sinks and sources

complexity of the system. The management of complexity associated with the supplier–customer system is important for manufacturing organizations as internal efficiency and profitability of organizations are influenced by the properties of the complexity that exists within the system. The information demands on Controllers that manage the system decrease as the operational complexity of the system decreases.

4.4. Policies for coping with complexity

An organization's attitude towards complexity management is key in the type of management strategy adopted and implementation policy pursued. The complexity management policies adopted by organizations can fall into four categories as indicated by Fig. 6.11, from which organizations have a choice of one or more of the following (Sivadasan *et al.* 2002*a–d*):

(1) export operational complexity to some other organization;
(2) charge for the service of coping with imported complexity;
(3) invest in precautionary systems that work to avoid complexity generation; or
(4) invest in sufficient resources to absorb complexity.

The implications of these four policies will be discussed in some detail below.

Exporting complexity. One way in which organizations try to cope with operational complexity is by transferring it to their suppliers and customers.

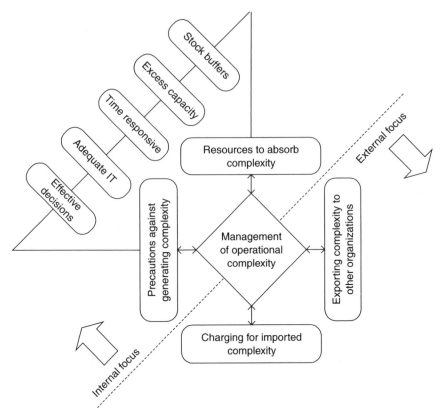

Fig. 6.11. Operational complexity managing policies

This phenomenon can be described in terms of exporting complexity. Thus, for example, organizations that alter their supplier delivery schedules due to changes in their internal production schedule can export complexity to their suppliers. Similarly, organizations that fail to deliver the required products at the expected time and in the requested quantity are exporting complexity to their customers. The justification for adopting the term is that such events generate additional information that needs to be transmitted to and managed by the importing organizations.

The extent to which organizations export complexity at the supplier–customer interface can be due to several factors including

(1) poor ability and insufficient resources internally to control and contain complexity;

(2) necessity of exporting complexity that has been imported from some other organization;

(3) imposition and control of the direction of complexity transfer by organizations with greater bargaining power; and
(4) internal culture of a 'them and us' divide in the supply relationship.

However, exporting complexity is not necessarily an effective response to dealing with supply chain issues, as these actions can have repercussions on the entire supply chain with direct implications for immediate partners. Suppliers can incur high operating costs where customer induced variations across forecasts and orders are internally accommodated. Suppliers can also export complexity to customers through the transfer of material by unreliable deliveries (in time or quantity) and sub-standard product quality. Customers can incur high revenue losses if supplier failures lead to plant stoppage. Unfortunately, the majority of the smaller and less powerful organizations may have neither the infrastructure nor the resources to absorb the additional variations and uncertainties transmitted to them, from suppliers or customers.

Suppliers can incur high precautionary costs in administering policies to buffer against imported customer complexity. These precautionary costs can include costs associated with building up inventories, investing in extra capacity, acquiring more powerful information management systems and training personnel to cope with a greater degree of decision flexibility. Ultimately, increased operating costs of the supplier would be passed on to the customers, where the supplier does not have the means to deal with them internally.

Customers can also incur high costs where complexity is exported to them. Complexity exported to customers, from suppliers, in the form of early deliveries, has costs associated with managing and monitoring the stock. Late or poor quality deliveries can at best delay internal production and at worst bring the customer's production to a halt. Precautionary measures taken by customers include cases where they may hold Goods-In inventory or operate a dual or multi-sourcing policy, where a choice of supply provides an opportunity for the complexity generated by one supplier to be absorbed by the flexibility of another supplier. These also carry costs.

Charge for imported complexity.   Organizations that manage imported complexity can charge the exporting organizations. This is beneficial to the non-exporting, exporting, and importing organizations within the chain. Identifying and specifically charging the exporting organizations will mean that non-exporting organizations will not be unfairly penalized as in the case where the costs of complexity are spread evenly between all organizations. In the case where exporting organizations pay for the complexity that they transfer, they can in return demand and expect a more predictable standard of service. In this case, armed with a quantification of the problem and provided with adequate resources, the importing organizations can focus on meeting the specific needs of the exporters.

It is proposed that charges for managing imported complexity can be set through premium rates or penalty rates.

1. Premium rates would provide supply chain partners with an option of paying a premium to cover for their complexity exporting behaviour. Premium rates would primarily act to charge customers who export demand complexity, through variations in demand. This may include premium rates for accepting late changes to the delivery requests or for delivering products on a fast turn-around basis as observed from the BAE SYSTEMS–Graphic case study (Sivadasan 2001).

2. Penalty charges would act to penalize supply chain partners who export supply complexity, through variations in supply. This would mainly take the form of penalty charges for failure to meet material delivery promises, such as quantity, timeliness, and quality. Often contractual agreements contain clauses detailing the penalty charges.

The premium rate charges are likely to be made by suppliers for adhering to the unpredictable and urgent change requirements made by customers. The penalty charges are likely to be made by customers for having to adjust to the unpredictable delivery characteristics of suppliers.

Investment to absorb or avoid complexity. The resources available to organizations determine their ability to absorb (or reduce) complexity internally and their capacity to take precautions against generating complexity. With respect to Fig. 6.11 the five resources of stock, capacity, time, IT systems, and decision making are considered and detailed below. These resources have different costs and benefits attached to them.

Stock holding. Many organizations continue to manage large levels of finished goods stock. This is often in response to operational complexity. Holding huge amounts of inventory can be a costly way to manage complexity. Moreover, large buffer stocks do not necessarily facilitate better management of complexity. Often the opposite can be true, as high inventory levels can often obscure the real complexity within the system. The complexity of stock is not necessarily linked to the size of the stock, but instead to the uncertainty associated with the variations in the stock.

Scheduling with excess capacity. An alternative to building up stock mountains is to allow some spare production capacity to be scheduled into the system to accommodate any uncertainty within the system. The use of excess capacity is often considered wasteful, as production resources may stand idle for some or most of the time.

Operating with time buffers. Planning time buffers into the logistics, production, and scheduling system also accommodates uncertainties. However, the competitive advantages presented by time compression (Towill 1996; Mason-Jones and Towill 1999) have persuaded many organizations to reduce time buffers, at the cost of being more prone to variations.

Investing in Information Technology. Supply chain IT systems, such as extended enterprise resource planning (ERP) tools, have the potential to facilitate tighter inter-firm links through facilitating increased information sharing. From a practitioner perspective, the use of IT systems should lead to reduced information complexity and associated costs. However, investment in IT does not automatically lead to a reduction in cost or in information complexity. The main drawbacks of present information systems include fragmentation and incompatibility of different systems, parameter settings that have become invisible or inaccessible, poor coordination with shop floor manufacturing processes, and issues regarding the security of data.

Nurturing effective decision-making. This is, perhaps, the most critical of all resource advantages available to organizations. Developing effective decision-making and schedule repair and management skills among personnel within the control and scheduling functions helps organizations to manage complexity (Calinescu *et al.* 2001). For any given set of resources, poor decision-making can contribute to complexity generation.

The first three complexity management policies of stock holding, scheduling with excess capacity, and operating with time buffers, ultimately have a trade-off attached to them. Where organizations strive for leanness by cutting back on stock, working to full capacity and pursuing time compression policies there is often a conflict with agility. In response to this conflict, organizations often resort to heavy investment in IT systems to manage complexity. The shortcomings of IT systems are often met by an increased reliance on decision-making systems.

The management of complexity associated with the supply chain is important for manufacturing organizations as internal efficiency and profitability of organizations are influenced by the operational complexity that exists within the system. The management policies adopted by organizations have implications for the operational complexity of the supply chain system. In order to create an efficient supply interface the transfer of operational complexity from one organization to another should be effectively controlled. For this, it is important that companies can identify and understand operational complexity-inducing activities and actions. Furthermore, organizations need to be aware of the implications of transferring operational complexity across the supplier–customer interface and the trade-offs that exist across the various operational complexity management policies.

5. Measuring complexity

Section 5.1 will briefly introduce the measurement techniques that may be used to assess quantitatively the complexity of an organization. Some specific results from case studies will be presented briefly in Section 5.2.

5.1. Measurement techniques

The methodology for measuring the complexity of a supplier–customer systems comprises five phases as shown in Fig. 6.12. Prior to the actual collection of data (phase 4), a period of preparation (phase 1) and case familiarization (phase 2) must be undergone to establish the design factors (phase 3).

1. The preparation phase is critical in building a solid foundation, to ensure that the project 'hits the floor running' at the familiarization phase. The main areas considered at the preparation stage of a complexity case study, include sufficient background research on the organization, adequate planning of the entire study, internal organization of the research group, and external coordination with the collaborating company.

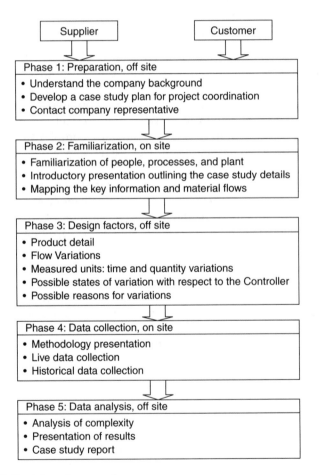

Fig. 6.12. Methodology framework

2. Prior to conducting measurements within organizations, a familiarization phase is necessary. The duration of this phase can vary with the size of the plant, the number of researchers involved, and the scope and the detail of the problem being addressed. This phase would include introductory presentations by the researchers to the key people at the organizations. The key people within the organizations included Controllers of potential Flow Variations to be monitored and other decision-makers and management figures. The aim of the familiarization phase is to identify the links between the key people, information flows, and material flows; provide details on, and samples of, the documents received, sent, and generated; clarify the typical time sequence of tasks within the organization; and highlight key organizational issues.

3. The information obtained from the familiarization phase is used to define a number of design factors prior to the data collection. The design factors are in line with the measurement variables identified in Section 3.1. After considering the design factors and before actually collecting the data, a presentation of the methodology to the organization is required, including a summary of the findings from the familiarization and the design factors phases. The presentations allow for organizational feedback, providing verification on the design factors and clarification of the data requirements from the Controllers.

4. In addition to the factors that determine the duration of the familiarization phase, the data collection duration is also determined by the number and nature of the Flow Variations and products monitored, and the lead times of production, order and delivery. The data required for measuring the operational complexity of supplier–customer systems are monitored on an event-triggered basis. For event-based data monitoring, all information regarding the event can be monitored at the frequency at which it occurs. The frequency of the measurements also has an influence on the duration of the study. The accuracy of the measured operational complexity depends initially on the number of data points observed and the number of out-of-control states occupied (Roulston 1999). The measurement error decreases as the number of data points increases and as the number of observed out-of-control states decreases. Based on estimates of the number of possible states of occurrence, frequency of monitoring, and the probability of being out-of-control, the number of data points required for a tolerated error bias can then be estimated (Sivadasan 2001).

5. For data analysis, each monitored Flow Variation is counted as an occurrence by product and reason as defined by the in- and out-of-control state boundaries classified by the Controllers of each Flow Variation. One of the principal advantages of the operational complexity analysis resides in its capacity to compare a wide scope of variations on a common scale. Once the data is gathered a number of analyses can be conducted by sorting and selecting the appropriate flows, product groups, and reasons.

The systematic application of the methodology allows the quantification, comparability, and hence prioritization of key areas of complexity. The measures provide industry with a quantitative basis on which they could take actions to scrutinize identified areas of high complexity.

5.2. *Generic case study findings*

Two case examples are given here to illustrate the powerful insights that can be obtained from the application of Equation 2 to analyse supply chain complexity across supplier–customer systems. The first case investigated is that of a Unilever bottle-filling plant and its key bottle supplier, ALPLA. With reference to Puttick (1994), Unilever–ALPLA may be placed within the commodity quadrant according to low product complexity and low environmental uncertainty. However, in the Unilever–ALPLA case the environmental uncertainty can also be high, since promotions are common within the fast moving consumer goods industry. The second case investigated is that of a BAE SYSTEMS PCB final assembly area and Graphic, its key bare PCB supplier. With reference to Fisher (1997), the BAE SYSTEMS–Graphic interface consists of innovative products operating in a responsive supply interface.

The findings of the first complexity case study considered the complexity of the Unilever–ALPLA system before and after a 'through-the-wall' integration programme. The results present evidence to suggest that before integration, the operational complexity of the supplier–customer system was managed through holding excess inventory; after integration, it was managed through increased flexibility (1997). Furthermore, the information-theoretic analysis suggests that the operational complexity of the customer–supplier system had increased as a result of integration (Sivadasan *et al.* 2002*a–c*).

The BAE SYSTEMS–Graphic case study investigated the impact of short-turn-around product requests made by BAE SYSTEMS on the complexity of the supply interface. The results present evidence to suggest that Graphic was able to manage the increased complexity of short-turn-around products because it was able to calculate and charge a premium price, as discussed in Section 4.4.2.

These complexity case studies demonstrate that the operational complexity measurement methodology is adaptable to low volume, make to order, batch manufacturing supplier–customer systems such as Graphic–BAE SYSTEMS, as well as to high volume, fast moving consumer goods manufacturing supplier–customer systems such as ALPLA–Lever.

6. Summary and Conclusion

The information-theoretic measure of operational complexity provides a means of understanding, analysing, and evaluating supply chain complexity by considering supplier–customer links. It provides a single integrated measure of operational complexity in terms of bits per unit time period or bits per unit occurrence, which allows for comparability. The measure defines operational complexity as being equivalent to the expected amount of information required to describe the system, where we define a system that requires more information to describe its state as being operationally more complex.

The general findings from the case studies have been used to develop frameworks of the complexity at supplier–customer interfaces and internally within each organization. At the interface, the dynamics of imported and exported operational complexity and the complexity absorbing nature of interface information flows can be modelled. Furthermore, it is shown that a mismatch across supplier–customer systems can occur where both organizations have a tendency to export complexity. Internally, the dynamics of absorbing and generating complexity and the prioritization of operational complexity by specific details such as product can be measured. The extent to which organizations import, export, generate, and absorb operational complexity can be used to identify complexity sinks and sources within the supply chain.

Several operational complexity management policies are identified which include exporting complexity, charging for complexity, absorbing complexity, and taking precautions against complexity. The measurement of operational complexity, and the identification and quantification of its constituent parts provide management with powerful insights into the dynamic operations of the system. The operational complexity measurement methodology presented can be used as a tool to guide organizations in selecting the appropriate policies to match the operational complexity experienced by the system. The methodology provides a model of how information and material variations can be managed, as a means of controlling the operational complexity of the system.

References

CALINESCU, A., EFSTATHIOU, J., SIVADASAN, S., and HUACCHO HUATUCO, L. (2001). 'Information-Theoretic Measures for Decision-Making Complexity in Manufacturing'. *Proceedings of the 5th World Multi-Conference on Systemics, Cybernetics and Informatics (SCI 2001)*, Orlando, FL, USA, X: 73–8.

—— —— —— SCHIRN, J., and HUACCHO HUATUCO, L. (2000). 'Complexity in Manufacturing: An Information Theoretic Approach'. *Proceedings of the International Conference on Complex Systems and Complexity in Manufacturing*, Warwick University, UK, 30–44.

Cox, A. (1999). 'Power, Value and Supply Chain Management'. *Supply Chain Management: An International Journal*, 4/4: 167–75.

—— (2001). 'Managing in Supply Chain Power Regimes'. *Proceedings of the UK Symposium on Supply Chain Alignment: Leading-Edge Thinking in Demand Network Alignment (DNA)*. Liverpool: Liverpool University.

DESHMUKH, A. V., TALAVAGE, J. J., and BARASH, M. M. (1998). 'Complexity in Manufacturing Systems, Part 1: Analysis of Static Complexity'. *IIE Transactions*, 30/4: 35–44.

EFSTATHIOU, J., TASSANO, F., SIVADASAN, S., SHIRAZI, R., ALVES, J., FRIZELLE, G., and CALINESCU, A. (1999). 'Information Complexity as a Driver of Emergent Phenomena in the Business Community'. *Proceedings of the International Workshop on Emergent Synthesis*, Kobe University, Japan, 1–6.

EVANS, S. (2001). 'Supply Chain Customer Satisfaction and the Impact of New Product Introduction'. *Proceedings of the UK Symposium on Supply Chain Alignment: Leading-Edge Thinking in Demand Network Alignment (DNA)*. Liverpool: Liverpool University.

FISHER, M. L. (1997). 'What Is the Right Supply Chain Product for You?' *Harvard Business Review*, 75/2: 105–16.

FORRESTER, J. W. (1961). *Industrial Dynamics: Systems Dynamics Series*. Cambridge, MA: MIT Press.

FRIZELLE, G. (1998). *The Management of Complexity in Manufacturing*. London: Business Intelligence.

—— and WOODCOCK, E. (1995). 'Measuring Complexity as an Aid to Developing Operational Strategy'. *International Journal of Operation and Production Management*, 15/5: 26–39.

HARLAND, C. M. (1996). 'Supply Chain Management: Relationships, Chains and Networks'. *British Journal of Management*, 7/1: S63–S80.

LEE, H. L., PADMANABHAN, V., and WHANG, S. (1997). 'Information Distortion in a Supply Chain: The Bullwhip Effect'. *Management Science*, 143/4: 546–58.

MACBETH, D., and FERGUSON, N. (1994). *Partnership Sourcing: An Integrated Supply Chain Approach*. London: Pitman Publishers.

MASON-JONES, R., and TOWILL, D. R. (1998). 'Shrinking the Supply Chain Uncertainty Circle'. *IOM Control*, 24/7: 17–22.

—— —— (1999). 'Total Cycle Time to Compression and the Agile Supply Chain'. *International Journal of Production Economics*, 62/1: 61–73.

PUTTICK, J. (1994). 'Modern Manufacturing'. Warwick Manufacturing Group, Warwick University.

ROULSTON, M. S. (1999). 'Estimating the Errors on Measured Entropy and Mutual Information'. *Physica D*, 125/3–4: 285–94.

SHANNON, C. E. (1948). 'A Mathematical Theory of Communication'. *Bell System Technical Journal*, 27: 379–423.

—— and WEAVER, W. (1949). *The Mathematical Theory of Communication*. USA: University of Illinois Press.

SIVADASAN, S. (2001). 'Operational Complexity of Supplier-Customer Systems', D.Phill. Thesis, Oxford.

—— EFSTATHIOU, J., FJELDSOE-NIELSEN, L., CALINESCU, A., and SCHIRN, J. (1999a). 'A Transaction Costs Approach to the Assessments of the Information Complexity of Supply Chains'. *Proceedings of the 15th National Conference in Manufacturing Research (NCMR 1999)*. Bath: University of Bath, 253–7.

—— —— SHIRAZI, R., FJELDSOE-NIELSEN, L., and CALINESCU, A. (1999b). 'Information Complexity as a Determining Factor in Evolution of the Supply Chain'. *Proceedings of the International Workshop on Emergent Synthesis*. Kobe University, Japan: 237–42.

—— —— CALINESCU, A., SCHIRN, J., and FJELDSOE-NIELSEN, L. (2000). 'The Costs of Complexity', *Manufacturing Engineer*, 79/3: 109–12.

—— —— HUACCHO HUATUCO, L., and CALINESCU, A. (2001). 'Complexity Associated with Supplier-Customer Integration'. *Proceedings of the 17th National Conference on Manufacturing Research (NCMR 2001)*, UK: University of Cardiff.

—— —— CALINESCU, A., and HUACCHO HUATUCO, L. (2002*a*). 'Operational Complexity of Supplier-Customer Systems: An Information-Theoretic Measure', *Journal of Operations Research Society*, forthcoming.

—— —— —— —— (2002*b*). 'Policies for Managing Operational Complexity'. *Proceedings of the International Conference on Complex Systems and Complexity in Manufacturing*. Cambridge: Cambridge University.

—— —— FRIZELLE, G., SHIRAZI, R., and CALINESCU, A. (2002*c*). 'An Information-Theoretic Methodology for Measuring the Operational Complexity of Supplier-Customer Systems'. *International Journal of Operations and Production Management*, 22/1: 80–102.

STERMAN, J. (1992). 'Teaching Takes Off, Flight Simulators for Management Education'. *OR/MS Today*, October: 40–4.

TOWILL, D. R. (1996). 'Time Compression and Supply Chain Management: A Guided Tour'. *Supply Chain Management: An International Journal*, 1/1: 15–27.

7

Supply Chain Learning

JOHN BESSANT

1. Introduction—why supply chain learning matters

It is a truism to say that organizations need to innovate to survive. Unless they are prepared to change what they offer (product/service) and the ways in which they create and deliver that offering (process innovation) there is a real risk that they will be overtaken by other players in what is clearly a turbulent and uncertain competitive environment. In extreme cases firms may have to undergo radical shifts from their original operations—for example, Nokia's moves from paper and pulp activities or Mannesmann's evolution from making steel tubes to mobile telecommunications. The German firm Preussag began life in 1917 as a public sector lead mining and smelting operation in Prussia, yet less than a century later had become the main actor in the European tourism industry with activities in airlines, travel agencies, and hotels.

Although these are exceptional and dramatic shifts the underlying innovation imperative is clear—and the mortality rate of firms which fail to change worryingly high (de Geus 1996). Innovation needs to be continuous in nature and implies a constant process of learning through various mechanisms and opportunities including research and development, technology transfer, alliances, and collaborations, and day-to-day operational experience (Hamel 2000).

The theme of innovation is usually considered with the individual enterprise as the unit of analysis but it is becoming clear that it has significant implications at the inter-firm level. Creating new products, especially of the higher knowledge complex type requires innovative behaviour and management at the system level (Hobday 1994; Marceau 1994; Miller *et al.* 1995; Tidd 1997; Oliver and Blakeborough 1998). Pursuing the 'lean' agenda, driving out waste and improving quality, speed, and other performance dimensions within a supply chain is increasingly seen as a shared activity involving the whole chain or network (Lamming 1993; Womack and Jones 1997; Hines *et al.* 1999).

In systems theory terms there is a need both for systems *optimization*—where innovative efforts are targeted at doing whatever the system does better, towards a theoretical optimum—and for systems *development*, where innovative efforts are targeted at moving the system forward, opening up new territory. These two forms of innovation need to occur in complementary fashion, the one pushing the envelope and the other ensuring optimum performance within it.

The challenge in supply networks—as systems involving multiple players but with some element of common purpose—is to ensure these parallel innovation activities can happen on a continuing basis. This focuses our attention on the question of supply networks not as static entities configured to deliver operational performance but also as learning systems. This chapter explores the extent to which what we will term supply chain learning (SCL) can take place and how it might be managed in active fashion rather than emerge as a random and occasional by-product.

2. What has to be learned?

2.1. The innovation agenda

It will be useful to reflect briefly on the nature of the learning challenge at the inter-firm level. Typically firms need to explore an 'innovation agenda' which can be summarized in Table 7.1; a robust portfolio would include projects concerned not only with optimizing—'do what we do better'—but also with developing—doing something different. We can apply a similar approach to looking at the innovation agenda at the level of an inter-firm system, and, as the cells in Table 7.1 indicate, there are significant challenges involving shared learning and capture and deployment of knowledge at the system level in new products, processes, etc.

2.2. Effective inter-firm learning and innovation

As Table 7.1 indicates there is extensive scope for inter-firm innovation, and a growing body of evidence suggests that there are considerable systemic benefits to be achieved. For example studies of 'collective efficiency' have explored the phenomenon of clustering in a number of different contexts (Piore and Sabel 1982; Humphrey and Schmitz 1996; Nadvi 1999; Porter 1997). From this work it is clear that the model is widespread—not just confined to parts of Italy, Spain, and Germany but diffused around the world—and under certain conditions, extremely effective. For example, one town (Sialkot) in Pakistan plays a dominant role in the world market for specialist surgical instruments made of stainless steel. From a core group of 300 small firms, supported by 1500 even smaller suppliers, 90 per cent of production (1996) was exported and took a

Table 7.1. The innovation agenda

	'Do better' innovation	'Do different' innovation
Product/Service innovation—change in what is offered	This includes incremental product development. For example, the Bic ball-point was originally developed in 1957 but remains a strong product with daily sales of 16 million units. Although superficially the same shape closer inspection reveals a host of incremental changes that have taken place in materials, inks, ball technology, safety features, etc. Achieving this has required considerable interorganizational activity—for example, close work with suppliers, links to research and technology providers, joint ventures on development projects with other producers, etc.	Radical shift to new product concept—for example, the replacement of horse-based transport with the motor car. In making such a jump the pattern of relationships between organizations—as suppliers and users of knowledge, specialist skills and equipment, etc.—requires radical transformation. Creating a new product concept requires multiple inputs from different perspectives and players
Process innovation—change in the ways in which it is created and delivered	Incremental improvements in key performance parameters—for example, cost reduction, quality enhancement, time reduction, etc. A good example of incremental process innovation can be found in the 'lean production' field where intra- and inter-firm efforts to drive out waste have led to sometimes spectacular performance improvements—but essentially achieved within the same envelope established by the original process (Womack and Jones 1997) Achieving these improvements is increasingly a function of being able to mobilize learning and exchange of ideas across players in the value stream or supply network	Radical shifts to new process routes—for example, the Bessemer process for steel-making replacing conventional charcoal smelting, the Pilkington float glass process replacing grinding and polishing, the Solvay continuous process for alkali production replacing the batch mode Leblanc process, etc. In each of these cases the inter-firm challenge is one of reconfiguring what goods/services are supplied in relation to the new process Much of the relevant knowledge for new process development is held by these players and success depends on early and extensive involvement and shared learning

Table 7.1. (*Continued*)

	'Do better' innovation	'Do different' innovation
Position innovation— change in the context in which it is applied	Launching of a product or deployment of a process in a new context—for example, opening up new market segments In mobile telephones the shift has taken place from a business tool to a leisure and recreation aid, with considerable incremental product and process development (ring tones, cartoon displays, text messaging) emerging as a result of such positional innovation Moving into such new positions requires reconfiguration of existing relationships and the establishment of new networks	Creating completely new markets rather than extending and deepening existing segments Moves of this kind require extensive learning about market needs and characteristics, but also requires cooperation and shared learning among firms creating products and services for the new market As Christensen points out, entering new markets can involve building radically new relationships and exploiting what might hitherto have been weak links (Christensen 1997)
Paradigm innovation— change in the underlying mental models surrounding it	Changes in underlying business models—for example, Bausch and Lomb recently reoriented themselves from 'eye wear' to 'eye care' In the process existing networks of relationships among actors in field like fashion design and manufacture and distribution of sunglasses and spectacles give way to new ones built around medical centres, specialist technology suppliers, and intermediary distribution	New business or industry model—for example, 'mass production' versus 'craft production' (Perez and Freeman 1989) Such shifts bring dramatic challenges to networks of players where wholesale reconfiguration of roles and requirements in terms of skills and capabilities takes place

20 per cent share of the world market, second only to Germany. Collective efficiency of this kind relies heavily on shared learning and development.

Conceived in 1993 as a response to the 1992 oil crisis, Cost Reduction Initiative for the New Era (CRINE) was a joint effort involving government and key industry players in the UK oil and gas sector representing contractors, suppliers, consultants, trade associations, and others. The original goal was to enable, by 1996, an across-the-board cost reduction of 30 per cent for offshore developments, and this was to be achieved by a sector-wide effort rather than individual actions.

The project was successful on a number of dimensions—for example, by 1997 the cost of field developments had fallen by 40 per cent on a barrel/barrel basis—and attracted significant international attention and emulation. As a consequence, CRINE-based programmes are now under development or in operation in Brazil, Mexico, Venezuela, India, and Australia. Significantly the participants felt that the model was worth maintaining and as a result the CRINE Network was established in 1997 and the LOGIC programme in 2000—Leading Oil and Gas Industry Competitiveness—with the new goal of international competitiveness replacing that of cost reduction. The stretching target for the industry is to increase its share of the non-UK market to 5 per cent; in 1996 this stood at only 1 per cent, indicating a relative weakness in international competitiveness. (Significantly this position had already improved by 1998 to 2.4 per cent, reflecting the industry's growing capabilities, partly supported by CRINE activities.)

The current mode of operation is one of 'supported networking', where players from regional and national government (e.g. DTI, Scottish Enterprise), major operators, trade and research bodies, and academic and other groups provide various forms of support (financial, technical, etc.) to a network made up of the main actors in the supply chain. A small coordinating group manages the network activities and the whole is steered by a representative body drawn from the above players. Activities cover a broad front, including awareness and communications via newsletters, websites, etc., workshops and conferences, technical projects and other initiatives: 'Since its inception CRINE has had a dramatic effect on the safety, efficiency and economics of North Sea oil and gas field development and operation', was the response of one senior manager (Chambers 1996).

A learning network has been established to help the emerging South African automotive components supply industry improve its competitiveness. Using a process of benchmarking to identify key areas for development, linked to regular inputs of training and plant level change projects the industry has managed to close the gap against suppliers from outside the country to the extent that in a number of key areas the country is a net exporter. Significantly, while the sector as a whole has been going through a process of rapid learning and development the rate of improvement amongst firms which are members of this actively managed learning network appear to be significantly higher than the industry average (Kaplinsky 2001).

In each of the above examples the gains emerged as a result of shared and cooperative activities and in particular shared learning processes. Inter-firm learning of this kind represents a significant potential resource but we need to understand further the dynamics and problems involved in making it happen.

3. The trouble with learning . . .

Most work on learning has been carried out at the level of the individual but in recent years there has been growing interest in the concept of 'learning organizations'. It can be argued that it is only the individuals within an organization who can learn but there is some evidence for viewing organizations as capable of learning behaviour which extends beyond that of individuals and which emulates key activities like experimentation, association, and remembering (Hedberg 1981). In particular learning can be viewed as a cyclical process involving a combination of experience, reflection, concept formation, and experimentation (Kolb and Fry 1975). Over time this process builds and consolidates the organization's knowledge base which can offer a source of competitive advantage.

Learning is not, however, an automatic property of organizations and problems include lack of motivation to enter the cycle and incomplete movement around it. Equally, it can be assisted by structures, procedures, etc. to facilitate the operation of the learning cycle—for example, through challenging reflection, facilitated sharing of experiences, or planned experimentation. These need to take into account that learning involves both tacit and formal components (Polanyi 1967; Nonaka 1991), and that it may take place in 'adaptive' mode—learning to do what we do a little better—or it may involve reframing and radical change in which the perception of the problems to be solved and the potential set of solutions change (Kuhn 1962; Argyris and Schon 1970; Bessant 1998). Table 7.2 summarizes some of the key blocks to learning and the problems underlying them.

Although much of the discussion on learning organizations is concerned with structures and processes within particular firms there is an emerging strand which deals with the theme of inter-firm learning. This aspect of learning has something in common with the principles of learning within groups instead of at the individual level. In particular, the active participation of others in the process of challenge and support is recognized as a powerful enabling resource and was developed into a widely used approach termed 'action learning' (McGill and Warner Weil 1989). This concept stresses the value of experiential learning and the benefits which can come from gaining different forms of support from others in moving around the learning cycle. Part of the vision of Revans, one of the pioneers of the concept, involved the idea of 'comrades in adversity', working together to tackle complex and open-ended problems (Revans 1983; Pedler, Boydell, and Burgoyne 1991).

The potential benefits of shared learning include the following and the problems underlying them:

- in shared learning there is the potential for challenge and structured critical reflection from different perspectives
- different perspectives can bring in new concepts (or old concepts which are new to the learner)
- shared experimentation can reduce perceived and actual costs risks in trying new things
- shared experiences can provide support and open new lines of inquiry or exploration

Table 7.2. Key blocks of learning

Learning block	Underlying problem
Lack of entry to the learning cycle	Perceived stimulus for change is too weak Firm is isolated or insulated from stimulus Stimulus is misinterpreted or underrated Denial—'it's not really happening' or ' it won't affect us'
Incomplete learning cycle	Motivation to learn is present but process of learning is flawed Emphasis given to some aspects—for example, experimentation—but not to all stages and to sequence
Weak links in the cycle	Reflection process is unstructured or unchallenging Lack of access to or awareness of relevant new concepts Risk avoidance leads to lack of experimentation Lack of sharing or exchange of relevant experiences—parochial search for new ideas 'Not invented here' effect
Lack of learning skills or structure	Lack of supporting and enabling structures and procedures
Knowledge remains in tacit form	Lack of mechanisms for capturing and codifying learning
Repeated learning	Lack of mechanisms for capturing and codifying learning leads to repetition of same learning content
Learning is infrequent, sporadic, and not sustained	Mechanisms for enabling learning are not embedded or absent

- shared learning helps explicate the systems principles, seeing the patterns—separating 'the wood from the trees'
- shared learning provides an environment for surfacing assumptions and exploring mental models outside of the normal experience of individual organizations—helps prevent 'not invented here' and other effects.

Arguably inter-organizational learning has much to offer and the experience of regional clusters of small firms provides one important piece of evidence in support of this. The ability of small producers in sectors like textiles or ceramics to share knowledge about product and process technology and to extend the capabilities of the sector as a whole is recognized as central to their abilities to achieve export competitiveness. In the case of Italian furniture, for example, a dominant position in world trade has been achieved and sustained over nearly 25 years—yet the average firm size is less than twenty employees (Piore and Sabel 1982; Best 1990).

Other configurations of 'learning network' are available, each of which offers potential traction on the learning problem and benefits both to individual members and to the system as a whole. Table 7.3 gives some examples.

Table 7.3. Outline typology of learning networks

Type	Learning target	Examples
Professional	Increased professional knowledge and skill = better practice	Professional institution and its individual members
Sector-based association of firms with common interests in the development of a sector	Improved competence in some aspect of competitive performance—for example, technical knowledge	Trade association Sector-based research organization 'Industry forum' initiatives
Topic-based	Improved awareness/knowledge of a particular field—for example, a new technology or technique in which many firms have an interest	'Best practice' clubs
Region-based	Improved knowledge around themes of regional interest—for example, SMEs learning together about how to export, diffuse technology, etc.	'Clusters' and local learning cooperatives
Supplier or value stream-based	Learning to achieve standards of 'best practice' in quality, delivery, cost reduction, etc.	Particular firms supplying to a major customer or members of a shared value stream
Government-promoted networks	National or regional initiatives to provide upgrades in capacity—knowledge about technology, exporting, marketing, etc.	Regional development agencies, extension services, etc.
Task-support networks	Similar to professional networks, aimed at sharing and developing knowledge about how to do a particular—especially novel—task	Practitioner networks

Source: Based on Holti and Whittle (1998); Bessant and Tsekouras (2000a, b).

4. The potential of SCL

One of these configurations of considerable interest as an inter-firm learning system is the supply chain or network. There are several reasons for such interest:

- there is a commonality of interest, focused on delivering value to a particular customer, and improvement of this core process along a supply chain
- there are potential benefits to sharing the learning experience, including risk reduction, transfer of ideas, shared experiment, etc.
- scope for innovation (both product and process) exists within individual firms in the chain/network, especially (but not exclusively) among lower tiers
- there is motivation for more advanced firms to help weaker firms improve since the overall system effectiveness depends upon this
- there is motivation for weaker players to participate in learning since their continued involvement in the supply chain/network depends on their upgrading
- there are issues of systemic effectiveness which lie in the inter-firm area rather than within the control or responsibility of individual enterprises and thus require some measure of joint problem-solving.

In considering the potential for SCL we need to recognize the different types of learning which might take place via this mechanism. These range from relatively simple, incremental additions to a current knowledge set—for example, new regulations—through to complex new approaches which will involve experiment and adaptation. Work by the Tavistock Institute (Holti and Whittle 1998) examining 'learning networks' in the construction industry suggests a distinction between 'operational learning' and 'strategic learning'.

1. Operational learning is when an organization tackles problems by applying established models or ways of thinking. This tends to give rise to incremental improvements to existing ways of doing things.
2. Strategic learning is when an organization approaches a problem with a completely new model or way of thinking. The learning is about a fundamentally different way of doing things (Holti and Whittle 1998).

The distinction—equivalent to the *optimising/do better* versus *development/do different* innovation mentioned earlier—is important in considering the use of SCL as a means for transferring 'best practice' across a supply network since much of what needs to be transferred is often of a 'strategic' nature in these terms. The problem is exacerbated by the fact that not all the relevant knowledge will be available in codified or embodied form (as in a manual or a new piece of equipment). Instead, much of it will be tacit in nature, something which is difficult to communicate and articulate and which often can only be learned through experience and practice.

Arguably, SCL can be applied to both types of learning but whereas much operational and codified learning can be transferred through simple and often one-way communication along the chain, strategic and tacit learning may require more active (and interactive) intervention.

In similar fashion we need to recognize that there are different modes in which supply chain learning can be enabled. At one level it can involve a one-to-one relationship between two players in a chain—for example, a customer and a key supplier. At the other end of the spectrum from such dyadic relationships are multi-firm groupings—clusters or networks—where there is some element of shared learning—for example, a supplier club involving all or a large proportion of suppliers to a particular firm. In between we might have gradations—for example, into levels of multi-firm involvement (such as a customer firm working with a group of two or three suppliers to develop a new way of working).

Linking these two frameworks, we can construct a simple matrix (Fig. 7.1) which highlights the different modalities under which different forms of SCL might be used. In this model simple dyadic relationships may be sufficient for operational learning but some form of learning network with shared learning features may be more important in more complex strategic learning.

There is clear potential in achieving and sustaining learning networks of this kind. One of the most notable examples is the case of Toyota where an active supplier association has been responsible for sustained learning and development over an extended period of time (Dyer and Nobeoka 2000). Hines reports on other examples of supplier associations which have contributed to sustainable growth and development in a number of sectors, particularly engineering

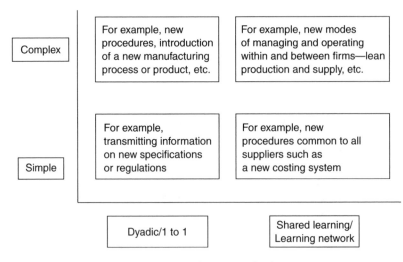

Fig. 7.1. Different learning types and modes in supply chains

Table 7.4. Sample benefits realized from SCL in six UK value chains

	Benefits to SCC	Benefits to first-tier	Benefits to second
Semiconductor equipment	—Sales quadrupled over 10 years —Incoming deliveries in kanbans: increased from 30% to 80% in 3 years	—On time delivery: 87% (1997), 100% (1998) —Scrap (internal and external): 1.5% (1995), 0.15% (1999) —Stockturns: 20 (1995), 40 (1999) —Set up time as % production time: >15% (1995), 10% (1999)	—Sales: grown 29% since 1995 —Stockturns: 8.5 (1996), 10.7 (1998) —Lead time: weekly (1996), next day delivery (1999)
Oil and gas	—The adoption of best practices through the supply chain may have generated saving of £1 billion	—First-tier supplier benefited as it saved 5% of total costs	—First-tier supplier helped the second-tier supplier cut down lead time from 14 weeks to only 16 days
Computer	—Cost reductions —Reduction of the number of first-tier suppliers from around 1,000 to nearly 200 —Reduced the time to market and increased profit margins and revenues		—Second-tier supplier now concentrates on technological capabilities which has increased the profit margins of the company
Chemical A	—The alliance has achieved total savings of 6%, which was jointly shared by the alliance and Chemical A —Productivity has grown by 4–5%	—Suppliers now have access to better equipment while all drivers are trained in defensive driving	—
Chemical B	—Quality and delivery time of materials has improved leading to cost savings throughout the supply chain	—Customers reduced inventory and in other targeted areas	

Table 7.4. (*Continued*)

	Benefits to SCC	Benefits to first-tier	Benefits to second
Aerospace	—Quality and delivery time of materials has improved leading to cost savings throughout the supply chain and relationships between participating companies has been enhanced	—Improved processes and reduced interface issues leading to delivery, quality, and responsiveness improvements	Use of SPC techniques to improve quality

and automotive (Hines *et al.* 1999). Marsh and Shaw describe collaborative learning experiences in the wine industry including elements of SCL, while the AFFA study reports on other experiences in the agricultural and food sector in Australia (AFFA 1998; Marsh and Shaw 2000). Case studies of SCL in the Dutch and UK food industries, the construction sector, and aerospace provide further examples of different modes of SCL organization (Fearne and Hughes 1999; AFFA 2000; Dent 2001).

To illustrate the potential of SCL we have data from six UK SCL networks studied in depth (Bessant, Kaplinsky, and Lamming 2001). Most of the cases we reviewed indicated improvements both for the main customer and its suppliers, confirming that SCL programmes can, in principle, be 'win-win' programmes. Table 7.4 lists several of the benefits firms realized from the programmes.

5. Implementation

There is, as can be seen from the preceding examples, growing evidence to underline the potential of SCL. But, as a recent UK government report indicates, 'learning is not a natural feature of business networks. It is unlikely to thrive unless it is part of the emergent new models for inter-company collaboration which stress trust, co-operation and mutual dependence' (UK Cabinet Office 2000). In other words there is a high risk that this will become simply another 'fashion' in operations management rather than a genuine platform for interorganizational development.

That said, it is clear that there is extensive experimentation taking place around SCL. In some cases the impetus for change comes from enlightened individual firms within the supply chain/network—usually the focal firm which acts as a leader/coordinator. In others the impetus comes from a sector-level initiative and is facilitated by a relatively neutral enabling agency—examples of this might be the SMMT's Industry Forum programme, the SCRIA programme in the aerospace sector or the Oil and Gas Forum in that industry. (Recent government policy has provided for the establishment of up to thirteen sector-based partnership initiatives in the United Kingdom, DTI/CBI 2000.) There is evidence of growing international activity along these lines and of state support for regional and national SCL initiatives—for example, the South African Sector Partnership fund.

Where SCL takes place there does appear to be evidence of gains at both individual enterprise level and at the system level. However, such reported initiatives are still confined to relatively high tiers in the chain/network and there is little direct involvement of SMEs (arguably the group which could benefit most from the approach). In the following section we will look in a little more detail at some of the common themes which emerge around the setting up and running of SCL.

6. SCL—the experience so far

What emerges from this early experimentation? The first is that there seems to be a model of supply chain learning in which a coordinating or central firm takes the lead. This firm tends to go through a number of generally (but not necessarily) sequential steps, as outlined below:

- a 'wake up call', with the drivers varying in different sectors and in different parts of the world
- the adoption of new organizational procedures within firms in response to this wake-up call (mainly in the quality and materials management areas)
- these internal changes are soon recognized to be of limited effectiveness unless the supply chain (and indeed the customer base) simultaneously undergoes complementary changes
- the rationalization of the vendor base (or the customer base), so that these complementary changes can more easily be implemented and synchronized
- the communication to vendors (and customers) of the new requirements which changing market conditions require
- mandating change in behaviour among suppliers (and customers)
- assisting suppliers (and customers) to achieve these new performance levels in their own activities in the design of a SCL programme, its running and in sustaining it over time
- assisting suppliers (and customers) to aid their own suppliers (and customers) in similar processes of change in the various tiers of the chain
- developing the ability to learn from suppliers and customers, not just to teach them.

These steps pass through processes of internal change and the recognition of the role played by the supply/customer base, and then to mandating change amongst suppliers. But SCL proper only really occurs once the coordinating firm plays an active role in *assisting* processes of learning amongst other firms in the value chain, and proceeds further when it recognizes that it also has something to learn from these firms.

A second core point to recognize is that there appear to be three distinct stages in SCL:

- a set-up phase where a variety of drivers converge around a commitment to action, often led by a champion individual or agency
- an operating phase in which the learning framework becomes established and begins to address the chosen learning agenda
- a sustaining phase where the challenge of maintaining momentum surfaces and where there is a high risk of failure.

Importantly the activities required and the key problem issues confronted at each of these stages differ. Table 7.5 gives some examples of the experiences (not always positive) of six SCL programmes which we have studied in depth. From this it can be seen that at the outset the challenges centre around acquiring resources and mobilizing commitment—but this is often facilitated by a shared sense of crisis. The role of active agents and champions—often from outside the network and with a perceived neutral status—is also significant. In the CRINE example mentioned earlier the impetus came from a widespread recognition of the weak competitive position of the United Kingdom sector as a whole, while the SMMT Industry Forum was established as a response to similar concerns in the UK automotive components sector. Set-up can also emerge through shared perception of common opportunity—for example, the possibility of entering new markets—through upgrading of capabilities across a supply chain/network (Kaplinsky *et al.* 2001).

Initial operation tends to be driven along particular paths often set by the lead or coordinating firm and there is a risk that other players in the network will not really 'buy-in' to the model or will become disappointed in some way with the learning processes. Early operations are supported by goodwill and the momentum from the set-up stage; over time this can be reinforced or diluted. Much depends here on the extent to which the initiative is founded on good supplier relationships and particularly a basis of trust (DTI/CBI 2001).

The sustaining phase is the most difficult since it is here that the initial impetus needs to be replaced with something able to maintain longer-term momentum and to take on the characteristics of shared ownership and direction.

These experiences resonate with other reported cases of SCL. For example, although the CRINE project was perceived to be a success overall there were concerns among small and medium sized players in particular. Its top down

Table 7.5. Implementing SCL programmes in the six value chains

	SCL Driver	Setting up	Running	Sustaining
Semiconductor equipment	Improving supplier quality	The pilot scheme began with local firms and with suppliers with a high transaction cost	Teams were set up with equal numbers from Semi-equip and supplier Teams set joint targets and hold regular reviews	The supply chain programe is not focusing proactively on SCL
Oil and gas	Comprehensive supply management	The programme set out to establish long-term contracts with contractors Best practices were proces-soriented and directed at the relationship between the customer and supplier	Commitment to share information Close collaboration between the SCC and its contractors Setting up cooperative schemes to improve the entire supply chain Measurement systems captured visible results such as cost savings	Annual reviews of supplier performance and assessing management practices
Computer	Improving all facets of supplier activities	Company outsources many activities leading to a dependency on the capabilities and performance of suppliers Critical supplies are managed globally SCC controls all supply tier contracts, that is, first-tier suppliers are not entirely	Transparency and information flows increased between firms Geographic proximity important as SCC pushes suppliers to open an office close by (even within its own premises)	Openness and transparency of information flows play an important role Moving from a need to exercise best practices related to quality and inventory to best practices that assist the provision of

Table 7.5. (Continued)

	SCL Driver	Setting up	Running	Sustaining
		free to choose second-tier suppliers Procurement guidelines stating how firms will be granted supplier status		services, technology development, and organizational learning.
Chemical A	increase the efficiency of transport and logistics	Workshops were organized to answer two key questions: —How to create a breakthrough in performance? —What can be done to realize this? Initial entry was to reduce costs across Europe by improving transport coordination Transporting firms (i.e. suppliers) formed an alliance to coordinate transport logistics with the SCC	Chemical A provided organizational framework Suppliers had to work through one representative, forcing suppliers to link together Culture of supplier competition had to be changed to culture of cooperation Supplier alliance created proposals for the terms and conditions of the alliance Costing developed into an open book approach with the SCC	Chemical A has agreed to a long-term agreement with supplier alliance The structure of the alliance is enabling each supplier to be effective as each company has a clear role Regular monthly meetings take place among the participants and information flows continuously between the companies
Chemical B	Reducing inventories and improving	External assistance from a consulting body was sought	Chemical B used an open book approach	Improvement projects were used with defined

	interfaces throughout the supply chain	for supply chain models Reviewed total global inventory How to reduce the total level of inventory for everyone in the chain? Inventory was reduced gradually with greater reductions occuring as customer confidence grew	to counter concerns about losing the security of holding large inventories	measures and objectives Upon completion, new projects were built on the previous project result but alignment with new business unit objectives was ascertained
Aerospace	Improving quality, delivery performance, and responsiveness of suppliers	Aerospace adopted the approach used in a previous collaboration and adapted it to their suppliers Senior management commitment key as the programme required significant resourses	Suppliers undertake self-assessment, Aerospace also performs a detailed assessment Results fed into a continuous improvement plan created by supplier, which is monitored by Aerospace over time Free assessments and training for suppliers. Exposure visits by supplier staff to other firms also arranged Suppliers have the opportunity to improve their business, and develop a long-term relationship	Programme has changed over time and now looks to incorporate functions such as finance and human resource development Difficult to get second and third-tier suppliers into the programme Programme relaunched to ensure current relevance and generate increased interest

Table 7.6.　Learning points in the six value chains

	Supply chain learning
Semiconductor equipment	Evidence of the development of learning capabilities in one of the first-tier suppliers Problem solving techniques were used by suppliers forming teams together with staff from the customers. But, in important respects, the SCC is itself a poor role model and learning is thus limited within the first tier
Oil and gas	Constant dialogue between the customer and the suppliers has led to better understanding among all parties Day-to-day work activities generate issues which are then incorporated into the strategic issues Supply chain issues are moving from practices related to material management toward soft ones such as services Suppliers recognize that a two-way learning process has occurred with (a) SCC adopting some of the supplier's techniques and (b) the supplier taking on practices first used by the SCC
Computer	The SCC establishes a set of standardized evaluations that are applicable to all suppliers This tool is used to benchmark all suppliers providing similar inputs The results are communicated to all suppliers. This practice gives clear advantage to the SCC during the bargaining processes No system implemented to measure the performance of the entire chain Creation of the supplier alliance improved relationship between all the suppliers and the chemical company enabling improved information transfer and understanding of requirements
Chemical A	Supplier alliance may prove to have a long-term benefit to suppliers (too early to determine) The concept of a supplier alliance is very useful in the transportation industry and there are prospects of transferring the initiative within the industry
Chemical B	Customer introduced six sigma SPC into SCC's manufacturing plants. This was not a structured mechanism of transferring best practice but a one-off occurrence Chemical B does not want to be responsible for passing initiatives beyond their direct customers or first-tier suppliers
Aerospace	The business assessments highlight areas for improvements and suggested tools and techniques that can be used to satisfy these requirements Suppliers were able to implement changes Some suppliers have transferred the Business Assessment into a Continuous Improvement Plan. The supplier takes ownership of the plan and is responsible for delivery Suppliers have not taken a consistent approach towards disseminating tools and techniques or lessons learnt to their own suppliers and do not feel responsible for dissemination to their second and third-tier suppliers

character meant that they often felt excluded from decision-making or involvement in planning (SQW and OTM Ltd 1997).

One indicator of sustainability in SCL will be the extent to which learning capabilities have been fostered—in other words, are the players in the network/chain learning to learn? Our results from detailed case studies bear out those of other researchers which suggest that at present SCL does not yet move far along the chain and in particular is not having a great impact on lower tiers and particularly the SMEs which often occupy such locations. Table 7.6 gives some examples of reported development of learning capabilities.

7. Enabling and constraining factors

Making SCL happen is clearly not easy, especially as we move beyond the initial set-up phase. Once the momentum provided by a shared sense of crisis or the support from external sources to configure a new arrangement has dissipated it needs to be replaced by structures, processes and a commitment to long-term sustainability and development of learning (Kaplinsky *et al.* 1999).

Effective SCL appears to be enabled or constrained by factors such as those listed in Table 7.7.

Some examples of how such blocks and enablers operate at the level of particular cases are given in Table 7.8.

Table 7.7.   Enabling and constraining factors in SCL

Enabling factors	Constraining factors
Firm foundation in good practice within the lead enterprise	Lack of trust /long-term relationships between firms in the chain
Firm foundation in good supply management—partnerships, cooperative relationships, etc.	Lack of awareness of sector problem or of 'best practice' solutions—problem of the underlying culture 'Best practice' is itself weakly developed in lead firm
Presence of lead firm or SCL champion	Lack of consensus or shared perspective on problem or solution
Presence of effective facilitation	Lack of structures and facilitation
Relevant measurement framework to guide learning	Lack of strategic focus
Structured operating arrangements and clarity of responsibilities and roles	Weak long-term sustainability

Table 7.8. Blocks and enablers to SCL

	Enablers	Blocks
Semi conductor	—Visit to the shop floor of customers and suppliers by production staff —Joint teams, involving a combination of management and production staff from both plants —Extensive communication by fax, 'faxbans', and through the use of e-mail, but no plans for the introduction of EDI proper —In general, large firms are more difficult to influence than small firms, since they have lower degree of dependence —Proximate suppliers are much easier to work with	—The slow and inconsistent pace of change within semiconductor equipment and some of its first-tier suppliers —Low levels of trust and the reluctance to become too dependent on suppliers/customers —A lack of systematic overview to the problems of supply chain learning —Absence of a proactive culture, both in relation to the broader problem of supply chain development, and the more specific challenges, which arise in promoting SCL
Oil and gas	—Senior management commitment —The existence of external bodies (e.g. CRINE) actively involved in the transmission of information on a collective and individual basis —Disposition to learn from suppliers —Avoiding an over-prescriptive approach towards suppliers —Willingness to learn from experiences from different industries —Focus on other aspects apart from price to assess suppliers and to ensure the sustainability of supply chains —Commitment on the part of the SCC to learn from suppliers and to accept that some answers to the supplier's malpractice could be found in their own malpractice —Development of high quality procurement areas —Periodic revision of objectives and measurement systems —Practising open-book type of relationship with the suppliers	—Lack of right skills —Time constraint —Incompatibility between what the SCL manager wants to promote and the objectives of particular parts of the company —Arrogance of some SCC managers —Some of the results of SCL are not easy to identify and sometimes are attributed to other activities
Computer	—High level of trust between the elements of the chain —Crystal clear objectives, methods of performance assessment and contracts —Uninterrupted flow of useful information —Physical proximity —Use of IT to communicate within and between firms	—Cultural differences between companies and within parts of the same company —Lack of processes to record the lessons obtained through SCL —External problems that impede the disclosure of information (e.g. legal procedures and poor protection of property rights in other countries)

Chemical A	—Suppliers linked to other SCL initiatives (networking) —Helping the suppliers to 'see the benefits of SCL all the time' —'Trust, trust and trust' between all the participating companies —Visible benefits and increasing awareness of the strength of the alliance —The SCC, an extremely big player with a good reputation was offering a long-term contract —Full commitment from all the participants —Continued consistent reviews against set targets —Seeing the bigger picture, that is, how the companies can jointly benefit when working together —Structured and organized approach of the participating companies	—Failure to understand the problem and see joint benefits from all parties' points of view —Protecting own corner instead of looking for the bigger picture —Failure to work with competitors —Failure to change culture, both within the SCC and other firms in the supply chain
Chemical B	—Trust and openness about fears and concerns —Obtaining prior agreement to any changes being made —Ability to see and share the benefits —Being a major supplier itself, the coordinating customer is willing to listen to its own suppliers —Senior Management commitment to release existing and employ new resources, and to support the initiative	—People protecting their own corner of the company and not having the vision to see the company benefits —Not being involved in the change —Slow project start-up leads to limited involvement and quick loss of interest —Inability to trust other participants —Lack of willingness to become involved due to the perceived restriction of investing in only one supplier
Aerospace	—The consideration that SCC is a major customer —Skilled and dedicated resources within the SCC —Structured approach, tools, and techniques transferred —Responsibility of the improvement plan lies with the company to which it relates —Visibility of the results achieved through using the approach, tools and techniques —Consistency in measures across first-tier suppliers enabling comparisons to be made and awards to be given —Assessments and participation in the programme and sharing of the tools and techniques was all free of charge and financial benefits generated were not all appropriated by the SCC	—Multiple assessments due to different customer requirements —Inadequate knowledge and skilled resource in suppliers —Inadequate availability and consistency of SCC's support —Inability to disseminate further than the first tier of suppliers —The approach of searching for one-size-fits-all solutions —Low cost culture of the aerospace industry creating destructive preconceptions

8. A model framework for developing SCL

As we noted earlier, SCL is still in its infancy and the subject of extensive experimentation. But there does seem to be some convergence around the experience, both in terms of confirming the significant potential it has and also the ways in which it develops and can be shaped and influenced. Based on this we can sketch out a framework within which SCL might be established within a particular context, and this section looks briefly at the questions which need to be addressed.

8.1. Set-up stage

The key issue at this stage is to provide focus and shared motivation to learn from and with others. As suggested earlier, this is often achieved as a result of a shared awareness of crisis or, to a lesser extent, of opportunity. As we have already discussed the question of 'governance' is raised and in the absence of a strong lead firm it is often difficult to find a focus or sustain momentum in SCL. Evidence suggests that an important activating and catalytic role can be carried out by key agencies such as business associations or government in focusing awareness and facilitating the development of a shared response. There is a need to move beyond building a shared vision, however, to identify key learning targets, network membership, network purpose, and primary modes of operation. Generating agreement at an early stage on specific targets for success and measurement frameworks to track progress towards these is a critical factor in obtaining commitment rather than simply enthusiasm on the part of network members.

8.2. Operation stage

Having established key structures and targets, the operating processes need to be explored and translated into ways of working. Our research suggests eight core processes have to be considered, and mechanisms developed for making these happen and for reviewing and improving them (Bessant *et al.* 2000). These are outlined in Table 7.9 and provide the focus for the development of formal operating mechanisms to allow the network to deliver on its learning objectives.

In addition, the difficulties of creating and running processes where the locus of control is not within a single enterprise need to be considered. It is easy for lead firms to assume a directing role but this may undermine the effectiveness of the processes and ultimately lead to withdrawal by other players.

Table 7.9. Eight core processes in interorganizational networking

Process	Underlying questions
Network creation	How the membership of the network is defined and maintained
Decision-making	How (where, when, who, etc.) decisions get taken
Conflict resolution	How (and if) conflicts are resolved
Information processing	How information flows and is managed
Knowledge capture	How knowledge is articulated and captured to be available for the whole network
Motivation/ commitment	How members are motivated to join/ remain in the network—for example, through active facilitation, shared concerns for development, etc.
Risk/benefit sharing	How the risks and benefits are shared
Integration	How relationships are built and maintained between individual representatives in the network

8.3. Sustaining stage

The final stage emerges once the network is established and has been operating for some time. The initial momentum provided by a shared sense of crisis or opportunity and initial goodwill (and possibly support funding) will have faded and the challenge is then posed to network members as to whether they remain committed or leave the network. Since membership is usually on a voluntary basis or involving low level financial and contractual commitments, exit is a strong possibility unless there is a sense of continuing advantage to be gained from participation. Several factors become relevant at this stage.

First is the potential for reviewing and redefining the purpose—relaunching the network. In the case of CRINE, for example, the initial goals of cost reduction were, to a large extent, achieved. The perception, especially among major players in the industry, was that the learning network effects had been valuable and should be further extended and so a steering group defined a number of new initiatives—(first in 1997) the CRINE Network with an explicit focus on upgrading along the supply chain and then in 1999 the LOGIC—Leading Oil and Gas Competitiveness programme, with the new goal of increasing global market share for UK firms in the industry. The positive momentum of the first phase was linked to a reframing of a new challenge with a continuing sense of underlying crisis.

Measurement and feedback also provides an input mechanism for sustaining SCL. For example, the use of 'best practice' benchmark data provides a continuing sense of performance gaps around which learning can be focused—an approach used extensively in the aerospace case study outlined above.

Facilitation and external support for the process can also assist with sustainability by providing a continuous review and organizational development process for the network. Operating processes like those outlined in Table 7.9 can be adapted and developed to take into account concerns and to give less experienced participants in the network a sense of share ownership and ability to shape and direct the network.

It is also clear that structural forms can help—for example, the relative longevity of the Toyota model probably owes much to the formal structure and requirements placed upon suppliers to participate.

Overall, it seems that the sustainability question links closely to the perception among members that learning and development is taking place. This suggests that attention paid to ensuring completion of the learning cycle, providing a combination of experience sharing, challenging, and structured reflection (accompanied by measurement), development, and diffusion of key concepts and active and shared experimentation will be critical.

9. Conclusions

SCL represents a part of a wider managerial problem for the twenty-first century. Increasingly emphasis is shifting to the inter-firm level as the unit of operation; businesses are increasingly about integrated and interconnected systems and managers need to learn new and complementary skills to deal with them. But systems do not behave as individual enterprises, the locus of control may vary widely, the assumption of shared goals and aspirations is untenable—in short, networks and systems pose significant new questions. We have looked at one aspect of the problem—the difficulties involved in trying to organize purposive learning systems along the supply chain, across the supply network.

SCL is still in its infancy although early experiences underline the significant potential which it offers. Almost all SCL activities seem at present to be focused on system optimization—enabling the players in the network to do what they do better. Most programmes are built around trying to spread 'best practice' and raise the overall level of performance through a variety of mechanisms which facilitate learning. There remains a considerable challenge for extending such learning to more strategic activities and to addressing the question of 'do different' innovation—for example, in evolving alternative and radical new product or service offerings.

Even at this early stage in the development of SCL it is clear that such learning will not emerge automatically or as a by-product from long-term supply partnerships. Rather there is a need for structures, operating processes, measurement systems, and continuing facilitation and development. In some ways the analogy might be drawn with groups and teams; simply assembling a group of people with a common purpose does not lead to high levels of performance or even to minimal achievements of the shared task. Teams emerge as a consequence of the evolution of norms and processes and their development can be aided and supported by a variety of team-building inputs. In the same way the achievement of the full potential of SCL is likely to require conscious and active investment in such interorganizational development and in research to support it.

References

AFFA (Australian Government Department of Agriculture, Fisheries and Forestry) (1998). *Chains of Success*. Canberra: AFFA.

—— (2000). *Supply Chain Learning: Chain Reversal and Shared Learning for Global Competitiveness*. Canberra: AFFA.

ARGYRIS, C., and SCHON, D. (1970). *Organization Learning*. Reading, MA: Addison Wesley.

BESSANT, J. (1998). *Developing Learning Networks*. London: 2nd IPSERA Conference on Strategic Purchasing and Supply.

—— KAPLINSKY, R., and LAMMING, R. (2001). 'Enabling Learning in Supply Chains', in *What Really Matters in Operations Management—8th Annual Conference of European Operations Management Association*. Bath: University of Bath.

—— and TSEKOURAS, G. (2001). 'Developing Learning Networks'. *A.I. and Society*, 15/2: 82–98.

—— HARLAND, C., LAMMING, R., and OLIVER, N. (2000). *Report on Inter-organisational Networking project*. Swindon: Engineering and Physical Sciences Research Council.

BEST, M. (1990). *The New Competition*. Oxford: Polity Press.

CHAMBERS, N. (1996). The *Future of the Offshore Oil and Gas Industry*. London: CRINE/DTI.

CHRISTENSEN, C. (1997). *The Innovator's Dilemma*. Cambridge, MA: Harvard Business School Press.

DE GEUS, A. (1996). *The Living Company*. Boston, MA: Harvard Business School Press.

DENT, R. (2001). *Collective Knowledge Development, Organisational Learning and Learning Networks: An Integrated Framework*. Swindon: Economic and Social Research Council.

DTI/CBI (Department of Trade and Industry/ Confederation of British Industry) (2000). *Industry in Partnership*. London: DTI/CBI.

—— (2001). *Supply Chain Learning—a Resource for Management*. London: 'Fit for the Future', DTI/CBI.

DYER, J., and NOBEOKA, K. (2000). 'Creating and Managing a High-performance Knowledge sharing Network: The Toyota Case'. *Strategic Management Journal*, 21/3: 345–67.

FEARNE, A., and HUGHES, D. (1999). 'Success Factors in the Fresh Produce Supply Chain: Insights from the UK'. *Supply Chain Management*, 4/3: 120–27.

HAMEL, G. (2000). *Leading the Revolution*. Boston, MA: Harvard Business School Press.

HEDBERG, B. (1981). 'How Organisations Learn and Unlearn', in H. Nystrom and W. Starbuck (eds.), *Handbook of Organisation Design*. Oxford: Oxford University Press.

HINES, P., LAMMING, R., JONES, D., COUSINS, P., and RICH, N. (1999). *Value Stream Management: The Development of Lean Supply Chains*. London: Financial Times Management.

HOBDAY, M. (1994). *Complex Product Systems*. Brighton: Science Policy Research Unit, University of Sussex.

HOLTI, R., and WHITTLE, S. (1998). *Guide to Developing Effective Learning Networks in Construction*. London: CIRIA/Tavistock Institute of Human Relations.

HUMPHREY, J., and SCHMITZ, H. (1996). 'The Triple C Approach to Local Industrial Policy'. *World Development*, 24/12: 1859–77.

KAPLINSKY, R. (2001). 'Learning Networks in the South African Auto Components Industry'. *Innovation News*, 5–6. University of Brighton: Centre for Research in Innovation Management.

——BESSANT, J. LAMMING, R., ROSS, A., and VAUGHAN, R. (1999). *Case Studies of Using Supply Chains to Transfer Best Practice*. London: Department of Trade and Industry.

——MORRIS, M., BARNES, J., and DUNNE, N. (2001). *Globalisation and Upgrading: Innovation and Learning in the Wood Furniture Value Chain*. Vienna: UNIDO.

KOLB, D., and FRY, R. (1975). 'Towards a Theory of Applied Experiential Learning', in C. Cooper (ed.), *Theories of Group Processes*. Chichester: John Wiley,

KUHN, T. (1962). *The Structure of Scientific Revolutions*. Chicago: University of Chicago Press.

LAMMING, R. (1993). *Beyond Partnership*. London: Prentice-Hall.

MARCEAU, J. (1994). 'Clusters, Chains and Complexes: Three Approaches to Innovation with a Public Policy Perspective', in R. Rothwell and M. Dodgson (eds.), *The Handbook of Industrial Innovation*. Aldershot: Edward Elgar, 3–12.

MARSH, I., and SHAW, B. (2000). *Australia's Wine Industry. Collaboration and Learning as Causes of Competitive Success*. Working paper. Melbourne: Australian Graduate School of Management.

McGILL, I., and WARNER WEIL, S. (1989). *Making Sense of Experiential Learning*. London: Open University Press.

MILLER, R., HOBDAY, M., LEROUX-DEMERS, T., and OLLEROS, X. (1995). 'Innovation in Complex Systems Industries: The Case of Flight Simulation'. *Industrial and Corporate Change*, 4/2: 363–400.

NADVI, K. (1999). 'The Cutting Edge: Collective Efficiency and International Competitiveness in Pakistan'. *Oxford Development Studies*, 27/1: 81–108.

NONAKA, I. (1991). 'The Knowledge–Creating Company'. *Harvard Business Review*, 69/6: 96–104.

OLIVER, N., and BLAKEBOROUGH, M. (1998). 'Innovation Networks: The View from the Inside', in J. Grieve Smith and J. Michie (eds.), *Innovation, Co-operation and Growth*. Oxford: Oxford University Press.

PEDLER, M., BOYDELL, T., and BURGOYNE, J. (1991). *The Learning Company: A Strategy for Sustainable Development*. Maidenhead: McGraw-Hill.

PEREZ, C., and FREEMAN, C. (1989). 'Structural Crises of Adjustment, Business Cycles and Investment Behaviour', in G. Dosi, C. Freeman, L. Soete, R. Nelson, and G. Silverberg (eds.), *Technical Change and Economic Theory*, London: Frances Pinter.

PIORE, M., and SABEL, C. (1982). *The Second Industrial Divide*. New York: Basic Books.

POLANYI, M. (1967). *The Tacit Dimension*. London: Routledge and Kegan Paul.

PORTER, M. (1997). *Location, Knowledge Creation and Competitiveness. Knowledge Capitalism: Competitiveness Re-evaluated*, Boston, MA: Academy of Management.

REVANS, R. (1983). *Action Learning*. Buckingham: ICMB/G, Wills Publisher.

SQW and OTM Ltd (1997). *Improving SME Relationships in the UK Oil and Gas Industry*. London: Department of Trade and Industry.

TIDD, J. (1997). 'Complexity, Networks and Learning: Integrative Themes for Research on Innovation Management'. *International Journal of Innovation Management*, 1/1: 1–22.

UK Cabinet Office (2000). *Learning Across Business Networks*. London: Department of Trade and Industry.

WOMACK, J., and JONES, D. (1997). *Lean Thinking*. New York: Simon and Schuster.

8

Supply Chain Transparency

RICHARD LAMMING, NIGEL CALDWELL, AND WENDY PHILLIPS

1. Introduction

1.1. The simplistic idea, the paradox, and the challenge

Behind the basic principle of supply chain management and much of the rhetoric of cooperation within 'chains' is a bland simplification of the commercial interface between customer and supplier. This chapter provides a conceptual challenge that reveals and criticizes this simplification and explains a practical approach that offers a strategic alternative for managing in the customer–supplier interface and introduces the concept of *value transparency*.

Since supply chains (or, more realistically, supply networks) are made up of organizations linked by relationships, the concept of value transparency may also be of relevance to managing supply within the broader focus (the network) and also challenging to established practices that are associated with it. Development of the concept has been based upon field research and longitudinal observation of practices and contingencies within supply relationships.

We know that, paradoxically, established business practices associated with managing purchasing and supply often tend to block or corrupt actual or potential interorganizational capabilities (Lamming *et al.* 2001). This chapter discusses how even what may be perceived as more recent or 'modern' practices appear to include this paradox. Over time our research has suggested that concentration upon leveraging the vantage points of customer or supplier (Lamming 1996), as opposed to concentrating upon leveraging the potential of the relationship, appears endemic to supply relationships (Lamming *et al.* 2000).

We suggest not only that issues of power, dominance, and game playing create noise, bilateral cost, and waste in the customer–supplier interface, but that industrial, social, and technological trends increasingly militate against attempts to maintain 'commercial secrets'. As a collateral issue to our principal focus, we observe that the Internet is playing a significant role in driving out traditional wastes (and postures) in global procurement as well as giving both buyers and sellers access to more information (and thence, knowledge) than ever before.

In this chapter, we propose the concept of *value transparency*, a radical form of information sharing, managed by and between customer and supplier, on a strictly delineated project-by-project basis, as a method for going beyond, and improving upon, traditional managerial practices in supply interfaces. In place of openly adversarial or customer-dominated relationships (and here we will discuss the role of the rhetoric mentioned earlier), value transparency is put forward as a potential source of competitive advantage. That is to say, the customer sees the supplier not as a supplicant but as a critical resource, the value of whose knowledge can only be fully utilized through two-way information sharing.

We define value transparency as 'the creation, nurture and delivery of value for the benefit, and thus continued existence, of both parties' (Lamming *et al.* 2001). This goes beyond the two-way sharing of information suggested in the original formulation of *cost* transparency (Lamming 1993), recognizing valuable properties of the relationship itself and involving managed risk for both parties, with identifiable additional returns. It also addresses two important issues that arose from the earlier development of cost transparency: the difficulty in reaching agreement on the type and extent of sensitive information that is to be shared, and the assumption that each party has both the technical and organizational capabilities necessary to exploit this information in a manner that will bring about operational improvements and commercial benefits.

1.2. Structure of this chapter

Under the title 'What We Know . . .' we trace the origins of transparency in supply, as originally proposed in the conceptualization of *lean supply* (Lamming 1993). Turning to what we know about practice, we briefly explore the origins of supply chain management, exposing the nature of the principal flawed management practice, open-book negotiation, which is then criticized in some detail. Addressing 'What We Don't Know . . .' we explain what the concept is not, enabling us to differentiate transparency from established system level definitions of the term. 'Key Developments for Practice' are contained in our explanation of the principles and practical issues of value transparency, while 'Key Developments for Theory . . .' are discussed with the help of a new conceptual model. We focus on some 'Key Developments for Pedagogy' including the need for educators to go beyond current texts and constantly question current practice before finishing with a discussion on the 'Consequences and Conclusions.'

2. What we know: the current state of knowledge

2.1. *The origins of the concept: lean supply and cost transparency*

Originating from research in the late 1980s, the concept of transparency in supply relationships arose (as *cost* transparency) during the development of the lean supply paradigm (Lamming 1993). Originally based upon extensive work in the global automotive industry (Womack, Jones, and Roos 1990), the lean supply paradigm includes the application of radical techniques (i.e. doing new things differently, rather than the old things better) in removing activities deemed wasteful (adding no value to the product or service, or the process of its delivery). It is important to note that no apparently redundant factor is taken as prima facie necessarily wasteful by the lean approach. Indeed, high inventory levels may be necessary for agility in responding to market dynamics, while idle time may be necessary for learning to take place in a system; neither would necessarily detract from the leanness of the system. (In other words, no differentiation is made between leanness and agility when considering supply interfaces.) Early work on lean supply focused on less traditional concerns, suggesting that much so-called 'professional' purchasing might actually be responsible for maintaining wasteful practices. Observation revealed that these practices were adding cost and time to processes, reducing the ability of the organizations (customer and supplier) to respond to market signals (i.e. making them less lean and agile). The focus of lean supply at the interface, ruthless in its attack on systemic waste, often contradicts aspects of conventional and modern purchasing which were previously considered to be practical skills to be encouraged and 'perfected'. Thus, transparency originated as a lean idea, aimed at removing waste and excising flawed practice. The waste that was targeted was often in the form of wasted opportunities in the supply relationship which, if exploited, might provide value to both parties in return.

In the mid-1990s, a second phase of action research was conducted in a variety of UK companies outside the automotive industry revealing the difficulties organizations might face in trying to implement cost transparency (Lamming *et al.* 2000). The principal outcome of this case-based work was the identification of organizational *inhibitors* to transparency, classed as *structural* or *operational*. The conclusion was that effective implementation of the concept would be facilitated by the *removal* of parts of a system (inhibitors), rather than introduction of new mechanisms (it did not appear appropriate, for example, to introduce a 'transparency manager'). This chimes with the lean principle of waste removal.

Conducted between 1998 and 2000, the third phase of the research involved working with a large high-technology systems manufacturer in the aerospace industry. As reported below, the practical outcome of this research not only contributed towards a clearer understanding of the conceptual and practical complexity and nature of transparency but also generated a formal *framework for discussion*. Current work is refining this framework, again working with manufacturing firms (EPSRC grant GR/N 38916/01). Based on case studies in four high-technology manufacturers (in a variety of industries) and their suppliers, the framework is being developed into a formal conceptual model. This will lead to the design of practical methods for managers to use in supply relationships.

The concept of *cost* transparency within the development of lean supply relationships, was defined as the 'sharing of costing information between customer and supplier including data which would traditionally be kept secret by each party, for use in negotiations. The purpose of this is to make it possible for customer and supplier to work together to reduce costs (and improve other factors)' (Lamming 1993). It was also proposed that the 'customer should require only directly relevant data and should be able to justify any and all requests (i.e. rather than requiring *carte blanche*)'. Costs are used here as a proxy for all assets involved at the interface and also the creation, nurture, and delivery of value. It is important to note that the term 'transparency' is used here to refer to *two-way* exchange of information, that is, the customer shares data with the supplier about its own operations, as well as requiring the supplier to 'open its books', to an agreed degree and for a specific purpose. This would require the removal of the inhibitors mentioned above. As we have said, such a radical approach is openly critical of the practice known as 'open-book negotiation'. This is discussed below but first it is necessary to relate the concept to what we know about the origins of supply chain management.

2.2. *Supply chain management and the 'always right' customer*

Earlier chapters in this book have dealt with the origins, development, and popular key concepts within supply chain management. Here we are highlighting how, in many accounts of supply chain management, the focal firm or lead organization in a supply chain is presented as the omnipotent (and ubiquitous) 'conductor' of a chain or network of resources (i.e. other autonomous organizations and firms). This is an intuitively appealing picture, and one that may be identified, for example, in the case of high street grocery chains whose severe demands upon suppliers of fresh food products, *inter alia*, are well known. It is tempting from examples such as this, to infer that supply chain management is all about gaining and exploiting economic power.

Perhaps one part of this view stems from initial attempts to validate supply chain approaches by reference to Japanese *keiretsu*, where focal firm dominance was common (Ellram and Cooper 1993). In Western interpretations, the *keiretsu* approach was taken to include supply relationships dominated by the customer, with a relentless focus on cost reduction (as envisaged and defined by the customer).

It is also germane that the term 'supply chain management' was coined in the 1970s by Western management consultants working with large and powerful business organizations. In such organizations, the prospect of managing resources beyond the firm boundaries and that offered a central role for their own management skills had an inherent appeal for managers. The attraction of coordinating interorganizational supply processes without resorting to outright ownership or taking a stake in suppliers was bolstered by the adoption in isolation of two elements of the *keiretsu*, open-book negotiation, and supplier development. Both techniques worked well in the Japanese example due to the senior–junior nature of their relationships (i.e. the customer actually could develop its suppliers) (Lamming 1993).

Extending this principle generally to business systems (in which suppliers must operate within commercial axioms and manage themselves with autonomy, and where customers do not automatically know best about how suppliers should develop), left a basic flaw in the practices of supply chain management as the idea developed.

2.3. The absurdity of open-book negotiation

The concept of open-book negotiation appears to spring from the fundamental tension in interorganizational relationships between sellers and buyers. This tension exists between two irreconcilable needs. The first of these is the need on the part of the seller to differentiate the good or service being sold, in order to charge for added value (i.e. worthwhile properties above basic specification), thus enhancing both immediate profit and long-term interest from the buyer. ('Of course my product costs more—because it is better!') The need on the part of the buyer is the reverse—to 'commoditize' the good or service so that standard value may be bought for the lowest price. It appears easier to cajole buyers into recognizing differentiation than to force suppliers to standardize, and the profession of sales and marketing has arisen specifically to do this. Buyers, meanwhile, realize that real added value may warrant paying more (acceding to differentiation) but that attractive but trivial features should be eschewed. This tension has, of course, always been the basic premise of buying and selling.

The advent of mass production in the late nineteenth century, and its dominance of the twentieth century, led to many extraordinary (and often absurd) behaviours in buyers—the 'profession' that grew to deal with the proliferation of sales tactics. Perhaps the strangest of these behaviours was generated by Gordon Selfridge's famous marketing aphorism *'The customer is always right'*. Given the nature of the tension discussed above, it is easy to see that this is a sales trick. If the seller can convince the customer that they are infallible and then convince them that *they* (the customer) have identified trivial features of the product as valuable, then the customer will naturally believe that they are right to think this way, and thus pay too much for the actual value being provided. It is alarming to observe professional buyers repeating Selfridge's subversive mantra, believing as a consequence that they should receive service from suppliers that reflects their infallibility—including the illusion that they can 'manage' the supplier to meet their requirements. As with most self-delusion, the denouement is usually painful and expensive.

To operationalize this principle, as part of the mass production–supply chain management canon (purchase orders, specifications, tough negotiations amounting in some sectors to plain arrogance and rudeness) customer organizations have developed the practice of *open-book negotiation*. Simply put, if the customer is always right and the performance of the relationship is suboptimal (e.g. the price of the good being bought is too high), then the customer's intervention in the supplier's operational processes should reveal ways of improving the situation (for the customer, by lowering prices, and imputably for the supplier, in the form of better efficiency). The basic principle is thus for the customer to ask the supplier to 'open its books' to reveal process factors, largely represented by costs (as proxies for, say, process times, physical space allocation, management superstructure, communications requirements, etc.) and submit to ideas that are suggested by the customer. In practice, it does not take long in such situations for it to become clear that the customer (represented by the buyer—often a poorly qualified commercial person with long but narrow experience) does not in fact understand the information being presented in the 'books'. If, say, a manufacturer of motor cars were to conduct the process with a supplier of machined parts, it might be accepted that *adequatio* (the ability, or 'adequateness', to understand what is being set before one—see Schumacher 1978) existed on the part of the customer (who probably knows something about the production of machined parts). Many other situations in which the practice is applied reveal no natural link between the expertise in the buyer and the operations of the supplier. Despite this, open-book negotiation is widely practised.

To address this anomaly, some customers seek to develop *intelligence* in their purchasing—building generic cost models for specific supply markets and sometimes employing (or consulting with) specialists in the subject, in order to mount an attack on the supplier's professed cost structures. A second order problem may arise here, however, stemming from the need for internal support departments to justify their existence. For example, if a 'Purchasing Intelligence Office' produces a guide price which the buyer should pay for an item from a supplier, it may be seen by the buyer as an implicit slur on their professional ability. A natural tension therefore builds between the buyer and the Purchasing Intelligence Office, especially when the former is formally required to use the services of the latter. The intelligence office has power over the buyer—if the guide price is not revealed until after the initial negotiation, they may suggest that a test may be made of the buyer's professional competence. Once the buyer's best price is known, it is quite possible for the Purchasing Intelligence Office to alter its estimate (before revealing it), thus indicating that the buyer had not achieved the best price through negotiation.

This has the double 'advantage' of making the buyer look bad and justifying the existence of the Purchasing Intelligence Office. A stand-off thus arises, with neither side prepared to tell the other their best price for the item, so the buyer goes into the open-book negotiation without much support.

The supplier, meanwhile, has realized the true purpose of open-book negotiation: it is an attempt by the customer to drive down prices by whatever means possible. There is a fundamental reason why this is unacceptable to the supplier but it is not simply a matter of the need for secrecy and the protection of a 'scarce asset' (their knowledge, tacit as well as codified). By requiring the supplier to 'open their books', the customer is asking them to take a risk. The customer is not beholden to the supplier beyond the immediate contract (which may not even be in place at this point) and, once in possession of process data, is quite likely to 'leak' critical information to the supplier's competitors, in order to encourage them to reduce prices, etc. (the well-known 'Dutch auction'). The customer, meanwhile, takes no risk.

The benefits of the exercise, however, are principally to be gained by the customer. The benefits for the supplier (typically proclaimed by the customer as part of heralding the process) are limited to retention of the business and, implicitly, improvements in efficiency (which may presumably be exploited by achieving greater margins on business with other customers, who do not 'help' the supplier by intervening in this way). In fact, in reducing process costs (if this were really to happen) and thus prices, the supplier might actually reduce its sales turnover if it retained the business—and quite possibly its profit (neither effect popular with shareholders).

This means that the customer is actually asking the supplier to take a risk in at least two ways (reduced sales figures and the threat of competitors receiving its data and thus nullifying competitive advantages it may have). The supplier would not survive long in business if it were constantly to take such risks without hedging. In the case of open-book negotiation the only hedging that is feasible is to 'fudge' or 'cheat'—to distort the figures contained in the 'open book'. Such cheating cannot be substituted by naïve 'trust' unless the customer is also taking a risk. When this is not done, the 'knowledge' gained by customers through open-book negotiation is inevitably corrupted and thus worse than useless (i.e. it is actually dangerous).

Another curious second-order problem results from this situation, again reflected in the behaviours of buyers. It is not difficult to work out the logic explained above, especially over several episodes of open-book negotiation. The buyer, however, is convinced that they are 'always right'. Two courses of action are open to the buyer: to blow the whistle, or to put their head in the sand. Given the other pressures on the buyer (including that of devices such as the Intelligence Office described above) it is perhaps forgivable that the buyer always takes the latter course. The buyer knows that the information (or knowledge) gained from the process is corrupt, but decides to live with it because that is what the system requires.

For these reasons (and several more) open-book negotiation appears to be nonsense in practice, resulting in excessively high process costs in purchasing and supply (Barry 1998). The key to breaking out of the formalized nonsense lies with the buyer: they must take a risk. Developing practice from open-book negotiation to transparency raises two key issues. The first is: which factors should be an agreed part of the negotiation and which are to be hidden from view? The second issue concerns the implicit assumption that increased bilateral information sharing will lead to lower costs (and other improvements). That is to say, there is an assumption that there are areas on each side of a business interface which when linked by transparency of relevant information (from each side) may lead to increased profitability for one or both parties. These two issues are treated below by relating them to aspects of dyadic supply relationships, progressing from totally hidden to totally transparent areas (see Table 8.1). However, before exploring transparency in supply relationships further, due to the widespread adoption and use of the term 'transparency' it is first necessary to differentiate the way that transparency functions in supply from other common usages.

3. What we do not know: priorities in research

When research identifies a conceptual flaw in practice it must go back to the origins of the concept to check that its provenance is sound. Before presenting transparency as the product of our work, therefore, we should briefly consider the gap in knowledge that led to its development. Also, since we are using a common word in a specific manner, we need to explain our meaning.

3.1. What value transparency is not

National and regional governments often espouse the concept of transparency. This is true, for example, of the European Commission, which has as one of its stated aims, a commitment to transparency in its processes and structures. This is reflected in UK government pronouncements and in calls from various pressure and special interest groups. The rise of the Internet has also raised interest in the concept of transparency—in areas of administration it is often positively associated with greater democracy and accountability.

Others view transparency with suspicion, associating it with the famous 'all-seeing eyes' of Foucauldian discipline regimes, where transparency took the form of oppressive surveillance (in the design of prisons) and Orwell's 'Big Brother' (of *1984*) (Foucault 1977, 1980). The same drive may be seen in business but with widely different implications, impacts, and processes, including challenges to managers that go beyond the pressures on certain types of margins visible in e-supply.

In seeking to manage transparency in supply relationships, we need to distinguish business or commercial relationship management from those system-wide approaches evident in governments, banking, commissions on national and international issues, and even much commodity-based Internet trading. Inherent in viewing transparency fundamentally as a *property* of a system is a claim that the entire relationship between two organizations could be termed transparent. Such a view may be possible or necessary where issues of democratic access and privilege are paramount although it has often been observed that too much transparency (literally providing a wall of 'information') is an effective way of hiding things.

However, where transparency is applied as a resource in supply relationships, it is based upon a more selective and particular application of the concept: as an *element* of the supply relationship (that managers in a specific, focused relationship may decide to utilize in a variety of forms, for specific purpose). According to this definition, transparency might be only one of several elements utilised in the specific relationship, along with others such as agreed procedures, equity sharing, joint patents, and so on.

Development of transparency in the meta-systems of governments and electronic markets is seen, at least in theory, to distribute or share the benefits of greater openness as widely as possible. Transparency in supply, as proposed here, is particular to a context, to a relationship associated with a *particular* project (product or service). Our hypothesis is that the net effect of this particularism may be to reduce market (and margin) pressures for the parties to a commercial relationship by developing value for them that would be unavailable in simple market-based transactions (Dyer and Singh 1998). Thus, the value in the relationship that may be realized through managed transparency attenuates the need to develop other sources of value (for each party at the expense of the other) through conventional techniques.

System-level views of transparency tend to emphasize an inevitable and inexorable commoditization process at work and the benefits of 'demystification' of arcane, obtuse, or possibly illegal practices. Clearly, transparency as described here might lead to demystification. However, more importantly, in recognizing and harnessing the unique capabilities of an individual customer and an individual supplier, the relationship itself becomes a shield from system level forces. In essence, in removing the neoclassical economist's concept of perfect information, transparency in supply distorts competition. This chimes with the recognition of long-term relationships as sources of value rather than the classic definition of them as 'market failures'. What is ultimately emphasized is value creation in the relationship rather than provision of a product or service; what is at issue is configuring that value, not simply identifying costs. Our research, therefore, tracks the refinement of the initial idea—cost transparency—into the proposed concept of *value transparency*.

One of the claims made by proponents of the Internet is that it will create transparency through wider information sharing. Pressure groups, governments (at both national and regional levels), and customers are aware of the 'democratic' principles inherent in the concept of transparency. In business, transparency has largely been viewed as an additional (but perhaps ultimately the most significant) pressure on margins. Thus, e-commerce systems moved quickly from simple electronic data interchange (EDI—in the 1980s) in which purchase orders, invoices, payments, and so on, could be made 'paperless' through online ordering systems accessing suppliers' catalogues (1990s) to exchanges and online auctions (2000). Current applications can indeed be seen as markets in which buyers and sellers know the market price. We do not yet know the implications of this for supply management. The role of information exchange or sharing, however, will clearly be great.

The need for sharing sensitive information and tacit knowledge is recognized as one of the basic reasons for establishing a firm. The restriction on opportunism of individuals (e.g. to sell secrets to others) via regulations and motivations couched in organizational mechanisms is clearly an effective way of consolidating the development of assets and supporting growth. In such a situation, commercial transparency is easily limited to the boundary of the firm—trade secrets are not traded. Traditional ways of capturing knowledge locked in firms include merger, acquisition, and espionage. Where the firm in question is a supplier of goods and services, the customer organization seeks to gain the *benefits* of such knowledge as a result of efficient playing of the market. In this view, the need for the supplier firm to retain its knowledge, protecting it from competitors, is assumed to be eclipsed by the need for that firm's outputs to be competitive.

As the need for concentration on specific competencies is introduced by economic forces including pressure on prices and costs from fierce international competition, so the realization dawns that an organization does need to know what is going on in other firms—especially its suppliers—without resorting to acquisition. Thus, the idea of transparency across firm boundaries arises. When the focus is enlarged to encompass the network within which the organization operates, the degree of complexity increases although the principle remains the same. As Möller and Halinen note, 'knowledge generation about networks is not unproblematic, as networks are highly non-transparent' (Möller and Halinen 1999).

4. Key developments for practice

4.1. Putting value transparency into practice

Once the mass production oriented assumption that the customer is always right is jettisoned, it becomes plain that in the interorganizational supply relationship, ideas for improvement may not only be forthcoming from the customer; the supplier also may be expected to contribute to mutual benefit.

While the customer employs simple economic power, however, there can be no possibility of this, other than that represented in squeezed prices, where the supplier may be expected to cheat as far as possible and give the minimum actual value. The market knowledge necessary to control such a relationship (with great numbers of suppliers) would appear to be impossible to contain in practice (although seductive in theory). Given this, the conditions under which genuine transparency and data exchange might be achieved would appear to require some sharing of risk and benefits. In revealing its own operating dimensions and costs to the supplier, the customer is sharing knowledge on its value-adding processes. This is a risk in both the basic sense of 'leakage'—exactly as described above in the opposite direction—and in the more complex form of forward integration on the part of the supplier (who might, for example, suggest the outsourcing of some of the customer's activities). It may even be that the supplier can suggest an overall cost reduction in a process which accommodates a unit price increase—something that might severely tax the comprehension of a traditional buyer.

As the customer 'opens up' to the supplier, the risk must be contained carefully and justified. Other functional managers within the customer's organization may be adversely affected by this process (as the supplier blows whistles on slack practices) and may be expected to oppose the process with guile (Åhlström and Karlsson 1996). Thus, a *carte blanche* approach would seem inappropriate (even though this may have been previously espoused in dealing with the supplier's 'open books'); only if requests for sensitive information are justified may accurate, uncorrupted data be expected in response. As both 'sides' are trusting the other with their information, there is a power balance. In ceding its apparent power, the customer is enabling the supplier to lower its guard; in effect, it is trading intelligence rather than assuming it may be achieved through threat or use of power. In fact the 'cost' of this may be negative—the benefits and cost savings are the payback for the investment. Transparency is achieved through two-way exchange of sensitive data for specific purposes of improvements in the dyad itself (the actual process change might take place in either company—or both).

4.2. Managing value transparency—a range of modes

To characterize the concept of value transparency in practice between two organizations, we employ a metaphor taken from geology. It has the inherent limits of all metaphors but is used here only after extensive trials in industry, where it has been very enthusiastically received (Lamming, Caldwell, and Harrison 1999).

The metaphor adopts the characteristics of minerals in terms of the amount of light that can pass through them. Since value transparency is a dynamic but manageable property of a relationship, not a characteristic or attribute, it does not need to be in action all the time. Rather, it may be selected as a useful element in a relationship for a particular purpose (i.e. a project). Its dynamism means that we may expect different types of transparency to be possible and by extension, the selection of several ways of configuring and using these different types.

In the metaphor, light is analogous to information in the supply relationship, since it must be transferred if the proposed mutual benefits are to arise. *Transparency* in a substance allows light to pass through without distortion; so, in some parts of a relationship, at some times, some information may pass from one party to another without corruption. *Translucency* in a mineral allows shapes and forms to be observed but obscures detail. Thus, in a relationship, outline information may be shared in a translucent manner without the inner workings of a system being shown (cf. 'black box' in shared engineering or design) again in a contingent, manageable manner. *Opaqueness* in a mineral will prevent all light from passing; similarly some information in a relationship may not be shared with the other party, but honesty in revealing this constraint is respected as a form of transparent behaviour. Working with these forms of transparency in a project plan it should be possible to decide jointly (i.e. supplier and customer together in a boundary-spanning project team) what types of sharing are necessary and practicable, how they might be combined, and how they may need to change over the stages of the project.

Thus, in practice, rather than 'being transparent' (or opaque or translucent) in a general manner, in the context of a specific purpose or project, a supply relationship is likely to contain (or require) all three characteristics in a variety of locations at different times (or stages in the project). In each case, selection of a manner of information exchange, characterized by the types of transparency in the metaphor, is justified by a specific purpose within a project plan. These three characteristics are likely to be distributed over the range of interface processes, for example, purchase manager with sales manager; design engineer with design engineer; operations manager with operations manager; director with director. We suggest that planning a project or relationship on the basis of what needs to be shared and in what manner, at what time, for the purpose to be achieved and potential (or latent) value to be realized, constitutes *managing value transparency*.

It is important to be clear that, in identifying a continuum from 'opaqueness' (no knowledge on either side) to 'transparency' (full but finite knowledge of a 'localized' topic) we are not suggesting that there is a 'designed path' or 'mandated route' for supply relationships themselves from opaque to transparent, even in the context of a specific project. In practice the matter is not iterative but more complex. For example (following the metaphor), a fundamentally non-transparent part of a relationship could develop 'fissures' of total value transparency from a long-term relationship between boundary-spanning personnel in the two organizations.

Table 8.1. Manageable modes of exchange in value transparency as derived from a geological metaphor

	Opaque	Translucent	Transparent
Geology: light shining on or through a piece of mineral	Light can neither penetrate the surfaces nor pass through the structure of the substance	Light can enter and exit the surfaces of the substance and pass through its structure, but is distorted or partly obscured in the passage	Light enters and exits the surfaces or the substance and passes through its structure without alteration
In supply management: (information existing in or shared between two organizations)	For any of a variety of reasons, information cannot be shared by party with the other between the parties on this subject but this constraint is acknowledged by both parties.	Restricted information on this subject may be shared, for example, but interface conditions or partial data Used in value transparency this is positive but limited collaboration If used tactically, it may be akin to 'cheating'	Information regarding this subject is shared candidly, on a selective and justified basis Development of information may lead to shared knowledge and collaborative abilities

In practice, therefore, the exchange modes employed in value transparency as it is presented here relate to aspects of a relationship as identified within a project (Table 8.1). The project-focused relationship is seen as combining points on the continuum from opaque (cf. 'arms length') to transparent, where information is freely shared (e.g. a common database or shared intranet). We use 'information' as an initial proxy for value being added (for one or both parties) through the relationship interface.

In addition to the manageable forms of two-way information sharing, there are two further, *unmanageable* states, at least in terms of the supply relationship. The first of these is *dazzle*, beyond value transparency, where too much information is presented and the receiver cannot deal with it (this may be accidental or deliberate—for example, politicians often employ such a tactic by shrouding a request for information in a plethora of facts and figures). The second is *black hole*, where the factors are so deeply buried or complex it is not possible to explain or share them.

5. Key developments for theory

5.1. A conceptual model for using value transparency in supply relationships

The conceptual model depicted in Fig. 8.1 aims to explain how value transparency might exist and be employed within a dyadic supply relationship and thus, eventually, within the supply network. The two parties to the dyad, A and B, are shown to the left and the right of the diagram. The relationship between them, for this specific encounter (development or delivery of a product or service), is the elliptical area bounded by the heavy, broken line. Note that it is assumed that many such relationships may exist between A and B simultaneously, with different complexions, i.e. a productive, congenial and collaborative relationship may be associated with one product or service while a quite different, adversarial, secretive and corrupted affair might characterize the supply or development of another. Logically, therefore, it is not meaningful to speak of 'the relationship' between the two parties in a homogeneous sense, other than as an amalgam or ganglion of diverse relationships that might be bundled together to form it.

Reflecting its origins in innovation and technological imperatives, the model of value transparency begins with the external *selection environments* of the two parties. These contain structural, regulatory, and legislative factors, the strengths and weakness of competitors, technologies (in the widest sense), market demands and unfulfilled needs, and so on (Lamming *et al.* 2002). The coincidence of potential for radical development lies in each of the two environments (which neither party can exploit alone) and provides the spark of originality for the relationship. The potential value for both parties lies in the differences

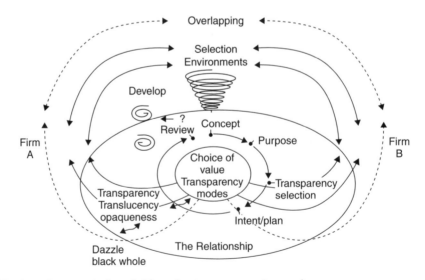

Fig. 8.1. A conceptual model for value transparency in supply

between the two environments (i.e. one would not otherwise contain, or perhaps even be aware of, the other). These overlapping environments are represented by four sets of two-way arrows. The upper pair show the interplay between the internal decision-making (the neoclassical focus) and the external environment before the relationship (or the interruption to it that is represented by the new input from the overlap) operates. The lower two sets of arrows show the same process during and after the relationship interlude. In both cases the flows represented by the arrows are the result of inward reflection and outward scanning by the two parties. In the latter case, however, 'outward' refers to the relationship, rather than the external environment.

The model presents the coalescent formation of an idea or a proposal as a whirlpool, metaphorically collecting ideas from the external environment that may be understood and exploited by A and B only through collaboration. The whirlpool descends into the relationship as a proposal for a new product variant, service development, process improvement, and so on. To give the proposal life, the two parties plan a project of implementation, represented by the circular arrows within the relationship space. Note that the ellipse represents an overlap between the organizations, representing the notion of a dynamic operating space that is partly in 'no man's land', 'owned' jointly by both parties but secured into each through boundary-spanning teams.

The first stage of implementation, or exploitation, is the identification of the expected returns to both parties (the basis for an internal business case in each party, to justify the investment about to be made, and a joint case referring to the success of the relationship based upon this project). This is the concept stage; the parties discuss the idea and prioritize actions. It is at the concept stage, for instance, that the allocation of intellectual property rights would be discussed and possibly pre-collaboration agreements might be drawn up lodging what each party already knows about the issue (both standard practices in pre-competitive collaborative product development).

If the cases are sound (and approved by the necessary processes in each firm) the concept develops into a purpose, the mission statement for the project that will deliver the benefits of the concept. This process is a mutual identification of an opportunity in the supply market which might lead to business benefits for both parties. Once this has passed through a formal preparation (including risk assessment and cost–benefit analysis, skills audit, etc.) the extent and nature of value transparency required for each stage of the project may be planned. This includes the choice of value transparency modes that are to be employed at each stage of the project in order to deliver the purpose. Thus, for example, knowledge of a factor that must remain opaque for one side in the first stage may be required in, say, the third stage. This could be accommodated by phasing the exchange to avoid delays or guesswork on one side and, on the other side, embarrassment or the need to hedge risks by corrupting data. By planning the value transparency as a variable, manageable resource for the project, both sides are able to reduce the surprises and conflicts that might normally impede such work, precipitating a return of the costs of 'cloak and dagger working'.

The processes of value transparency selection, intent, and planning may be expected to overlap and assume an iterative nature. Following their completion, the project of exploitation takes place, generating the knowledge flows referred to above, in addition to its central purpose. At the final review of the project, the decision might be made to end the engagement or to extend the concept to new purposes. This might be inward consolidation (installing the concept as a feature of the organization, represented by the inward spiral) or the reverse, taking the concept to a greater purpose, perhaps with expanded expectations.

Note that the conceptual challenge of value transparency is the identification of forms of value within the relationship which, while perhaps inevitably linked to established terminology (exchange, utility, place, etc.) may be operationalized in useful managerial terms.

6. Developments in pedagogy

6.1. A challenge for developing knowledge

The challenge for educators presented by conceptual developments such as that associated with value transparency lies in the need for innovation to inspire education. The pedagogy associated with supply chain management is typically reliant upon observation and analysis of practice, action research, modelling and framing, and attention to strategic imperatives. In order to include radical approaches into pedagogy, therefore, it is necessary to delimit the educational process to allow creative destruction of current practices and fundamental questioning of established ideas, no matter how much has been invested in them by protagonists, not for how long. Much supply management pedagogy takes its origins from Ronald Coase's epochal article, over 60 years ago (Coase 1937; Williamson and Masten 1999) and Williamson's seminal work, beginning in the 1970s. Both these, and the heated criticism of the latter that continues to this day, represent the destruction of established ideas—a profound challenge for pedagogy. If supply chain management is a flawed metaphor based upon linear development of established ideas, then concepts such as value transparency must be seen as discontinuities and accommodated by pedagogy that embraces exploratory thought, not trammelled teaching. Just as the research associated with the topic is typically action research based (inductive, phenomenological, qualitative), so teaching must become similarly open and interpretive.

7. Consequences and conclusions

7.1. Changes in practice

Recasting the management of supply relationships—increasingly being termed 'SRM'—as a shared responsibility rather than the domain of the customer entails many changes in practice. Principal among the consequences of a move to value transparency would be:

1. Recognition of the value of supplier expertise—tapping into current but unused interface resources, notably by involving suppliers to a greater extent than before, this chimes with the lean principle of not wasting opportunities to capture latent value in the relationship.
2. Acceptance of a dynamic management space (the relationship) rather than a linear development (e.g. such as that implied by the concept of supplier development towards goals set by a customer).
3. The sharing of risks, including the customer engaging in a managed risk with the supplier, in pursuit of defined rewards.
4. The need for structured knowledge management: the information shared using transparency is convertible into knowledge by the process of thinking and understanding.
5. Managing supply management (or purchasing, procurement, etc.) in the case of a strategic supplier may become a matter of project management rather than the established role of daily tasks. Buyers employed in this new role will need new skills—principally those of writing business cases, managing risks, and project management.

7.2. Conclusions

The chapter has distinguished between *value transparency* and *open-book negotiation*. The proposed concept of transparency presents a more developed and holistic approach to risk than the traditional one dictated by the customer. With regard to knowledge management, transparency appears to require reflexivity, whereas open-book approaches appear static and concerned with the treatment (or management) of existing knowledge—working '*on*' knowledge, whereas transparency is concerned with dynamics and potentials, that is working '*with*' knowledge.

This is a radical challenge; without addressing such challenges, supply chain management may remain simply a set of managerial techniques rather than becoming a genuine field of knowledge.

References

ÅHLSTRÖM, P., and KARLSSON, C. (1996). 'Change Processes Towards Lean Production—The Role of Management Accounting'. *International Journal of Production & Operations Management*, 16/11: 42–56.

BARRY, C. (1998). 'Choosing Qualitative Data Analysis Software'. *Sociological Research Online*, 3/3: U59–U75.

COASE, R. H. (1937). 'The Nature of the Firm'. *Economica*, 4/16: 386–405.

DYER, J. H., and SINGH, H. (1998). 'The Relational View: Cooperative Strategy and Sources of Interorganizational Competitive Advantage'. *Academy of Management Review*, 23/4: 660–79.

ELLRAM, L. M., and COOPER, M. C. (1993). 'The Relationship Between Supply Chain Management and Keiretsu'. *International Journal of Logistics Management*, 4/1: 1–12.

FOUCAULT, M. (1977) *Discipline and Punish*. London: Allen Lane.

—— (1980). *Power/ Knowledge*. Brighton, Sussex: The Harvester Press.

LAMMING, R. C. (1993). *Beyond Partnership: Strategies for Innovation and Lean Supply*. Harlow, UK: Prentice Hall.

—— (1996). 'Squaring Lean Supply with Supply Chain Management'. *International Journal of Operations and Production Management*, 16/2: 183–96.

—— CALDWELL, N. D., and HARRISON, D. A. (1999). 'A Conceptual Model of Transparency in Supply Relationships'. *Working paper presented at British Academy of Management*, Manchester: Metropolitan University.

LAMMING, R. C., JONES, O., and NICHOL, D. (2000). 'Transparency in the Value Stream: From Open-Book Negotiation to Cost Transparency', in P. Hines, R. C. Lamming, D. Jones, P. Cousins, and N. Rich (eds.), *Value Stream Management*, Harlow: Prentice Hall, 273–302.

—— —— —— and PHILLIPS, W. E. (2001). 'Transparency in Supply Relationships: Concept and Practice'. *Journal of Supply Chain Management*, 37/4: 4–10.

—— HAJEE, D., HORRILL, M., KAY, G., LI, M., MACGREGOR, S., NEWNES, L., STANIFORTH, J., and TOBYN, M. (2002). 'Lessons From Co-development of a Single Vessel Processor: Methodologies for Managing Innovation in Customer–supplier Networks'. *International Journal of Technology Management*, 23/1-3: 21–39.

MÖLLER, K., and HALINEN, A. (1999). 'Business Relationships and Networks: Managerial Challenges of Network Era'. *Industrial Marketing Management*, 28/5: 413–27.

SCHUMACHER, E. F. (1978). *A Guide for the Perplexed*. London: Abacus Books.

WILLIAMSON, O. E., and MASTEN, S. E. (1999). *The Economics of Transaction Costs*. Northampton, MA: Edward Elgar.

WOMACK, J. P., JONES, D. T., and ROOS, D. (1990). *The Machine that Changed the World*. New York: Maxwell Macmillan.

9

Supply Chain Relationships

CHRISTINE HARLAND, LOUISE KNIGHT, AND PAUL COUSINS

1. Introduction

This chapter explores the evolution of understanding of supply relationships from several academic perspectives. First, we evaluate the key issues addressed through the different approaches, and consider their contributions. Then, we focus on more recent cross-disciplinary research that offers a more holistic understanding of the structure and content of supply interaction in different contexts, overcoming some of the limitations of previously fragmented research. Research in supply relationships has developed from a focus on more tangible aspects of relationships. Here, we argue that there are significant, less tangible aspects that also need to be examined if we are to develop a more comprehensive, detailed, and integrated understanding of the many facets and forms of supply relationships. Also, research in supply relationships was traditionally mainly conducted in high volume, low variety manufacturing industries, particularly automotive and electronics, whereas more recently a broader spread of types of supply relationships in different sectors has been examined.

Since the 1980s it has been appreciated that different relationships may be required for different products/services in different contexts. Notably, Kraljic (1983) developed a portfolio approach in which the appropriate relationship type was contingent upon a combination of the value and the criticality of the product/service being purchased. We argue that this 'relationship positioning' technique oversimplifies relationships. We also challenge the wisdom of research claiming to focus on 'the relationship' as a unit of analysis. Relationships are complex, multi-stranded arrangements of exchange between different actors in the short, medium, and long terms. We discuss recent research that views relationships as processes involving social, informational, and technological exchange over time, in addition to short-term transactions of products, services, and payments, giving rise to accrual of corporate social capital resources, such as trust and reputation, for both parties. We conclude that an integration of different perspectives of relationships provides a richer understanding than single perspective studies have achieved to date.

Supply relationships have provided an interesting focus of study for researchers with various epistemological and axiological perspectives. Some of those perspectives have concentrated on more tangible aspects of relationships, such as the volume and timing of materials and information flows, product quality improvement, and cost minimization. Others have focused on less tangible aspects, such as the perception of service quality, trust, and power. Some research has addressed the flows or exchanges between the parties to a supply relationship, while other research has examined the nature of the relationship itself as a quasi-organization, and the changing nature of the parties to that relationship. These various perspectives are discussed in this chapter.

Although any categorization of research is necessarily imperfect, grouping work according to subject area provides a clear understanding of the fragmented evolution of research into supply relationships. In the next sections, we examine four approaches to understanding supply relationships grounded in the disciplines of operations management, industrial economics, purchasing and supply, and industrial marketing.

2. Operations management

Early texts in operations management concentrated on the tasks performed by the production manager (Meredith *et al.* 1989), mostly within the organization. Mayer (1962) chose to omit externally oriented decisions from his text on production management, on the basis that production managers would play only a minor role in such decisions. Wild (1971) was one of the few operations management authors who included a chapter on purchasing and supply. Operations management texts from the 1990s have covered logistics, purchasing, and materials management and procurement (see, for example, Schmenner 1990; Meredith 1992; and Slack *et al.* 1995), as relationships with suppliers have increasingly been recognized as part of the subject of operations management.

Research on inventory management addressed exchange of information and materials replenishment between buyers and suppliers; earlier stochastic based replenishment systems led to short-term crisis management of suppliers to satisfy shortages arising from inaccuracies of independent demand forecasting systems (Orlicky 1975). From the 1960s, deterministic calculation of materials requirements with suppliers was possible through the use of Materials Requirements Planning systems (Wight 1982; Vollman, Berry, and Whybark 1989), and with distributors through Distribution Resource Planning systems (Martin 1983). Logistics authors such as Bowersox, Closs, and Helferich (1986), and Christopher (1992) also focused on exchange of information and materials in relationships, though they tended to examine immediate relationships with distributors, rather than suppliers.

Within operations management, there is evidence of interest in the importance of supply relationships through Deming's fourteen points for quality improvement (Deming 1982, though they were developed in the 1940s) and the whole Total Quality Management movement led by Deming (1982), Juran (1988), and Crosby (1979). Deming argued that firms should work more closely with fewer suppliers, to enable clear and unambiguous communication flows to take place, allowing buyer, supplier, and customer to realize the maximum amount of synergy from their relationship, and therefore achieve competitive advantage for all parties involved in the transaction (Macbeth and Ferguson 1994). The Deming ethos is based on timely and acceptable inputs to the organization and focuses on productivity and efficiency, rather than profitability per se. A concentration on productivity and efficiency will, according to Deming, lead to overall improvement levels in long-term sustainable competitive advantage and profitability (Nishiguchi 1994)—a view substantiated by the subsequent success of Japanese companies today as discussed in Womack, Jones, and Roos (1990).

The Total Quality Management movement that significantly improved quality of inbound supplies enabled the implementation of Just-in-Time (JIT). From an inventory management perspective, JIT is a physically based replenishment system appropriate to relatively high volume, routinized exchange relationships, where suppliers replenish to the rate demanded by production (i.e. a 'pull' approach) rather than to an information system generated schedule ('push' approach) (Harrison 1992). However, to achieve JIT required integration of many subsystems within supplying and buying organizations, including design and production engineering, materials management, production planning and control and quality management (Hahn, Pinto, and Bragg 1983). As Deming (1982: 33) points out, purchasers should '. . . end the practice of awarding business on the basis of price tag alone. Purchasing must be combined with design of product, manufacturing, and sales to work with the chosen suppliers.'

Hayes and Wheelwright (1984) and Hill (1989) externalized Operations Management at a more strategic level through considering vertical integration and sourcing as operations decisions, and asking such questions as:

1. What boundaries should a firm establish over its activities?
2. How should it construct its relationships with other firms—suppliers, distributors, and customers—'outside' its boundaries?
3. Under what circumstances should it change its boundaries or these relationships, and what will be the effect on its competitive position?

So, progressively, operations management authors have broadened their interest beyond the firm to include relationships with suppliers. Predictably, they have focused on operational exchanges, primarily of materials and information, to improve operational objectives of dependability, flexibility, speed, cost, and quality (Slack *et al.* 1995). This firm-to-firm based operational perspective of relationships is different to that taken by industrial economists.

3. Industrial economics

Discussion of alternative forms of organization to vertical integration or market can be traced back as far as Marshal (1923). Since then various authors have identified different intermediate types of relationships in markets, notably Williamson (1975, 1985, 1986), Richardson (1972), and Blois (1972). In a groundbreaking paper, Coase (1937) considered the internal and external workings of a firm, highlighting that a firm can source supplies and services either internally from itself or externally from other firms. Crediting the start of this relationship work to Coase, Williamson (1975) has developed it and made the most significant contribution to the area. Williamson categorized different forms of market organization on a scale ranging from market (no interdependence) through relational exchanges (some interdependence) to hierarchy (ownership). While economists such as Richardson (1972) and Blois (1972) had identified the continuum of relationship types prior to this, it was Williamson's classification and theories that appear to be most widely recognized.

The trend away from vertical integration as a relationship type was reported from the mid-1980s. For example, Thackray (1986) reported on vertical disintegration in manufacturing industries including automotive, machine tools, video recorders, industrial robots, optics, consumer appliances, and medical equipment manufacturing. Porter (1988) found that over 60 per cent of acquisitions in entirely new fields through vertical integration were later divested. Significant evidence was provided for the increasing incidence of buy rather than make strategies at this time (e.g. Dirrheimer and Hubner 1983; Child 1987; Kumpe and Bolwijn 1988; Gadde and Håkansson 1990).

Underpinning the industrial economics perspective of relationships is the concept of Transaction Cost Economics (TCE) (Williamson 1975, 1985). TCE theory explores markets and hierarchies within governance structures, indicating an appropriate type of relationship to a particular economic environment. TCE assumes that firms are opportunistic, driven by self interest, and that managers within firms have a limited ability to handle complex situations, that is, a bounded rationality (Simon 1957). TCE has been criticized in two major areas. First, it assumes that firms are solely motivated by economic considerations; other more social motivations such as trust, reputation and status are largely ignored. Second, TCE fails to explain why recurrent subcontracting exists. In an effort to counter the recurrent subcontracting argument Williamson (1985) developed the term 'obligation contracting', where the key characteristic in the exchange was 'asset specificity'. He proposed that if long-term investments were incurred between two companies then they would be inclined to an obligation exchange as switching costs would be high. Porter (1980: 124) uses the same argument of high switching costs for avoiding such exchanges and selecting vertical integration rather than relationship. Williamson (1975) defined four clear types of asset specificity: human, site, physical, and dedicated. In the absence of asset specificity, Williamson argues that obligation contracting is unlikely to occur because the winning bidder would have no advantage over the non-winners, as switching costs would be low and the winning bidder would constantly have to meet competitive bids from qualified rivals.

The industrial economics perspective of relationships is, not surprisingly, founded on economic considerations. While operations management academics concentrated on improving quality, speed, dependability, flexibility, and cost through relationships, industrial economists sought to improve price; this reflects the key difference between taking a firm or a market-based perspective of supply relationships. Purchasing and supply academics have tended to combine the operations management/firm based performance view and the industrial economics market perspective.

4. Purchasing and supply

The traditional purchasing and supply literature took a rational, negotiated approach to purchasing from suppliers, optimizing the best combination of the 'Five Rights': 'to purchase the right quantity of material, at the right time, in the right quantity, from the right source, at the right price' (Baily and Farmer 1985). Buyers were encouraged to take an adversarial position to suppliers using a variety of negotiation techniques to gain control (see, for example, England 1967; Westing, Fine, and Zenz 1976; Lee and Dobler 1977). The emphasis was on buying decisions and activities, and the organization of the purchasing function.

It is only relatively recently that purchasing texts have examined trading of a longer-term nature with suppliers, as 'relationships'. Authors of these texts, such Cox (1996), Ellram (1990), and Macbeth and Ferguson (1994), all appear to have been heavily influenced by the industrial economics perspective. Ellram (1991) defined supply chain management as an intermediate market form between acquisition (hierarchy) and transaction (market). Macbeth and Ferguson (1994: 106) placed relationships on a continuum ranging from vertical integration to the pure market.

Focus in the purchasing and supply arena on longer-term relationships was evident from the 1990s onwards as attention was moved to 'partnerships'. Cousins (1991) defined a partnership as 'the sharing of risks and rewards, of technology and innovation, leading to a reduction in costs, improvements in delivery and quality and the creation of sustainable competitive advantage' thereby integrating industrial economics and operations management perspectives. Partnerships with suppliers relate to what Contractor and Lorange (1988) termed 'vertical quasi-integration'. Lamming (1993) referred to the buyer–supplier relationship as a 'quasi-firm': 'the management of lean supply chains may require both collaborators to view the relationship as a "quasi-firm" with its own organizational structure and goals, communication mechanisms and culture'.

Burt and Doyle (1994) highlighted how Western firms have looked at the success of their Japanese counterparts and seen how they reduce costs with closer working relationships with their suppliers. Lamming (1993) proposed that, in the West, perceptions of partnership are based on profitability and cost reduction whereas the partnership philosophy should be based on improving productivity and efficiency; this view is underpinned by the operations management perspective of the total quality movement.

Lorange and Roos (1992) identified that in a partnership, the supplier is a stakeholder in the customer's organization. Cyert and March (1963) defined stakeholders as either 'internal' or 'external' to the firm. Internal stakeholders include managers, trade unions, etc., while the external influencers include government, legislators, suppliers, and so on. In this view, the supplier will have a profound effect on the production and supply of the buying firm's product—that is, the perceived quality and reliability of the buying firm's product is highly dependent on the supplier. More importantly, internal stakeholder status should give both firms equal access to information that is important to the relationship, such as production schedules, forecasts, promotional activity plans, and even more strategic information about directional change of either firm. This consideration of stakeholders and richer elements of exchange indicates some integration of social aspects of relationships.

Partnership is a long-term process and should not be viewed as an instant cost saving exercise but rather as an investment (Kanter 1989), which is very much how Japanese manufacturers viewed relationships with suppliers. Japanese buying organizations recognized that suppliers were the experts in their own field of technology, and that they could draw upon this expertise to create synergies with their own organizations. This model involves viewing the supplier as 'co-producer', working with fewer suppliers per customer and customers per supplier; developing long-term relationships; managing close interaction among all functions; sharing physical proximity; and agreeing blanket contracts (Nishiguchi 1994; Cousins 2002).

In Slack *et al.* (1995: 544), Harland provided a categorization of exchange in different types of relationships, as shown in Table 9.1.

One of the main failings of the work on 'partnerships' was its promotion of partnerships as being somehow good and right and adversarial relationships as being traditional, and therefore outdated, and a bad approach to dealing with suppliers. Kraljic (1983) proposed a contingency, portfolio, approach to determining the appropriate form of relationships, which has been adopted and adapted by many others, such as Ring and Van de Ven (1992). Typically, two contextual dimensions are selected and related to one another on a 2-by-2

Table 9.1. Types of relationships

Relationship type	Exchange elements	Examples
Integrated hierarchy	People materials, goods and services, technologies, information, money, equity	Single product firm, for example, paper, aluminium
Semi-hierarchy	People, materials, goods and services, technologies, information, money, equity, centralized control, divisional reporting	Multi-divisional firm, holding company, for example, chemicals, food
Co-contracting	Medium/long-term contract, technologies, people, specifications, materials, goods, services, knowledge	Co-makership, joint venture, for example, automotive
Coordinated contracting	Specification, payment, planning and control information, materials	Projects, for example, construction
Coordinated revenue links	Contract, performance measures, specification of processes and products/services, brand package, facilities, training	Licensing, franchising, for example, fast food chains
Long-term trading commitment	Reservation of future capacity, goods and services, payments, demand information	Single and dual source, blanket order, for example, electronics
Medium-term trading commitment	Partial commitment to future work, reservation of capacity, goods and services, specifications	Preferred suppliers, for example, defence
Short-term trading commitment	Goods and services, payment, order documentation	Spot orders, for example, stationery purchases

matrix to provide four categories of relationships. Users of the technique can then analyse their supplier or customer relationships and identify the appropriate relationship strategy. Authors, such as Sako (1992), Dore (1983, 1987), and Lamming (1993), concur that a portfolio of relationships is essential to a firm, with the appropriate type of relationship depending on the parties involved, the external environmental conditions (Burt and Doyle 1994: 5) and the parties' overall willingness to enter into a particular form of relationship.

However, particularly as firms have rationalized their supply bases, two organizations may often exchange a range of products and services. For example, in one case study of two firms linked as buyer and supplier in the aerospace industry, Cousins (2002) found that there were over 1,500 interfaces between them, on a variety of products, service, and commodities. If we consider, for example, Kraljic's dimensions of product/service value and criticality, exchange of some products/services may justify an adversarial relationship, while others may require high degrees of collaboration, cooperation, and co-development. So, one type of relationship between the buying and selling organizations may not be appropriate. This challenges a basic premise of much of the purchasing and supply work on relationships that tends to view *the relationship* as a unit of analysis, whereas in fact there may be many relationships between two firms, and they are dynamic, not stable.

Not only might there be several relationships between two organizations around different products and services, but also often many individuals are involved in establishing and maintaining a supply relationship. Managers in different positions with different roles may form relationships with other managers in the dyadic relationship partner. Engineers in both firms may work closely and collaboratively on designing a new product or developing a major project, to the extent that interpersonal relationships across organizational boundaries may be more cooperative than internal relationships between functions in the buying organization (Knight 2000: 125–8), while buyers may treat salespeople adversarially. In public sector procurement, suppliers can question the value of collaborating on innovation projects, if they are later to be subjected to competitive tendering for volume orders.

Purchasing and supply academics have, to some extent, drawn on theory from operations management, industrial economics and, to a lesser extent, organizational behaviour, but they have only relatively recently examined longer-term interaction in relationships. Marketing academics have developed concepts that help to understand interaction in relationships.

5. Industrial Marketing

The field of marketing is primarily concerned with consumer marketing, but there is a sector within the discipline that focuses on 'industrial marketing', marketing to industrial buyers. Within this, in Europe, the Industrial Marketing and Purchasing (IMP) Group, dominated by industrial marketers, has developed an 'interaction approach' to the study of industrial markets and supply relationships, which has proved to be highly influential. It is based on continuous exchange relationships occurring between a limited number of identifiable actors (Håkansson and Snehota 1989) and incorporates aspects of interorganizational theory (Van de Ven, Emmit, and Koenig 1975) and work of the 'new institutionalists' from industrial economics (Williamson 1975).

This approach models a supply relationship as 'frequently long term, close and involving a complex pattern of interaction between and within each company' (The IMP Group 1982), and defines four key variables of relationships:

(1) the elements and process of interaction which include short-term exchanges of products/services, payment, information, and social interaction, and longer-term institutionalization and adaptation;

(2) the parties involved in the interaction (organizations and individuals);

(3) the atmosphere affecting and affected by the interaction;

(4) the environment in which the interaction takes place.

Each of these variables is subdivided into elements, as shown in Fig. 9.1.

This model is particularly useful in analysing relationships of strategic importance which are characterized by their longevity, high levels of inter-dependence, and multiple interfaces (Knight 2000: 124)—precisely the type of relationship that is of increasing interest to academics and practitioners because of the rise in outsourcing and partnership working. The central theme of this model, which is lacking or underdeveloped in other approaches to supply relationships, is 'embeddedness' (Dacin, Ventresca, and Beal 1999). It sets the short-term, more operational exchanges in the context of long-term adaptation. It recognizes the role of interpersonal relations in the interorganizational rela-tionship, and the impact of sociability and solidarity (Goffee and Jones 1996) between individuals on economic relations. It enables a more integrated view of social, commercial, technological, and operational factors. It addresses the market and strategic context of the relationship. The model allows a rich analy-sis of supply relations, which has been used extensively in empirical research. However, much of the IMP Group's work has been aimed at theoretical develop-ment, with relevance to practice as a secondary interest (Easton 2000).

In general, the industrial economic and industrial marketing approaches to supply relationships have developed knowledge that is more theoretically robust but less relevant to practice, while the operations management and purchasing and supply approaches have developed knowledge of relevance to practice that

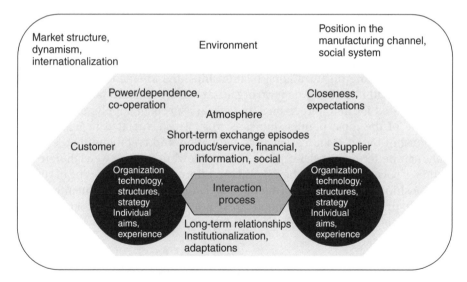

Fig. 9.1. IMP's interaction model

Source: The IMP Group (1982).

is less theoretically robust. However, since the 1990s, perhaps aided by the advent of electronic access to databases of academic publications, there has been a considerable growth in research which integrates these different approaches and draws on a wide range of other disciplines in the social sciences. In the next part of this chapter, we review some of this work, showing the contribution it can make to improving our understanding of supply relationships.

6. Integrative approaches for examining supply relationships

There are several ways in which research of supply relationships can be seen as 'integrative'. Research may draw on more than one of the knowledge bases developed in the four fields described above. There is, however, also an increasing interest in the interorganizational domain from academics in many other disciplines including sociology, economics, and public policy, centred on a common interest in networks (Mayntz 1993; Powell and Smith-Doerr 1994; Araujo and Easton 1996; Kickert, Klijn, and Koppenjan 1997). This research provides new opportunities for novel contributions, as theories and principles from these disciplines are 'translated' to the context of interorganizational relations.

Research can also be seen as integrative if it covers more than one system level, considering, for example, individuals within interorganizational relationships, or relationships within networks of relationships. Finally, researchers may use a variety of research methods to explore supply relationships, possibly combining quantitative, large-sample surveys with qualitative, in-depth case studies. Evidently, projects may be integrative in more than one way.

There is both increasing recognition of the importance of 'strategic' customers and suppliers, and increasing interdependence between organizations as they engage in longer-term, higher value, and higher risk relationships. In these sorts of interorganizational relationships, the interactions of individual employees within and between two organizations are critical. Many researchers are interested in the interpersonal and social aspects of supply relationships, and one of the most popular topics is trust. Trust is related to many other relationship-based resources such as reputation and credibility that, collectively, can be termed 'social capital'. In the following section, we elaborate the notion of social capital and show how it can inform our understanding of supply relationships. The discussion is intended to demonstrate the value of integrative research, through a specific example; there are, of course, many other concepts that can usefully serve as the basis for integrative research.

7. (Corporate) social capital and supply relationships

The notion of social capital was initially applied to individuals within communities and organizations (Coleman 1990; Burt 1992). Leenders and

Gabbay (Leenders and Gabbay 1999; Gabbay and Leenders 2001*a*) have recognized, however, that it is also relevant to organizations within networks, and have proposed the concept of *corporate* social capital (CSC): 'the set of resources, tangible or virtual, that accrue to organizations through social *structure*, facilitating the attainment of organizational goals' (Gabbay and Leenders 2001*a*: 8)

Less formally, corporate social capital can be described as resources that are available to an organization because of its relationships with others. Some authors focus on resources *within* relationships, such as trust, reputation, and credibility, whereas others also treat resources that become available *through* relationships—for example, information—as forms of social capital resources. The absence of such resources, when social structure prohibits and obstructs action and consequently the attainment of goals, is seen as social liability (Gabbay and Leenders 2001*a*: 6).

Trust is often singled out as a key resource (Araujo and Easton 1999) which provides increased 'opportunities, access to resources and flexibility' (Uzzi 1997: 43–5). Trust enables access to resources that can be used to help achieve organizational goals; these include information in excess to that which is exchanged in an economic transaction (Uzzi 1997), support and advice (Knoke 1999), financial capital (Uzzi and Gillespie 1999) and intellectual capital (Nahapiet and Ghoshal 1998). Of all the different forms of social capital, trust seems to have had the most attention from researchers of supply relationships. It is often recognized as an important element in successful, strategic relationships with suppliers, but rarely analysed in any depth.

One important exception is Mari Sako's (1992) work, in which she defined three categories of trust:

Contractual Trust. The trust that the supplier (or other party) will adhere to the points of the contract as agreed. This covers both explicit and implicit agreements.
Goodwill Trust. The trust that the other party will, if required, perform tasks in excess of the agreed terms and conditions.
Competence Trust. The trust that the other party has the ability to be able to produce what the contract requires.

Another exception is Lane and Bachmann's (1996) comparative study of trust in supplier relations in Germany and Britain, based on the work of Luhmann (1979) and Zucker (1986). They focus on the institutional context for trust, for example, the extent of reliance on legal regulation.

There has been greater interest in trust from those studying business-to-business relationships from a marketing perspective but, as Blois' review (1999) demonstrates, there are many problems with much of this work that undermine its value to the development of both theory and practice. For example, the definitions of trust are often incompatible and sometimes conflicting, and are usually based on prior marketing research, rather than being grounded in more robust theories of trust developed in philosophy and sociology; the important notion of trustworthiness (Dasgupta 1988) is not recognized; uncritical assumptions are made about the transferability of conceptualizations of interpersonal trust to interorganizational trust (exceptions include Doney and Cannon 1997; Zaheer, McEvily, and Perrone 1998) and a failure to recognize that the complexity and fragility of trust make direct questioning about trust an unreliable approach to research.

Reputation is also an important element of business relations (Macaulay 1963). Cousins (1992) included 'current reputation' as one of ten attributes that are important in a buyer/supplier partnership. Aspects of reputation such as 'word of mouth' (Parasuraman, Zeithaml, and Berry 1988) and 'external communications' (Zeithaml, Parasuraman, and Berry 1990) are examined in service management research. Zeithaml, Parasuraman, and Berry (1990) examined credibility as a contribution to both expected service and perceived service. In earlier work credibility was merged with competence, courtesy, and security within the dimension of service quality termed 'assurance' (Parasuraman, Zeithaml, and Berry 1985); their definition and explanation of assurance was later expanded to 'the knowledge and courtesy of employees and their ability to convey trust and confidence' (Parasuraman, Zeithaml, and Berry 1988).

A further problem that prevents prior research from forming a cohesive, comprehensive body of knowledge is that much of it is based on empirical studies which only partially cover the vast spectrum of interorganizational supply relations. Purchasing studies tend to be based in the manufacturing sector, and the majority of service management and marketing studies focus on relations with individual consumers (see, for example, Swan, Trawick and Silva 1985; Sako 1992; Morgan and Hunt 1994; Lane and Bachmann 1996; Doney and Cannon 1997; Zaheer, McEvily, and Perrone 1998). The former tend to neglect service-based relations, the latter tend to neglect business-to-business relations and both have yet to address adequately supply to the public sector.

In terms of the research process, as well as being difficult to address directly (Smeltzer 1997; Blois 1999), resources such as trust and reputation are difficult to examine because they are enmeshed with other resources and their accrual is context specific (Araujo and Easton 1999). For example, reputation and trust are not the same, but they are intimately related to one another, and a good reputation in one setting may be of little relevance in another.

In summary, the quality of some prior research is undermined by fundamental problems such as inadequate definitions, and inappropriate assumptions and methods. Prior research which is more robust gives only partial coverage of the scope of supply relations, and our knowledge base is therefore fragmented. Like Gabbay and Leenders, we believe that social capital and, in particular, corporate social capital provide a vital opportunity to integrate future research in the field of supply relations. Based on the contributions of authors to two volumes edited by Gabbay and Leenders (Leenders and Gabbay 1999;

Gabbay and Leenders 2001*b*) and our own experience using the concept of CSC to reanalyse data on relations in supply networks (Harland and Knight 2001*a*), we suggest that it offers a conceptual framework which

(1) is theoretically robust (though not unproblematic—see Gabbay and Leenders 2001*a*);

(2) enables an integration of analysis of 'bundles' of social capital resources, in relation to structures, actions, and goals;

(3) reflects a network perspective, which emphasizes the structural and temporal embeddedness of actors in networks of relations over time (Knoke 1999);

(4) explicitly recognizes the issue of how individuals' social capital accrues to organizations (Araujo and Easton 1999; Pennings and Lee 1999; Gabbay and Leenders 2001*a*: 8–16);

(5) can serve as a 'bridge' between research focusing on different forms of interorganizational relations (e.g. supply, innovation, and political relations);

(6) incorporates both the positive aspects of resources such as trust, and negative aspects such as the absence of trust and distrust;

(7) recognizes the dynamic character of relations and networks, which constantly change as part of 'normal' interaction and through actors' purposive actions (Gabbay and Leenders 2001*a*);

(8) accommodates both qualitative and quantitative empirical inquiry.

This framework allows us to develop an integrated approach to the study of the social aspects of long-term, complex relationships which complements more established economic perspectives. In terms of practice, while the notion of 'relationship management' is sound for the specific relationships, the management of social capital is useful for both single relationships and an organization-centred view of the management of its relationships collectively.

In advocating corporate social capital as a framework for integrating supply relationship research, we wish to emphasize three points. First, that we are not suggesting that researchers should adopt a single, common definition of concepts such as trust. We expect the variety of perspectives on such topics among economists, philosophers, and sociologists to be reflected by variety among supply relationship researchers. However, future research would benefit from better-grounded and more critical analysis and, by framing studies of trust, reputation, etc. within social capital theory, there is less risk of inappropriately abstracting these social resources from related concepts. Second, though the discussion above tends to focus on social resources, the concept relates resources, social structure, and the attainment of goals; this link of resources and structure to goals is important. The value of social capital is context specific; social capital in a supply relationship cannot meaningfully be considered without examining the activities and goals of the relationship.

Social capital, or liability, arising through relationships is significant in so far as it affects current and future capability. Using the CSC framework can help supply relationship researchers to place their work in the field of business strategy and public policy. Third, as previously mentioned, there are other theories that can be deployed in integrative research; one example with which we are familiar is role theory (Zurcher 1983; Hales 1986; Stewart 1989; Fondas and Stewart 1994; Uzzi 1996; Harland and Knight 2001*b*).

8. Conclusions

In this chapter we have explored the evolution of research and knowledge in supply relationships, from its fragmented, subject-based origins, to a more integrative, multidisciplinary perspective. We have also considered the benefits of these developments, and suggested how they be continued.

Supply relationships involve complex webs of interactions between individuals—director to director, senior sales manager to senior buyer, engineer to engineer, and so on. Directors may view a relationship as long term and collaborative, though day-to-day ordering decisions may be conducted by buyers and sales people in a short-term, adversarial way. Suppliers of a range of products/services may find that their product/services may fit into different quadrants of a Kraljic-type purchasing portfolio. In such cases, it seems to make little sense to view the links between two firms as a single, uniform relationship. These interactions may be quite different in style and may be better represented as *several* relationships of different *types*. They are also dynamic, and will change over time. Researchers should explicitly identify their unit(s) of analysis when examining supply relationships.

It may be more meaningful to view and examine relationships as processes (Easton and Lundgren 1992), rather than as a quasi-organization or structure. These processes consist of interwoven elements of short-term exchanges of materials, services, information, payments, and social interaction, as well as longer-term adaptation and institutionalization. They result in accrual of resources such as trust, reputation, status, and credibility for each party to the relationship. Over time, these resources, or liabilities, have an impact on relationship processes, in a recursive manner.

While the IMP Group's annual conference typically has a selection of papers on the breakdown and cessation of relationships, the 'downside' of relationships, and 'normal' relationships and organizational practices are neglected fields of study. As supply relationship researchers, we tend to focus on, for example, trust, rather than distrust (but see Hedaa 1993 for an interesting exception); investigate relationships which are (perceived to be) successful, rather than failed relationships, despite the importance of learning from mistakes; seek to understand 'best practice' in leading companies' 'strategic' relationships, rather than develop a good understanding of what is 'normal' in 'average' companies. The body of knowledge on supply relationships could be significantly developed by research that explicitly addresses what is negative and normal, as well the 'best'. Achieving this will require different approaches to specifying and conducting projects: making the case to funders of research about a project's relevance and contribution will be more difficult; participants may be more reluctant to reveal valuable data; and this, in turn, will require different forms of engagement with them, for example long-term participant-observation, rather than questionnaire surveys and interviews.

Recent research on social capital, innovation, learning, and value in supply relationships is founded on concepts and theories from a wide range of disciplines. Other research is integrative in that it examines supply relationships as embedded in networks of relationships, critically linked to public policy and business strategy, and constituted of multiple interpersonal bonds and product/service transactions. To undertake such work, academics need to learn about other disciplines, both in terms of the 'content' of the disciplines' knowledge bases and their discourses. They must also contend with much greater complexity, if they are to achieve contributions considered robust by their peers in the various disciplines. The discussion presented in this chapter suggests that it is worth facing these challenges, since integrative approaches can provide far richer understanding of supply relationships.

References

ARAUJO, L., and EASTON, G. (1996). 'Networks in Socio-economic Systems: A Critical Review', in D. Iacobucci (ed.), *Networks in Marketing*. London: Sage, 63–107.

—— —— (1999). 'A Relational Resource Perspective on Social Capital', in R. T. H. A. J. Leenders and S. M. Gabbay (eds.), *Corporate Social Capital and Liability*. London: Kluwer Academic Publishers, 68–87.

BAILY, P., and FARMER, D. (1985). *Purchasing Principles and Management* (5th edn). London: Pitman.

BLOIS, K. (1972). 'Vertical Quasi-Integration'. *Journal of Industrial Economics*, 20/3: 253–72.

—— (1999). 'Trust in Business to Business Relationships: An Evaluation of its Status'. *Journal of Management Studies*, 36/2: 197–215.

BOWERSOX, D. J., CLOSS, D. J., and HELFERICH, O. K. (1986). *Logistical Management* (3rd edn). Oxford: Macmillan Publishing.

BURT, D., and DOYLE, M. (1994). *The American Keiretsu: A Strategic Weapon for Global Competitiveness*. Homewood, IL: Irwin.

BURT, R. S. (1992). *Structural Holes: The Social Structure of Competition*. Cambridge, MA: Harvard University Press.

CHILD, J. (1987). 'Information Technology, Organization and the Response to Strategic Challenges'. *California Management Review*, 29: 35–50.

CHRISTOPHER, M. G. (1992). *Logistics and Supply Chain Management*. London: Pitman.

COASE, R. (1937). 'The Nature of the Firm'. *Economica*, 4/16: 386–405.

COLEMAN, J. S. (1990). *The Foundations of Social Theory*. Boston, MA: Harvard University Press.

CONTRACTOR, F., and LORANGE, P. (1988). *Cooperative Strategies in International Business*. Lexington: Lexington Books.

COUSINS, P. (1992). 'Purchasing A Professional Approach'. *Purchasing and Supply Management* (September): 20–3.

COUSINS, P. (1991). 'Purchasing Partnerships: The Way Forward?' *Purchasing and Supply Management*: 23–31.

—— (2002). 'A Conceptual Model for Managing Long-term Inter-organisational Relationships'. *European Journal of Purchasing and Supply Management*, 8/2: 71–82.

COX, A. (1996). 'Relational Competence and Strategic Procurement Management'. *European Journal of Purchasing and Supply Management*, 2/1: 57–70.

CROSBY, P. (1979). *Quality is Free*. New York: McGraw-Hill.

CYERT, R., and MARCH, J. (1963). *A Behavioural Theory of the Firm*. NJ: Prentice Hall.

DACIN, T., VENTRESCA, M., and BEAL, B. (1999). 'The Embeddedness of Organizations: Dialogue and Directions'. *Journal of Management*, 25/3: 317–56.

DASGUPTA, P. (1988). 'Trust as a Commodity', in D. Gambetta (ed.), *Trust: Making and Breaking Cooperative Relations*. Oxford: Blackwell, 3–13.

DEMING, W. E. (1982). *Out of the Crisis*. Cambridge, MA: MIT Centre for Advanced Engineering Study.

DIRRHEIMER, M., and HUBNER, T. (1983). *Vertical Integration and Performance in the Automotive Industry*. Boston, MIT: Paper presented at 'The Future of the Automobile' Forum.

DONEY, P. M., and CANNON, J. P. (1997). 'An Examination of the Nature of Trust in Buyer-Seller Relationships'. *Journal of Marketing*, 61/April: 35–51.

DORE, R. (1983). 'Goodwill and the Spirit of Market Capitalism'. *British Journal of Sociology*, 34/4: 459–82.

—— (1987). *Taking Japan Seriously*. Stamford: Stamford University Press.

EASTON, G. (2000). 'Is Relevance Relevant?'. *Proceedings of the 16th Annual IMP Conference*, Bath, September.

—— and LUNDGREN, A. (1992). 'Changes in Industrial Networks as Flow Through Nodes', in B. Axelsson and G. Easton (eds.), *Industrial Networks: A New View of Reality*. London: Routledge, 88–104.

ELLRAM, L. (1990). 'The Supplier Selection Decision in Stratetgic Partnerships'. *Journal of Purchasing and Materials Management*, 26: 8–14.

—— (1991). 'Supply Chain Management: The Industrial Organization Perspective'. *International Journal of Physical Distribution and Logistics Management*, 21/1: 13–22.

ENGLAND, W. B. (1967). *Procurement Principles and Practice* (5th edn). Homewood, IL: Richard D. Irwin.

FONDAS, N., and STEWART, R. (1994). 'Enactment in Managerial Jobs: A Role Analysis'. *Journal of Management Studies*, 31/1: 83–103.

GABBAY, S. M., and LEENDERS, R. T. H. A. J. (1999). 'CSC: The Structure of Advantage and Disadvantage', in R. T. H. A. J. Leenders and S. M. Gabbay (eds.), *Corporate Social Capital and Liability*. London: Kluwer Academic Publishers, 1–14.

—— —— (2001a). 'Social Capital of Organizations: From Social Structure to the Management of Corporate Social Capital'. *Research in the Sociology of Organizations*, 18: 1–20.

—— —— (eds.) (2001b). 'Social Capital of Organizations'. *Research in the Sociology of Organizations*, 18: 1–20.

GADDE, L. E., and HÅKANSSON, H. (1990). 'The Changing Role of Purchasing', in Research Developments in International Industrial Marketing and Purchasing: *Proceedings of 6th IMP Conference*, Milan.

GOFFEE, R., and JONES, G. (1996). 'What Holds the Modern Company Together?' *Harvard Business Review*, 74/6: 133–48.

HAHN, C., PINTO, P., and BRAGG, D. (1983). 'Just-in-Time Production and Purchasing'. *Journal of Purchasing and Materials Management*, 19: 2–10.

HÅKANSSON, H., and SNEHOTA, I. (1989). 'No Business is an Island: The Network Concept of Business Strategy'. *Industrial Journal of Management*, 5/3: 187–200.

HALES, C. (1986). 'What Do Managers Do? A Critical Review of the Evidence'. *Journal of Management Studies*, 23/1: 88–115.

HARLAND, C. M., and KNIGHT, L. (2001a). 'Supply Strategy: A Corporate Social Capital Perspective'. *Research in the Sociology of Organizations*, 18: 151–83.

—— —— (2001b). 'Supply Network Strategy: Role and Competence Requirements'. *International Journal of Operations and Production Management*, 21/4: 476–89.

HARRISON, A. (1992). *Just-in-Time Manufacturing in Perspective*. New Jersey: Prentice Hall.

HAYES, R., and WHEELWRIGHT, S. C. (1984). *Restoring our Competitive Edge: Competing the Learning Organization*. New York: Free Press.

HEDAA, L. (1993). 'Distrust, Uncertainties and Disconfirmed Expectations in Supplier–Customer Relationships'. *International Business Review*, 2/2: 191–206.

HILL, T. (1989). *Manufacturing Strategy: Text and Cases*. London: Macmillan.

The IMP Group (1982). 'An Interaction Approach', in H. Håkansson (ed.), *International Marketing and Purchasing of Industrial Goods*. Chichester: John Wiley, 10–27.

JURAN, J. M. (1988). *Juran on Planning for Quality*. New York: Free Press.

KANTER, R. M. (1989). *When Giants Learn to Dance*. London: Simon and Schuster.

KICKERT, W., KLIJN, E. H., and KOPPENJAN, J. (eds.) (1997). *Managing Complex Networks: Strategies for the Public Sector*. London: Sage.

KNIGHT, L. (2000). 'Learning to Collaborate: A Study of Individual and Organizational Learning, and Interorganizational Relationships'. *Journal of Strategic Marketing*, 8/2: 121–38.

KNOKE, D. (1999). 'Organizational Networks and Corporate Social Capital', in R. T. H. A. J. Leenders and S. M. Gabbay (eds.), *Corporate Social Capital and Liability*. London: Kluwer Academic Publishers, 17–42.

KRALJIC, P. (1983). 'Purchasing Must Become Supply Management'. *Harvard Business Review*, 61/5: 109–17.

KUMPE, E., and BOLWIJN, P. T. (1988). 'Manufacturing: The New Case for Vertical Integration'. *Harvard Business Review*, 66/2: 75–81.

LAMMING, R. C. (1993). *Beyond Partnership: Strategies for Innovation and Lean Supply*. London: Prentice Hall.

LANE, C., and BACHMANN, R. (1996). 'The Social Construction of Trust: Supplier Relations in Britain and Germany'. *Organization Studies*, 17/3: 365–95.

LEE, L., and DOBLER, D. W. (1977). *Purchasing and Materials Management*. New York: McGraw Hill.

LEENDERS, R. T. H. A. J., and GABBAY, S. M. (eds.) (1999). *Corporate Social Capital and Liability*. London: Kluwer Academic Publishers.

LORANGE, P., and ROOS, J. (1992). *Strategic Alliances*. Oxford: Blackwell Publishers.

LUHMANN, N. (1979). *Trust and Power*. Chichester: John Wiley and Sons.

MACAULAY, S. (1963). 'Non-contractual Relations in Business: A Preliminary Study'. *American Sociological Review*, 28/1: 55–66.

MACBETH, D., and FERGUSON, N. (1994). *Partnership Sourcing: An Integrated Supply Chain Management Approach*. London: Financial Times Pitman Publishing.

MARSHAL, A. (1923). *Industry and Trade*. London: Macmillan.

MARTIN, A. J. (1983). *Distribution Resource Planning*. New Jersey: Prentice Hall.

MAYER, R. (1962). *Production Management*. New York: McGraw Hill.

MAYNTZ, R. (1993). 'Modernization and the Logic of Interorganizational Networks', in J. Child, M. Crozier, and R. Mayntz (ed.), *Societal Change Between Market and Organization*. Aldershot: Avebury, 3–18.

MEREDITH, J. R. (1992). *The Management of Operations: A Conceptual Emphasis*. Chichester: John Wiley and Sons.

—— RATURI, A., GYAMPAH, K. A., and KAPLAN, B. (1989). 'Alternative Research Paradigms in Operations'. *Journal of Operations Management*, 8/4: 297–326.

MORGAN, R. M., and HUNT, S. D. (1994). 'The Commitment-Trust Theory of Relationship Marketing'. *Journal of Marketing*, 58/3: 20–38.

NAHAPIET, J., and GHOSHAL, S. (1998). 'Social Capital, Intellectual Capital and the Organizational Advantage'. *Academy of Management Review*, 23/2: 242–66.

NISHIGUCHI, T. (1994). *Strategic Industrial Sourcing*. Oxford: Oxford University Press.

ORLICKY, J. (1975). *Material Requirements Planning: A New Way of Life in Production and Inventory Management*. New York: McGraw Hill.

PARASURAMAN, A., ZEITHAML, V. A., and BERRY, L. L. (1985). 'A Conceptual Model of Service Quality and its Implications for Future Research'. *Journal of Marketing*, 49/4: 41–50.

—— —— —— (1988). 'SERVQUAL: A Multiple Item Scale for Measuring Consumer Perceptions of Service Quality'. *Journal of Retailing*, 64/1: 12–40.

PENNINGS, J. M., and LEE, K. (1999). 'Social Capital of Organization: Conceptualization, Level of Analysis, and Performance Implications', in R. T. H. A. J. Leenders and S. M. Gabbay (eds.), *Corporate Social Capital and Liability*. London: Kluwer Academic Publishers, 43–67.

PORTER, M. E. (1980). *Competitive Advantage Strategy: Techniques for Analysing Industries and Competitors*. New York: Free Press Macmillan.

—— (1988). 'From Competitive Advantage to Corporate Strategy'. *McKinsey Quarterly*, 2: 35–66.

POWELL, W., and SMITH-DOERR, L. (1994). 'Networks and Economic Life', in N. Smelser and R. Swedberg (eds.), *The Handbook of Economic Sociology*. Chichester: Princeton University Press, 368–402.

RICHARDSON, G. B. (1972). 'The Organization of Industry'. *Economic Journal*, 82/327: 883–96.

RING, P. S., and VAN DE VEN, A. H. (1992). 'Structuring Co-operative Relationships Between Organizations'. *Strategic Management Journal*, 13/7: 483–98.

SAKO, M. (1992). *Prices, Quality and Trust: Interfirm Relations in Britain and Japan*. Cambridge: Cambridge University Press.

SCHMENNER, R. W. (1990). *Production/Operations Management: Concepts and Situations*. New York: Maxwell Macmillan International.

SIMON, H. A. (ed.) (1957). *A Study of Decision-Making Processes in Administrative Organizations*. New York: Free Press.

SLACK, N., CHAMBERS, S., HARLAND, C. M., HARRISON, A., and JOHNSTON, R. (1995). *Operations Management*. London: Pitman.

SMELTZER, L. (1997). 'The Meaning and Origin of Trust in Buyer–supplier Relationships'. *International Journal of Purchasing and Materials Management*, Winter: 40–48.

STEWART, R. (1989). 'Studies of Managerial Jobs and Behaviour: The Ways Forward'. *Journal of Management Studies*, 26/1: 1–10.

SWAN, J. E., TRAWICK, I. F., and SILVA, D. W. (1985). 'How Industrial Salespeople Gain Customer Trust'. *Industrial Marketing Management*, 14/3: 203–11.

THACKRAY, J. (1986). 'America's Vertical Cutback'. *Management Today*, June, 74–77.

Uzzi, B. (1996). 'The Sources and Consequences of Embeddedness for Economic Performance of Organizations: The Network Effect'. *American Sociological Review*, 61/August: 674–98.

—— (1997). 'Social Structure and Competition in Interfirm Networks: The Paradox of Embeddedness'. *Administrative Science Quarterly*, 42/1: 37–69.

—— Gillespie, J. J. (1999). 'Corporate Social Capital and the Cost of Financial Capital: An Embeddedness Approach', in R. T. H. A. J. Leenders and S. M. Gabbay (eds.), *Corporate Social Capital and Liability*. London: Kluwer Academic Publishers, 446–59.

Van de Ven, A. H., Emmit, D. C., and Koenig, R. (1975). 'Frameworks for Interorganizational Analysis', in A. R. Negandhi (ed.), *Interorganizational Theory*. Kent, OH: Kent State University Press.

Vollman, T. E., Berry, W., and Whybark, D. C. (1989). *Manufacturing Planning and Control Systems*. Homewood, IL: Dow Jones Irwin.

Westing, J. H., Fine, I. V., and Zenz, G. J. (1976). *Purchasing Management: Materials in Motion*. New York: John Wiley.

Wight, O. W. (1982). *The Executive's Guide to Successful MRP II*. Englewood Cliff, New Jersey: Prentice Hall.

Wild, R. (1971). *Production and Operations Management*. Austin, Texas: Holt, Rinehart and Winston.

Williamson, O. (1975). *Markets and Hierarchies: Analysis and Antitrust Implications*. New York: Free Press.

—— (1985). *The Economic Institutions of Capitalism: Firms, Markets, Relational Contracting*. New York: Free Press.

—— (1986). *Economic Organization*. Brighton, UK: Wheatsheaf Books.

Womack, J. P, Jones, D. T., and Roos, D. (1990). *The Machine that Changed the World*. Oxford: MacMillan International.

Zaheer, A., McEvily, B., and Perrone, V. (1998). 'Does Trust Matter? Exploring the Effects of Interorganizational Trust on Performance'. *Organization Science*, 9/2: 141–59.

Zeithaml, V. A., Parasuraman, A., and Berry, L. L. (1990). *Delivering Service Quality: Balancing Customer Expectations and Perceptions*. New York: Free Press.

Zurcher, L. (1983). *Social Roles: Conformity, Conflict and Creativity*. London: Sage Publications.

Zucker, L. (1986). 'Production of Trust: Institutional Sources of Economic Structure, 1840–1920', in B. Staw and L. Cummings (eds.), *Research in Organizational Behavior*. Greenwich, CT: JAI Press, 53–111.

10

The Green Supply Chain

ROBERT D. KLASSEN AND P. FRASER JOHNSON

1. Introduction

The natural environment continues to be a challenging supply chain management issue. Not only does it directly impact competitiveness through traditional
performance measures such as cost and quality, but also the range of stakeholders extends well outside traditional suppliers and customers (Monczka and
Trent 1995; Lamming and Hampson 1996). As a result, current research and
managerial practice related to environmental issues has expanded from a narrow focus on pollution control within a single firm to include a larger set of
interorganizational management decisions, programmes, tools, and technologies that prevent pollution before its generation. Because of the systemic nature
of many environmental concerns, significant improvement, both in terms of
competitiveness and environmental performance, is only possible through concerted efforts that affect the broader network of interconnected buyers and
suppliers, otherwise termed a supply chain.

Notable examples of firms that have begun to successfully integrate
environmental management practices within their supply chain include Xerox,
DaimlerChrysler, 3M, and Kodak. Xerox's Asset Recycle Management Program
successfully diverts 90 per cent of all materials and components for its end-of-life
photocopiers through reuse, remanufacturing, and recycling. The company
estimates that this programme generated annual savings of $300–400 million
(Hart 1997). Meanwhile, DaimlerChrysler estimates that it saved $4.7 million per
year at one manufacturing facility in Michigan through the implementation of a
new scrap management system set-up by OmniSource (Hoeffer 1999). Scrap
metal from DaimlerChrysler is returned to steel suppliers and recycled.

These examples illustrate that corporate approaches to improving environmental performance cannot be undertaken in isolation; instead, environmental
management must be linked with the particular supply chain management
strategy adopted. As a starting point, opportunities for environmental management within the supply chain extend beyond auditing suppliers for conform-
ance to environmental procedures or working with product engineers to

substitute materials to facilitate recycling. The resource-based view of the firm provides one theoretical lens for proposing that the alignment and integration of environmental management orientation with a comprehensive supply chain management strategy provides a source of competitive advantage (Hart 1995; Bowen *et al.* 2001). Thus, it is not realistic for a firm to proactively move forward on environmental improvement without a corresponding proactive supply chain strategy. The real challenge for research and practice is first to identify approaches to integration, and second to understand how the process varies with the supply chain strategy.

The objective of this chapter is to present a framework for alignment and integration of environmental management within supply chain management. First, we briefly examine how research has viewed environmental management orientation, which comprises multiple dimensions relevant to supply chain management. Doing so prompts a more detailed examination of five green supply chain practices that are being used to varying degrees by management: environmental certification; pollution prevention; reverse logistics; life cycle assessment (LCA); and design for the environment. A conceptual framework is presented that illustrates how and when these practices can be applied within a supply chain context. Finally, opportunities for future research are discussed.

2. Environmental management orientation

Over the past decade, conceptual models, case studies, and survey research have compiled a diverse and growing body of literature that helps to characterize the development of environmental management in a firm. Yet, even the terminology varies widely. At the firm level, researchers have used terms such as response pattern (Logsdon 1985), maturity profile (Marguglio 1991), developmental stages (Hunt and Auster 1990), environmental processes (Lawrence and Morell 1995), environmental strategy (Petulla 1987), and environmental management systems (Dillon and Fischer 1992), among others (Kolk and Mauser 2002). Within the operations management literature, environmentally conscious manufacturing strategies (Sarkis 1995), eco-manufacturing strategy (Newman and Hanna 1996), and environmental management orientation (Klassen 2001) also have been used.

Despite the variety of terms, the concepts and their respective definitions have much in common. Furthermore, the recent international formalization of ISO 14001 has begun to force some consensus about the management aspects that must be considered. Based on earlier research (Hunt and Auster 1990; Dillon and Fischer 1992; Post and Altman 1992; Lawrence and Morell 1995) and paralleling the elements in ISO 14001 (Clements 1997), environmental management orientation has been defined as the set of objectives, plans and mechanisms that determine the responsiveness of operations to environmental issues (Klassen 2001). For example, if management anticipates new environmental issues, moves ahead of public pressure, integrates environmental concerns throughout the manufacturing process and supply chain, and generally exhibits characteristics of environmental leadership, a more proactive orientation has been adopted. Case research indicates that firms can change their orientation over time, with internal factors including values of senior management (Logsdon 1985; Petulla 1987) and plant outlook (Klassen 2001), and the availability of resources and opportunities (e.g. new products or facilities) (Lawrence and Morell 1995).

At an aggregate level, this construct covers the spectrum from a basic reactive orientation to a sophisticated proactive orientation. At least three factors contribute to the overall degree of proactiveness for individual members of the supply chain: systems analysis and planning; organizational responsibility; and management controls (Klassen 2001). Systems analysis and planning is assessed from the scope and depth of integration of environmental issues into product and process planning, and generally ranges from none to extensive. Systems analysis is necessary because environmental management must encompass the supply chain from supplier to customer. The second factor, organizational responsibility, captures the level of involvement of frontline personnel in environmental issues, and ranges from none to extensive. Finally, management controls—including auditing, monitoring, and follow up—also ranges from none to extensive. Taken together, these three characteristics provide an overall, general assessment of how proactive individual supply chain members are.

3. Green supply chain management

Extending these ideas to interorganizational linkages along the supply chain (Fig. 10.1), environmental regulation of both the firm and its suppliers remains an important factor that focuses management attention on environmental supply chain management (Beckman, Bercovitz, and Rosen 2001). Resulting managerial action has traditionally focused on resisting the imposition of external restrictions—particularly regulation—in order to minimize cost, improve efficiencies and increase quality. In general, this view can be labelled

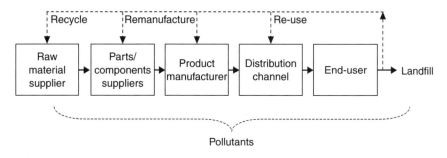

Fig. 10.1. The reverse supply chain

a Constraint perspective (Angell and Klassen 1999). As a result, supply chain members, both individually and collectively, tend to make small changes, so as to minimize any disruption to existing processes. The most straightforward path toward environmental improvement, often directed by regulation, is to capture pollutants and wastes at the end of process, otherwise termed end-of-pipe pollution control. Recently, this Constraint perspective has expanded to include longer segments of the supply chain through 'take-back' regulations (e.g. Germany), which at a minimum, forces manufacturers to be responsible for the downstream, post-consumption fate of products and packaging (Cairncross 1992).

However, both researchers and managers are beginning to move away from simply viewing environmental issues as a constraint toward viewing them as another component that must be fundamentally integrated into supply chain management (e.g., Beckman, Bercovitz, and Rosen 2001; Lamming *et al.* 2001), termed here an integrative perspective. In their boundary-spanning role, supply chain managers can play a critical role in assessing the impact of product and process changes on the natural environment. To date, much of the emphasis has been on upstream suppliers, with the use of terms such as green or environmental purchasing (Min and Galle 1997), green value chain practices (Handfield *et al.* 1997), spectrum of environmental management programmes (Beckman, Bercovitz, and Rosen 2001), and green supply (Bowen *et al.* 2001)—all of which implicitly or explicitly focus on improved environmental performance through better supply chain management. For example, environmental purchasing has been narrowly described as the involvement of the purchasing function in supply chain management activities in order to facilitate recycling, reuse, and resource reduction (Carter and Carter 1998), whereas green supply more broadly encompasses all supply management activities that attempt to improve the environmental performance of purchased inputs (Bowen *et al.* 2001).

Simultaneously, a somewhat separate body of literature has begun to mature around reverse logistics, defined as the materials management activities needed to perform product recovery (Fleischmann *et al.* 1997; Stock 1998) including the upstream movement of materials and source reduction (Carter and Ellram 1998). Several types of operations can be involved in product recovery, such as reuse, remanufacturing, and recycling, at both the product and component level (Gupta 1995; Thierry *et al.* 1995). If the concept of reverse logistics is broadened to include the relationships between manufacturing firms and end-users (i.e. final customer in the supply chain) (Florida 1996), the concept of a reverse supply chain emerges (Barry, Girard, and Perras 1993). Drawing together these concepts, van Hoek (1999) has argued that integration aimed at minimizing the overall environmental impact, that is, 'ecological footprint', of both the forward and reverse supply chains should be termed green supply chain management (GSCM).

Thus, GSCM has at least four important elements. First, it involves interaction between the buying firm and its upstream suppliers, ideally to achieve sustained improvements in environmental performance (Handfield *et al.* 1997). Second, the interaction also extends downstream, ideally to the extent that the end-user becomes a supplier of used products or components (Vachon, Klassen, and Johnson 2001). Third, the manufacturing firm gathers environmental information on suppliers, possibly through audits or external certification, for example, ISO 14000 (Walton, Handfield, and Melnyk 1998; Bowen *et al.* 2001). Finally, GSCM does not just solely rely on suppliers to improve environmental performance, but integrates internal and external environmental systems and investments (Geffen and Rothenberg 2000), both upstream and downstream. Although the direction of causality can be debated, GSCM is more likely to develop from integrated, partnership-oriented supply chain relationships (Florida 1996), rather than vice versa, because environmental improvement still tends occur as ancillary investment.

3.1. Development of capabilities

Stronger green supply chain management has been linked by several researchers to the development of underlying strategic resources, drawn from the theoretical grounding of the resource-based view of the firm (Bowen *et al.* 2001). These strategic resources, in turn, enable the implementation of green supply chain practices, discussed in the following section.

Strategic resources that generate sustained competitive advantage are defined as assets, capabilities, and organizational processes controlled by a firm that add value, are rare, difficult to imitate and have few substitutes (Barney 1991). These resources have been classified as physical, human, organizational, technological, financial and reputational (these categories are not necessarily exhaustive or mutually exclusive) (Grant 1991). The development and control of a firm's specific resources either can be acquired (Black and Boal 1994) or can be path dependent and accumulate over time (Dierickx and Cool 1989). Moreover, the competitive advantages generated by different forms of resources vary with the stability of the business environment: tradeable, property-based resources conferred competitive advantage in more stable business environments, whereas knowledge-based resources offered greater benefit in uncertain business contexts (Miller and Shamsie 1996). Finally, others differentiate between resources, which are the basic building blocks (e.g. employee skills), and capabilities, which are bundles of resources brought to bear on value-added tasks (Hart 1995; Bowen *et al.* 2001).

The theoretical implications for environmental management are multifaceted. In terms of outcome, environmental and economic performance are related because strategic capabilities yield multiple competitive advantages. Thus, proactive environmental policies and strong environmental performance have been linked with better economic performance (e.g. Bragdon and Marlin 1972; Klassen and McLaughlin 1996; Russo and Fouts 1997). In fact, Hart (1995) went further and proposed that future competitive advantage might be increasingly rooted in capabilities that facilitate environmentally sustainable activity.

Initial firm-level research highlighted several specific organizational capabilities related to proactive environmental management: continuous improvement, cross-functional management, and stakeholder integration (Hart 1995). This set was subsequently extended to include the deployment of physical assets and technology, organizational culture, interfunctional coordination and intangible resources (i.e. appeal to green customer segments and political acumen) (Russo and Fouts 1997). For green supply chain management, strategic capabilities include processes, systems, networks, and culture, all of which foster both external and internal integration (de Bakker and Nijhof 2002). More specific, tactical capabilities include interfunctional coordination; partnering with suppliers; knowledge of environmental issues; strong technical skills for purchasing; and detailed purchasing policies (Bowen *et al.* 2001).

When these contributions are considered collectively for green supply chain management, the varied use of the term capabilities tends to mix the level of analysis (e.g. corporate versus functional), the scope (e.g. culture versus knowledge) and the form (e.g. relationship versus policies). As a result, these capabilities are not directly comparable in terms of either the difficulty to achieve or the likely impact on performance. Thus, an overview of particular green practices that relates directly to the supply chain is helpful to better structure our understanding of their cumulative nature.

4. Green supply chain practices

In general, environmental practices represent actions and programmes within the firm that improve environmental performance, remediate problems, and minimize any environmental burden. For supply chain management, boundary-spanning environmental practices remain particularly challenging, as two or more organizations must actively work to coordinate and integrate their management and technological systems. Termed green supply chain practices, five such practices are environmental certification, pollution prevention, life-cycle assessment (LCA), design for the environment, and reverse logistics practices. As a result, the adoption of any, or ideally all, of these green supply chain practices requires particular supply chain capabilities, thereby forming both a theoretical and practical bridge between a firm's environmental management orientation and supply chain strategy. The following sections briefly describe these practices within the context of supply chain management.

4.1. Environmental certification

In contrast to regulatory demands, an increasing array of voluntary standards, certification protocols and codes of practice have emerged to ensure that management is addressing environmental considerations and improving environmental performance. These certifications can take on various forms, ranging from product specific eco-labels, which may rely on a comparative environmental LCA, to management-based practices that employ third-party audits (International Institute for Sustainable Development 2001). Both have implications for managing supply chain, as they can be used to position products and services with customers, as well as select preferred suppliers.

Product certifications, also referred to as eco-labels, were the first programmes to gain recognition with consumers, as recognizable symbols were introduced into the marketplace. Based on at least a partial LCA, individual products or product classes are identified based on their reduced environmental impact, with additional specific measures that may assess production and/or use. The German eco-labeling of a 'Blue Angel' established the basis for other national and international programmes following its introduction in 1977 (Hartwell III and Bergkamp 1992). More recent eco-label programmes include: European Union Eco-Label (i.e. flower), Swedish Environmental Choice, Nordic Swan, Canadian EcoLogo, US Green Seal, Japanese Eco-Mark, French *NF Environnement* (OECD 1997).

More recently, specific standards have been developed for the management systems that underlie effective environmental management rather than individual products. Based on the pioneering British Standards Institute's BS 7750, two related standards have emerged: Eco-Management and Audit Scheme (EMAS) from the European Union and ISO 14001 from the International Organization for Standardization. In reality, ISO 14000 has expanded to become a family of over twenty standards that cover aspects of any strong environmental management system (i.e. 14001), including auditing (14011), labelling (14021), performance evaluation (14031), and LCA (14040), to note several (ISO 1998).

In many ways, ISO 14000 parallels the ISO 9000 quality standard (Puri 1996). As a result, ISO 14000 has encouraged the application of continuous improvement models such as plan-do-check-act (PDCA) to foster environmental improvement, with some empirical support for coordinated implementation (Corbett and Kirsch 2001; King and Lenox 2001). Of principal interest to supply chain practice and research is the ISO 14001, where early evidence links certification with better corporate performance (Montabon *et al.* 2000).

In addition, an increasing number of guiding principles or codes of practice have been developed, which emphasize broad environmental and social objectives. For example, the Coalition for Environmentally Responsible Economies (CERES), a US non-profit organization, has advanced ten principles of conduct that promote investment policies that are environmentally, socially, and financially sound (www.ceres.org). Adoption by suppliers of the CERES principles indicates a commitment to such objectives as protection of the biosphere, sustainable use of natural resources, reduction of wastes, and energy conservation. A similar approach is codified in the Business Charter for Sustainable Development from the International Chamber of Commerce (ICC) (www.iccwbo.org). Finally, the Triple Bottom Line encourages companies to expand traditional reporting to take into account not just financial outcomes, but also environmental and social performance (Elkington 1998; International Institute for Sustainable Development 2001).

4.2. Pollution prevention

Historically, much attention on improving environmental performance has emphasized capturing pollutants. Pollution control is the capture and treatment of pollutants and harmful by-products at the various stages along a supply chain, either immediately after their generation or later. To accomplish this, additional operations or equipment must be added to the end of an existing process, which generally leaves the product and supply chain virtually unaltered.

In contrast, pollution prevention emphasizes approaches that involve fundamental changes to the basic product or manufacturing processes along the supply chain. Pollution prevention reduces or eliminates pollutants by using a cleaner alternative than traditional means (Freeman *et al.* 1992; OECD 1995). Popularized by 3M under the banner Pollution Prevention Pays (3P), the company has saved over $800 million since its inception in 1975.

Pollution prevention can provide net positive benefits because of the potential to 'build in' better environmental performance at lower cost rather than fixing it as an afterthought, as with pollution control (Schmidheiny 1992; Porter and van der Linde 1995). The fundamental rethinking of a product or manufacturing process also places fewer constraints on the means of achieving environmental improvement, thereby offering greater opportunity for innovation. Some management systems, such as improved housekeeping practices, also might be considered pollution prevention (Hart 1995; Statistics Canada 1996). However, from an operational perspective, there are theoretical and practical advantages to separate structural changes (i.e. product and physical process) from infrastructural changes (i.e. management practices and systems) because of the form, cost, and scope (Hayes and Wheelwright 1984), and a similar distinction is helpful for pollution prevention (Klassen and Whybark 1999).

Pollution prevention frequently requires concerted efforts that extend beyond the manufacturing operations of a single plant to suppliers and buyers, or even across a broader supply chain network. Thus, stronger supply chain integration allows suppliers greater access and influence in downstream operations, and can leverage supplier expertise to improve implementation of the more environmentally friendly product or process configurations (Geffen and Rothenberg 2000). While a growing body of literature has highlighted the competitive benefits of pollution prevention relative to pollution control for individual firms and manufacturing plants (Royston 1979; Hart 1995; Klassen and Whybark 1999; Reinhardt 1999), the extension to a more complex supply chain performance demands further empirical investigation.

4.3. Reverse logistics

An environmental strategy adopted by companies over the past decade—
termed product stewardship—has been to internalize environmental costs and
risks during manufacturing, use, and post-consumption. While many managers
still tend to view the supply chain as a one-way, downstream flow of materials
and services, effective product stewardship requires companies to manage its
reverse supply chain, the upstream flow of consumed goods and by-products.

Two major outcomes may result from adoption of product stewardship.
First, the environmental impact of the product can be reduced during its manufacture or consumption. Second, product recovery and/or disposal can be
introduced to manage the product at the end of its useful life.

Managing the reverse supply chain challenges firms to establish a broad set
of activities, such as managing inter-firm relationships and cross-functional
integration, to accommodate two-way flows of materials. Several types of operations and processes are involved in reverse supply chains, including repair
and re-use, remanufacturing, and recycling. Figure 10.1 represents a simplified
reverse supply chain model, although reverse supply chains can take many
different forms and involve a large number of stakeholders.

In all cases, at a minimum, materials must be collected and transported
upstream. Thus, two critical interfaces in the reverse supply chain are at the
end-user (e.g. consumer), where the flow is reversed, and where the reverse
flow must be integrated with the forward flow (Vachon, Klassen, and Johnson
2001). The first critical interface is at the end of the product's useful life, where
it must either be directed to a landfill or enter the reverse supply chain. For
example, product proliferation at the end of the forward supply chain can ham-
per product recovery and collection of used products. The second critical interface is where the used product is reintroduced into the forward supply
chain—such as distribution, product manufacturer, component suppliers, or
raw material levels (Fig. 10.1). The challenges encountered at this interface may
include quality control, planning and scheduling, cost control and measurement, and inventory management and logistics (Fleischmann *et al.* 1997).

Within the reverse supply chain, various activities or combinations of activities take place—re-use, repair, remanufacturing, or recycling. Recycling returns
materials to a commodity state, where their identity is lost. It involves systems
and processes that support collection, sorting, processing, decontamination,
and disassembly. In contrast, remanufacturing returns product functionality to
an acceptable level of quality or performance, while preserving its basic identity.
Remanufacturing can involve processes such as disassembly, refurbishing,
parts replacement, and reassembly.

Reverse supply chains can take one of two basic forms: open or closed-loop.
Closed-loop reverse supply chains are characterized by product manufacturers
actively involved in the product recovery process in order to extend the useful
life or to control and manage final disposition or disposal. For example, Xerox's

Asset Management programme facilitates such a chain (Krut and Karasin 1999). In contrast, open-loop reverse supply chains involve less ownership and product stewardship, and involve the existence of a secondary market for products or by-products. One example is the North American steel industry and the more than 1,000 ferrous scrap brokers and processors that provide a wide range of services, including collection, reprocessing, transportation, and reselling of the material. This reverse supply chain network helps support an overall recycling rate of 68 per cent for steel in North America (Johnson 1998).

4.4. Life-cycle assessment

As firms along a supply chain become increasingly sophisticated toward environmental issues, a more detailed assessment of the environmental burden of its products and processes is possible. The methods associated with quantifying the environmental burden and impact of a product, process or service is termed environmental LCA, which ideally encompasses cradle-to-grave (Fava *et al.* 1991; Hart 1995). Because an LCA includes extraction and processing of raw materials, manufacturing, transportation and distribution, use/re-use/maintenance, recycling, and final disposal, it can offer important information for designing and managing the supply chain.

Depending on the objectives and scope of analysis, the development and use of LCA has tended toward two possible outcomes: comparison versus improvement (Klassen and Greis 1993). The first focuses on identifying environmentally preferable product or process alternatives (Klöpffer and Rippen 1992), that in turn, may influence customer purchasing patterns based on the degree and form of any environmental impact (Hartwell III and Bergkamp 1992). Not surprising for the supply chain, packaging systems have received a great deal of attention (Curran 1992). Eco-labelling programmes, a subset of environmental certifications discussed later, are frequently based on a comparative LCA, and attempt to leverage marketplace forces to displace environmentally harmful alternatives. A comparative LCA can also form the basis for new public policies (Huppes 1988).

Alternatively, LCA can be used as a tool to identify the stages of the product's life-cycle that have a particularly strong negative impact on the environment, and thus, where improvements would be most beneficial. The results are then used by firms for internal evaluation, industry benchmarking and management decision-making, as one factor in selecting among alternative materials and processes or in modifying existing systems. The application of improvement LCAs to new products, along with their manufacturing processes and suppliers, can help to identify environmental impacts before the products are actually introduced into the marketplace (Keoleian and Menerey 1993). LCA also has been promoted as one means of evaluating pollution prevention options (Freeman *et al.* 1992), thereby improving the allocation of limited management time and financial resources within the supply chain.

4.5. Design for the environment

Early involvement of the supply function in the product design process can provide benefits for the organization (Stuart 1991). Research in new product development has started to study approaches to the process of, and outcomes from, the inclusion of the natural environment in decision-making. Design for the environment (DfE), otherwise termed green product design, is an important element in environmental management (Dechant and Altman 1994), with potential benefits including less waste, greater productivity, and higher levels of innovation (Porter and van der Linde 1995). The shift from regulatory-driven pollution control, to pollution prevention product technologies, necessitates changes in engineering design, research, and education (Navinchandra 1990; OECD 1995).

Using DfE, it is possible to identify less costly and more effective opportunities to minimize the environmental impacts of both manufacturing processes and products during use. A life-cycle assessment is one approach to provide specific input data to DfE. In addition, specific elements focus on particular environmental impacts or benefits, such as increased recyclability, simpler disassembly, and increased energy efficiency. While it might appear that environmentally friendly design should be well accepted, significant hurdles remain because DfE and LCA are unfamiliar to product designers and not well integrated with other design tools along the supply chain (Smith and Melnyk 1996; Lenox *et al.* 2000).

Sustainable product–service systems have been proposed as the next evolutionary step beyond DfE toward sustainable development. Rather than optimize the environmental and competitive factors of products and processes, a radical and creative rethinking to focus on the desired end-use function has the potential for dramatic reductions in environmental impact (Roy 2000). For example, a sustainable floor covering system moves to transform durable carpet tiles into a service. Whereas carpet tiles are usually sold and installed, floor covering is leased. As the flooring wears out, old tiles would be broken down and remanufactured and installed as new tiles as part of the lease fee. Another example, a sustainable transport system is likely to involve changing from private car-based travel to improved public transportation systems, to vehicle sharing schemes, to hybrid electric vehicles and bicycles, and to the replacement of some travel with electronic communication. Thus, the supply network could become oriented toward particular consumer outcomes, such as shared services product-life extension services, and demand side management.

5. Supply chain orientation

Before giving more specific consideration of the alignment and integration of environmental and supply chain management, it is important to summarize briefly several critical issues related to supply chain management. Recall that a supply chain has been defined as 'the integration of business processes from end user through original suppliers that provides products, services and information that add value for customers' (Cooper, Lambert, and Pagh 1997: 2). Activities within the supply chain incorporate sourcing, inbound logistics, operations, outbound logistics, and after-market service (Mabert and Venkataramanan 1998). Consequently, supply chain management includes elements of procurement, logistics, and marketing activities.

Supply chains are made up of independent organizations working together to provide value for the end consumer. Considerable research has been conducted that examines the nature of supply chain relationships, such as partnerships and alliances (e.g. Landeros and Monczka 1989; Stuart 1993; Maloni and Benton 1997; McIvor and McHugh 2000) and functional development (e.g. Ellram and Carr 1994; La Londe 1994; Masters and Pohlen 1994).

The term supply chain orientation refers to the management philosophy that underlies efforts to create coordinated interactions among members across a supply chain, which extends recent research (Shin, Collier, and Wilson 2000). At one extreme, a weak supply chain orientation is primarily *transactional* in nature; at the other extreme, a strong orientation emphasizes the supply *network*, with *partnership* positioned between these two extremes. There has been growing interest over the past decade concerning supply chain orientation and its effects on performance (Lee and Billington 1992; Trent and Monczka 1998; Dong, Carter, and Dresner 2001). Supply chain orientation is affected by the degree of integration (i.e. number of tiers in the supply chain) and the upstream or downstream direction of integration (Frohlich and Westbrook 2001).

A transactional orientation represents the most basic, weakest degree of development. The primary objective is trouble avoidance, where materials, goods, and services arrive as planned at the lowest acquisition cost. Under a transactional orientation, opportunities for synergies between supply chain partners are ignored in favour of short-term profit opportunities. For example, sourcing relationships are driven by price, and distribution is regarded as a cost centre. As a result, little competitive advantage is sought or expected from the firm's supply chain. This is similar to Stage 1 companies described by Bowersox and Daugherty (1987) for the logistics function and the clerical role of the purchasing function described by Leenders and Johnson (2002). Frohlich and Westbrook (2001) referred to low levels of supplier and customer integration as 'inward facing' organizations.

The next stage of a stronger supply chain management orientation involves establishing relations with key supply chain partners to capture potential synergies. The partners can either be upstream or downstream in the supply chain, similar to the periphery-facing organizations described by Frohlich and Westbrook (2001). The motivation for entering into supply chain relationships can be opportunities for improved quality, lower inventory levels, or increased flexibility (Corbett, Blackburn, and Wassenhove 1999). Important projects are typically championed by a functional executive, and may be as simple as a close working relationship or formal partnership between a buyer and seller. This intermediate stage is a termed partnership orientation, and extends the opportunities for the firm from trouble avoidance to creating competitive advantage within limited aspects of the firm's operations.

Under a partnership orientation, the supply chain orientation is focused on supporting organizational goals and strategies, although organizational goals and strategies may fail to reflect adequately the competitive opportunities in the supply chain. This stage is similar to the Stage II companies described by Bowersox and Daugherty (1987), the partnership/relational stage described by Giunipero and Brand (1996), and the professional supply organization described by Leenders and Johnson (2002).

The most advanced stage is network orientation, where strategic opportunities in the supply chain are reflected in corporate strategy and the firm strongly integrates both the upstream and downstream elements of its supply chain, similar to the 'outward-facing' orientation described by Frohlich and Westbrook (2001). Firms with a network orientation require support from the firm's executive leadership, who understand and appreciate the strategic opportunities in supply chain management, and are prepared to become directly involved in major supply chain initiatives, make appropriate invest-ments in capital and organizational talent, invest in systems and technology to support supply chain strategies, and benchmark supply chain management practices with the objective of achieving world-class performance. Giunipero and Brand (1996) described this stage as supply chain management, while Bowersox and Daugherty (1987) used the term Stage III firms and Leenders and Johnson (2002) used the term meaningful involvement.

Firms that adopt a network orientation strive to achieve competitive advant-age from their supply chain. The potential benefits are well documented and include lower costs through inventory reduction and component substitution, reduced lead time and improved customer service from improved commun-ication and forecasting, and increased market share through innovative product design and faster time-to-market.

While some research suggests a developmental progression along the con-tinuum (e.g. Bowersox and Daugherty 1987), more recent research suggests that supply chain orientation can be subject to change in either direction, with movement either towards network or transactional orientation (Johnson, Leenders, and Fearon 1998). Using a strong supply chain orientation to create competitive advantage requires constant attention and top management sup-port. Consequently, change in executive leadership and/or adoption of a new business strategy may result in a change in supply chain orientation (Leenders and Johnson 2002).

6. Bridging supply chain and environmental management orientation

Supply chain orientation, environmental orientation, and the resulting green supply chain practices can be linked with a basic conceptual framework (Fig. 10.2). Contingency theory proposes that firms perform better when their strategies are properly aligned with the business context (Chandler 1962). Taken one step further down in the organization, corporate strategy then drives both the firm's supply chain orientation (transactional to network) and its environmental orientation (reactive to proactive). Finally, successful development and implementation of green supply chain practices (i.e. environmental certification, pollution prevention, LCA, DfE, and reverse logistics) is the product of alignment.

Based on contingency theory, firms are expected to achieve superior performance through the proper alignment of supply chain orientation and environmental orientation. Empirical evidence has recently emerged to help assess these capabilities (de Bakker and Nijhof 2002) and has positively linked supply management capabilities, environmental orientation, and green supply chain practices (Bowen *et al.* 2001). In other words, environmental and supply chain practices must be viewed as mutually supportive. The areas plotted on the matrix in Fig. 10.3 demonstrate the progressive capabilities of the firm as it advances up the continuum from transactional supply chain orientation/reactive

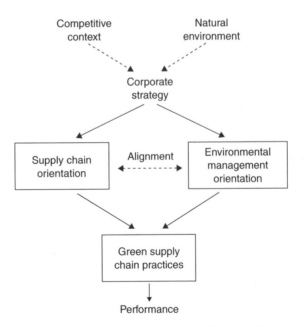

Fig. 10.2. Environmental management orientation and supply chain orientation

environmental orientation to a network supply chain orientation/proactive environmental orientation.

However, two important challenges limit the degree of alignment and integration. First, for many firms, primary responsibility for these two areas resides in different functional areas, such as separate purchasing and environment, health, and safety (EH and S) groups, for supply chain and environmental issues, respectively. Second, as noted earlier, interorganizational coordination further compounds the complexity of aligning environment and supply chain management.

Thus, a transactional supply chain orientation limits the potential improvement possible from the firm's green supply chain practices. Without cross-boundary partnerships, green supply chain practices are limited to practices that require little cooperation from other supply chain stakeholders, such as recycling and certification. Attempting to implement advanced practices, such as DfE or LCA, while not impossible, can be extremely difficult and are less likely for firms with a transactional supply chain orientation. For example, data from upstream and downstream supply chain members may not be available (e.g. systems analysis and planning), opportunities to monitor effectiveness of environmental programmes can be difficult (e.g. management controls), and the emphasis on lowest cost may inhibit or limit such activities (e.g. organizational responsibility).

Supply chain partnerships can either be upstream or downstream focused. In the partnership mode, firms can cooperate to create mutually beneficial relationships that support the interorganizational coordination for by-products and used components, in conjunction with reverse logistics. Implementing reverse logistics and associated remanufacturing or re-use programmes requires appropriate equipment, people, and systems. Such relationships must be stable and exist over the long term to facilitate the cost effective movement of materials upstream in the supply chain as well as develop dependable markets for the remanufactured goods. Again, a transactional orientation is not likely to have the stable relationships or the long-term perspective necessary to make such practices efficient or effective.

Finally, firms with a network orientation are concerned with the delivery of goods and services from end users back to original commodity suppliers. If management has simultaneously developed a proactive environmental orientation, the systems analysis and planning, organizational responsibility, and management controls can be fully leveraged by supply chain managers. Thus, firms in the upper left area (Fig. 10.3) can use sophisticated green supply chain practices. Design for the environment and life-cycle assessment provide opportunities to manage products from cradle to grave, and provide potential opportunities to reduce waste, improve productivity, increase customer satisfaction, lower total costs, and eliminate risks. Such practices are consistent with the philosophy of network orientation, as it seeks to capture the broadest possible range of benefits from its supply chain. These firms are capable of

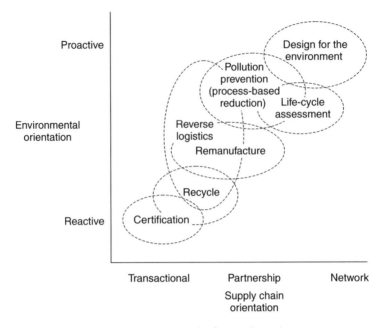

Fig. 10.3. Aligning environmental and supply chain orientation

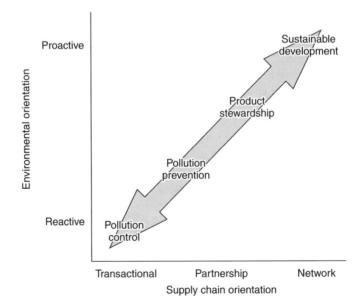

Fig. 10.4. Building capabilities toward sustainability

making decisions that balance overall supply chain performance, which includes environmental factors.

The framework provided in Fig. 10.3 should be interpreted to suggest that capabilities across the supply chain orientation scale are cumulative, not mutually exclusive. It is this cumulative nature that yields a competitive advantage (Hart 1995) and allows significant progression toward broad-scale sustainability (Fig. 10.4). Thus, firms that have a network orientation can make use of practices such as recycling and certification. However, if such a firm fails to develop a proactive environmental management orientation, opportunities to establish new competitive advantages are being missed.

7. Future research directions

As we look toward the future, the framework presented in this chapter provides at least three significant opportunities for continuing theoretical and empirical research. The first research opportunity is related to the relationships between corporate strategy, supply chain orientation, and environmental management orientation. Such research can examine the impact of competitive context and the natural environment on corporate strategy, and the implications for supply chain and environmental orientation. As part of this research, formal processes and organizational structures that favour the alignment and integration of supply chain orientation and environmental orientation can be explored.

Second, the theoretical and empirical research of others laid the foundation for the model presented here (Fig. 10.2), with a diverse set of increasingly complex green supply chain practices (i.e. environmental certification, pollution prevention, reverse logistics, LCA, DfE). Furthermore, the framework suggests that alignment between the environmental and supply chain orientations is predicted to translate into specific green supply chain practices (Fig. 10.3). However, the precise ordering of these practices, and the understanding of which practices that are necessary, but not necessarily sufficient, for the development of others, promises to improve managerial application.

Consequently, testing the relationship between supply chain orientation, environmental orientation, and green supply chain practices represents another research opportunity. This research can examine the theory that alignment between supply chain orientation and environmental orientation permits leveraging particular green supply chain practices. For example, case-based research can be used to compare firms with various levels of alignment to test this theory. A particularly interesting research opportunity would be to compare firms with alignment between their supply chain orientation and environmental management orientation to firms where misalignment exists.

Third, the supply chain and environmental management literatures suggest that superior practice leads to superior performance (e.g. for environment, Klassen and Whybark 1999; for supply chain, Carter, Kale, and Grimm 2000;

Shin, Collier, and Wilson 2000), which could extend to sustainable development (Fig. 10.4). Consequently, a final research opportunity is to critically examine the joint impact of aligning environmental management orientation and supply chain orientation for broad measures of firm performance. The theoretical basis and initial empirical work to date support the framework, but significant research is needed to understand both the benefits of alignment and the costs of misalignment, which may not be symmetrical. In a related fashion, a comparison of the relative performance of firms at different positions within the framework would provide management with practical assistance in building both capabilities and implementing green supply chain practices.

References

ANGELL, L. C., and KLASSEN, R. D. (1999). 'Integrating Environmental Issues Into the Mainstream: An Agenda for Research in Operations Management'. *Journal of Operations Management*, 17/5: 575–98.

BARNEY, J. (1991). 'Firm Resources and Sustained Competitive Advantage'. *Journal of Management*, 17/1: 99–120.

BARRY, J., GIRARD, G., and PERRAS, C. (1993). 'Logistics Planning Shifts Into Reverse'. *The Journal of European Business*, 5/1: 34.

BECKMAN, S., BERCOVITZ, J., and ROSEN, C. (2001). 'Environmentally Sound Supply Chain Management', in C. N. Madu (ed.), *Handbook of Environmentally Conscious Manufacturing*. Boston, MA: Kluwer Academic Publishers, 363–83.

BLACK, J. A., and BOAL, K. B. (1994). 'Strategic Resources: Traits, Configurations and Paths to Sustainable Competitive Advantage'. *Strategic Management Journal*, 15/5: 131–48.

BOWEN, F., COUSINS, P. D., LAMMING, R. C., and FARUK, A. C. (2001). 'The Role of Supply Management Capabilities in Green Supply'. *Production and Operations Management*, 10/2: 174–89.

BOWERSOX, D. J., and DAUGHERTY, P. J. (1987). 'Emerging Patterns of Logistical Organization'. *Journal of Business Logistics*, 8/1: 46–59.

BRAGDON, J., and MARLIN, J. (1972). 'Is Pollution Profitable?' *Risk Management*, 19/4: 9–18.

CAIRNCROSS, F. (1992). 'How Europe's Companies Reposition to Recycle'. *Harvard Business Review*, 70/2: 34–42.

CARTER, C. R., and CARTER, J. R. (1998). 'Interorganizational Determinants of Environmental Purchasing: Initial Evidence From the Consumer Products Industries'. *Decision Sciences*, 29/3: 659–84.

—— and ELLRAM, L. M. (1998). 'Reverse Logistics: A Review of the Literature and Framework for Future Investigation'. *Journal of Business Logistics*, 19/1: 85–102.

—— KALE, R., and GRIMM, C. M. (2000). 'Environmental Purchasing and Firm Performance: An Empirical Investigation'. *Transportation Research. Part e, Logistics and Transportation Review*, 36E/3: 219–28.

CHANDLER, A. D. (1962). *Strategy and Structure: Chapters in the History of the Industrial Enterprise*. Cambridge, MA: MIT Press.

CLEMENTS, R. B. (1997). *Complete guide to iso 14000*. Englewood Cliffs, NJ: Prentice Hall.

COOPER, M. C., LAMBERT, D. M., and PAGH, J. D. (1997). 'Supply Chain Management: More Than a New Name for Logistics'. *International Journal of Logistics Management*, 8/1: 1–14.

CORBETT, C. J., and KIRSCH, D. A. (2001). 'International Diffusion of iso 14000 Certification'. *Production and Operations Management*, 10/3: 327–42.

—— BLACKBURN, J. D., and WASSENHOVE, L. N. V. (1999). 'Partnerships to Improve Supply Chains'. *Sloan Management Review*, 40/4: 71–82.

CURRAN, M. A. (1992). 'Epa's Life-cycle Methodology'. Risk Reduction Engineering Laboratory, Office of Research and Development, US Environmental Protection Agency.

DE BAKKER, F., and NIJHOF, A. (2002). 'Responsible Chain Management: A Capability Assessment Framework'. *Business Strategy and the Environment*, 11/1: 63–75.

DECHANT, K., and ALTMAN, B. (1994). 'Environmental Leadership: From Compliance to Competitive Advantage'. *Academy of Management Executive*, 8/3: 7–27.

DIERICKX, I., and COOL, K. (1989). 'Asset Stock Accumulation and Sustainability of Competitive Advantage'. *Management Science*, 35/12: 1504–11.

DILLON, P. S., and FISCHER, K. (1992). *Environmental Management in Corporations: Methods and Motivations*. Medford, MA: Tufts Center for Environmental Management.

DONG, Y., CARTER, C. R., and DRESNER, M. E. (2001). 'Jit Purchasing and Performance: An Exploratory Analysis of Buyer and Supplier Perspectives'. *Journal of Operations Management*, 19/4: 471–83.

ELKINGTON, J. (1998). *Cannibals With Forks: The Triple Bottom Line of 21st Century Business*. Tony Creek, CT: New Society Publishers.

ELLRAM, L. M., and CARR, A. (1994). 'Strategic Purchasing: A History and Review of the Literature'. *International Journal of Purchasing and Materials Management*, 30/2: 10–18.

FAVA, J. A., DENISON, R., JONES, B., CURRAN, M. A., VIGON, B., SELKE, S., and BARNUM, J. (eds.) (1991). *A Technical Framework for Life-cycle Assessments*. Washington, DC: Society of Environmental Toxicology and Chemistry (SETAC).

FLEISCHMANN, M., BLOEMHOF-RUWAARD, J. M., DEKKER, R., VAN DER LAAN, E., VAN NUNEN, J. A. E. E., and VAN WASSENHOVE, L. N. (1997). 'Quantitative Models for Reverse Logistics: A Review'. *European Journal of Operational Research*, 103/1: 1–17.

FLORIDA, R. (1996). 'Lean and Green: The Move to Environmentally Conscious Manufacturing'. *California Management Review*, 39/1: 80–105.

FREEMAN, H., HARTEN, T., SPRINGER, J., RANDALL, P., CURRAN, M. A., and STONE, K. (1992). 'Industrial Pollution Prevention: A Critical Review'. *Journal of the Air and Waste Management Association*, 42/5: 617–56.

FROHLICH, M. T., and WESTBROOK, R. (2001). 'Arcs of Integration: An International Study of Supply Chain Strategies'. *Journal of Operations Management*, 19/2: 185–200.

GEFFEN, C. A., and ROTHENBERG, S. (2000). 'Suppliers and Environmental Innovation'. *International Journal of Operations and Production Management*, 20/2: 166–86.

GIUNIPERO, L. C., and BRAND, R. R. (1996). 'Purchasing's Role in Supply Chain Management'. *International Journal of Logistics Management*, 7/1: 29–37.

GRANT, R. M. (1991). 'The Resource-Based Theory of Competitive Advantage: Implications for Strategy Formulation'. *California Management Review*, 33/3: 114–35.

GUPTA, M. C. (1995). 'Environmental Management and its Impact on the Operations Function'. *International Journal of Operations and Production Management*, 15/8: 34–51.

HANDFIELD, R. B., WALTON, S. V., SEEGER, L. K., and MELNYK, S. A. (1997). 'Green Value Chain Practices in the Furniture Industry'. *Journal of Operations Management*, 15/4: 293–315.

HART, S. L. (1995). 'A Natural Resource-based View of the Firm'. *Academy of Management Review*, 20/4: 986–1014.

—— (1997). 'Beyond Greening: Strategies for a Sustainable World'. *Harvard Business Review*, 75/1: 66–76.

HARTWELL R.V., III, and BERGKAMP, L. (1992). 'Eco-labeling in Europe: New Market-related Environmental Risks?' *International Environment Reporter*, 15/19: 623–32.

HAYES, R. H., and WHEELWRIGHT, S. C. (1984). *Restoring Our Competitive Edge: Competing Through Manufacturing*. New York: John Wiley and Sons.

HOEFFER, E. (1999). 'The Worst is Over'. *New Steel*, 15/1: 48–51.

HUNT, C. B., and AUSTER, E. R. (1990). 'Proactive Environmental Management: Avoiding the Toxic Trap'. *Sloan Management Review*, 31/2: 7–18.

HUPPES, G. (1988). New Instruments for Environmental Policy: A Perspective'. *International Journal of Social Economics*, 15/3–4: 43–50.

International Institute for Sustainable Development (2001). Business and Sustainability Development: A Global Guide, 2001.

ISO (International Organization for Standardization) (1998). *Iso 14000—meet the whole family!* Geneva, Switzerland: ISO.

JOHNSON, P. F. (1998). 'Managing Value in Reverse Logistics Systems'. *Transportation Research—Part E*, 34/3: 217–27.

—— LEENDERS, M. R., and FEARON, H. E. (1998). 'Evolving Roles and Responsibilities of Purchasing Organizations'. *International Journal of Purchasing and Materials Management*, 34/1: 2–11.

KEOLEIAN, G. A., and MENEREY, D. (1993). *Life Cycle Design Guidance Manual: Environmental Requirements and the Product System*. Cincinnati, OH: Risk Reduction Engineering Laboratory, Office of Research and Development, US Environmental Protection Agency.

KING, A. A., and LENOX, M. J. (2001). 'Lean and Green? An Empirical Examination of the Relationship Between Lean Production and Environmental Performance'. *Production and Operations Management*, 10/3: 244–56.

KLASSEN, R. D. (2001). 'Plant-level Environmental Management Orientation: The Influence of Management Views and Plant Characteristics'. *Production and Operations Management*, 10/3: 257–75.

—— and GREIS, N. P. (1993). 'Managing Environmental Improvement Through Product and Process Innovation: Implications of Environmental Life Cycle Assessment'. *Industrial and Environmental Crisis Quarterly*, 7/4: 293–318.

—— and McLAUGHLIN, C. P. (1996). 'The Impact of Environmental Management on Firm Performance'. *Management Science*, 42/8: 1199–214.

—— and WHYBARK, D. C. (1999). 'The Impact of Environmental Technologies on Manufacturing Performance'. *Academy of Management Journal*, 40/6: 599–615.

KLÖPFFER, W., and RIPPEN, G. (1992). 'Life Cycle Analysis and Ecological Balance: Methodological Approaches to Assessment of Environmental Aspects of Products'. *Environment International*, 18/1: 55–61.

KOLK, A., and MAUSER, A. (2002). 'The Evolution of Environmental Management: From Stage Models to Performance Evaluation'. *Business Strategy and the Environment*, 11/1: 14–31.

KRUT, R., and KARASIN, L. (1999). *Supply Chain Environmental Management: Lessons from Leaders in the Electronics Industry*. Washington, DC: US–Asia Environment Program, US Agency for International Development.

LA LONDE, B. J. (1994). 'Evolution of the Integrated Logistics Concept (ch. 1)', in J. F. Robeson, W. C. Copacino, and R. E. Howe (eds.), *The Logistics Handbook*. New York: Free Press.

LAMMING, R., and HAMPSON, J. (1996). 'The Environment as a Supply Chain Management Issue'. *British Journal of Management*, 7/(Special Issue): S45–S62.

—— COUSINS, P. D., BOWEN, F. E., and FARUK, A. C. (2001). *Environmentally Sound Supply Chain Management: A Guide for Managers*. Oxford: Chandos Publishing.

LANDEROS, R., and MONCZKA, R. M. (1989). 'Cooperative Buyer/seller Relationships and a Firm's Competitive Posture'. *Journal of Purchasing and Materials Management*, 25/3: 9–18.

LAWRENCE, A. T., and MORELL, D. (1995). 'Leading-edge Environmental Management: Motivation, Opportunity, Resources, and Processes', in J. E. Post (ed.), *Research in Corporate Social Performance and Policy, Supplement*, 1. Greenwich, CT: JAI Press Inc., 99–126.

LEE, H. L., and BILLINGTON, C. (1992). 'Managing Supply Chain Inventory: Pitfalls and Opportunities'. *Sloan Management Review*, 33/3: 65–73.

LEENDERS, M. L., and JOHNSON, P. F. (2002). *Major Changes in Supply Chain Responsibilities*. Tempe, AZ: Center for Advanced Purchasing Studies.

LENOX, M., KING, A., and EHRENFELD, J. (2000). 'An Assessment of Design-for-Environment Practices in Leading US Electronics Firms'. *Interfaces*, 30/3: 83–94.

LOGSDON, J. M. (1985). 'Organizational Responses to Environmental Issues: Oil Refining Companies and Air Pollution', in L. E. Preston (ed.), *Research in Corporate Social Performance and Policy*, 7. Greenwich, CT: JAI Press Inc, 47–71.

MABERT, V., and VENKATARAMANAN, M. (1998). 'Special Research Focus on Supply Chain Linkages: Challenges for Design and Management in the 21st Century'. *Decision Sciences*, 29/3: 537–52.

MALONI, M. J., and BENTON, W. C. (1997). 'Supply Chain Partnerships: Opportunities for Operations Research'. *European Journal of Operational Research*, 101/3: 419–29.

MARGUGLIO, B. W. (1991). *Environmental Management Systems*. New York: M. Dekker.

MASTERS, J. M., and POHLEN, T. L. (1994). 'Evolution of the Logistics Profession (ch. 2)', in J. F. Robeson, W. C. Copacino and R. E. Howe (eds.), *The Logistics Handbook*. New York: Free Press.

McIVOR, R., and McHUGH, M. (2000). 'Partnership Sourcing: An Organization Change Management Perspective'. *Journal of Supply Chain Management*, 36/3: 12–20.

MILLER, D., and SHAMSIE, J. (1996). 'The Resource-based View of the Firm in Two Environments: The Hollywood Film Studios From 1936 to 1965'. *Academy of Management Journal*, 39/3: 519–43.

MIN, H., and GALLE, W. P. (1997). 'Green Purchasing Strategies: Trends and implications'. *International Journal of Purchasing and Materials Management*, 33/3: 10–17.

MONCZKA, R. M., and TRENT, R. J. (1995). *Purchasing and Sourcing Strategy: Trends and Implications*. Tempe, AZ: Center for Advanced Purchasing Studies.

MONTABON, F., MELNYK, S. A., SROUFE, R., and CALANTONE, R. J. (2000). 'Iso 14000: Assessing its Perceived Impact on Corporate Performance'. *Journal of Supply Chain Management*, 36/2: 4–16.

NAVINCHANDRA, D. (1990). *Steps Toward Environmentally-Compatible Product and Process Design: A Case for Green Engineering*. Pittsburgh, PA: Carnegie Mellon University.

NEWMAN, W. R., and HANNA, M. D. (1996). 'An Empirical Exploration of the Relationship Between Manufacturing Strategy and Environmental Management'. *International Journal of Operations and Production Management*, 16/4: 69–87.

OECD (Organisation for Economic Cooperation and Development) (1995). *Technologies for Cleaner Production and Products*. Paris, France: OECD.

—— (1997). *Eco-labelling: Actual Effects of Selected Programmes*. Paris, France: OECD.

PETULLA, J. M. (1987). 'Environmental Management in Industry'. *Journal of Professional Issues in Engineering*, 113/2: 167–83.

PORTER, M. E., and VAN DER LINDE, C. (1995). 'Green and Competitive: Ending the Stalemate'. *Harvard Business Review*, 73/5: 120–33.

POST, J. E., and ALTMAN, B. W. (1992). 'Models of Corporate Greening: How Corporate Social Policy and Organizational Learning Inform Leading-edge Environmental Management', in J. E. Post (ed.), *Research in Corporate Social Performance and Policy*, 13. Greenwich, CT: JAI Press Inc., 3–29.

PURI, S. C. (1996). *Stepping up to ISO 14000: Integrating Environmental Quality with ISO 9000 and TQM*. Portland, OR: Productivity Press.

REINHARDT, F. L. (1999). 'Bringing the Environment Down to Earth'. *Harvard Business Review*, 77/4: 149–57.

ROY, R. (2000). 'Sustainable Product-service Systems'. *Futures*, 32/3–4: 289–99.

ROYSTON, M. G. (1979). *Pollution Prevention Pays*. New York: Pergamon Press.

RUSSO, M. V., and FOUTS, P. A. (1997). 'A Resource-based Perspective on Corporate Environmental Performance and Profitability'. *Academy of Management Journal*, 40/3: 534–59.

SARKIS, J. (1995). 'Manufacturing Strategy and Environmental Consciousness'. *Technovation*, 15/2: 79–97.

SCHMIDHEINY, S. (1992). *Changing Course: A Global Business Perspective on Development and the Environment*. Cambridge, MA: MIT Press.

SHIN, H., COLLIER, D. A., and WILSON, D. D. (2000). 'Supply Management Orientation and Supplier/buyer Performance'. *Journal of Operations Management*, 183: 317–33.

SMITH, R. T., and MELNYK, S. A. (1996). *Green Manufacturing: Integrating the Concerns of Environmental Responsibility with Manufacturing Design and Execution*, 44. Dearborn, MI: Society for Manufacturing Engineering.

Statistics Canada (1996). *Environmental Protection Expenditures in the Business Sector, 1994*. Ottawa, ON.

STOCK, J. R. (1998). *Development and Implementation of Reverse Logistics Programs*. Oak Brook, IL: Council of Logistics Management.

STUART, F. I. (1993). 'Supplier Partnerships: Influencing Factors and Strategic Benefits'. *International Journal of Purchasing and Materials Management*, 29/4: 22–8.

—— (1991). 'Purchasing in an R and D Environment: Effective Teamwork in Business'. *International Journal of Purchasing and Materials Management*, 27/4: 29–34.

THIERRY, M., SALOMON, M., VAN NUNEN, J., and VAN WASSENHOVE, L. N. (1995). 'Strategic Issues in Product Recovery Management'. *California Management Review*, 37/2: 114–35.

TRENT, R. J., and MONCZKA, R. M. (1998). 'Purchasing and Supply Management: Trends and Changes Throughout the 1990s'. *International Journal of Purchasing and Materials Management*, 34/4: 2–11.

VACHON, S., KLASSEN, R. D., and JOHNSON, P. F. (2001). 'Customers as Green Suppliers: Managing the Complexity of the Reverse Supply Chain', in J. Sarkis (ed.), *Green*

Manufacturing and Operations: From Design to Delivery and Back. Sheffield, UK: Greenleaf Publishing.

VAN HOEK, R. I. (1999). 'From Reversed Logistics to Green Supply Chains'. *Supply Chain Management*, 4/3: 129–34.

WALTON, S. V., HANDFIELD, R. B., and MELNYK, S. A. (1998). 'The Green Supply Chain: Integrating Suppliers into Environmental Management Processes'. *International Journal of Purchasing and Materials Management*, (Spring): 2–11.

11

The Ethical Supply Chain

STEVE NEW

1. Introduction

'Business ethics' has become an important feature of commercial life, and—in terms of publishing and consulting—a major industry in its own right. Most MBA courses pay attention to the subject, and corporate mission statements are full of noble declarations of ethical intent and high moral purpose. The field remains, however, one of heated controversy, and is the subject of a vast and incoherent literature (see as examples: Bowen 1953; Friedman 1970; Heald 1970; Davis 1973; Anshen 1974; Holmes 1976; Schreyögg and Steinmann 1986; Shrivastava 1995; Woller 1996; Jones and Pollitt 1998; Wartick and Wood 1998). For some, the so-called Corporate Social Responsibility (CSR) movement is a major force for good in the world. For others, it is the epitome of corporate hypocrisy: '. . . when people talk of corporate social responsibility, it makes you want to gag' (Jain 2002).

This chapter is about one important but significantly under-theorized aspects of the broader topic: ethics in the supply chain. Although many of the 'classic' business ethics debates revolve around supply chains (e.g. the much-discussed Nike case—see UCMS 1999; HBS 2000; Wokutch 2001; Litvin 2003), many important theoretical 'chain-related' points are lost in the overall discussion, largely due to the conceptual miasma which fogs the supply chain literature. Despite the lack of rigorous theorizing, the idea of the 'ethical' supply chain is becoming an increasingly frequent topic of discussion (see Cowe 2002*a*, *b*; Kent 2002). There are five initial reasons why paying 'supply chain ethics' particular attention may be worthwhile.

First, supply chain issues are, unlike some other issues in business ethics, often central to an organization's activities, and are not an optional 'add on'. Worrying about supply chain ethics is not like worrying about whether an organization should contribute to arts in the local community or generally engage in 'good citizenship' (see Grunig 1979). Supply chain management is a central theme of contemporary management. Second, the increased globalization of production and consumption means that the chains in which consumers and organizations operate have become increasingly complex and geographically dispersed. This can be observed in the general trends towards outsourcing and the continuing disintegration of production systems (Feenstra 1998). Third, it is only through buyer–supplier interactions that pressure for improvement from end-consumers can be exerted back through the industrial system; one recent report (Strandberg 2002) describes a CSR 'ripple effect' which operates 'up and down the supply chain'. Fourth, supply chain ethics raise some interesting and complex theoretical issues: unlike many other aspects of corporate behaviour, the extent of managers' control over what happens in the chain is not straight-forward. Whereas accountability in a hierarchy might be clearly delineated, this is not so in chains of economic activity punctuated by commercial boundaries. Finally, supply chain ethics broadens out the discussion of business ethics from the narrow question of 'responsibility to whom?' to 'responsibility for what?' Much of the literature on business ethics concerns the extent to which firms should adopt notions of responsibility to stakeholders other than their owners (e.g. Donaldson and Preston 1995; Plender 1997; Harrison and Freeman 1999; Trevino 1999; Wolfe and Putler 2002). A large and significant literature also exists on the means by which firms might give account of themselves to these constituencies (Benston 1982; Gray, Owen, and Maunders 1988). However, this line of analysis has largely left untouched the more metaphysical question of how supply chain relationships might lead to a genuinely ethical responsibility for the actions of supply chain partners.

The focus of this chapter is rather narrow: it does not seek to review the area of business ethics as a whole, nor does it seek to deal with the specific arguments about, for example, the exploitation of workers in developing countries or child or forced labour. Rather, the focus is on a small but important set of theoretical questions that particularly apply in the context of supply chain relationships. Having offered this caveat, it may be helpful to offer three impressionistic images to set the scene for the discussion. First, imagine a laughing child—say, 13 years old—unwrapping a small gift at a family celebration. Maybe it is a small electronic game. The next image is of a child of the same age, thousands of miles distant, sat exhausted at a bench in a vast hall, laboriously silk screen printing the letters above the keys on the same toy. The final image is of a business executive, maybe a parent of the first child, waiting in an airport departure lounge, thinking about the contract just negotiated with the employers of the second child, and reflecting on the complex system which links the two children. These images alone tell us little about the ethical implications of such a system—but they may help suggest some of the questions of detail which might flesh out the following abstract discussion of principle.

The chapter is structured as follows. Section 2 introduces some foundational arguments, and introduces a simple model. The meat of the discussion follows in Section 3, in which three central concepts are explored (allocation of responsibility, information, and power). Section 4 offers some suggestions on the practical consequences of the discussion, and makes some recommendations for further research.

2. Ethics and the chain: foundational arguments and an initial model

2.1. Business, ethics, and the chain

It is a truism that in ethical terms, business has a bad press; indeed, a standard joke concerns the oxymoronic character of 'business ethics'. This can perhaps be traced to Aristotle's denunciation of *chrematisike*, trade for profit, although he approved of *oikomikos*, household trading (Solomon 1991). However, careful consideration of the nature of trade shows it to be deeply connected to morality and ethics; exchange processes require institutionalized social norms and expectations of behaviour (Arrow 1973; Hausman and McPherson 1993; Wood 1995; Moldoveanu and Stevenson 1998). However, there is no shortage of confusion in this domain, prompted in part by a conflation of prescriptive, idealized and descriptive accounts of 'the market'.

This point is key to making sense of the incoherence of the debates regarding business ethics. It arises because our understanding of market processes relies on significant simplification; economists' curves rely on sweeping and heroic assumptions, leaving the 'market' as a stylized abstraction that may bear little relation to the actual world. This is not to belittle the discipline of conventional economics, but merely to point out the daunting nature of its ambitions. In particular, economics is a totalizing paradigm: it embodies a conceptual reductionism which translates much of human action to its own internally consistent language, casting rich and complex interactions within a necessarily denuded symbolic discourse. Many writers have focused on the limitations of economic approaches to behaviour with varying degrees of sympathy for the broad intellectual project. Zafirovski and Levine (1999), for example, argue that market exchange is a dependent variable on concrete social–historical conditions, rather than being a 'human universal'. They argue that economists' preoccupation with the maximization of utility becomes a strategy for replacing a complex sociology with a simplistic but tractable psychology. In similar vein, Lie (1997) concludes that 'the economic approach is in this view incompatible with an elementary understanding of sociology', and goes on to discuss the absence of power in economic analysis. This point is explored in more detail by Rothschild (2002). For the current discussion, it is important to note that there are important differences between the complex supply chains that channel real goods and services around the world, and the abstracted and commodified 'market'. The very notion of 'supply chain' intrinsically brings with it an understanding of some supra-organizational entity which is constituted by more than a sequence of 'clean-in, clean-out' atomistic exchanges in impersonal price-taking markets.

This observation goes part of the way to explain much of the confusion in business ethics. 'Markets', in the abstract schema of economics, may well be amoral, but this does not necessarily have much bearing on markets and chain relationships as experienced by human beings. Arguments about the abstracted market that are phrased in its own terms are basically tautological (Gaulthier 1986; Hausman 1989; McCloskey 1994; Khalil 1997). However, the major cause of non-illuminating heat in the debates on business ethics is the concept that the 'pure market'—even if its descriptive powers are limited—has *prescriptive* value. In other words, the market has its own normative power to describe how the world *ought* to be. Buchanan (1985) summarizes some of the arguments that underpin this: first, there are deontic arguments in which the supremacy of the market is inferred from parallels with evolutionary processes in the natural world—a kind of social Darwinism (in other words, the market is good because it most closely resembles the order of nature; see Hofstader 1944; Jones 1980). These ideas are periodically fashionable, but in recent times tend to be played down in the articulated defences of the market. Second, there is what Buchanan characterizes as the 'argument from desert' (see Feinberg 1970): the market is good because it distributes benefits according to those who deserve them. Again, this is a line of thinking that tends not to be often presented in its positive form, although it is widespread in its negative version (e.g. 'government intervention favours the lazy or incompetent'). The third, and by far the most forcefully argued, moral imperative for the market comes from broadly utilitarian arguments about the maximization of social welfare; the market is simply the best way of organizing society and economic activity, and this practical advantage is seem by some to be so great that many of the fundamentally consequentialist defences crystallize into overriding deontic principles (Hayek 1948; Friedman 1962).

Untangling this variety of non-intersecting discourses is important for explaining why so much of the discussion of business ethics is so inchoate, and, in many cases, even silly. On the one hand, those wishing to argue against the imperialism of economic discourse can end up trapped inside the paradigm they are trying to critique; on the other, market advocates can be guilty of using the technical machinery of economic modelling as a smokescreen for basically existential political choices. Key questions of what the 'market' is 'maximizing', and for whom, can be lost in translation between description and prescription. Furthermore, arguments about distribution can become hopelessly entangled in debates about whether growth or increased consumption is desirable in the first place (see Douthwaite 1992; Lintot 1998).

Such confusion generates a heavy penalty across the entire field of business ethics, but is particularly damaging for the consideration of supply chain ethics; public debate is debased by the incoherence of arguments about issues that are clearly of importance. These emotive issues often hinge on notions of responsibility—a major theme of the argument below. However, to avoid some of the conceptual traps it is necessary to review some foundational arguments.

2.2. *Some foundational arguments*

Any exploration of ethics in the chain is problematic; this is due to the intrinsic philosophical complexity of the subject matter, and the difficulties of generalization. The argument proceeds by making some significant assumptions; the reader is asked for forbearance if some of these grate too much. Many of the positions are adopted merely for the purpose of avoiding cumbersome and repetitious qualification as the argument unfolds, and may be relaxed once the key points are developed. I will also not problematize the notion of the 'supply chain', which I have done in detail elsewhere (New 2003); for the most part I adopt a loose and intuitive definition, broadly in line with much other literature.

The first assumption is that it makes sense to talk about right and wrong. Robertson and Crittenden (2003) present a framework which points out that different moral philosophies might prevail in different cultural contexts, but the discussion here will proceed as if there is enough overlap in regard to fundamental moral issues that differences between geographic and cultural settings can be put to one side. This position is in line with many other writers (e.g. Sen 1999) and a detailed justification is provided by Spaemann (1989: chapter one). However, here I commit only to the *existence* of a fixed moral frame, but not to its *particular content*. A corollary of this position is that legal arguments can be informative but not determinative of the ethical analysis; things that might be legal might not be moral. This presumption of a final moral scale, against which actions might be judged, is of course out of line with the relativism associated with post-structuralism or post-modernism, although there are some insights from that literature which are pertinent to the discussion which will be touched on in the concluding section (see Caputo 1993; Anderson-Irwin 2001). I will also dodge the debate between duty ethics and virtue ethics (Statman 1997).

The second assumption is that it makes sense to think of corporate bodies as moral agents. This is an area of heated theoretical debate and is of great legal and conceptual significance, and has received a great deal of discussion in the literature (see French 1984; Kettunen 1984; Manning 1984; Werhane 1985; Ranken 1987; Garrett 1989; Pfeiffer 1990; Ewin 1991; Gibson 1995; Metzger and Dalton 1996; Moore 1999; Wilmot 2001). There are several justifications for making this assumption. Firms are credited with a legal status and a particular type of legal personhood; the very concept of limited liability exists to remove responsibility from individuals, and—like people—corporations can enter contracts, make commitments, and be the subject of law. Furthermore, in practice, it is impossible to even talk about organizations for very long without engaging in some sort of anthropomorphism—and we do this without any second thought at all in regard to other collective entities (e.g. Manchester United, the French), tacitly ascribing some version of unified agency. It seems only sensible that corporations are talked about in the same way. Regardless of any theoretical argument that might be made that could absolve the corporation from moral responsibility, people talk and act as if 'blaming Nike' or 'feeling grateful to the hospital' or 'loyal to the firm' made sense. An enormous literature exists—and a great deal of human effort is expended—on the notions of corporate behaviour and corporate culture, both of which are premised on the organization being more than the sum of its parts, exhibiting characteristics above and beyond those of its constituent elements. A final argument might be made following the same theme, pointing to the fact that, when we regard people as the location of moral agency, we are also dealing with some sort of collective entity, either in terms of 'minds' (Minsky 1988) or in terms of the collection of organs and cells of which we are made (McKay 1974; Maturana and Varela 1980). It is possible to argue that the reductionism that insists on treating organizations as 'just people' leads equally to saying that people are 'just cells' or 'just DNA', leaving ethical argument stranded on the barren rocks of irresolvable arguments about free will and determinism.

2.3. A simple model

In order to develop the argument, a simple model is presented in Fig. 11.1. The purpose of the diagram is to help consider the various loci of ethical considerations in the chain, and, for simplicity, it deals with three supply chain actors, organizations A, B, and C; the arrow indicates the flow of goods through the chain.

Relationship.   The first element of the model relates to ethics at the level of the supply chain relationship: in other words, how corporate actors engage in trade

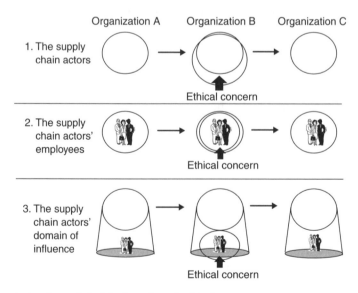

Fig. 11.1.   A simple model of the location of ethical concern

deal with one another. The locus of concern is the supply chain actor; is organization B being fairly treated by organizations A and C? For example, C might be engaging in sharp practice, such as deliberately lying to B about future volumes of work in order to try to drive down a price. Alternatively, A might be breaching B's commercial confidentiality by betraying sensitive information to another customer. Such issues are central to notions of fairness and trust between trading parties; good arguments can be made that at least some type of ethical regime is essential for trade to be possible at all. The understanding of the moral aspects of trade is deeply rooted in political and economic thinking; Jeremy Bentham (1780) writes of the moral obligation of the seller to the purchaser, for example, not to supply adulterated goods. This domain of supply chain ethics is relatively straightforward, and finds its way into the codes of practice of professional ethics for both buyers and sellers (Cooper, Frank, and Kemp 1997). Trade would collapse if market relationships were completely unethical, and organizations need to defend their reputations (Holley 1986; Vermillion, Lassar, and Winsor 2002).

This concept—that the relationship between corporate entities has a moral dimension—is interesting on several counts. On one hand, practitioners seem to talk readily in these terms, and, in the author's experience, often express strong moral judgements about their trading partners. Indeed, on occasion, buyers' and suppliers' mutual perceptions can be almost entirely framed by stark notions of good and evil. On the other hand, the construction of inter-corporate ethics in this way is relatively neglected in the theoretical literature, although there is much prescriptive material about how corporations (and, in particular, professional individuals) ought to behave. One strand of supply chain literature which does bring a theoretical element to this issue is that related to relationship marketing and partnership sourcing (e.g. Carter 2000; Carter and Jennings 2002). For some writers, long-term buyer–supplier relationships, based on cooperative mutual advantage, entail an intrinsic and significant ethical superiority over other ways of doing business (e.g. Kavall, Tzokas, and Saren 1999). Zukav (1995) takes this to an extreme position: 'In the commerce that is emerging, the relationship between customers and businesses will be the same as that between businesses and employees: businesses will strive for the well-being and spiritual development of their customers. Each company will offer what it is, along with what it produces, to its customers, and this total is what its customers will choose to purchase or not.' It is fair to point out, however, that this rhetoric of interorganizational morality is not always played out in practice, as perhaps illustrated by the story of the breakdown of the relationship between UK supermarket chain, Marks and Spencer, and its textile supplier, William Baird (see Blois 2003*a*, *b*). Furthermore, despite the apparent secular trend towards supply chain cooperation, at any point in time it is relatively easy to find examples of weary declarations that ethics of buying and selling are in tragic decline: for example, Pregmon (1998) declares: 'For those participants in the food logistics supply chain, the ethics of channel players has been recognizably getting worse for a long time'.

Employees. The second level of the model concerns ethics that extend not to the treatment of the corporate entity of the supplier or customer, but to the human beings that work for and constitute that organization. In other words, the ethical orbit includes the workers of the trading organization. Thus, in Fig. 11.1, organization C might take some interest in, or be ascribed some responsibility for, the workers in organization B. (It turns out that the discussion here will mostly concentrate on the buyer's ethical obligation in regard to the supplier's workforce, but it is possible for this to work downstream in the supply chain, too.) Furthermore, organization C might be ascribed responsibility not just for the working conditions for B's employees, but also those of A, and so on back up the chain.

Consideration of employment conditions within suppliers is the area of supply chain ethics that has probably received the greatest degree of attention, and is a major concern for many organizations. For example, there are widespread concerns about the global use of sweatshop labour (Appelbaum 1999; Emmelhainz and Adams 1999; Bachman 2000; Adams 2002; Frenkel and Scott 2002; Smith 2002; Arnold 2003; Miller 2003; Hartman, Shaw, and Stevenson 2003), and child and forced labour in particular (Lee-Wright 1990; Varley 1998; Arat 2002; Kolk and van Tulder 2002; Winstanley, Clark, and Leeson 2002). Although these have been the subject of concern and campaigns for many years, they remain serious problems: the International Labor Organization (ILO) estimates that there are 250 million child labourers globally, with 22,000 children dying annually in work-related accidents (Crace 2003).

The principal mode of expression for concern in this area has been the promotion of labour standards and codes of conduct. An example is the so-called Harkin-Engel Protocol, designed to bring about a system to stop abusive child labour in the global chocolate industry by 2005 (Graham and Guyton 2001; Renaut 2002). Although codes and standards are becoming widespread, there remain significant complexities in regard to their use (Diller 1999; van Tulder and Kolk 2001). The question of what standards should be applied is not at all clear. For example, conflicting arguments can be made about whether appropriate benchmarks should be western labour practices, or local practice (see Hartman, Shaw, and Stevenson 2003; Donaldson and Dunfee 1994, 1995, 1999). Furthermore, the Child Labor Coalition (2003) reports that 10 per cent of inspections against such codes reveal violations. Howard, Nash, and Ehrenfeld (1999) make similar observations in regard to the adoption of voluntary codes in regard to environmental health and safety.

While there is a clear secular trend of increasing employment protection and working standards in many developing countries, the trend is by no means uniform. One significant issue is the rapid growth of the so-called Export Processing Zones, special designated regions in developing countries in which imported materials receive some processing before re-export, and which often have particular exemptions from local employment laws. For example, Pakistan has excluded its zones from its standard industrial relations legislation (ILO 1998). Nor is the problem of working conditions confined to developing countries: Ng and Lim (2001) estimate 20,000 sweatshop workers in the San Francisco area of the United States. In addition to concerns about the 'upstream' supply chain, there have been concerns raised about the 'downstream' supply chain, best illustrated by the long-standing campaigns against Nestlé and the marketing and distribution of infant milk substitutes in developing countries (see Madeley 1999).

Others. The third level of the model relates to the ethical issues that apply not just to the workers employed by the suppliers, but also to the various constituencies affected by the suppliers' or customers' operations. These might include local residents suffering from pollution from a supplier's factories, animals used within the production process, or—in the widest sense—communities and society at large that might suffer because of the actions of the trading partner. An example is the problem of deforestation caused by tobacco production (see EIU 1983; Madeley 1999); to what extent might cigarette manufacturer B (in Fig. 11.1) be responsible for the damage caused to the local environment by farmer A? Alternatively, one might consider responsibility in the other direction, and a stark example is provided by Black (2001; see also Kettle 1998 and Barkan 2002): to what extent is manufacturer B (IBM) responsible for the use of its products by C (its prewar Nazi customers) in oppression and murder?

3. Responsibility and the chain

3.1. *Allocating responsibility*

Equipped with this simple model, it becomes possible to begin to develop to a theoretical approach to supply chain ethics. The discussion begins by focusing on a narrow but significant question: if an organization's trading partner behaves badly, to what extent can the first organization be deemed ethically responsible? A large number of writers comment on the fact firms end up being treated *as if* they were responsible, without exploring the detail of the argument (e.g. Maignan, Hillebrand, and McAllister 2002). Without deeper analysis, however, the discussion of supply chain ethics can rapidly collapse to a pragmatic exploration of corporate public relations.

For simplicity, I will tend to focus on the notion of a buyer's responsibility for its supplier's actions. This turns out to be the crux of many of the widely discussed business ethics cases; it is the fulcrum for many activist campaigns and an implicit aspect of many of the codes of conduct and ethical rhetoric adopted by corporations. But it is not a simple question. Neither of the polar answers 'not at all' and 'completely' are satisfactory, and it is useful to consider why this is so.

To begin with, the notion of 'responsibility' itself must be addressed. It is worth noting that while there is more to moral responsibility than causation, some model of the latter is a requirement for the former; Audi (1991) labels this point the 'traceability thesis'. The same author proceeds to differentiate simple *causal responsibility* from *role responsibility* (that which accrues from a position or function), and a more generalized *normative responsibility* (what Zimmerman 1988 calls 'appraisability'). For causal responsibility, there needs to be a comprehensible chain of cause and effect. Role responsibility is perhaps best illustrated by a life guard on the beach; by dint of the position, the person in that role acquires a particular form of responsibility for the safety of the bathers. Continuing the illustration, however, we might note that anybody on the beach might share some normative responsibility for someone calling for help, on the grounds of our generalized responsibility for one another. This simple scheme turns out to be a useful and informative framework, and helps greatly in unlocking arguments about the supply chain. However, Audi's analysis does not stop there, but goes on to point out that normative responsibility cannot be abjured by a claim about character ('I can't be held responsible for not helping, because it's not in my nature to notice people in distress'): Audi claims that normative responsibility can extend to a responsibility to generate, retain, and even anticipate those traits which pertain to our mutual care for one another.

The next stage in the argument considers the extent to which moral responsibility can be somehow be divided up and shared among participants in a situation. This is a problem that has received extensive attention in legal and philosophical literatures (Zimmerman 1985; Sverdlik 1987; May 1990). There are many precedents for construing a notion of a unit of blame, and then allocating fractions of this unit to a variety of participants. This notion is not unproblematic, but is in harmony with some established legal precedents in which, for example, courts might allocate to multiple parties varying percentages of blame for an industrial accident for the purposes of compensation. If the idea of the supply chain as a multi-tier system is taken seriously, one might even claim that some of the responsibility for a supplier's misdemeanours could be allocated to the customer, and then (in presumably diminishing proportions) to the customer's customers and so on.

Given that responsibility can be construed in these ways, to what extent does a buyer–supplier relationship—or a chain of such relationships—communicate ethical responsibility? Surprisingly, there is little extant literature on this precise topic. Santoro (2000) and Arnold and Bowie (2003) are exceptions, both claiming baldly that firms *are* responsible for their suppliers' behaviour. Santoro cites the principle of *respondeat superior*, whereby firms might be liable for the actions of employees: '. . . multinational corporations are morally responsible for the way in which their suppliers and subcontractors treat their workers'. The application of this principle, however, is not straightforward. *Respondeat superior*, associated with the notion of vicarious liability and the associated common law maxim *qui facit per alium facit per se* (he who acts through another is taken to have acted himself), is well established as the basis by which an employer may be held responsible for the actions of an employee. It underpins a great deal of the legal protection experienced by consumers, as it means that redress might be sought, not just from a particular employee, but from the supplying organization itself. It is not the case, however, that the translation of the principle from employee–employer to supplier–customer is unproblematic. First, the application of the concept even in its primary domain of the employment relationship turns out to be highly contingent on the particularity of the situation. Examples may be found in many jurisdictions in which individual cases have required significant modifications to the application of the principle. Although the concept has intuitive appeal and appears superficially sensible, it transpires to be complicated in practice, in some instances crediting employers with responsibilities that are generally acknowledged to be unfair, and in others providing sufficient loopholes for employers to sidestep reasonable obligations. For example, in the United Kingdom, the House of Lords recently reinforced an opinion from an earlier Court of Appeal judgement that the principle was intellectually and legally problematic (Clyde 2001); Deakin (2002) suggests that the emergence of the concept as such a powerful element of common law owes more to accident and historical convenience than rationality.

In terms of then extending the principle to the realm of customers and suppliers, several examples illustrate that it cannot be taken as an simple guide. In *Ontario Ltd.* v. *Sagaz Industries Canada Inc* (Grossman 2002) the Supreme Court of Canada decided that the principle of vicarious liability did not in general apply between a purchaser and an independent contractor, because of the relatively limited ability of the purchaser to control the supplier. In a US case, *Tauscher* v. *Puget Sound Power and Light Co*, it was deemed that the failure of an independent contractor to ensure the health and safety of its employees could not be blamed on the purchaser, the judgement stating that 'It is one thing to retain a right to oversee compliance with contract provisions and a different matter to so involve oneself in the performance of the work as to undertake responsibility for the safety of the independent contractor's employees' (see also *Hennig* v. *Crosby* 116 Wn.2d131, 1991). Barney, Edwards, and Ringleb (1992) examine the way in which firms might seek to use vertical disintegration as a mechanism for absolving themselves of responsibility for the dangers of workers exposed to hazardous materials. They found some evidence that supported the conjecture that firms may use the 'hiving off' of risky activities as a means of legal (and, implicitly, 'ethical') protection. They cite the case of Allied Chemicals and Life Science Products Company (*Wall Street Journal*, 1976); the former encouraged two of its employees to set up the latter as an independent concern, and, when the latter was sued for workplace exposure of toxins, the former was effectively protected from legal assault (see also Bethel and Liebeskind 1998).

Despite these legal examples, there is some scope for using the *respondeat superior* principle as a basis for thinking about supply chain ethics, and a good starting point is provided by the two main practical considerations that tend to be brought to bear in cases relating to employers and employees. The first of these principles is that the employer is generally vulnerable only if the employees actions were conducted as part of or in the scope of the employment. An employer is likely to be on reasonably safe grounds if the actions in question were nothing to do with the employee's proper work. The second principle is that the employer's culpability diminishes if she has taken reasonable precautions to prevent the employee doing the bad thing, and has not in some way encouraged the bad behaviour. In regard to this point, consider a salesperson who is found to have behaved in a threatening or intimidating way to a customer. If the employing organization has no standards or policies about customer relations, and—worse—if the salesperson is constantly fed corporate propaganda that nothing matters more than clinching a sale, and, say, this were to be reflected in the way the salesperson were remunerated and incentivized, then the employer would be fair game for the application of *respondeat superior*. If, on the other hand, the employer can point to systems, procedures, and training that seek to prevent this behaviour, the less culpability is likely to be ascribed.

Extending this principle to the supply chain case, it is clear that the key point is the extent to which one supply chain partner (again, it is easier to focus on the example of the buyer) is in the position of the *superior* to another. In other words, to what extent is a commercial relationship an effective analogue to the employment relationship? A moment's consideration of this point leads to the clear conclusion that this will be highly contingent, and have something to do with the interdependencies between the parties, and the relative power between them. In many cases, the analogy is absurd; a small firm who buys some software cannot plausibly be projected as some kind of 'employer' to Microsoft. On the other hand, Microsoft will have many suppliers for whom it is the dominant customer and over whom it has *de facto* if not *de jure* control. A key point here is that if it is sensible to start to use the language of supply chains, it is likely that analogy between employer and employee is going to be progressively more applicable.

In such cases, it is possible that a customer's responsibility might be judged to be stronger in cases where the supplier's actions are something directly to do with the business transacted between the parties. Suppose a supplier has multiple business units, one of which has outrageous employment practices. A customer of one of the other units will presumably have a lower degree of moral contamination than customers of the offending division. This seems relatively obvious, although does not let the customers entirely off the moral hook, as I shall explore later. The principle about the encouragement or discouragement of the offending behaviour provides more interesting food for consideration; for example, in the case of level two of the model in Fig. 11.1, one might note how the treatment of organization B's workforce might arise directly from the policies and demands of organization C. A commonly made case against the large multinational buying organizations in the textile industry, for example, is that their constant pressure for tighter deadlines and lower costs is translated directly into unbearable working conditions in their suppliers' factories. Even if a customer does not *force* the suppliers to respond to its demands in any particular way (the supplier could, arguably, simply use better technology or increase managerial efficiency), if the customer can foresee that its pressure will result in ethically problematic outcomes, the notion of vicarious responsibility becomes more applicable. To develop this notion, however, requires some consideration of two other important concepts—information and power.

3.2. *Responsibility and information*

A major question in the consideration of supply chain ethics, and the allocation of responsibility, is the extent to which information is accessible to actors in the chain (Roche 2003). Referring again to Fig. 11.1, can organization C be held responsible for the actions of organization A, if C is ignorant of what A does? To what extent does knowledge increase moral accountability? For the current discussion, the key information is about *provenance* (where does something come from?) and *practice* (under what conditions or with what impacts was it manufactured?).

In many ways, the issue of supply chain information for corporate buyers relates closely to the problems faced by end-consumers in obtaining and evaluating information about the things they buy. Consumers' interest in the origins of the things they buy is deeply contradictory. For some economists, it is taken as a article of faith that consumers have no interest whatsoever: Breton (1989) baldly asserts 'Consumers are indifferent about the provenance of the goods and services they consume'. Empirically, the evidence is mixed: recent research in many markets implies that consumers can be unaware of the issues, or if aware, concerned only to the point of a rather mild indifference (see reports, for example, by the Dangar Research Group (1999) and the Nordic Partnership (2002)). On the other hand, there is a long history of interest in 'ethical consumerism' ranging from eighteenth- and nineteenth- century concern about the slave-labour issues relating to sugar (Sussman 2000) and various initiatives to mark out products as ethically acceptable. For example, Addams (1899) describes an 1885 initiative to identify cigars made by unionized workforces with a blue ribbon, allowing consumers to give their encouragement to the free organization of labour. More recently, organizations and publications such as the Fair Trade Movement and *Ethical Consumer* magazine have gained a certain purchase on the consumers' imagination, although the proportion of consumption affected by these movements remains relatively small. A concern for the origins of products is not only an ethical issue, however, and the notion of 'provenance' is important in matters such as food safety—for example, in regard to British Beef and BSE, the so-called 'mad-cow' disease (see Henson and Northern 1998; Nugard and Storstad 1998; Morris and Young 2000; Weatherell, Tregear, and Allinson 2003)—and also aesthetics. Around the world, accepted museum gallery practice is that the display of artistic or 'heritage' material 'without provenance' is tantamount to condoning illicit trade in cultural property (see http://icom.museum/ethics_rev_engl.html). At auctions, old paintings may gain value by virtue merely of having been owned by particular individuals or having been hung in particular historic houses. In other words, for art, the nature of the supply chain becomes part of the identity of the artwork itself, a concept which raises interesting intellectual problems in regard to materialist philosophic approaches, and which connects closely with concepts of 'authenticity' (See Eco 1990). Even in regard to food, a product's origins may have aesthetic and cultural importance; a recent *Financial Times* restaurant review discusses a trend for customers to be told the precise farms from which food is procured: '. . . it is the source—rather than the sauce— that counts these days' (Selby 2003). Product origins play an important (if not complete) role in branding, and have done so for hundreds of years (Olins 2003). The argument that buyers are *in principle* indifferent to origins is absurd.

For consumers and for corporate buyers, the issue of defining provenance can be complex. As early as 1907, Gray was commenting on the way in which the industrial age leaves us in moral relation to vast numbers of people whom we will never know, but to whom we may yet have obligations: 'the paradox of impersonal ethics'. Supply chain structures are not easy to define, and the routes through which a product passes may be effectively impossible to trace. Supply chains in practice bear little relation to the simplified and symbolic presentations such as Fig. 11.1. This complexity, compounded by the commercial sensitivity of the data, means that it can be very difficult to map out the supply chains for even simple products. Even powerful organizations may find it difficult to know exactly the origin of their purchases beyond the first tier of supply. Firms may deal with thousands of first-tier suppliers, and so possibly millions of suppliers in the further stages of the chain. A good example of this is the chocolate industry, where cocoa supplied to European retailers is sourced through a supply chain ending in a complex network of between 1.2 and 1.5 million West African cocoa farms (see www.fhidc.com/cocoa/index.asp). Furthermore, the structure of supply chains may be opaque because of the 'grey market', in which firms' official channels of distribution are confounded—with or without the complicity of the manufacturer—by the importation of products from other geographic markets (Howell *et al.* 1986; Champion 1998; Prince and Davies 2000; Wood 2003).

The second difficulty is that even if the provenance of a product can be traced, then the moral evaluation of the practices by which it has been produced present complex informational difficulties. The lone consumer is ill-equipped to collate and interpret information about the working conditions of those in the chain, and even organized campaigning groups face difficulties; Dunne (1998) describes activists being ejected from supermarkets for systematically collecting data from product labels. Even in situations where the supply chain structure is simple and the number of firms is small, the idea that a buyer needs to undertake a full moral audit of the chain before making a purchase—and to maintain this level of audit during the course of the relationship—is implausible on grounds of cost and practicality, especially if some checking mechanism were needed to validate suppliers' own declarations of policy and behaviour. Even if information is provided by third parties or some kind of independent audit, buyers need to assure themselves of the reliability of this too; since the nineteenth century, for example, controversy has raged about the accuracy of claims regarding inhumane working conditions (Fox 1977).

Although the practical difficulties of establishing provenance and practice might be high, it is not the case that buying organizations operate in an information vacuum in regard to their suppliers (Monczka, Giunipero, and Reck 1981; Purdy and Safayeni 2000). Indeed, it is common for customers to investigate suppliers' production systems and financial standing (Moore 2002). In many industrial settings, an enormous amount of effort by purchasing, logistics, and quality personnel goes into close examination of suppliers' businesses, and analyses beyond the first tier are documented in several sectors. Making judgements about whether a supplier's workforce is subject to racist employment policies, for example, is not substantially different to making judgements about a supplier's quality or planning systems. What is clear, however, is that the extent of this interorganizational information collation varies widely, and it should not be expected that practice is uniform within industries or even within a single buying organization.

These observations lead to the consideration of Audi's point about traits: it can be argued that there is an ethical responsibility of actors to put themselves in a position to act ethically. Spaemann (1989: 31) goes further: 'Man can pretend to be blind and act as though he were not able to see. But he is responsible for his inability to see, both morally, and in our judiciary systems, legally.' Later in the same volume, he writes: 'It would be possible to define evil as a refusal to pay attention. There is a sense in which someone who acts badly does not know what he is doing. The point, though, is that he does not want to know. It is here, rather than in intentions which are obviously bad, that evil is to be found' (p. 69). So even if a buyer in the chain does not directly know about potential ethical concerns in the supply chain, there may be a responsibility to seek to know. In other words, the serious problems of finding out about provenance and practice do not necessarily absolve the buyer from ethical responsibility. Denying the possibility of supply chain ethical questions on the grounds of cost and difficulty is likely to be itself morally questionable. Note that this is not to say that ethical actions or policies are unproblematic or even achievable; what is being argued here is that the difficulty of identification of ethical issues does not mean that the ethical obligations evaporate. Understanding the extent of, and potential responses to, such obligations, however, are a different matter, and will be explored later in the discussion.

Various authors have addressed the issue of the denial of ethical responsibilities, and it is worth reviewing some of these ideas in the context of supply chain ethics. Cohen (2001) outlines several modalities of moral denial. First, he explores denial of responsibility, breaking these down into notions of obedience, conformity, and necessity. The 'obedience' argument—perhaps most famously characterized as the 'Nuremberg defence'—is that an actor's status as a servant of some higher entity absolves her of responsibility for actions. In the context of supply chain ethics, one can see this notion articulated in defences of supply chain practices which posit the 'customer' or the market as being in command. This, of course, relies on a reading of a theory of shared responsibility that denies the claimant's facility for independent action: an extreme form of corporate determinism. The notion of denial based on conformity is that an action is justified if everyone else does it, and, in supply chain ethics, is again an often-voiced defence of corporate practice. Again, it is a rather weak ethical position, even if factually supported. However, it is instantly undermined by the presence of any exemplar who does not conform to the practice in question. The third version of denial, necessity, is difficult to sustain in the context of commercial organizations in liberal democracies: no one is forced to make training shoes or consumer electronics, and organizations retain the option of doing something else, or even of not doing anything at all, rather than necessarily sharing responsibilities for wrong. Cohen's analysis goes on to consider the tactics of denial, and explores how defences of behaviour may be constructed. Again, it is interesting to see how these modes of argument may be applied to supply chain questions: denial of injury (e.g. 'the children enjoy working those long hours'), denial of the victim ('these people don't count, or they don't know any better'), condemnation of the condemners ('your raising of this issue is driven by a hatred of capitalism/a belief in protectionism'), appeal to higher loyalties ('the operation of the market is more important than some local suffering'), and moral indifference ('I do not believe in right and wrong/I do not believe that notions of morality affect this domain of life'). In over 12 years of exploring these ideas with students and practitioners, the author has encountered each one of these positions.

The consideration of the epistemology of supply chain ethics, then, can seem to be central to the understanding of the topic. However, where this argument leads is not clear without an analysis of what can be done in response to information. For this, it is necessary to review the issue of supply chain power.

3.3. Responsibility and power

The consideration of power raises two fundamental problems for supply chain ethics. The first—and perhaps the most compelling argument for those who might not wish to take the notion of supply chain ethics seriously—could be described as an argument about *limited influence*. *Even if* the structural linkages in the chain were traceable, and *even if* there were unequivocal cases of ethical misconduct, there is little that the buyer in the chain can do to affect anything. Given the high 'arborescence' of supply chains, there is little influence that a single player can exercise. This clearly applies in its most extreme form to the individual end-consumer; in an ironic twist to the notion of the rhetoric of the all-powerful final customer, whose whims and preferences are regularly invoked as the ultimate justification for the practices of industry, the solitary buyer at the end of the chain is rendered effectively powerless. This sense of helplessness is frequently expressed by corporations too, and used as mitigation when challenged on ethical issues: for example, Nike's European Director of Corporate Responsibility claims that the firm faces severe limitations on their influence with suppliers, stating that it normally takes less than 40 per cent of a factory's output, and sometimes as low as 2 or 3 per cent (Jones 2002). As Duff (1998) points out, it is obviously ridiculous to assign collective responsibility if one has no power.

The broad force of this type of argument is clearly valid, and is exacerbated by a second idea that might be labelled as an argument about *contestable consequences*. Even if power could be exercised, it might not be possible for it to be used in clear confidence that it would actually make things better. An illustrative example might be a US retailer who sources goods from, say, the Indian subcontinent. For the purpose of the argument, assume that the retailer discovers the fact that suppliers and their subcontractors are using child labour in a way that gives rise to (let us assume) clear moral concerns. Assume also that the retailer is in a position to directly influence the supplier, perhaps by threatening to source elsewhere. Can the retailer be sure that taking the ostensibly higher moral position will really bring about a situation that is ethically preferable? Even if power might be exercised, and the child labour stopped, would this actually benefit the children? Would it perhaps mean that poor families might just end up poorer? Is work in this factory better than the available alternatives? It is not the intention of this chapter to address the detail of the child labour/sweatshop debates (see Varley 1998; Bao 2002; Bender 2002) but the illustration serves to illustrate a general point—we cannot always know *a priori* the consequences of well-intentioned interventions. What might look like exploitative labour relations and inhumane working conditions might be some necessary stage for a society's industrial development (Litvin 2003). Another example might be the actions of food manufacturers to encourage suppliers of tuna fish to use techniques which do not kill dolphins: maybe the alternative methods cause some other unintended problem? Perhaps intervention makes things worse? Perhaps these judgements hinge on the estimation of probabilities and guesses about causal relationships? Zanardi (1990) discusses this general problem from the perspective of the consumer, but the issue applies similarly even to large corporate buyers. Accusations are frequently levelled at NGO and activist campaigns on supply chain issues along the lines that intervention will end up doing more harm than good (e.g. see Goodhart 1994 and Okonska's 2002 critique of the Oxfam 'Mugged' campaign in regard to labour conditions in global coffee production).

These two arguments—limited influence and contestable consequences—are powerful objections to the very notion of supply chain ethics. However, three broad counter-arguments can be formulated. The first is that although a buyer's power over the chain may be small, in some cases it is not. In many instances, buyers wield considerable influence over the chain, and exert a kind of 'ownership' over the chain. For example, the global coffee chain Starbucks talk in their ethical and environmental initiative *Commitment to Origins*™ about their close involvement with 'our farmers' (Starbucks 2003). The chairman of UK retailer Marks and Spencer, discussing supply chain ethics, declares: 'In trying to take the lead in this area, we have a natural advantage in that Marks and Spencer *controls its supply chain one hundred per cent*' (Vandevelde 2003, emphasis added). Many firms assume a role within the chain which involves extensive involvement in their suppliers' operations, through such means as supplier development programmes, and exert powerful influence over their supply chain in regard to operating procedures, quality systems, and logistics practices (Nishiguchi 1994; Bache *et al.* 1997; New 2003). Although the dynamics of inter-organizational power are complex, it is clear that there are many mechanisms of influence which range (adapting Hirschman's 1970 terms) from threats of 'exit' to the exercise of 'voice' (New *et al.* 2001 illustrate this point in regard to environmental issues). In other words, supply chain power in regard to ethical issues is not just about threatening to source elsewhere, but about the power to use influence: a director of a major charity comments that pressure directed at corporate purchasers should not be about demanding ethical purity in the chain: '. . . we don't want a boycott of the produce we have highlighted, or for the big stores to dump certain suppliers. We want them to work with their suppliers to improve conditions . . .' (Jury 1996). Examples of this kind of intervention are provided by Cowe (2002a).

The second argument is that, although the risk of misguided and counter-productive ethical policies is very real, this does not eliminate the need for the exercise of moral judgement. Indeed, a firm cannot avoid the ethical challenge because inaction is itself an ethical decision; it is only by clinging to a notion of a natural order of how organizations should act and interact, that one can maintain the fiction of morality being an alien concept in trading relations. If it were to be argued that firms are simply incapable of analysing the moral calculus of, say, eliminating child labour in the supply chain, then one would have to conclude that the firms are incapable of asserting the moral superiority of the status quo. In other words, arguments about the severe complexity of the ethical questions, for example, lead to the conclusion not that moral considerations are impossible, just difficult.

The third argument is that in some instances, *even if* the ethically driven actions were futile (because the actor had insufficient power), and/or *even if* the consequences were difficult to predict, they would be justified on fundamentally deontic grounds of unavoidable principle. This is a generally neglected position in the business ethics literature, but one which is arguable from the consideration of extreme cases. Even for those who believe the notion of corporate social responsibility to be suspect, it is normally possible to identify some outlying cases, in which sourcing from a particular supplier would breach moral sensibilities. Even the stalwart Friedmanites would baulk at knowingly purchasing from factories which, for example, used harsh forced labour or were run with the explicit purpose of funding terrorism. Although there are significant problems with this type of *reductio ad absurdum* argument, it is difficult to sustain the extreme position that ethics should never be brought into play. Where this line should be drawn is clearly a question of great contestability; the key point is that every individual and every organization is likely to have a 'line'. An important insight here is that the very notion of a 'supply chain' implies some kind of community—and there are some types of community with which moral actors will not want to be associated.

4. A concluding discussion

The preceding arguments point to a single broad conclusion: even though there are considerable practical obstacles, the notion of supply chain ethics cannot be swept away. The position that a supply chain actor can automatically disclaim responsibility for actions elsewhere in the chain does not stand up. To some extent, participants in a chain are ethically intertwined with the other participants, and buyers in particular will share some responsibility for the actions of suppliers. Claiming ignorance will not always do as a moral defence, as supply chain relationships, in contrast to the stylized interactions of pure price-driven markets, are defined and constituted by the exchange of information. Furthermore, the power to act and influence is often considerable.

On the other hand, there are unlikely to be simplistic solutions to ethical problems in the chain, and the way obligations are operationalized will be necessarily highly contingent. A small firm buying a toner cartridge for its laser printer, has an extremely limited scope for worrying about the ethical issues regarding the health and safety policies of the firm that manufactured it. Nike, on the other hand, has rather more influence on its Korean subcontractors' factories in China. But how far does this obligation go? Should Nike (and Nike's shareholders) forgo benefits by placing the rights and wages of its contractors'

Chinese workers above its own interests? To what extent should Nike be expected to sacrifice its own profitability by expending effort or restricting its actions in regard to supply chain ethics? Three arguments may be made which help delineate the scale of obligations.

The first argument draws on Scanlon's (1998) work on the obligations we bear to one another in society. Broadly, Scanlon argues that actors' duties to others need to be based on some kind of symmetry: we cannot impose a moral principle on A in regard to B that we would not apply the other way around. This 'social contractualism' leads to some fairly straightforward obligations about negative duties, such as avoiding harming others. For more positive duties, it also leads to some kind of balance between the penalty that A sustains in doing good to B and the benefit experienced by B. This line of argument—termed the Rescue Principle—can be illustrated by again invoking the idea of our response to someone drowning off the beach. We have an obligation to help, but if the likely cost to us is very high, and the chances of benefiting the other very small, then the nature of our obligation is constrained. This logic suggests that a major company, for example, could have an obligation to seek to improve its suppliers' wage rates, *if* the advantage to the workers was in relative terms significantly greater than the marginal cost to the buying firm. The obligation, though, is not open-ended; Scanlon's key insight is to counter the fallacy that once a moral obligation is identified it becomes a superordinate principle that trumps all self-interests of the obliged person. For supply chain ethics, this argument is profoundly important. Critics often seek to present business ethics as fundamentally antithetical to the pursuit of profits, with the introduction of other objectives and criteria for action acting as some fatal cancer that would rot the capitalist system. Scanlon's position, in contrast, means that ethics—including business ethics—involves a constant process of judgement about the balance of interests of self and others. Wener (2001) and Nagel (1999) provide interesting commentary on Scanlon's ideas.

A second argument can be made, which extends Scanlon's position by considering the benefits of trade and productive activity, not just to the supply chain participants, but to society at large. Unless one is prepared to make an argument against human creativity, collective endeavour and free exchange, one is bound to concede the fundamental ethical merit of organized trade in pursuit of profit (Flew 1976). This is not the same as Friedmanite market absolutism, but merely a position that includes within the moral frame the benefits arising from supply chain activity. It says that in the analysis of—say—the rights and wrongs of textile production in North Africa, there is scope for including in the evaluation the benefits that young Europeans get from having cheap jeans. It must be stressed that this does not mean that consumers' benefits override the exploitation of workers; it does mean that the complex moral judgements that must be made need to—in the spirit of supply chain analysis—entail some consideration of the whole system.

The third argument is one which emphasizes that, although participants in a supply chain may bear some responsibility for the actions of supply chain partners, we must not use this idea in a way which denies the dignity of moral action—and, indeed, the shame of wrong-doing—from those who are the principal culprits. In other words, even if Wal-Mart are to be deemed partially culpable for sourcing from suppliers who exploit the workforce, then it must not be forgotten that the prime responsibility is held by the suppliers themselves. Although activists and campaigns may have sound tactical reasons for targeting companies at particular points in the supply chain, questions of *realpolitik* should not be confused with genuine ethical analysis. One might sensibly criticize IBM for supplying equipment to the Nazis, but this is not to diminish the wickedness of the Nazis.

Early in this chapter, images of children making and receiving toys were presented to help frame the discussion. The analysis has presented an argument that the parent/executive in the vignette cannot put aside ethical considerations in the chain. The issues that have been explored in the chapter—responsibility, information, and power—are those that frequently arise *en passant* in discussion of supply chain ethics, and the conclusions drawn here point to significant challenges for practice and research. For practice, the conclusions are that the emergence of the supply chain motif brings with it a need for painstaking and careful inquiry. Forming closely synchronized and integrated global supply chains brings with it a type of ethical transaction cost; firms cannot seek to interweave their operations while keeping their morality in hermetically sealed units. The consequence is that organizations need to equip themselves with the managerial wherewithal to gather, process, and act on the ethical dimensions of business; this is more than public relations. However, the post-modern twist to the analysis is that even if the foundational assumptions (the meaningfulness of moral judgement, and the ascription of moral agency to corporations) are rejected, companies end up being judged by stakeholders and consumers as if they were valid. The vagaries of public opinion and the attention of activists can seize upon aspects of an organizations' supply chain operations at short notice; those organizations with a coherent moral intelligence are likely to be better placed to respond to these challenges.

References

ADAMS, R. J. (2002). 'Retail Profitability and Sweatshops: A Global Dilemma'. *Journal of Retailing and Consumer Services*, 9/3: 147–53.

ADDAMS, J. (1899). 'Trades Unions and Public Duty'. *The American Journal of Sociology*, 4/4: 448–62.

ANDERSON-IRWIN, C. (2001). 'Beyond Economy, or the Infinite Debt to the Other: Caputo and Derrida on Obligation and Responsibility'. *Journal of Social and Political Thought*, 1/3, online edition at www.yorku.ca/jspot/3.

ANSHEN, M. (1974). *Managing the Socially-Responsive Corporation*. New York: Macmillan.

APPELBAUM, R. P. (1999). *Los Angeles Jewish Commission on Sweatshops*. Los Angeles: LAJCS.

ARAT, Z. F. (2002). 'Analyzing Child Labor as a Human Rights Issue: Its Causes, Aggravating Policies, and Alternative Proposals'. *Human Rights Quarterly*, 24/1: 177–204.

ARNOLD, D. G. (2003). 'Exploitation and the Sweatshop Quandary'. *Business Ethics Quarterly*, 13/2: 243–56.

—— and BOWIE, N. E. (2003). 'Sweatshops and Respect for Persons'. *Business Ethics Quarterly*, 13/2: 221–42.

ARROW, K. (1973). 'Social Responsibility and Economic Efficiency'. *Public Policy*, 21: 303–17.

AUDI, R. (1991). 'Responsible Action and Virtuous Character'. *Ethics*, 101/2: 304–21.

BACHE, J., CARR, R., PARNABY, J., and TOBIAS, A. M. (1987). 'Supplier Development Systems'. *International Journal of Technology Management*, 2/2: 219–28.

BACHMAN, S. L. (2000). 'The Political Economy of Child Labor and its Impacts on International Business'. *Business Economics*, 35/3: 30–41.

BAKER, M. (2003). 'Raising the Heat on Business Over Human Rights'. *Ethical Corporation Online* 18 August, www.ethicalcorp.com/content.asp?ContentID=973.

BAO, X. (2002). 'Sweatshops in Sunset Park: A Variation on the Late 20th Century Chinese Garment Shops in New York City'. *International Labor and Working-Class History*, 61: 69–90.

BARKAN, E. (2002). *The Guilt of Nations: Restitution and Negotiating Historical Injustices*. New York: Norton.

BARNEY, J. B., EDWARDS, F. L., and RINGLEB, A. H. (1992). 'Organizational Responses to Legal Liability: Employee Exposure to Hazardous Materials, Vertical Integration and Small Firm Production'. *Academy of Management Journal*, 35/2: 328–49.

BENDER, D. (2002). 'Sweatshop Subjectivity and the Politics of Definition and Exhibition'. *International Labor and Working-Class History*, 61: 13–23.

BENSTON, G. J. (1982). 'Accounting and Corporate Accountability'. *Accounting, Organizations and Society*, 7/2: 87–105.

BENTHAM, J. (1780). *An Introduction to the Principles of Morals and Legislation*, chapter 16 section 55 (1970 edn). London: Burns and Hart.

BETHEL, J. E., and LIEBESKIND, J. P. (1998). 'Diversification and the Legal Organization of the Firm'. *Organization Science*, 9/1: 49–67.

BLACK, E. (2001). *IBM and the Holocaust: How America's Most Powerful Corporation Helped Nazi Germany Count the Jews*. London: Little, Brown.

BLOIS, K. (2003a). 'B2B Relationships—a Social Construction of Reality? A Study of Marks and Spencer and One of its Major Suppliers'. *Marketing Theory*, 3/1: 79–95.

—— (2003b). 'Is it Commercially Irresponsible to Trust?' *Journal of Business Ethics*, 45: 183–93.

BOWEN, H. R. (1953). *Social Responsibilities of the Businessman*. New York: Harper and Row.

BRETON, A. (1989). 'The Growth of Competitive Governments'. *The Canadian Journal of Economics*, 22/4: 717–50.

BUCHANAN, A. (1985). *Ethics, Efficiency and the Market*. Oxford: Clarendon Press.

CAPUTO, J. (1993). *Against Ethics: Contributions to a Poetics of Obligation with Constant Reference to Deconstruction*. Indianapolis: Indiana University Press.

CARTER, C. R. (2000). 'Ethical Issues in International Buyer–supplier Relationships: A Dyadic Examination'. *Journal of Operations Management*, 18/2: 191–208.

—— and JENNINGS, M. M. (2002). 'Social Responsibility and Supply Chain Relationships'. *Transportation Research. Part E*, 38E/1: 37–52.

CHAMPION, D. (1998). 'Marketing: The Bright Side of Gray Markets'. *Harvard Business Review*, 76/5: 19–22.

CHANDLER, G. (2003). 'UN Sub-commission's Draft Norms on the Responsibilities of Transnational Corporations'. *Ethical Corporation Online*, 2 September http://www.ethicalcorp.com/content.asp?ContentID=1024.

CLC (Child Labor Coalition) (2003). *2002 Child Labor State Survey*. Washington, DC: CLC.

CLARK, C. E. (2000). 'Differences Between Public Relations and Corporate Social Responsibility: An Analysis'. *Public Relations Review*, 26/3: 363–80.

CLYDE (2001). (Judgment by Lord Clyde) *Opinions of the Lords of Appeal for Judgment in the Cause of Lister and Others* v Helsey Hall Limited, 3 May (2001) UKHL 22.

COHEN, S. (2001). *States Of Denial: Knowing About Atrocities and Suffering*. Cambridge: Polity.

COOPER, R. W., FRANK, G. L., and KEMP, R. A. (1997). 'Ethical Issues, Helps and Challenges: Perceptions of Members of the Chartered Institute of Purchasing and Supply'. *European Journal of Purchasing and Supply Management*, 3/4: 189–98.

COWE, R. (2002*a*). 'The Market for High Standards'. *Financial Times*, 10 May, 12.

—— (2002*b*). 'Key Drivers for Sustainable Corporate Supply Chains'. *Ethical Corporation Online*, 22 July, www.ethicalcorp.com/content.asp?ContentID=151.

CRACE, J. (2003). 'Old Before Their Time'. *The Guardian* (Education Supplement) 10 June, 68.

Dangar Research Group (1999). *Do Consumers Care About Clothing Outworker Exploitation?* Sydney: Dangar Research Group.

DAVIS, K. (1973). 'The Case for and Against Business Assumption of Social Responsibilities'. *Academy of Management Journal*, 16/2: 312–22.

DEAKIN, S. (2002). *Evolution for Our Time: A Theory of Legal Memetics*. Working Paper 242, Cambridge: ESRC Centre for Business Research, University of Cambridge.

DILLER, J. (1999). 'A Social Conscience in the Global Marketplace? Labour Dimensions of Codes of Conduct, Social Labelling and Investor Initiatives'. *International Labour Review*, 138/2: 99–129.

DONALDSON, T., and DUNFEE, T. (1994). 'Towards a Unified Conception of Business Ethics: Integrative Social Contracts Theory'. *Academy of Management Review*, 19/2: 252–64.

—— —— (1995). 'Integrative Social Contracts Theory: A Communitarian Concept of Economic Ethics'. *Economics and Philosophy*, 11/1: 85–112.

—— —— (1999). *Ties that Bind*. Boston, MA: Harvard University Press.

—— and PRESTON, L. E. (1995). 'The Stakeholder Theory of the Corporation: Concepts, Evidence, and Implications'. *Academy of Management Review*, 20/1: 65–91.

DOUTHWAITE, R. (1992). *The Growth Illusion: How Economic Growth has Enriched the Few, Impoverished the Many and Endangered The Planet*. Bideford: Green Books.

DUFF, R. A. (1998). 'Responsibility', in E. Craig (ed.), *Routledge Encyclopedia of Philosophy* (online version). London: Routledge. www.rep.routledge.com/article/L085SECT4.

DUNNE, N. (1998). 'Wal-Mart Attacked for Supplier Labour Standards'. *Financial Times*, 31 June, 4.

ECO, U. (1990). *Travels in Hyperreality*. New York: Harcourt.

EIU (Economist Intelligence Unit) (1983). Tobacco and Food Crops Production in the Third World. London: EIU.

EMMELHAINZ, M. A., and ADAMS, R. J. (1999). 'The Apparel Industry Response to Sweatshop Concerns: A Review and Analysis of Codes of Conduct'. *Journal of Supply Chain Management*, 35/3: 51–7.

EWIN, R. E. (1991). 'The Moral Status of the Corporation'. *Journal of Business Ethics*, 10/10: 749–56.

FEENSTRA, R. C. (1998). 'Integration of Trade and Disintegration of Production in the Global Economy'. *Journal of Economic Perspectives*, 12/4: 31–50.

FEINBERG, J. (1970). *Doing and Deserving*. Princeton, NJ: Princeton University Press.

FLEW, A. (1976). 'The Profit Motive'. *Ethics*, 86/4: 312–22.

FOX, C. (1977). 'The Development of Social Reportage in English Periodical Illustration During the 1840s and Early 1850s'. *Past and Present*, 74: 90–111.

FRENCH, P. (1984). *Collective and Corporate Responsibility*. New York: Columbia University Press.

FRENKEL, S. J., and SCOTT, D. (2002). 'Compliance, Collaboration and Codes of Labor Practice'. *California Management Review*, 45/1: 29–49.

FRIEDMAN, M. (1962). *Capitalism and Freedom*. Chicago: University of Chicago Press.

—— (1970). 'The Social Responsibility of Business is to Increase its Profits'. *New York Times Magazine*, 33, 13 September, 122–6.

GARRETT, J. E. (1989). 'Unredistributable Corporate Moral Responsibility'. *Journal of Business Ethics*, 8/7: 535–45.

GAULTHIER, D. (1986). *Morals by Agreement*. Oxford: Oxford University Press.

GIBSON, K. (1995). 'Fictitious Persons and Real Responsibilities'. *Journal of Business Ethics*, 14/9: 761–7.

GOODHART, D. (1994). 'A Bid to Push the World to Rights'. *Financial Times*, 5 April, 14.

GRAHAM, L., and GUYTON, W. (2001). *Chocolate Industry Agreement*. At http://harkin. senate.gov/specials/20010110-chocolate-text.cfm.

GRAY, B. K. (1907). 'The Ethical Problem in an Industrial Community'. *International Journal of Ethics*, 17/2: 217–31.

GRAY, R. H., OWEN, D., and MAUNDERS, K. (1988). 'Corporate Social Reporting: Emerging Social Trends in Accountability and the Social Contract'. *Accounting, Auditing and Accountability Journal*, 1/1: 6–20.

GROSSMAN, N. (2002). 'Independent Contracting Relationship Saves Company from Liability'. *Workopolis.com*. Available at: http://globeandmail.workopolis.com/ servlet/Content/rprinter/20020131/ls20020131.

GRUNIG, J. E. (1979). 'A New Measure of Public Opinions on Corporate Social Responsibility'. *Academy of Management Journal*, 22/4: 738–64.

HARRISON, J. S., and FREEMAN, R. E. (1999). 'Stakeholders, Social Responsibility, and Performance: Empirical Evidence and Theoretical Perspectives'. *Academy of Management Journal*, 42/5: 479–85.

HARTMAN, L. P., SHAW, B., and STEVENSON, R. (2003). 'Exploring the Ethics and Economics of Global Labour Standards: A Challenge to Integrated Social Contract Theory'. *Business Ethics Quarterly*, 13/2: 193–220.

HASUMAN, D. M. (1989). 'Are Markets Morally Free Zones?' *Philosophy and Public Affairs*, 18/4: 317–33.

—— and MCPHERSON, M. S. (1993). 'Taking Ethics Seriously: Economics and Contemporary Moral Philosophy'. *Journal of Economic Literature*, 31/2: 671–731.

HAYEK, F. (1948). *Individualism and the Economic Order*. Chicago: University of Chicago Press.

HBS (Harvard Business School) (2000). *Hitting the Wall: Nike and International Labour Practices*. (Case study written by Burns, J. L., and Spar, D.) 9-700-047. Boston: HBS.

HEALD, M. (1970). *The Social Responsibilities of Business: Company and Community, 1900–1960*. Cleveland, OH: Case Western Reserve University Press.

HENSON, S., and NORTHERN, J. (1998). 'Economic Determinants of Food Safety Controls in Supply of Retailer Own-branded Products in the United Kingdom'. *Agribusiness*, 14/ 2: 113–26.

HIRSCHMAN, A. O. (1970). *Exit, Voice, and Loyalty: Responses to Decline in Firms, Organizations, and States*. Cambridge, MA: Harvard University Press.

HOFSTADER, R. (1944). *Social Darwinism in American Thought, 1860–1915*. Philadelphia: Beacon Press.

HOLLEY, D. M. (1986). 'A Moral Evaluation of Sales Practices'. *Business and Professional Ethics Journal*, 5: 3–21.

HOLMES, S. L. (1976). 'Executive Perceptions of Corporate Social Responsibility'. *Business Horizons*, 19/3: 34–40.

HOWARD, J., NASH, J., and EHRENFELD, J. (1999). 'Industry Codes as Agents of Change: Responsible Care Adoption by US Chemical Companies'. *Business Strategy and the Environment*, 8/5: 281–95.

HOWELL, R. D., BRITNEY, R. R., KUZDRALL, P. J., and WILCOX, J. B. (1986). 'Unauthorized Channels of Distribution: Gray Markets'. *Industrial Marketing Management*, 15/4: 257–63.

ILO (International Labour Organization) (1998). *Labour and Social Issues Relating to Export Processing Zones*. Geneva: ILO.

JAIN, S. (2002). 'What About Old-fashioned Ethics?', in N. Dhillon and A. Joshi (eds.), *Corporate Responsibility: A View from India*. Brussels: EU-India CSR Network, 44–6.

JONES, G. (1980). *Social Darwinism and English Thought*. Atlantic Highlands, NJ: Harvester.

JONES, H. (2002). 'Looking Beyond Europe', in N. Dhillon and A. Joshi (eds.), *Corporate Responsibility: A View from India*. Brussels: EU-India CSR Network, 22–4.

JONES, I., and POLLITT, M. (1998). *The Role of Business Ethics in Economic Performance*. Basingstoke: Macmillan Press.

JURY, L. (1996). 'Stores Urged to Stop Third World Exploitation'. *The Independent*, 28 October, 7.

KAVALL, S. G., TZOKAS, N. X., and SAREN, M. J. (1999). 'Relationship Marketing as an Ethical Approach: Philosophical and Managerial Considerations'. *Management Decision*, 37/7: 573–81.

KENT, T. (2002). 'Values-based Supply Chain Management: Whose Values, Whose Benefit?' *Ethical Corporation Online*, 26 September. www.ethicalcorp.com/content.asp?ContentID=185.

KETTLE, M. (1998). 'GM and Ford Face New Nazi Challenges'. *The Guardian*, 1 December, 15.

KETTUNEN, P. (1984). 'The Stages of Moral Responsibility of the Firm'. *Scandinavian Journal of Management Studies*, 1/2: 137–51.

KHALIL, E. L. (1997). 'Etzioni Versus Becker: Do Moral Sentiments Differ From Ordinary Tastes?' *De Economist*, 145/4: 491–520.

KOLK, A., and VAN TULDER, R. (2002). 'The Effectiveness of Self-regulation: Corporate Codes of Conduct and Child Labour'. *European Management Journal*, 10/3: 260–271.

LEE-WRIGHT, P. (1990). *Child Slaves*. London: Earthscan.

LIE, J. (1997). 'Sociology of Markets'. *Annual Review of Sociology*, 23/1: 341–60.

LINTOT, J. (1998). 'Beyond the Economics of More: the Place of Consumption in Ecological Economics'. *Ecological Economics*, 25/3: 239–48.

LITVIN, D. B. (2003). *Empires of Profit: Commerce, Conquest and Corporate Responsibility*. New York: Texere.

MACKAY, D. M. (1974). *The Clockwork Image*. London: Inter-Varsity Press.

MADELEY, J. (1999). *Big Business, Poor Peoples*. London: Zed Books.

MAIGNAN, I., HILLEBRAND, B., and MCALISTER, D. (2002). 'Managing Socially Responsible Buying: How to Integrate Non-economic Criteria into the Buying Process'. *European Management Journal*, 20/6: 641–8.

MANNING, R. C. (1984). 'Corporate Responsibility and Corporate Personhood'. *Journal of Business Ethics*, 3/1: 77–84.

MATURANA, H. R., and VARELA, F. G. (1980). *Autopoiesis and Cognition: The Realization of the Living*. Boston: D. Reidel Pub. Co.

MAY, L. (1990). 'Collective Inaction and Shared Responsibility'. *Nous*, 24/2: 269–78.

MCCLOSKEY, D. (1994). 'Bourgeois Virtue'. *The American Scholar*, Spring: 177–91.

METZGER, M. B., and DALTON, D. R. (1996). 'Seeing the Elephant: An Organizational Perspective on Corporate Moral Agency'. *American Business Law Journal*, 33/4: 489–500.

MILLER, J. (2003). 'Why Economists are Wrong About Sweatshops and the Antisweatshop Movement'. *Challenge*, 46/1: 93–122.

MINSKY, M. (1988). *The Society of Mind*. New York: Simon and Schuster.

MOLDOVEANU, M. C., and STEVENSON, H. (1998). 'Ethical Universals in Practice: An Analysis of Five Principles'. *Journal of Socio-Economics*, 27/6: 721–52.

MONCZKA, R. M., GIUNIPERO, L. C., and RECK, R. F. (1981). 'Perceived Importance of Supplier Information'. *Journal of Purchasing and Materials Management*, 17/1: 21–9.

MOORE, G. (1999). 'Corporate Moral Agency: Review and Implications'. *Journal of Business Ethics*, 21/4: 329–43.

—— (2002). *The Science of High-Performance Supplier Management*. New York: Amacom.

MORRIS, C., and YOUNG, C. (2000). 'Seed to Shelf, Teat to Table, Barley to Beer and Womb to Tomb: Discourses of Food Quality and Quality Assurance Schemes in the UK'. *Journal of Rural Studies*, 16/1: 103–15.

NAGEL, T. (1999). 'Review of *What We Owe to Each Other* by T. M. Scanlon'. *London Review of Books*, 21/3: 10–13.

NEW, S. J. (2003). '*Supply Chain Ontology*'. Working Paper. Oxford: Saïd Business School, University of Oxford.

—— GREEN, K., and MORTON, B. (2000). 'Buying the Environment: The Multiple Meanings of Green Supply', in S. Fineman (ed.), *The Business of Greening*. London: Routledge, 35–53.

NG, J., and LIM, J. H. (2001). 'Blood, Sweat, Tears—at a Price'. *Asian Week* 20–26 July, online edition. www.asianweek.com/2001_07_20/feature.html.

NISHIGUCHI, T. (1994). *Strategic Industrial Sourcing: The Japanese Advantage*. Oxford: Oxford University Press.

Nordic Partnership (2003). *No Writing on the Wall*. Copenhagen: Nordic Partnership.

NUGARD, B., and STORSTAD, O. (1998). 'De-globalisation of Food Markets? Consumer Perceptions of Safe Food'. *Sociologia Ruralis*, 38/1: 35–53.

OKONSKA, K. (2002). 'Oxfam is Full of Beans', *Wall Street Journal Europe*, 3 October, A12.

OLINS, W. (2003). *Wally Olins on Brand*. London: Thames and Hudson.

PFEIFFER, R. S. (1990). 'The Central Distinction in the Theory of Corporate Personhood'. *Journal of Business Ethics*, 9/6: 473–80.

PLENDER, J. (1997). 'A Stake in the Future: The Stakeholding Solution'. London: Nicholas Brealey.

POGGE, T. (ed.) (2001). *Global Justice*. Oxford: Blackwell Publishing.

PREGMON, M. (1998). 'Supply Chain Ethics: A Grocery Logistics System Epidemic'. *International Refrigerated Transport Association Newsletter*, 3/5. www.irta.org/irta_report_spring98.html.

PRINCE, M., and DAVIES, M. (2000). 'Seeing Red Over International Gray Markets'. *Business Horizons*, 43/2: 71–4.

PURDY, L., and SAFAYENI, F. (2000). 'Strategies for Supplier Evaluation: A Framework for Potential Advantages and Limitations'. *IEEE Transactions on Engineering Management*, 47/4: 435–50.

RANKEN, N. L. (1987). 'Corporations as Persons—Objections to the Goodpaster Principles of Moral Projection'. *Journal of Business Ethics*, 6/8: 633–7.

RENAUT, A. (2002). 'Chocolate has a Bitter Taste for Child Slaves'. *Trade Union World* 13 May. Available via www.icftu.org.

ROBERTSON, C. J., and CRITTENDEN, W. F. (2003). 'Mapping Moral Philosophies: Strategic Implications For Multinational Firms'. *Strategic Management Journal*, 24/4: 385–92.

ROCHE, J. (2003). 'Ethical Supply Chain Management—the Story so Far'. *Ethical Corporation Online*, 6 March. www.ethicalcorp.com/content.asp?ContentID=426.

ROTHSCHILD, K. W. (2002). 'The Absence of Power in Contemporary Economic Theory'. *Journal of Socio-Economics*, 31/5: 433–42.

SANTORO, M. A. (2000). *Profits and Principles: Global Capitalism and Human Rights in China*. Ithica: Cornell University Press.

SCANLON, T. (1998). *What We Owe to Each Other*. Cambridge: Harvard University Press.

SCHREYÖGG, G., and STEINMANN, H. (1986). 'Moral Issues in Business: The Case of Cabora Bassa'. *Scandinavian Journal of Management Studies*, 2/3–4: 213–29.

SELBY, A. (2003). 'Do You want Source with That?' *Financial Times*, 27 September, W9.

SHRIVASTAVA, P. (1995). 'Industrial/Environmental Crises and Corporate Social Responsibility'. *Journal of Socio-Economics*, 24/1: 211–27.

SMITH, J. (2002). *Internationally Binding Legislation and Litigation for the Enforcement of Labour Rights*. Report on the seminar organized by CCC and IRENE, Mülheim an der Ruhr, 26–28 June. Amsterdam: Clean Clothes Campaign.

SOLOMON, R. C. (1991). 'Business Ethics', in P. Singer (ed.), *A Companion to Ethics*. Oxford: Blackwell, 354–65.

SPAEMANN, R. (1989). *Basic Moral Concepts* (trans. T. J. Armstrong). London: Routledge.

Starbucks (2003). *Commitment to origins*™, www.starbucks.com/aboutus/origins.asp.

STATMAN, D. (ed.) (1997). *Virtue Ethics: A Critical Reader*. Edinburgh: Edinburgh University Press.

STRANDBERG, C. (2002). *The Future of Corporate Social Responsibility*. Vancouver: VanCity Credit Union.

SUSSMAN, C. (2000). *Consuming Anxieties: Consumer Protest, Gender and British Slavery, 1713–1833*. Stanford: Stanford University Press.

SVERDLIK, S. (1987). 'Collective Responsibility'. *Philosophical Studies*, 51/1: 61–76.

TREVINO, L. K. (1999). 'The Stakeholder Research Tradition: Converging Theorists–not Convergent Theory'. *Academy of Management Review*, 24/2: 222–7.

UCMS (1999). *Cruel Treatment: Working for Nike in Indonesia*. Jakarta: Urban Community Mission Survey Report.

VAN TULDER, R., and KOLK, A. (2001). 'Multinationality and Corporate Ethics: Codes of Conduct in the Sporting Goods Industry'. *Journal of International Business Studies*, 32/2: 267–83.

VANDEVELDE, L. (2003). 'Changing Fashion or Fashioning Change?'. Speech made to *Business in the Community's Annual Conference* 10 July. Available at: www.edie.net/gf.cfm?L=left_frame.htmlandR=www.edie.net/library/features/ENH 032.html.

VARLEY, P. (ed.) (1998). *The Sweatshop Quandary: Corporate Responsibility on the Global Frontier*. Washington DC: Investor Responsibility Centre.

VERMILLION, L. J., LASSAR, W. M., and WINSOR, R. D. (2002). 'The Hunt-Vitell General Theory of Marketing Ethics: Can it Enhance Our Understanding of Principal–agent Relationships in Channels of Distribution?' *Journal of Business Ethics*, 41/3: 267–85.

Wall Street Journal (1976). 'Allied Chemical gets Kepone fine of £13.3 million'. 6 October, 2.

WARTICK, S. L., and WOOD, D. J. (1998). *International Business and Society*. Oxford: Blackwells.

WEATHERELL, C., TREGEAR, A., and ALLINSON, J. (2003). 'In Search of the Concerned Consumer: UK Public Perceptions of Food, Farming and Buying Local'. *Journal of Rural Studies*, 19/2: 233–44.

WENER, L. (2001). 'Contractualism and Global Economic Justice', in D. Pogge (ed.), *Global Justice*. Oxford: Blackwell Publishers, 76–90.

WERHANE, P. H. (1985). *Persons, Rights and Corporations*. Englewood Cliffs, NJ: Prentice-Hall.

WILMOT, S. (2001). 'Corporate Moral Responsibility: What Can we Infer From Our Understanding of Organisations?' *Journal of Business Ethics*, 30/2: 161–9.

WINSTANLEY, D., CLARK, J., and LEESON, H. (2002). 'Approaches to Child Labour in the Supply Chain'. *Business Ethics: A European Review*, 11/3: 210–23.

WOKUTCH, R. E. (2001). 'Nike and its Critics: Beginning a Dialogue'. *Organization and Environment*, 14/2: 207–37.

WOLFE, R. A., and PUTLER, D. S. (2002). 'How Tight are the Ties that Bind Stakeholder Groups?' *Organization Science*, 13/1: 64–80.

WOLLER, G. M. (1996). 'Business Ethics, Society and Adam Smith: Some Observations on the Liberal Business Ethos'. *Journal of Socio-Economics*, 25/3: 311–32.

WOOD, G. (1995). 'Ethics at the Purchasing/Sales Interface: An International Perspective'. *International Marketing Review*, 12/4: 7–19.

WOOD, J. (2003). 'Grey Market Army Fears'. *The Grocer*, 26 July, 14.

ZAFIROVSKI, M., and LEVINE, B. B. (1999). 'A Socio-economic Approach to Market Transactions'. *Journal of Socio-Economics*, 28: 309–34.

ZANARDI, W. J. (1990). 'Consumer Responsibility from a Social Systems Perspective'. *International Journal of Applied Philosophy*, 5/1: 57–66.

ZIMMERMAN, M. (1985). 'Sharing Responsibility'. *American Philosophical Quarterly*, 22/2: 115–22.

—— (1988). *An Essay on Moral Responsibility*. Totowa, NJ: Rowman and Littlefield.

ZUKAV, G. (1995). 'Evolution and Business', in B. DeFoore and J. Renesch (eds.), *Rediscovering the Soul of Business*. San Francisco: Sterling and Stone, 9–32.

12

Postscript: Supply Chain Futures

ROY WESTBROOK AND STEVE NEW

1. Introduction

It seems appropriate at the end of a collection of this type to consider the possible futures for supply chains and their study. It also seems, if not so appropriate, at least allowable, for this brief postscript to the book to adopt a more speculative tone. Our observations are more provocation than prediction. Any reader resistant to reading on in that spirit had better close the volume now.

We consider four possible futures for supply chain management: marginalization, realization, rationalization (with its corollaries of codification and professionalization), and canonization.

2. Marginalization

The first possibility for the future of supply chain management is that it has none. In terms of its influence in management thought and its role in corporate activity, it faces only marginalization. The belief that we could manage supply chains, 'integrate' them, to the benefit of all parties and the environment, will be shown to be just that—a belief, something in which many people once had faith, but which could not survive scientific scrutiny. It would not, after all, be the first management breakthrough to be shown to be a fad. Any reader who has a collection of management books (at least, one not subject to regular culls), will have only to glance at her bookshelves to blush at her indiscretion in parting with hard won funds to purchase what can now be seen to be the intellectual equivalent of an astrological chart. Perhaps you regret once giving time to 'management by objectives' or seriously entertaining Oliver Wight's notion that 'MRP2 is the game plan for the whole company', a claim eerily foreshadowing some claims for supply chain management. Each reader will have their own list of defunct nostrums once held sacred, and yet, knowing that others still cling to the old gods, will fear to seem blasphemous by doubting the claims of the disciples. Why should not supply chain management turn out to be the cause of a powerful sect, able to silence doubters by force of numbers rather than persuasive argument?

This possible future marginalizes supply chain management as one of the fashionable ways of thinking about commercial activity in the late 1990s, which did not survive beyond 2010. Ideas are like products, they have to pass a market test; a test of their value for practitioners and academics (the latter, in the realm of ideas, are of course also practitioners, or so we like to think). If there is too little perceived value compared to earlier and later ideas, then the concept will ossify and be gradually abandoned. It is unlikely to be formally pronounced dead or withdrawn from circulation—one problem with management scholarship is that we never make any product recalls, never formally withdraw any dated or dangerous concepts. We prefer quietly to move on to the next new idea.

One variation of the 'no future' thesis is the possibility that supply chain management is an idea whose time has come—that is, its future is here—but will soon go. This is supported by the fact that it derives largely from the success of Japanese manufacturing since the 1970s. That phenomenon was much studied and progressively revealed as a series of core techniques, such as just-in-time and various approaches to quality management, and recodified into 'new' ideas such as lean production and supply chain management. Now these ideas are applied wherever in the world sophisticated manufacturers are found, and thus have been reintegrated once more into the broader notion of 'world-class manufacturing'. Supply chain management in this possible future becomes reabsorbed into a wider framework, and disappears as a significant independent mode of apprehending our economic world.

3. Realization

But possibility does not equate to plausibility. A more likely future, perhaps, is further realization, an increase in the reality (rather than rhetoric) of supply chain management. Chapter 4 of this book explored the possibility that the expression 'supply chain' itself presents, along with its metaphorical implications, an ontological conundrum, and the supply chain may be chimerical. But a chimera may become a reality. The omnipresence of the concept and the debates around it can lead to the creation of the thing itself. At a simpler level, we have seen this kind of realization in the way science fiction can become fact. Jules Verne's submarine and moon rocket were fictional artefacts long before they became realities. Intellectual activity focused upon a concept which, however erroneously, is assumed to represent the real world, can lead to the imperceptible creation of that reality. (It is imperceptible because, since its reality is preceded by an assumed reality, there is no discernible break in perception, no apparent moment of coming into being.) Note that this is different from proselytizing. We hope by discussing the benefits of a concept such as design for manufacture or ethical investing to encourage better practice, but we do not assume their pre-existence (rather the opposite), as we currently do in the case of supply chain management.

4. Rationalization

A still higher degree of plausibility applies to our next possible future: rationalization. In this scenario, the supply chain is already a reality (one to which most of the preceding chapters attest), and the future is one of ever-more rational development of the various aspects of the phenomenon, such as our contributors describe. As in the past, rationalization will be driven by technology. Internet technology will continue to facilitate the rapid transfer of information, and the increased efficiency of the bidding, purchasing, and payment processes. In a parallel development, tagging technologies will continue to enhance traceability and accountability, imposing ever greater transparency on the physical movements along a supply chain. If inventory exists in part because of our ignorance (we are not sure what we have, where more is to be found, or what customers will order, so we fill our warehouses), then fully rationalized supply chains offer us a world without superfluous stock. Both globalization and localization can be promoted with these technologies—'links' in the chain can be geographically distant, but the local economic infrastructure will be developed around the local link in the global chain.

This exciting, rational, ordered, and technological future is not without its problems. As in the past, there is scope for what looks splendid in terms of efficiency to look more dubious in terms of politics and economics. With industrial rationalization, we can expect concentration of power, and, potentially, some reaction against that power. Issues of governance will become increasingly urgent. Who owns the supply chain, when so few products are the outcome of a vertically integrated system owned by one corporation? If no one owns a supply chain, how can it be controlled and regulated by outside parties, such as governments, concerned with its local impact? Geopolitical debates, currently so preoccupied with terrorism and the role of states—will begin to revolve around the governance of transnational, multi-agent chains. When fundamental industries such as arms, food, water, and electricity supply are dominated by unregulated, global meta-organizations, how will national security be protected?

These areas are, of course, already the subjects of wide, and sometimes wild, speculation. But there are other corollaries to rationalization which, though humbler than geopolitics, may be as significant a part of this particular future. For the process of rationalization, if it follows earlier such processes, will be accompanied by two others: codification and professionalization. Codification (the description of, and discrimination between, various types of supply chain and supply chain management) is the work of the academic. Professionalization (the creation of a coherent set of skills qualifying individuals as members of a profession, and the systematic training and registration of such individuals) is the task of the practitioner.

Codification will focus on unbundling the generic concept of the supply chain, and will develop taxonomies of different supply chains, and related modes of supply chain management. This may be founded on sectoral differences (not everything is transferable from the automotive sector), or more subtle structural insights. To some of us, before we were exposed to a little biology, a whale was clearly a kind of fish, since it lived in the ocean. Only closer study of many creatures uncovered common mammalian characteristics which reveal greater insights into the true nature of mammals than their varied habitats. So with supply chains. Sector differences may be attractive and intuitive, the equivalent of habitat. But closer study of more varieties reveals differences and likenesses which help us predict behaviours and performance—a supply chain after all can be seen as a collection of human (indeed mammalian) activities, like any other economic phenomenon.

Professionalization has, of course, already begun. By definition, professional activity can be taught, and most of the authors in this volume are academics who teach supply chain management courses. Practitioners themselves attend conferences, join associations, subscribe to journals and newsletters, and develop notions of best practice—all aspects of professionalization (see Chapter 1). The importance of professionalization is that it is a step of social significance, and that it is generally irreversible. Socially, the professional class is distinct from non-professionals, and enjoys a degree of social status. A supply chain professional may perhaps in the future enjoy a social position not perhaps accorded to his predecessor, such as a purchasing manager. Professions, moreover, are often self-perpetuating, and may enjoy a longevity not always justified by their contribution. (Some might claim this has happened in the case of the accountancy profession.) Professions rarely disband, so this step of professionalization is likely to ensure the continuity of supply chain management as an essential part of corporate life.

5. Canonization

There is perhaps a final goal to this process, even beyond professionalization, and that is canonization. This term refers here not to an elevation to the company of saints. There is nothing about supply chain management which is inherently saintly, or wicked, despite the claims of some consultants for the former quality and some anti-globalization lobbyists for the latter. The sense of canonization here is one of entering the canon, the canon of approved modes of thinking about business, the collection of received wisdom on the appropriate means of conducting enterprise. The canon, in thought, or practice, or thought about practice, is what one generation passes to the next.

Central to the possibility of this canonized future is the claim that competition will be between supply chains rather than firms (see the openings of Chapters 1 and 4). This aggrandizement of the supply chain concept implies the removal of barriers that currently constrain our ability to manage supply chains themselves. At present two major limits to supply chain management development are our information systems and our managerial tools. Supply chain thinking continues to address information flow inefficiencies, for we need still more accurate data, immediately available wherever it is required. But our information systems continue to be modelled on the autonomy of the firm, not the interconnectedness of the supply chain. Similarly our management techniques, our methods, tools, and procedures for controlling people and processes, are largely concerned with control of what we own, with the firm. Much of the work described in this volume is concerned with dismantling these particular barriers, and it is likely that they will soon come down. But the future barriers will then be found on the wider stage of governance and its mechanisms—of supply chain boards with representatives of controlling parties in a federal structure perhaps. Here there will be limits to the possibilities of coordination, as managerial effort is torn between different allegiances and is subject to diminishing returns. Even if these barriers are overcome, one will remain, and that is in our own psychology as members of firms and other institutions. Our social identity and self-image is often bound up with the larger groups to which we belong—we are 'company men and women', IBM-ers, and so on. It is hard to see such allegiance being owed to a supply chain, without dramatic shifts in both the reality and perception.

Thus, there are indications that in terms of canonization, in establishing an hegemony over longer established ways of thinking, supply chain management is not yet there. Not every Board of a manufacturing company has a Supply Chain Director, and few professional managers feel it is as essential for them to understand supply chain management as it is for them to master finance or human resource management. This is reflected in the academic world. An MBA programme will normally contain a core course on operations management, while supply chain issues will be confined to one part of that course or even relegated to an elective course (i.e. one which students can elect not to take). Yet, one logical outcome of the claim that competition will be between supply chains rather than firms, is for supply chain management to be taught in the core of an MBA degree while operations management, which deals with the firm as the unit of study, is relegated to elective status (as it already is in some courses). One cannot understand the whole from study of one part, so study of the supply chain should supplant study of the firm. Likewise the Manufacturing Director should report to the Supply Chain Director. Canonization can thus imply usurpation. But then, this really is, if not the least plausible, surely not the most immediate, of all possible supply chain futures.

INDEX